Forget Me Not

7

ORIGINAL STORY:
Mag Hsu

ART:
Nao Emoto

CONTENTS

CHAPTER 40: **Nana and Nana 3**   2

CHAPTER 41: **Nana and Nana 4**   37

CHAPTER 42: **Nana and Nana 5**   69

CHAPTER 43: **The End 1**   103

FINAL CHAPTER: **The End 2**   148

Worst Company Ever:
A Major Record Company
That Openly Plagiarizes!!

THEME: BLOG

Like! (31)

Hello, everyone! ☼⸜

I've been... very upset recently.

The reason why is because a major record company stole a song by one of my close friends who is a singer-songwriter. 😨

Listen for yourself <u>here.</u>

...So, what did you think?
Aren't they practically the same? 😳😳😳

How could this possibly be forgivable?! 👹🔥

For those who would like to assist me with this, please leave a message for me in the comments.

CHAPTER 40: Nana and Nana 3

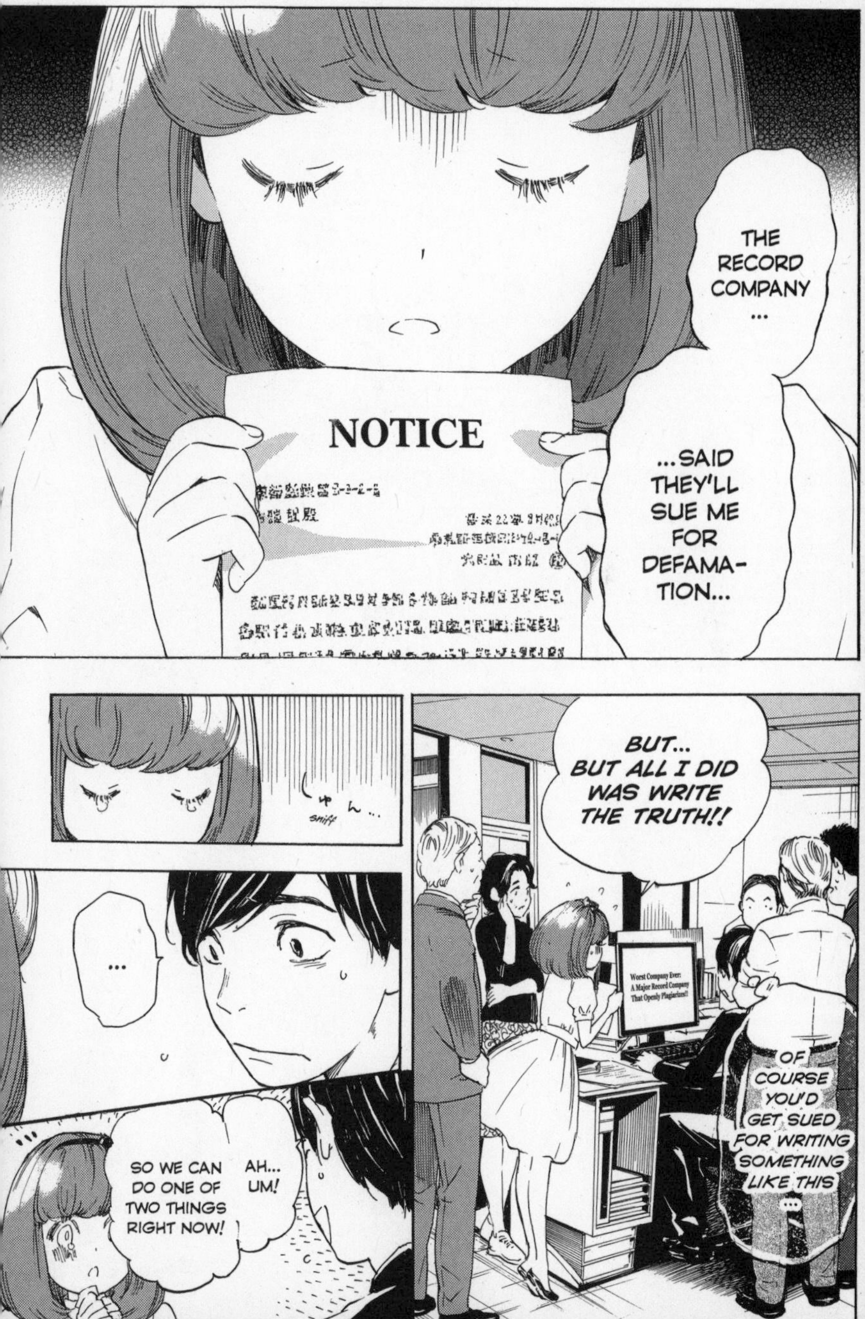
THE RECORD COMPANY...
...SAID THEY'LL SUE ME FOR DEFAMATION...
NOTICE
BUT... BUT ALL I DID WAS WRITE THE TRUTH!!
Worst Company Ever: A Major Record Company That Openly Plagiarizes!!
OF COURSE YOU'D GET SUED FOR WRITING SOMETHING LIKE THIS...
sniff
...
AH... UM!
SO WE CAN DO ONE OF TWO THINGS RIGHT NOW!

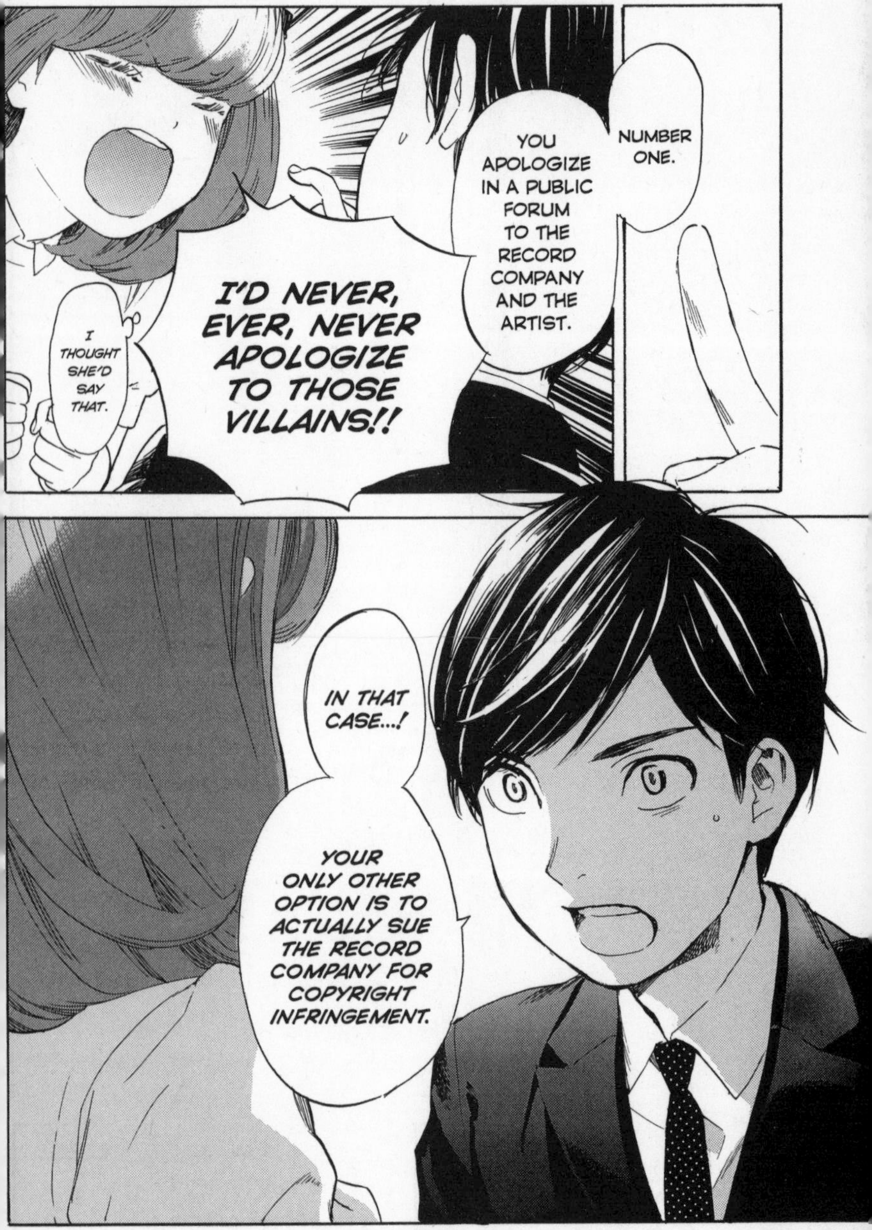
NUMBER ONE.
YOU APOLOGIZE IN A PUBLIC FORUM TO THE RECORD COMPANY AND THE ARTIST.
I'D NEVER, EVER, NEVER APOLOGIZE TO THOSE VILLAINS!!
I THOUGHT SHE'D SAY THAT.
IN THAT CASE...!
YOUR ONLY OTHER OPTION IS TO ACTUALLY SUE THE RECORD COMPANY FOR COPYRIGHT INFRINGEMENT.

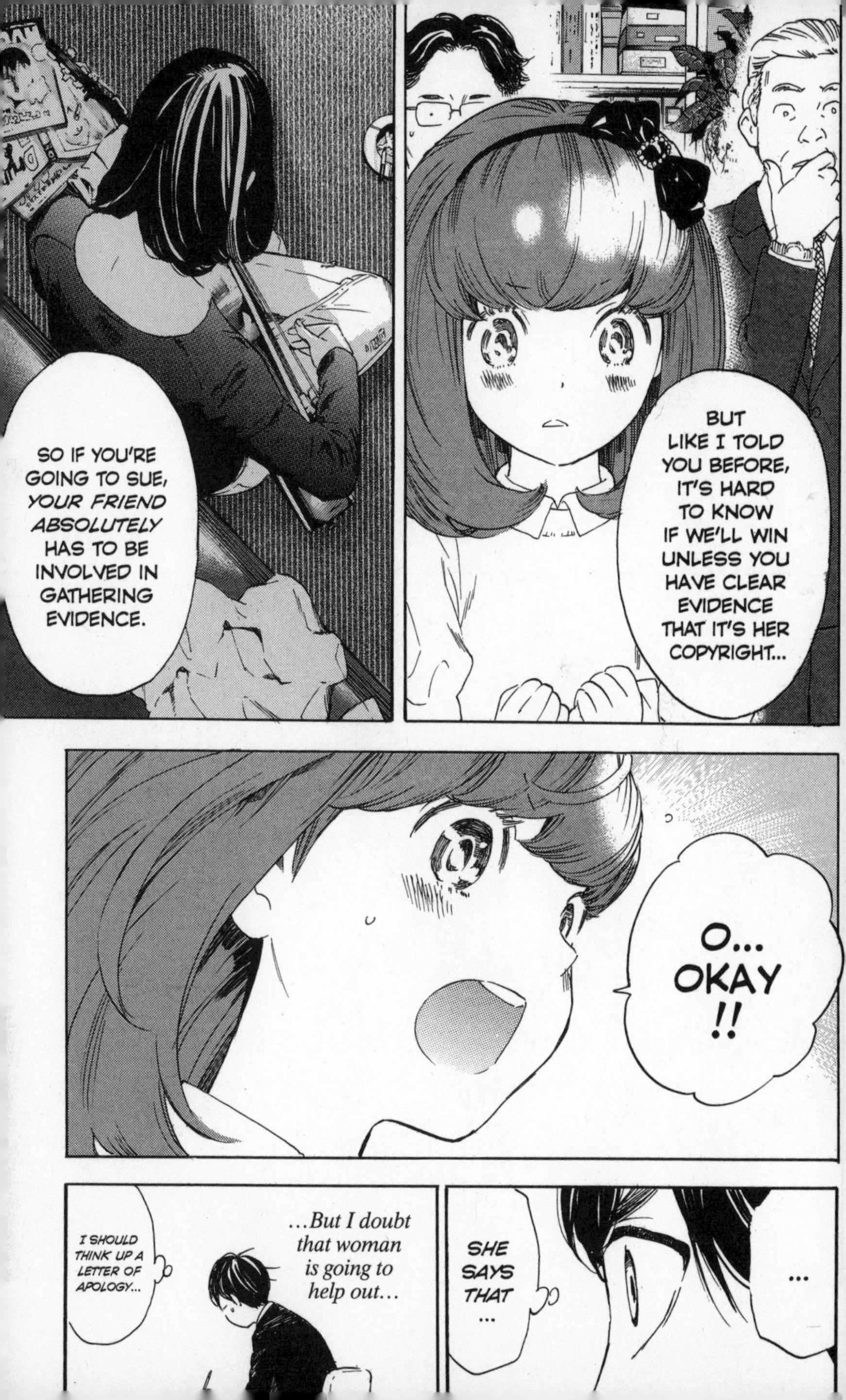
BUT LIKE I TOLD YOU BEFORE, IT'S HARD TO KNOW IF WE'LL WIN UNLESS YOU HAVE CLEAR EVIDENCE THAT IT'S HER COPYRIGHT...
SO IF YOU'RE GOING TO SUE, *YOUR FRIEND ABSOLUTELY* HAS TO BE INVOLVED IN GATHERING EVIDENCE.
O... OKAY !!
...
SHE SAYS THAT ...
...But I doubt that woman is going to help out...
I SHOULD THINK UP A LETTER OF APOLOGY...

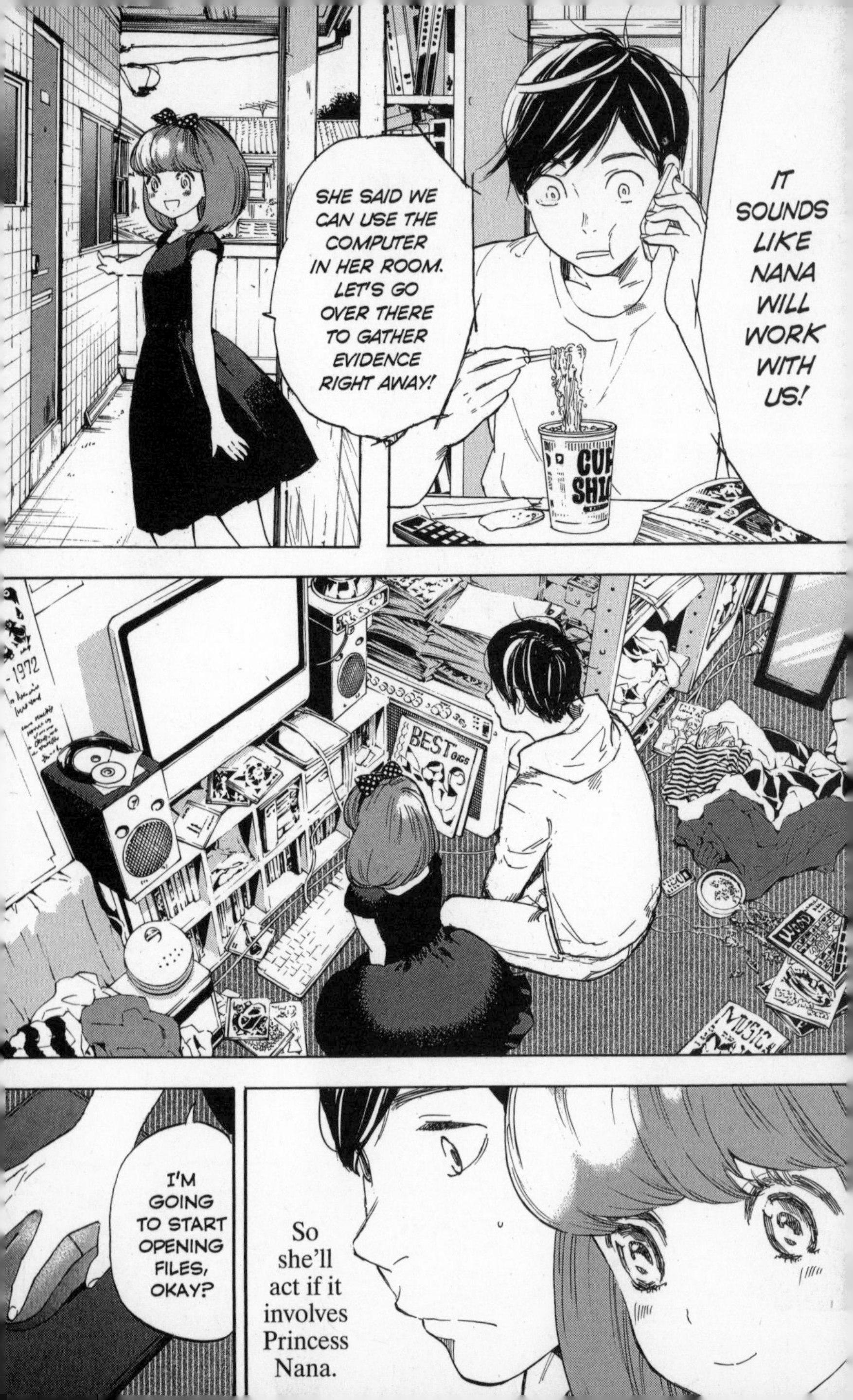
IT SOUNDS LIKE NANA WILL WORK WITH US!
SHE SAID WE CAN USE THE COMPUTER IN HER ROOM. LET'S GO OVER THERE TO GATHER EVIDENCE RIGHT AWAY!
So she'll act if it involves Princess Nana.
I'M GOING TO START OPENING FILES, OKAY?

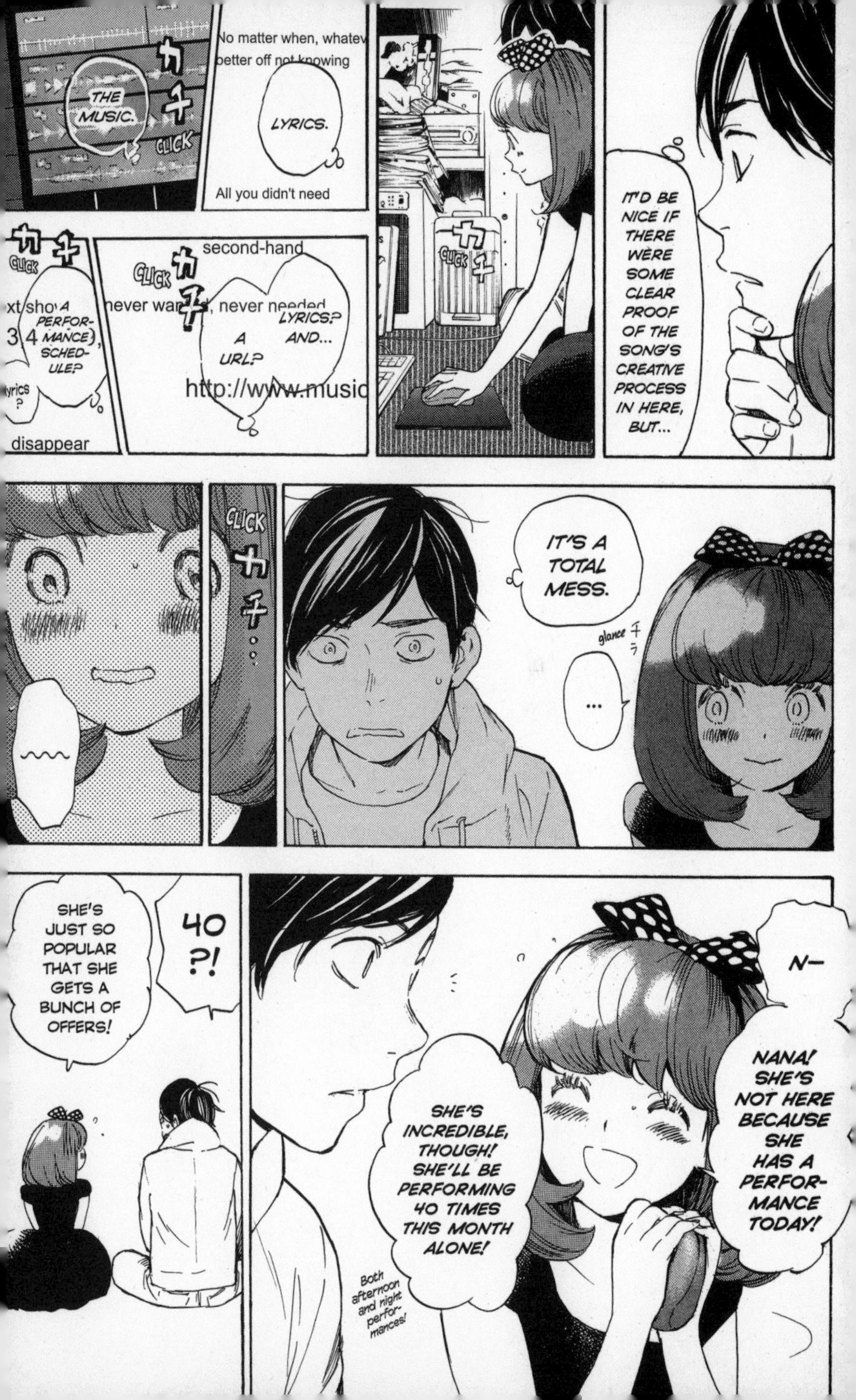
IT'D BE NICE IF THERE WERE SOME CLEAR PROOF OF THE SONG'S CREATIVE PROCESS IN HERE, BUT...
CLICK
No matter when, whatev
better off not knowing
LYRICS.
All you didn't need
THE MUSIC.
CLICK
CLICK
second-hand
never wa , never needed
LYRICS? AND...
A URL?
http://www.music
CLICK
A PERFORMANCE SCHEDULE?
disappear
IT'S A TOTAL MESS.
glance
...
CLICK
~~~
N—
NANA! SHE'S NOT HERE BECAUSE SHE HAS A PERFORMANCE TODAY!
SHE'S INCREDIBLE, THOUGH! SHE'LL BE PERFORMING 40 TIMES THIS MONTH ALONE!
Both afternoon and night performances!
40?!
SHE'S JUST SO POPULAR THAT SHE GETS A BUNCH OF OFFERS!
~~~

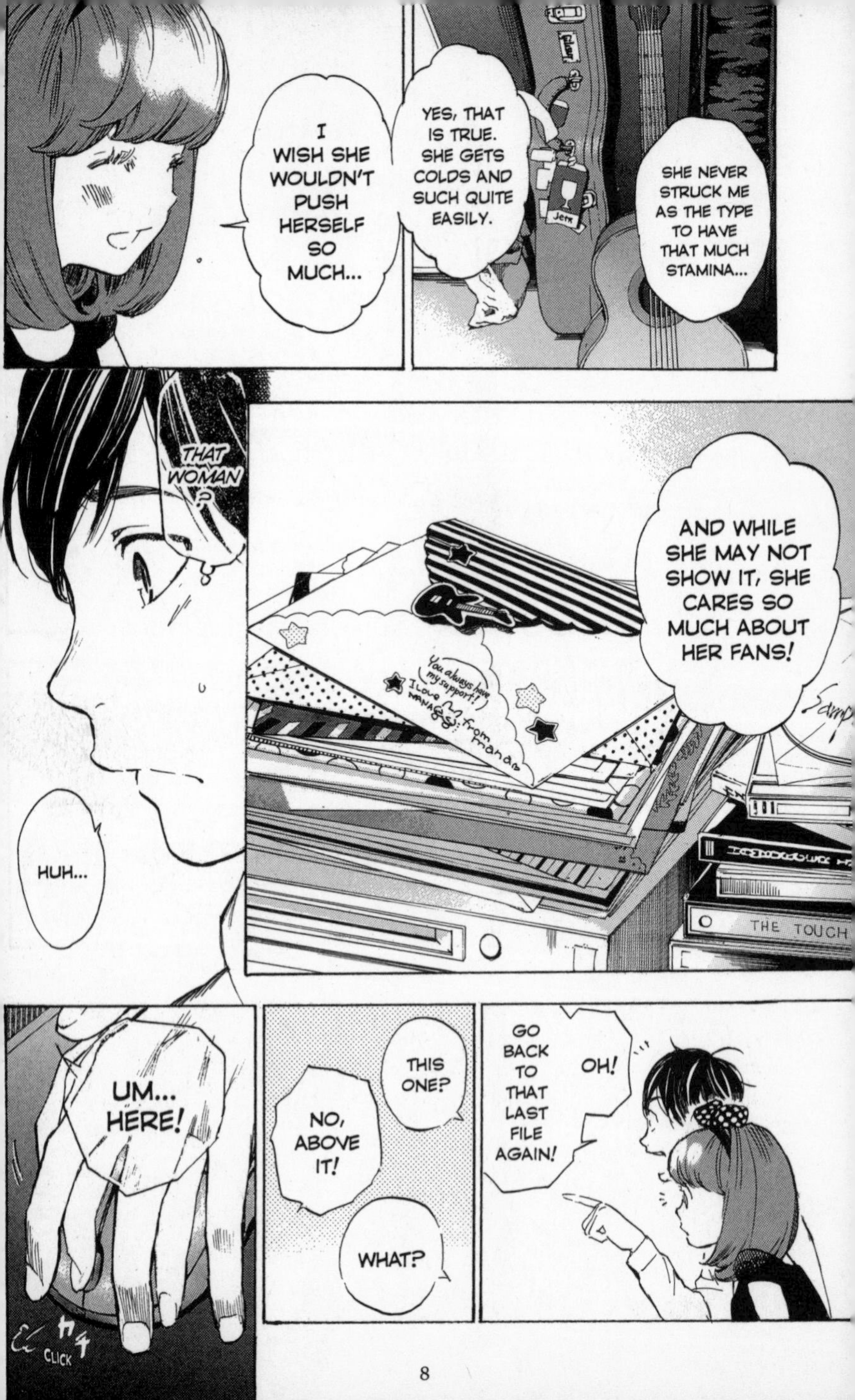

SHE NEVER STRUCK ME AS THE TYPE TO HAVE THAT MUCH STAMINA...
YES, THAT IS TRUE. SHE GETS COLDS AND SUCH QUITE EASILY.
I WISH SHE WOULDN'T PUSH HERSELF SO MUCH...
AND WHILE SHE MAY NOT SHOW IT, SHE CARES SO MUCH ABOUT HER FANS!
THE TOUCH
THAT WOMAN?
HUH...
OH!
GO BACK TO THAT LAST FILE AGAIN!
THIS ONE?
NO, ABOVE IT!
WHAT?
UM... HERE!
カチ CLICK

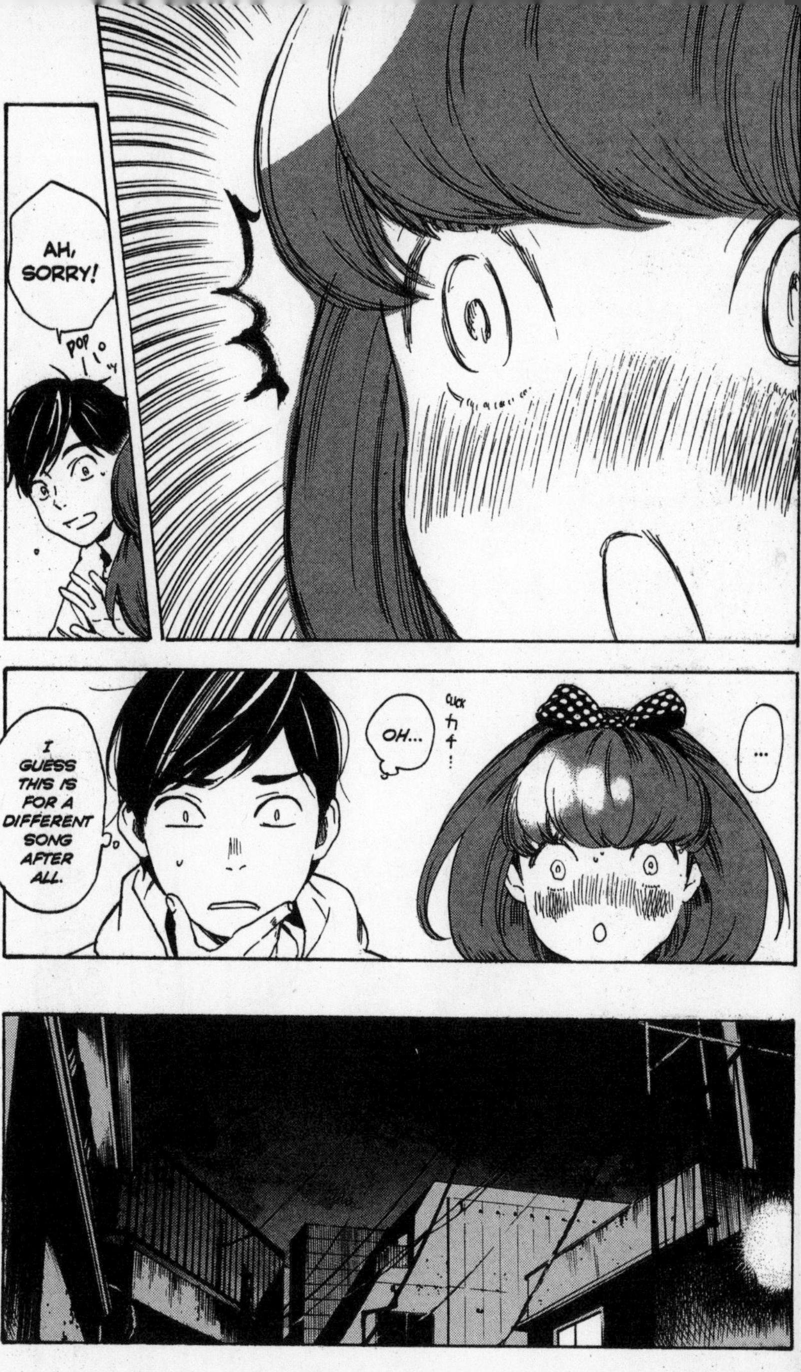
AH, SORRY!
POP
...
CLICK
OH...
I GUESS THIS IS FOR A DIFFERENT SONG AFTER ALL.

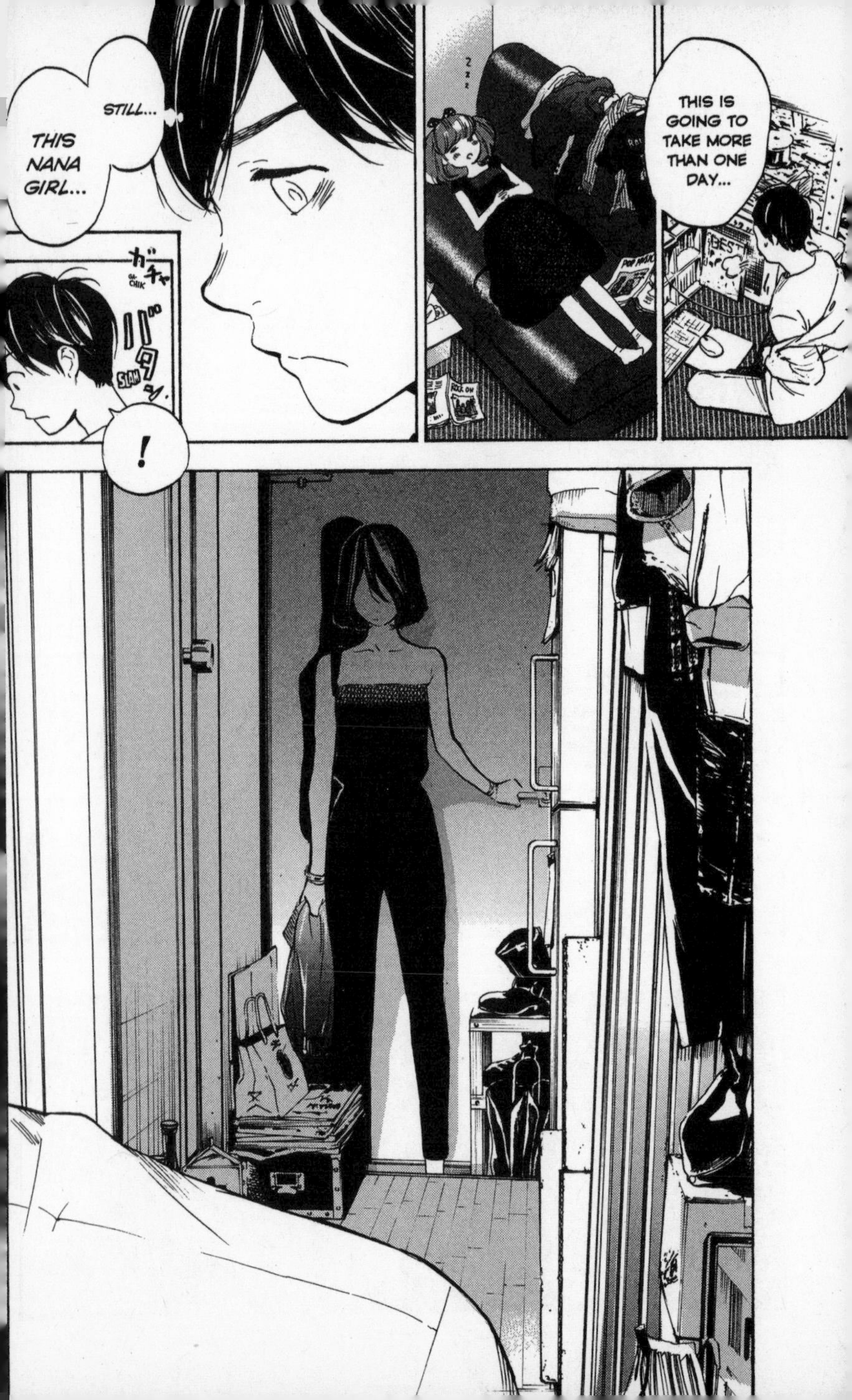
THIS IS GOING TO TAKE MORE THAN ONE DAY...
STILL...
THIS NANA GIRL...
ガチャ
GA-CHIK
SLAM
!

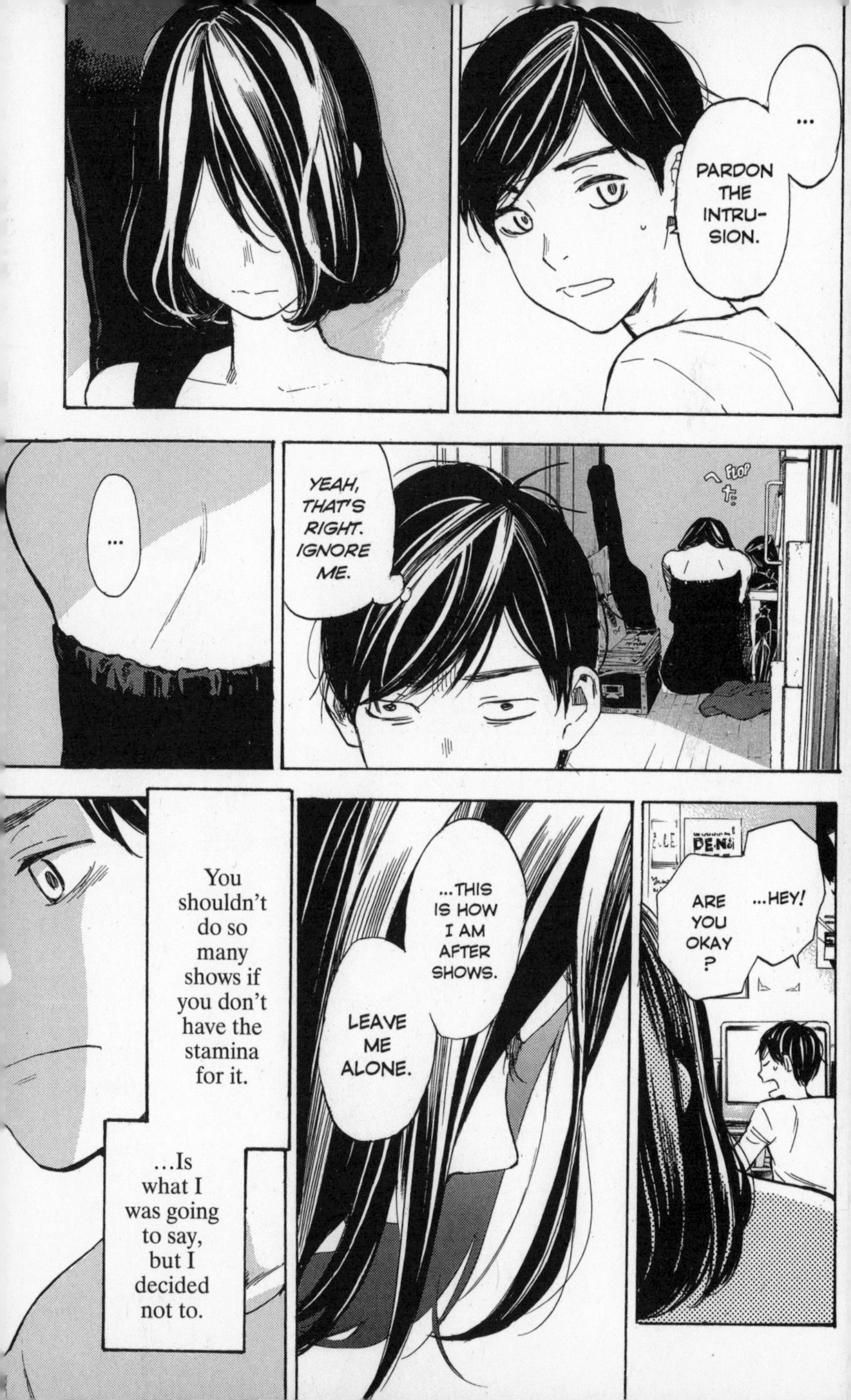
...
PARDON THE INTRU- SION.
FLOP
YEAH, THAT'S RIGHT. IGNORE ME.
...
...HEY!
ARE YOU OKAY?
...THIS IS HOW I AM AFTER SHOWS.
LEAVE ME ALONE.
You shouldn't do so many shows if you don't have the stamina for it.
...Is what I was going to say, but I decided not to.

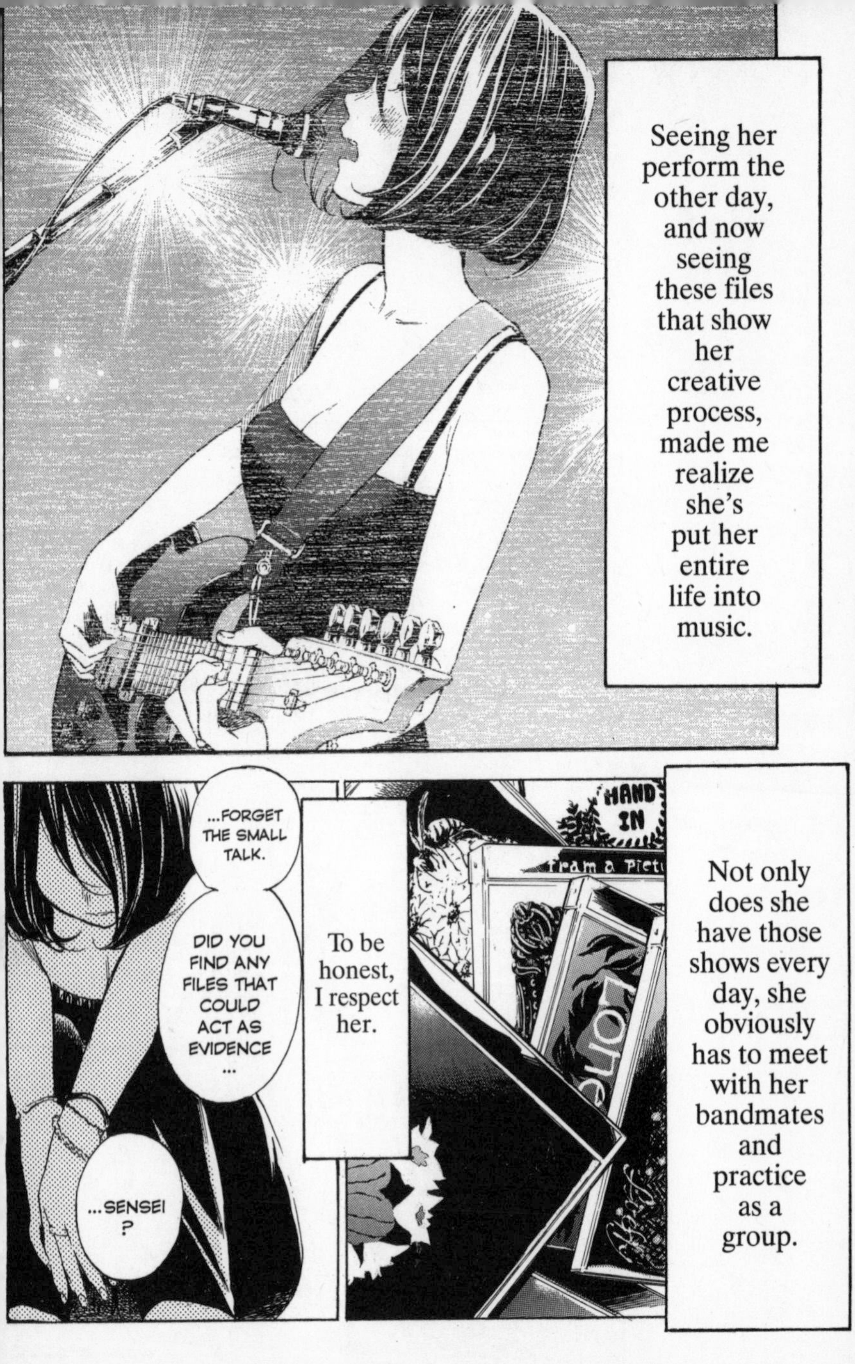

Seeing her perform the other day, and now seeing these files that show her creative process, made me realize she's put her entire life into music.
Not only does she have those shows every day, she obviously has to meet with her bandmates and practice as a group.
HAND IN
To be honest, I respect her.
...FORGET THE SMALL TALK.
DID YOU FIND ANY FILES THAT COULD ACT AS EVIDENCE ...
...SENSEI ?

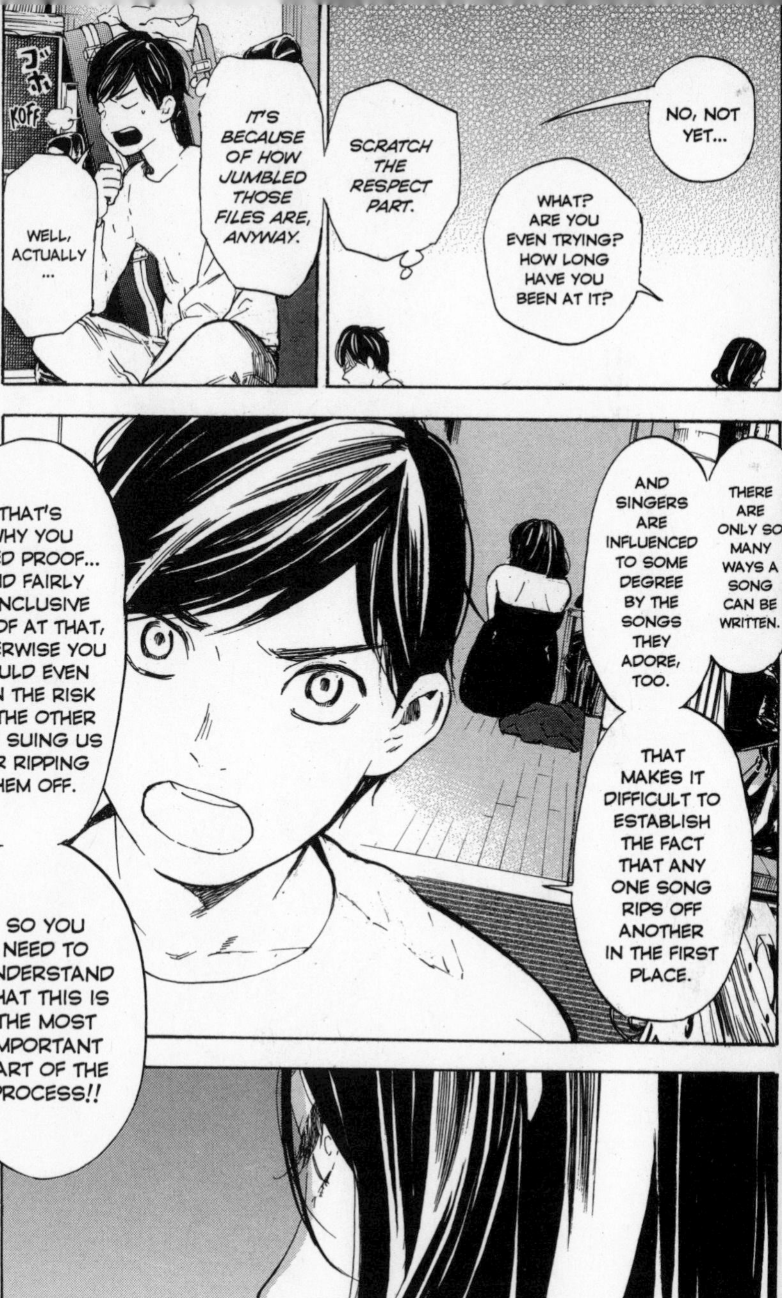
NO, NOT YET...
WHAT? ARE YOU EVEN TRYING? HOW LONG HAVE YOU BEEN AT IT?
SCRATCH THE RESPECT PART.
IT'S BECAUSE OF HOW JUMBLED THOSE FILES ARE, ANYWAY.
ゴホ
KOFF
WELL, ACTUALLY ...
THERE ARE ONLY SO MANY WAYS A SONG CAN BE WRITTEN.
AND SINGERS ARE INFLUENCED TO SOME DEGREE BY THE SONGS THEY ADORE, TOO.
THAT MAKES IT DIFFICULT TO ESTABLISH THE FACT THAT ANY ONE SONG RIPS OFF ANOTHER IN THE FIRST PLACE.
THAT'S WHY YOU NEED PROOF... AND FAIRLY CONCLUSIVE PROOF AT THAT, OTHERWISE YOU COULD EVEN RUN THE RISK OF THE OTHER SIDE SUING US FOR RIPPING THEM OFF.
SO YOU NEED TO UNDERSTAND THAT THIS IS THE MOST IMPORTANT PART OF THE PROCESS!!

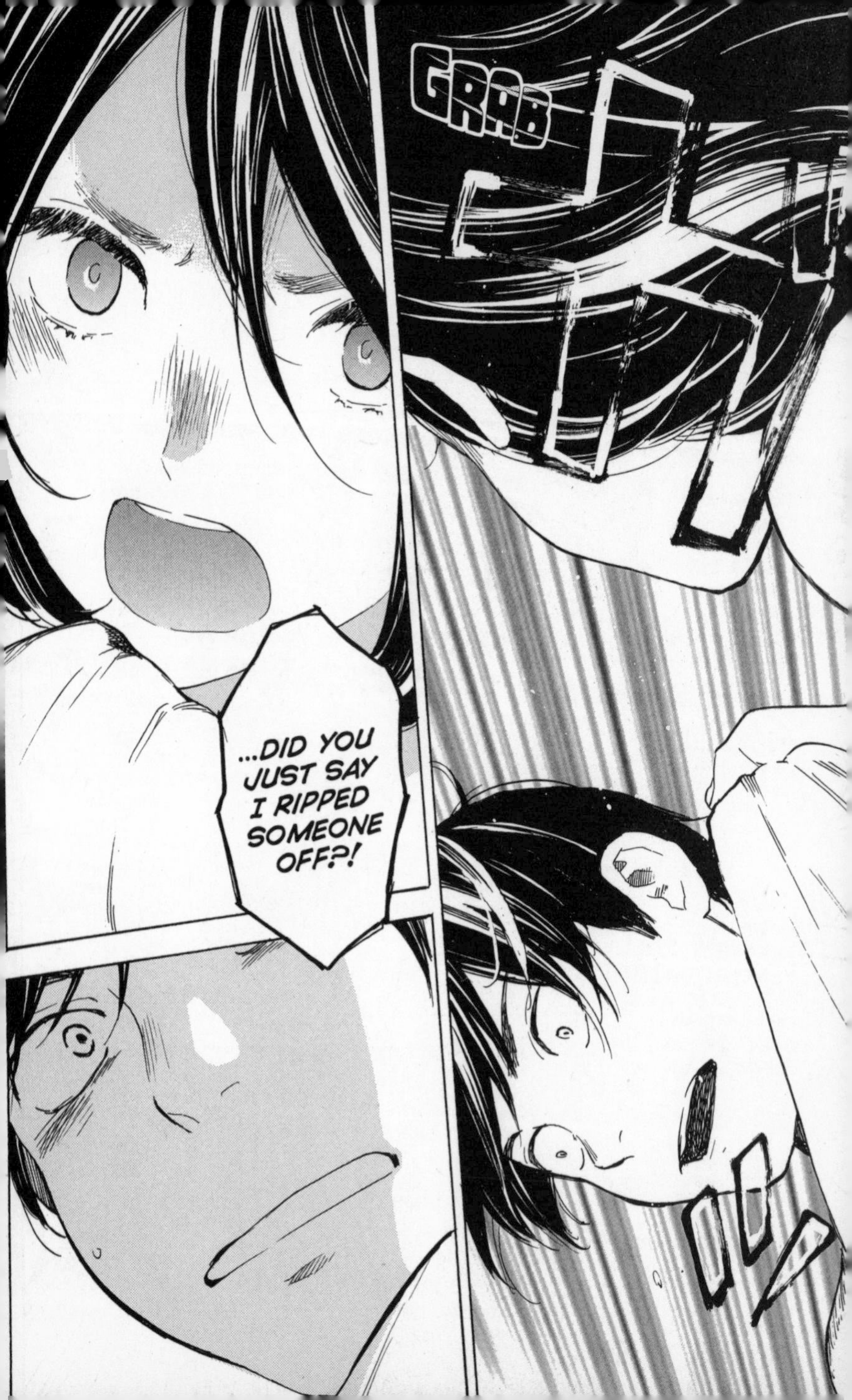
GRAB
...DID YOU JUST SAY I RIPPED SOMEONE OFF?!

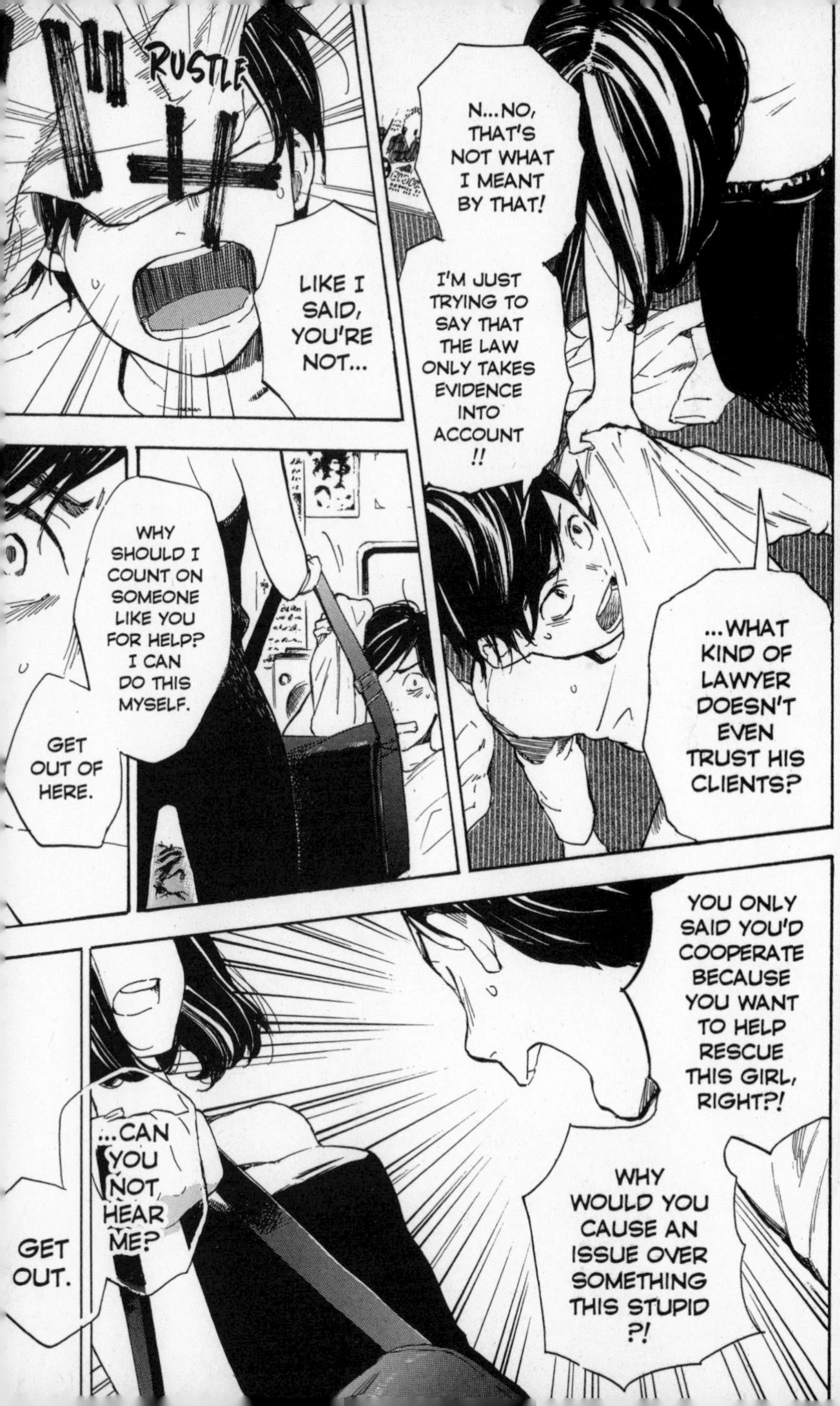
N...NO, THAT'S NOT WHAT I MEANT BY THAT!
I'M JUST TRYING TO SAY THAT THE LAW ONLY TAKES EVIDENCE INTO ACCOUNT!!
RUSTLE
LIKE I SAID, YOU'RE NOT...
...WHAT KIND OF LAWYER DOESN'T EVEN TRUST HIS CLIENTS?
WHY SHOULD I COUNT ON SOMEONE LIKE YOU FOR HELP? I CAN DO THIS MYSELF.
GET OUT OF HERE.
YOU ONLY SAID YOU'D COOPERATE BECAUSE YOU WANT TO HELP RESCUE THIS GIRL, RIGHT?!
WHY WOULD YOU CAUSE AN ISSUE OVER SOMETHING THIS STUPID?!
...CAN YOU NOT HEAR ME?
GET OUT.

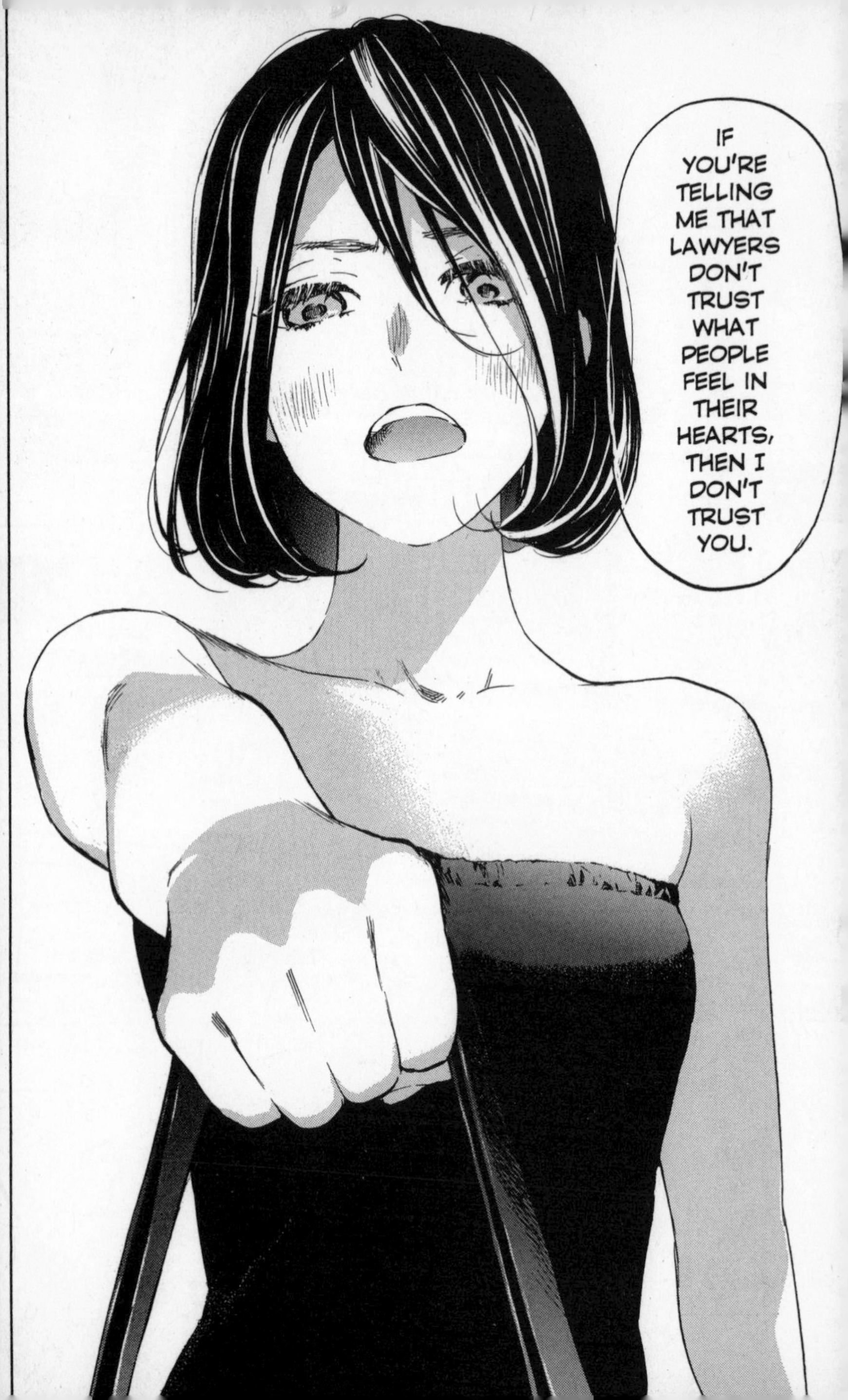
IF YOU'RE TELLING ME THAT LAWYERS DON'T TRUST WHAT PEOPLE FEEL IN THEIR HEARTS, THEN I DON'T TRUST YOU.

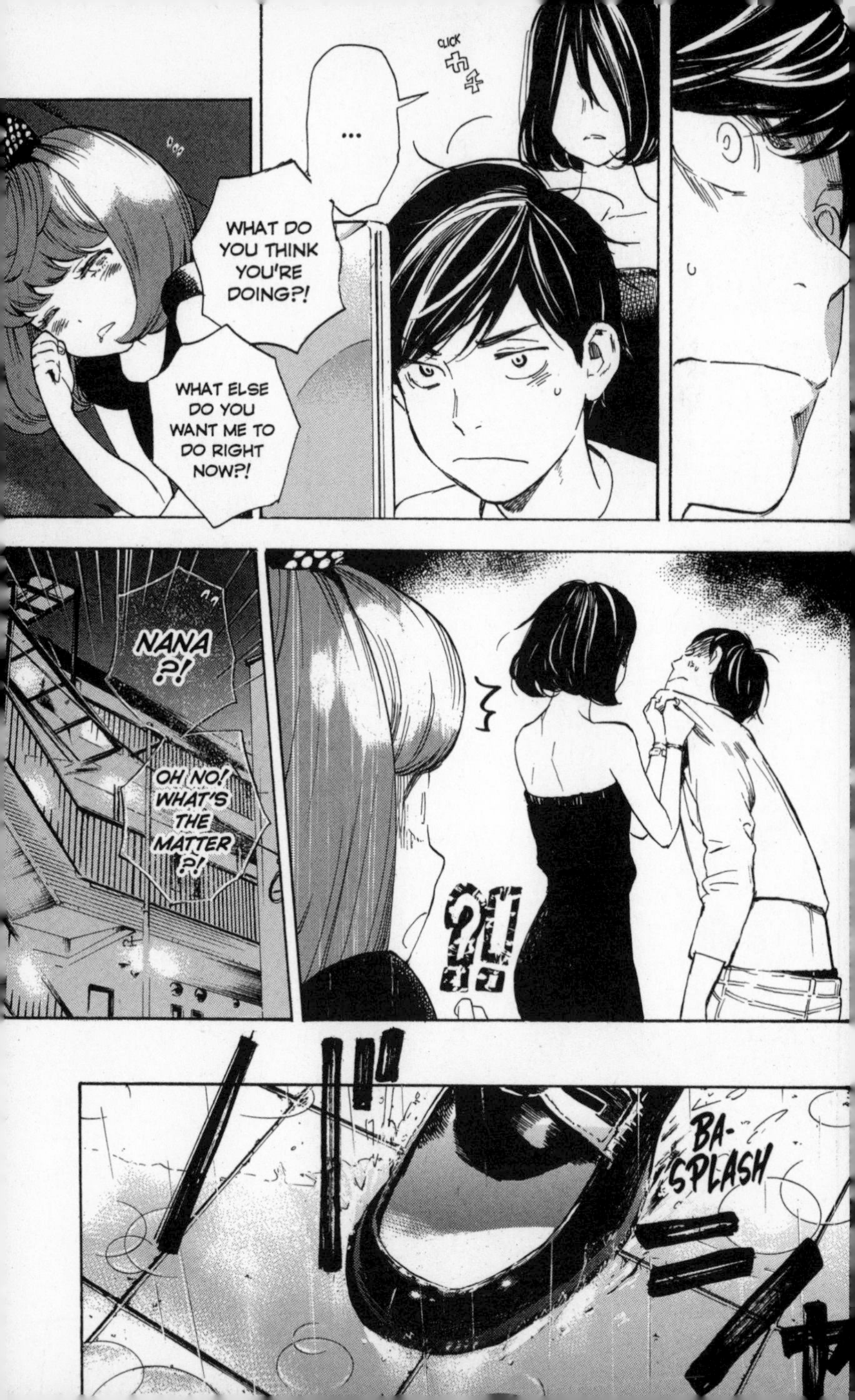
CLICK
...
WHAT DO YOU THINK YOU'RE DOING?!
WHAT ELSE DO YOU WANT ME TO DO RIGHT NOW?!
?!
NANA?!
OH NO! WHAT'S THE MATTER?!
BA-SPLASH

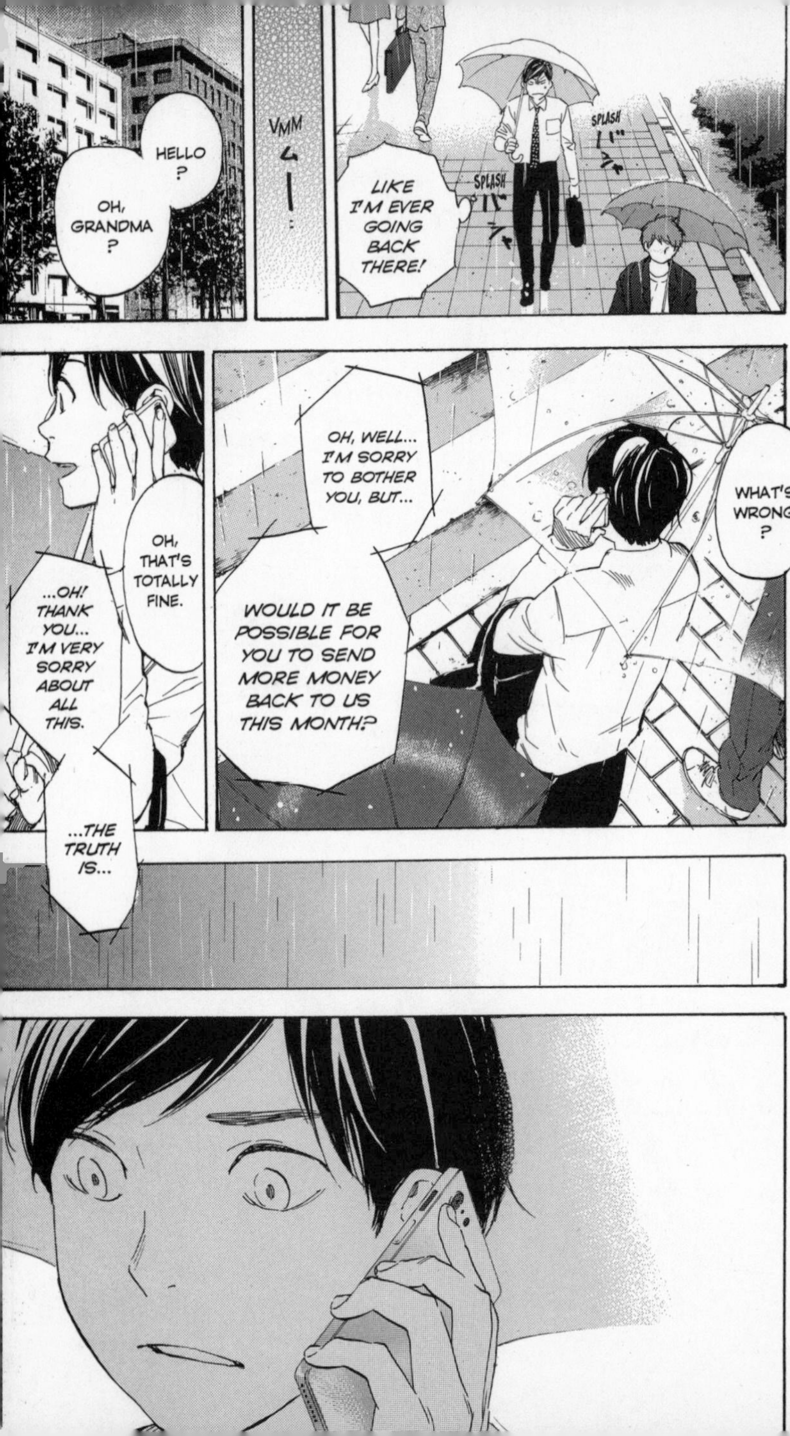
SPLASH
SPLASH
LIKE I'M EVER GOING BACK THERE!
VMM
HELLO?
OH, GRANDMA?
WHAT'S WRONG?
OH, WELL... I'M SORRY TO BOTHER YOU, BUT...
WOULD IT BE POSSIBLE FOR YOU TO SEND MORE MONEY BACK TO US THIS MONTH?
OH, THAT'S TOTALLY FINE.
...OH! THANK YOU... I'M VERY SORRY ABOUT ALL THIS.
...THE TRUTH IS...

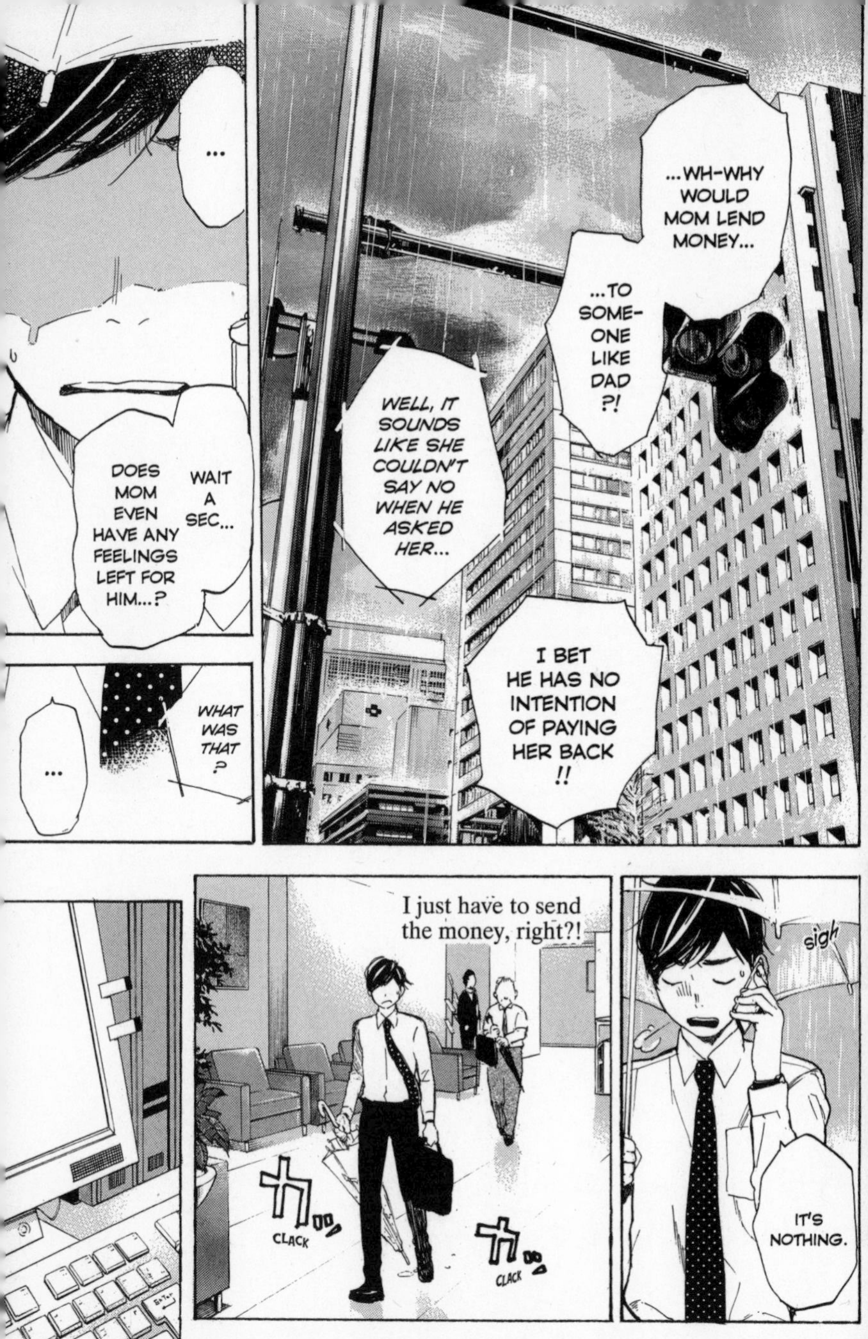
...WH-WHY WOULD MOM LEND MONEY...
...TO SOME-ONE LIKE DAD?!
WELL, IT SOUNDS LIKE SHE COULDN'T SAY NO WHEN HE ASKED HER...
I BET HE HAS NO INTENTION OF PAYING HER BACK!!
...
WAIT A SEC...
DOES MOM EVEN HAVE ANY FEELINGS LEFT FOR HIM...?
WHAT WAS THAT?
...
sigh
IT'S NOTHING.
I just have to send the money, right?!
CLACK
CLACK

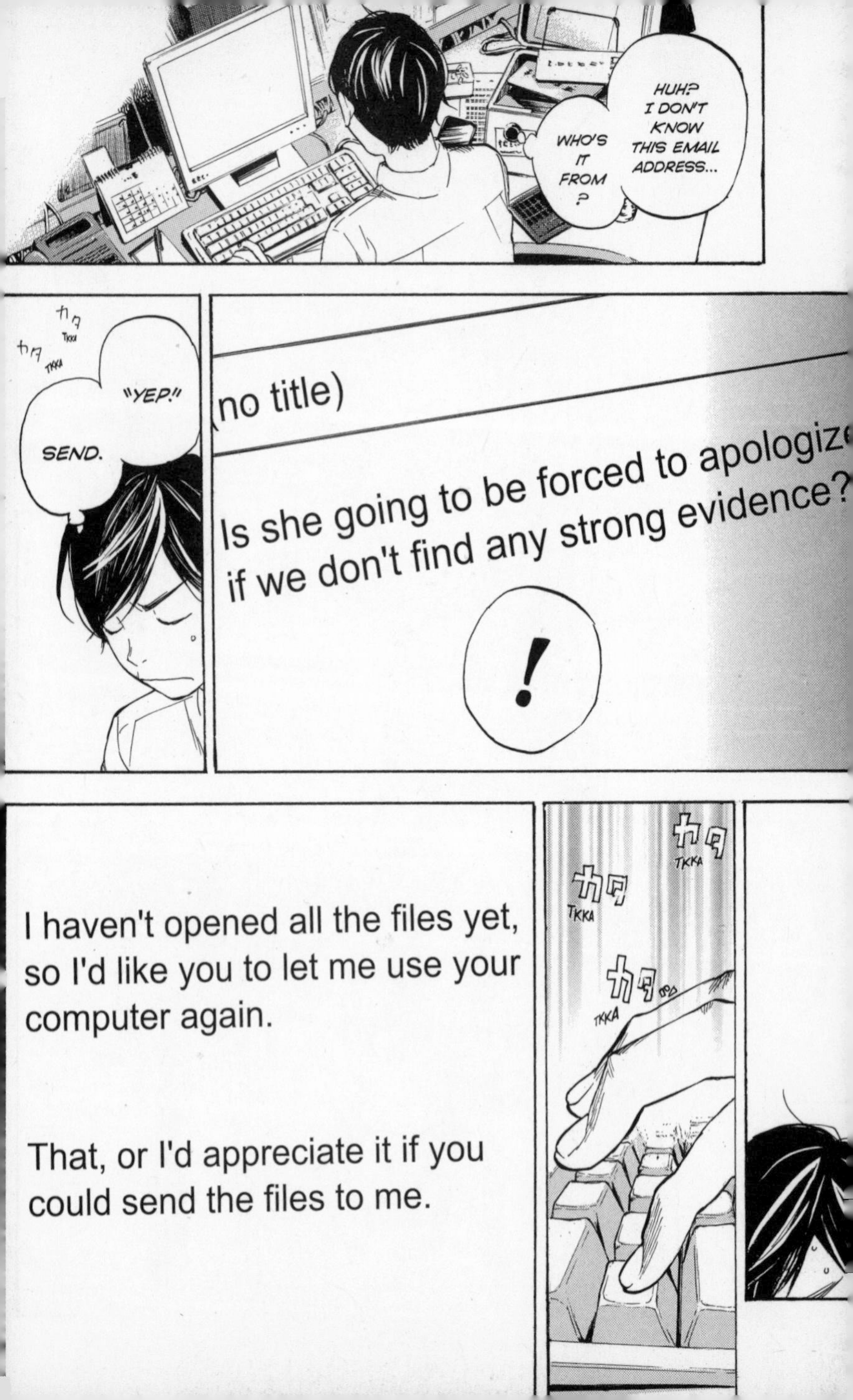

HUH? I DON'T KNOW THIS EMAIL ADDRESS...
WHO'S IT FROM?
(no title)
Is she going to be forced to apologize if we don't find any strong evidence?
!
カタ TKKA
カタ TKKA
"YEP!" SEND.
カタ TKKA
カタ TKKA
カタ TKKA
I haven't opened all the files yet, so I'd like you to let me use your computer again.
That, or I'd appreciate it if you could send the files to me.

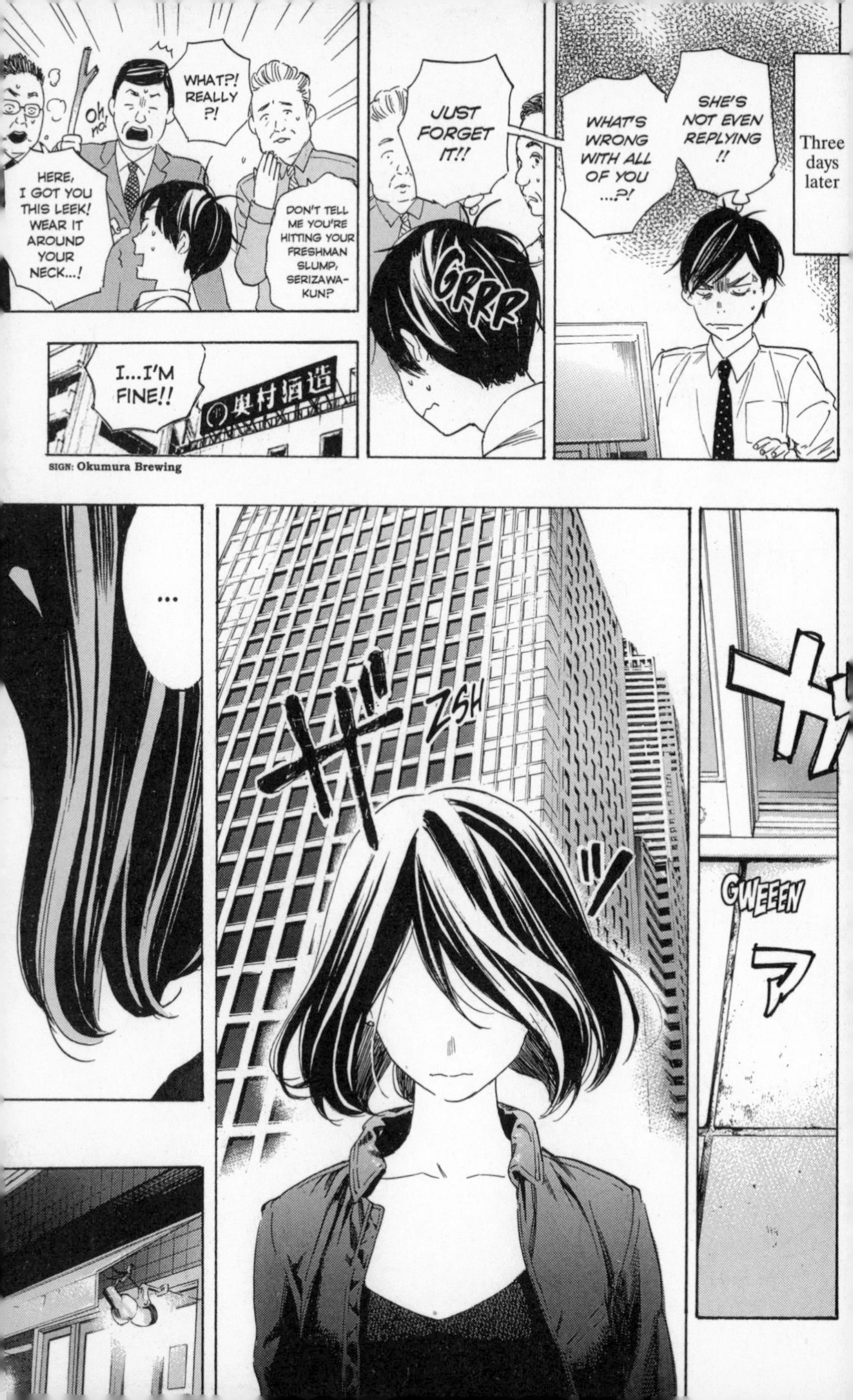
Three days later
SHE'S NOT EVEN REPLYING!!
WHAT'S WRONG WITH ALL OF YOU...?!
JUST FORGET IT!!
GRRR
WHAT?! REALLY?!
Oh, no!
DON'T TELL ME YOU'RE HITTING YOUR FRESHMAN SLUMP, SERIZAWA-KUN?
HERE, I GOT YOU THIS LEEK! WEAR IT AROUND YOUR NECK...!
I...I'M FINE!!
奥村酒造
GWEEEN
ア
ZSH
...

SIGN: Okumura Brewing

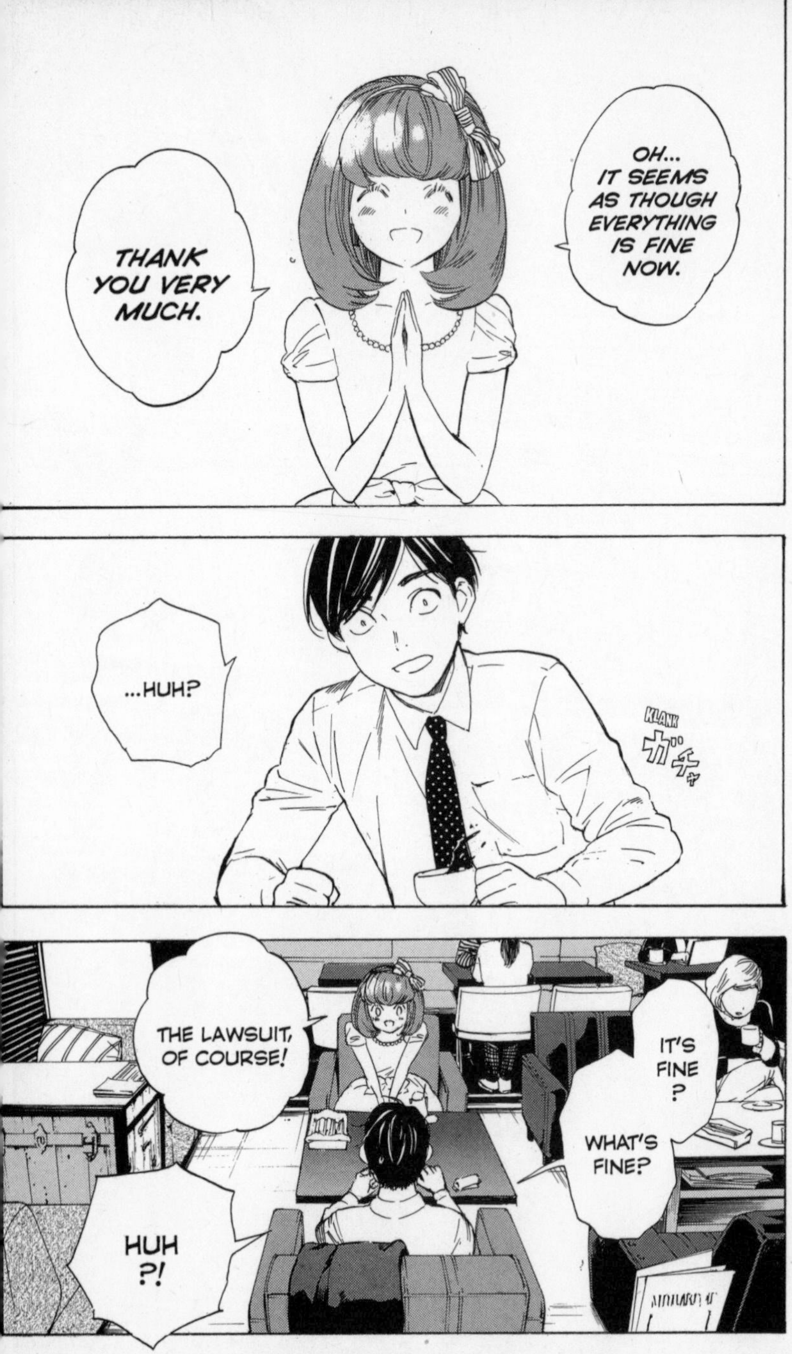
OH... IT SEEMS AS THOUGH EVERYTHING IS FINE NOW.
THANK YOU VERY MUCH.
KLANK ガチャ
...HUH?
IT'S FINE?
WHAT'S FINE?
THE LAWSUIT, OF COURSE!
HUH?!

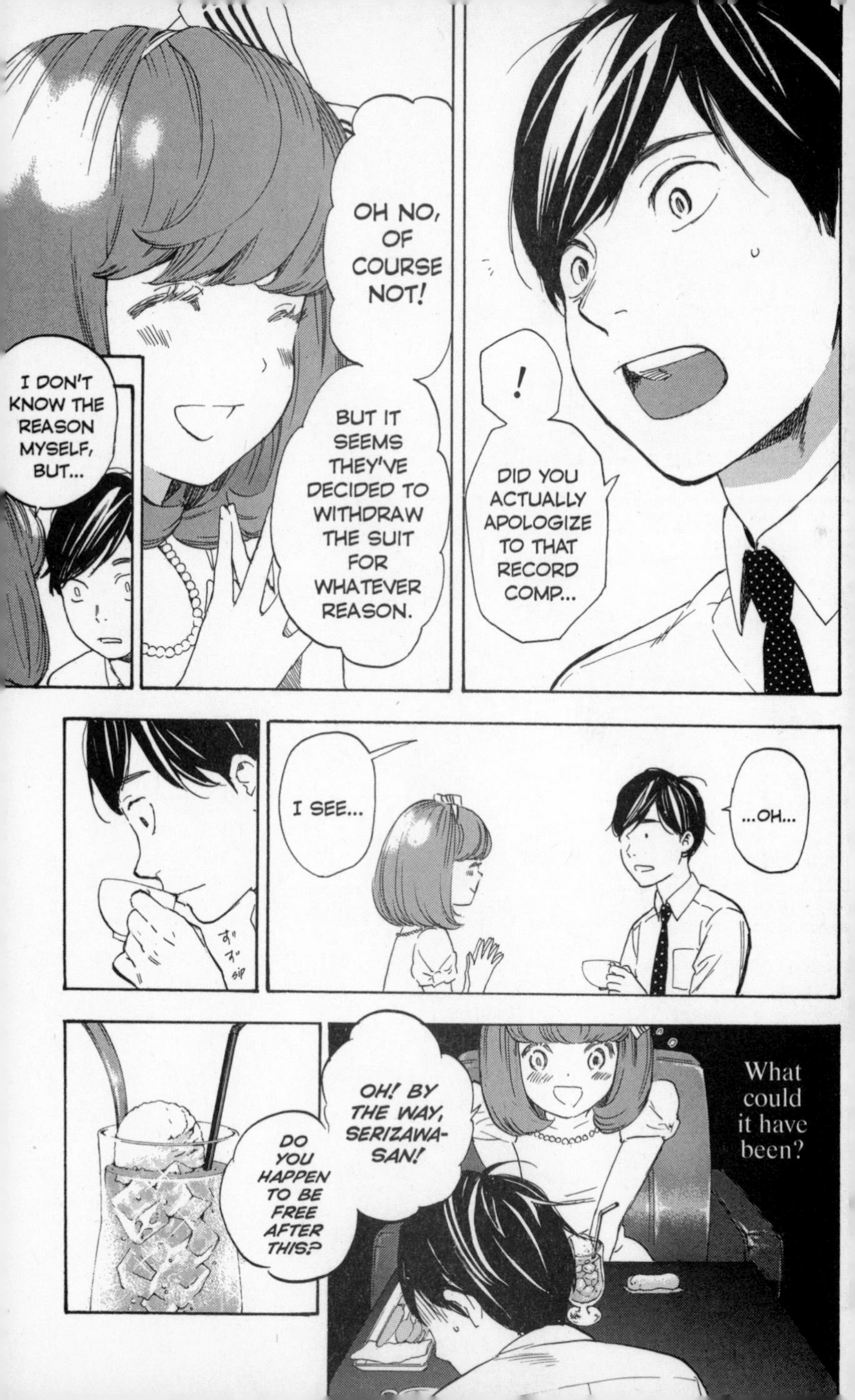
!
DID YOU ACTUALLY APOLOGIZE TO THAT RECORD COMP...
OH NO, OF COURSE NOT!
BUT IT SEEMS THEY'VE DECIDED TO WITHDRAW THE SUIT FOR WHATEVER REASON.
I DON'T KNOW THE REASON MYSELF, BUT...
...OH...
I SEE...
ずず
sip
What could it have been?
OH! BY THE WAY, SERIZAWA-SAN!
DO YOU HAPPEN TO BE FREE AFTER THIS?

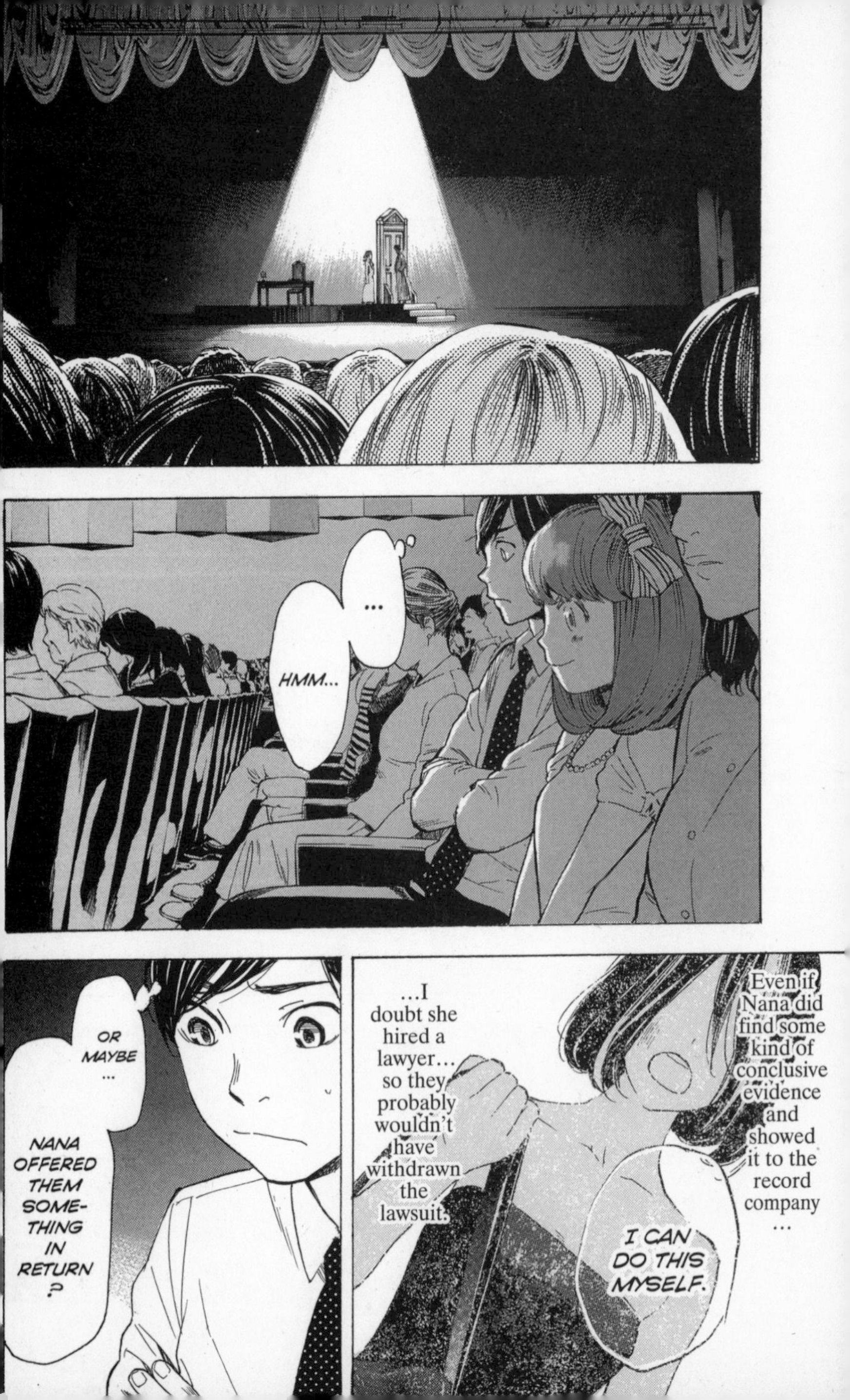
...
HMM...
Even if Nana did find some kind of conclusive evidence and showed it to the record company…
…I doubt she hired a lawyer… so they probably wouldn't have withdrawn the lawsuit.
I CAN DO THIS MYSELF.
OR MAYBE…
NANA OFFERED THEM SOMETHING IN RETURN?

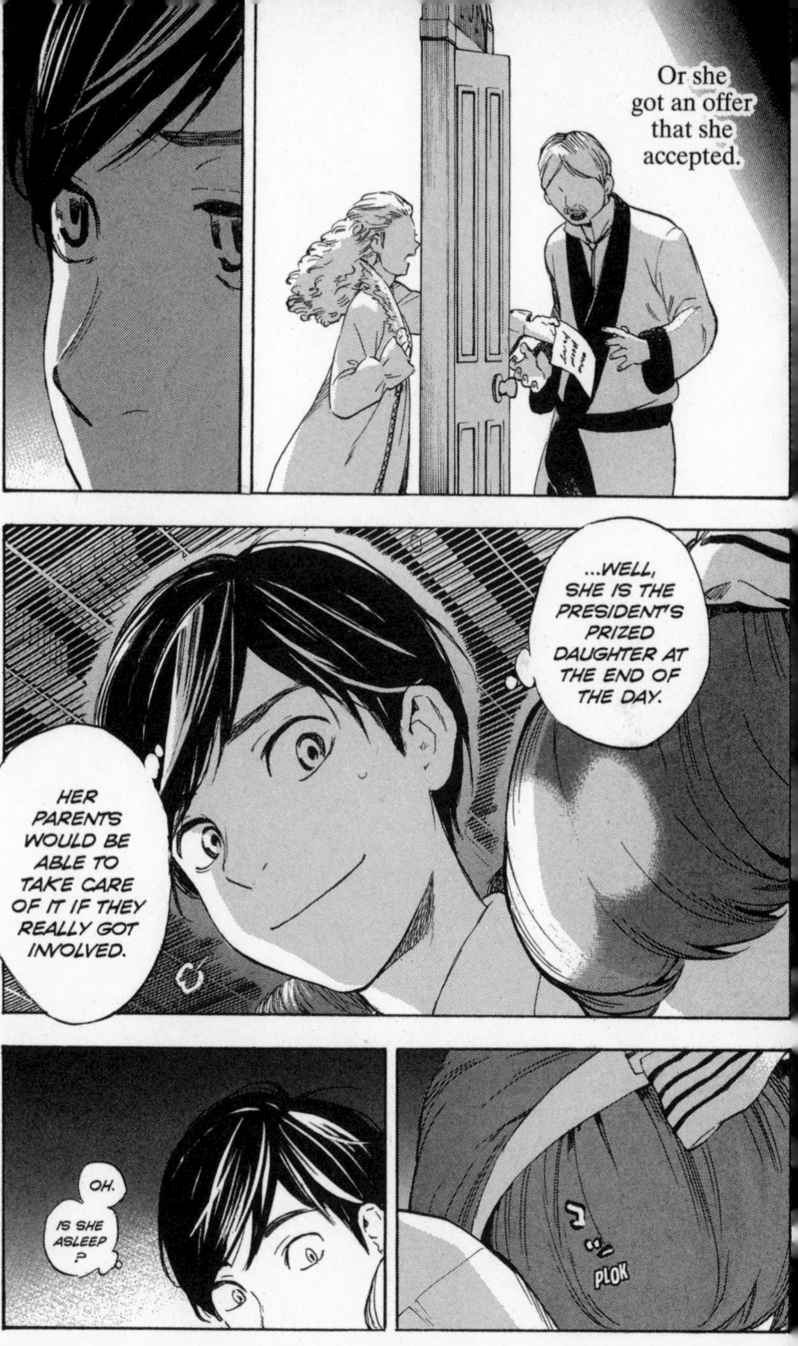
Or she got an offer that she accepted.
...WELL, SHE IS THE PRESIDENT'S PRIZED DAUGHTER AT THE END OF THE DAY.
HER PARENTS WOULD BE ABLE TO TAKE CARE OF IT IF THEY REALLY GOT INVOLVED.
PLOK
OH.
IS SHE ASLEEP?

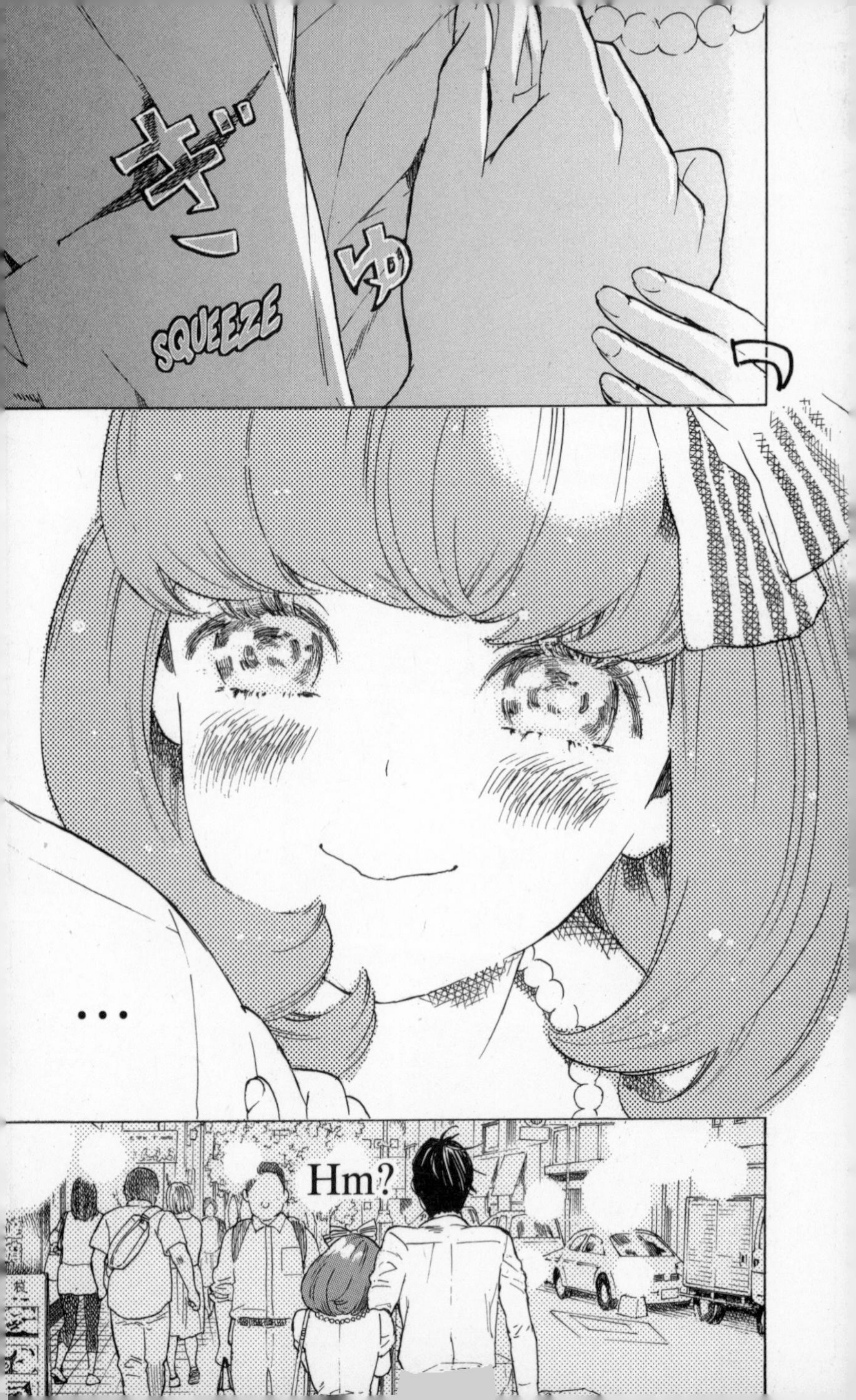
SQUEEZE
...
Hm?

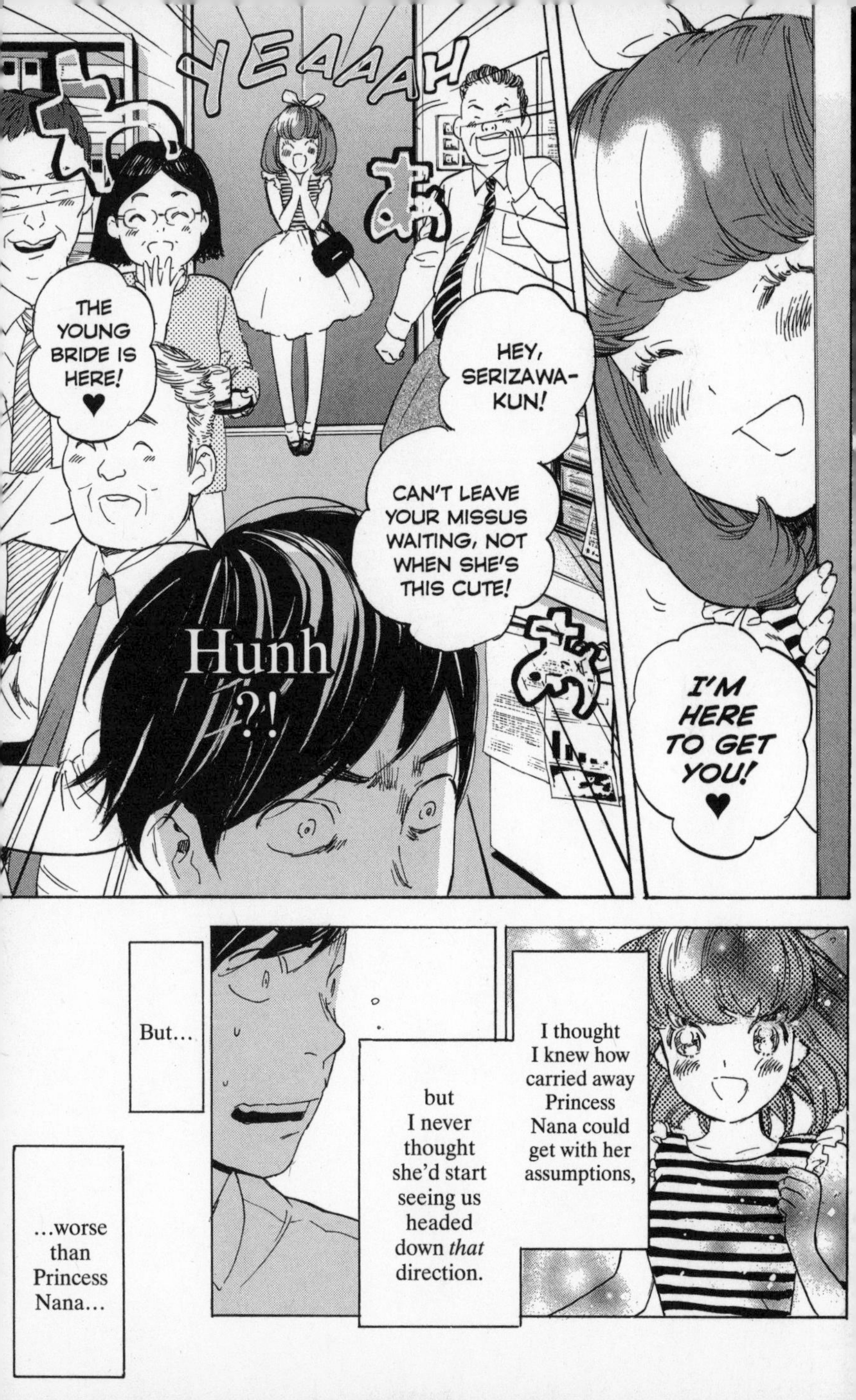
I'M HERE TO GET YOU! ♥
YEAAAH
THE YOUNG BRIDE IS HERE! ♥
HEY, SERIZAWA-KUN!
CAN'T LEAVE YOUR MISSUS WAITING, NOT WHEN SHE'S THIS CUTE!
Hunh ?!
I thought I knew how carried away Princess Nana could get with her assumptions,
but I never thought she'd start seeing us headed down *that* direction.
But…
…worse than Princess Nana…

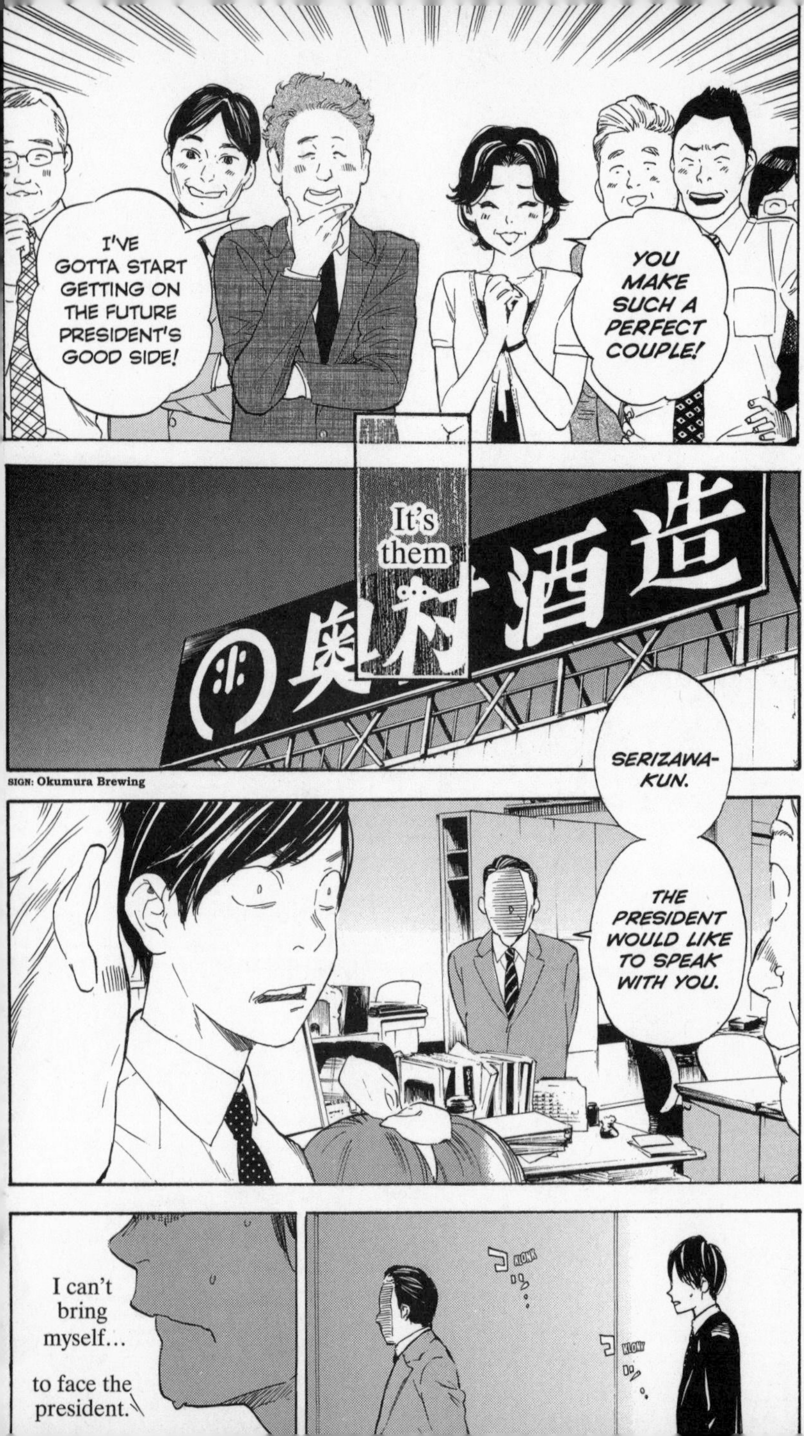
YOU MAKE SUCH A PERFECT COUPLE!
I'VE GOTTA START GETTING ON THE FUTURE PRESIDENT'S GOOD SIDE!
It's them
SERIZAWA-KUN.
THE PRESIDENT WOULD LIKE TO SPEAK WITH YOU.
KLONK
KLONK
I can't bring myself...
to face the president.
SIGN: Okumura Brewing

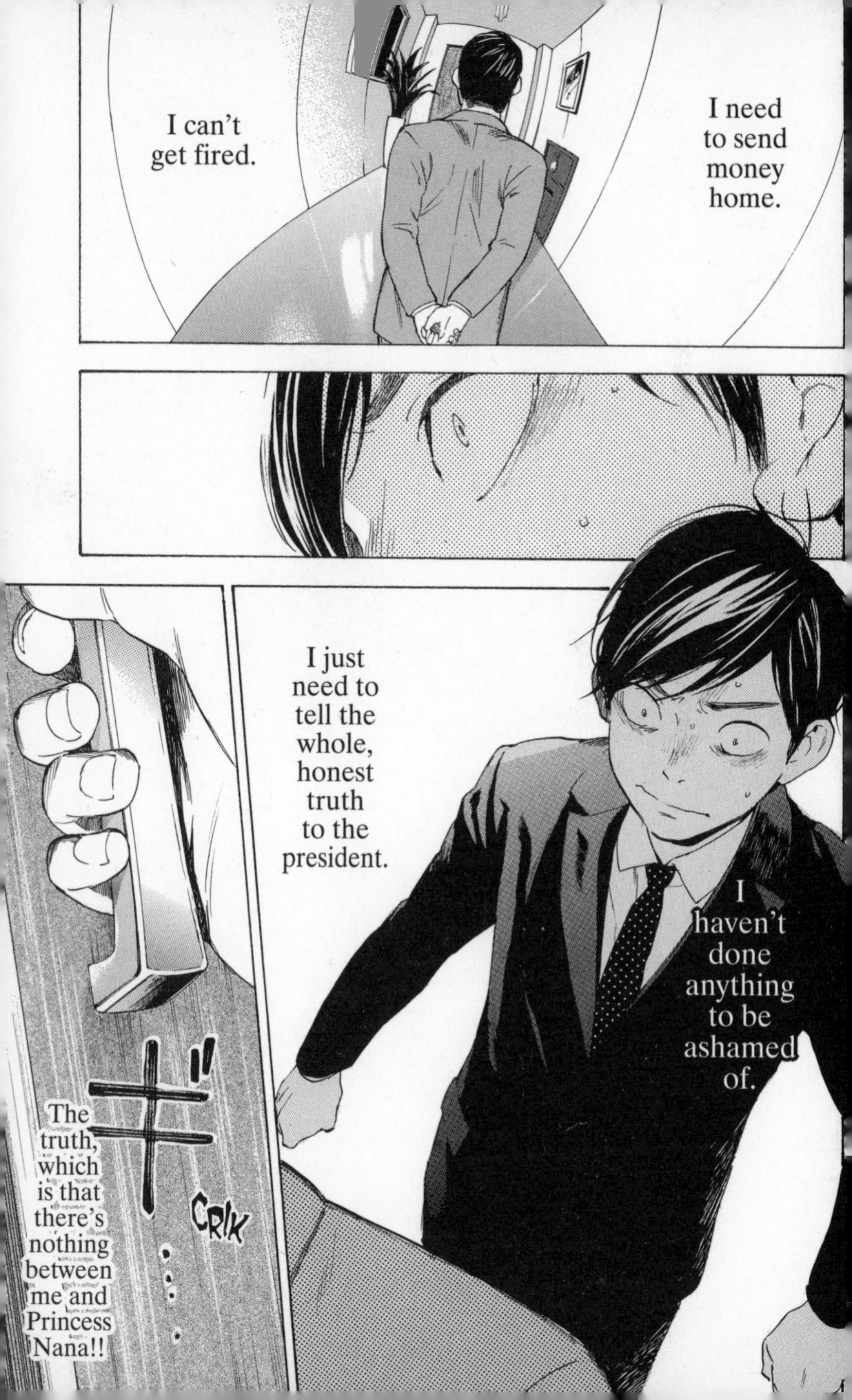

I need to send money home.
I can't get fired.
I just need to tell the whole, honest truth to the president.
I haven't done anything to be ashamed of.
CRIK
...
The truth, which is that there's nothing between me and Princess Nana!!

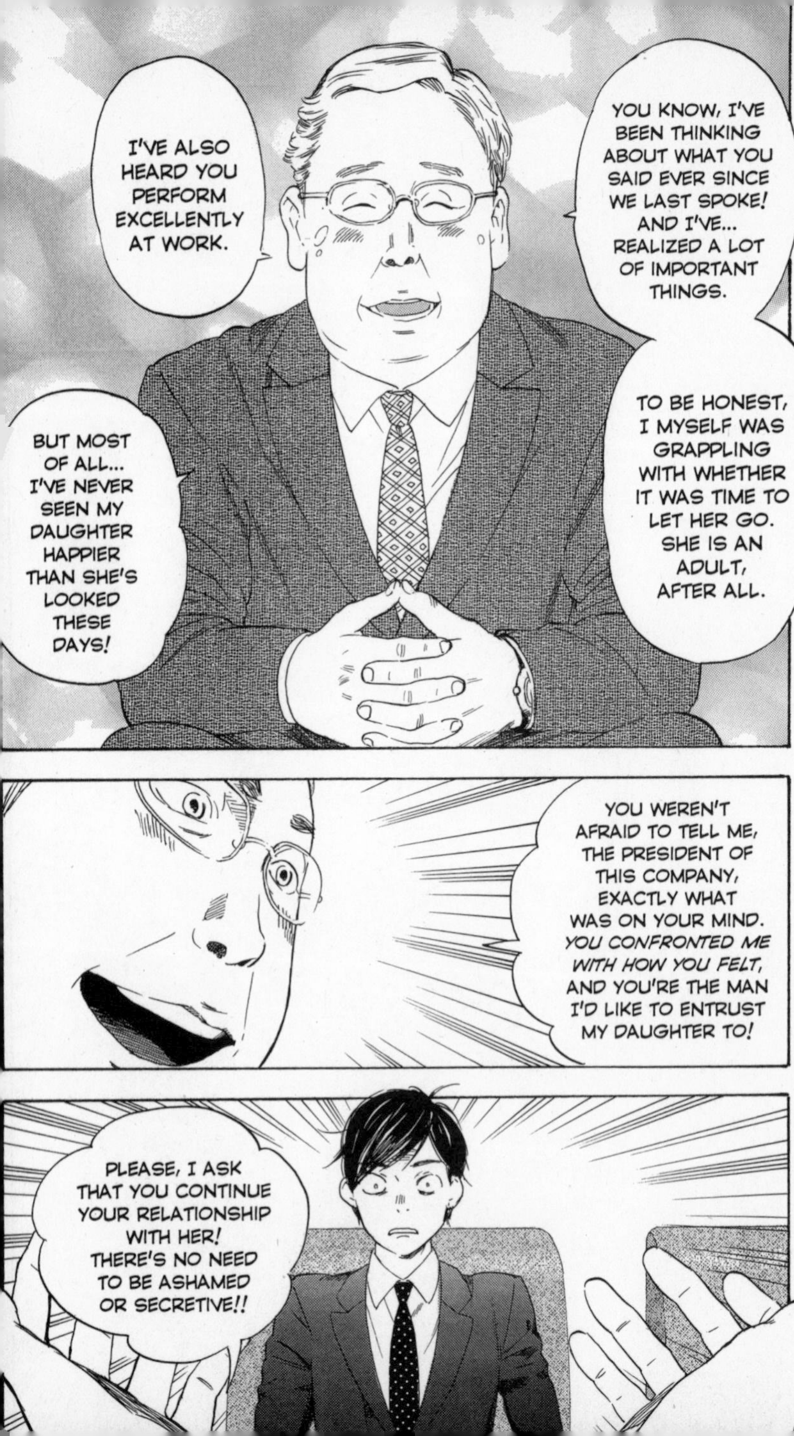
YOU KNOW, I'VE BEEN THINKING ABOUT WHAT YOU SAID EVER SINCE WE LAST SPOKE! AND I'VE... REALIZED A LOT OF IMPORTANT THINGS.
I'VE ALSO HEARD YOU PERFORM EXCELLENTLY AT WORK.
TO BE HONEST, I MYSELF WAS GRAPPLING WITH WHETHER IT WAS TIME TO LET HER GO. SHE IS AN ADULT, AFTER ALL.
BUT MOST OF ALL... I'VE NEVER SEEN MY DAUGHTER HAPPIER THAN SHE'S LOOKED THESE DAYS!
YOU WEREN'T AFRAID TO TELL ME, THE PRESIDENT OF THIS COMPANY, EXACTLY WHAT WAS ON YOUR MIND. *YOU CONFRONTED ME WITH HOW YOU FELT,* AND YOU'RE THE MAN I'D LIKE TO ENTRUST MY DAUGHTER TO!
PLEASE, I ASK THAT YOU CONTINUE YOUR RELATIONSHIP WITH HER! THERE'S NO NEED TO BE ASHAMED OR SECRETIVE!!

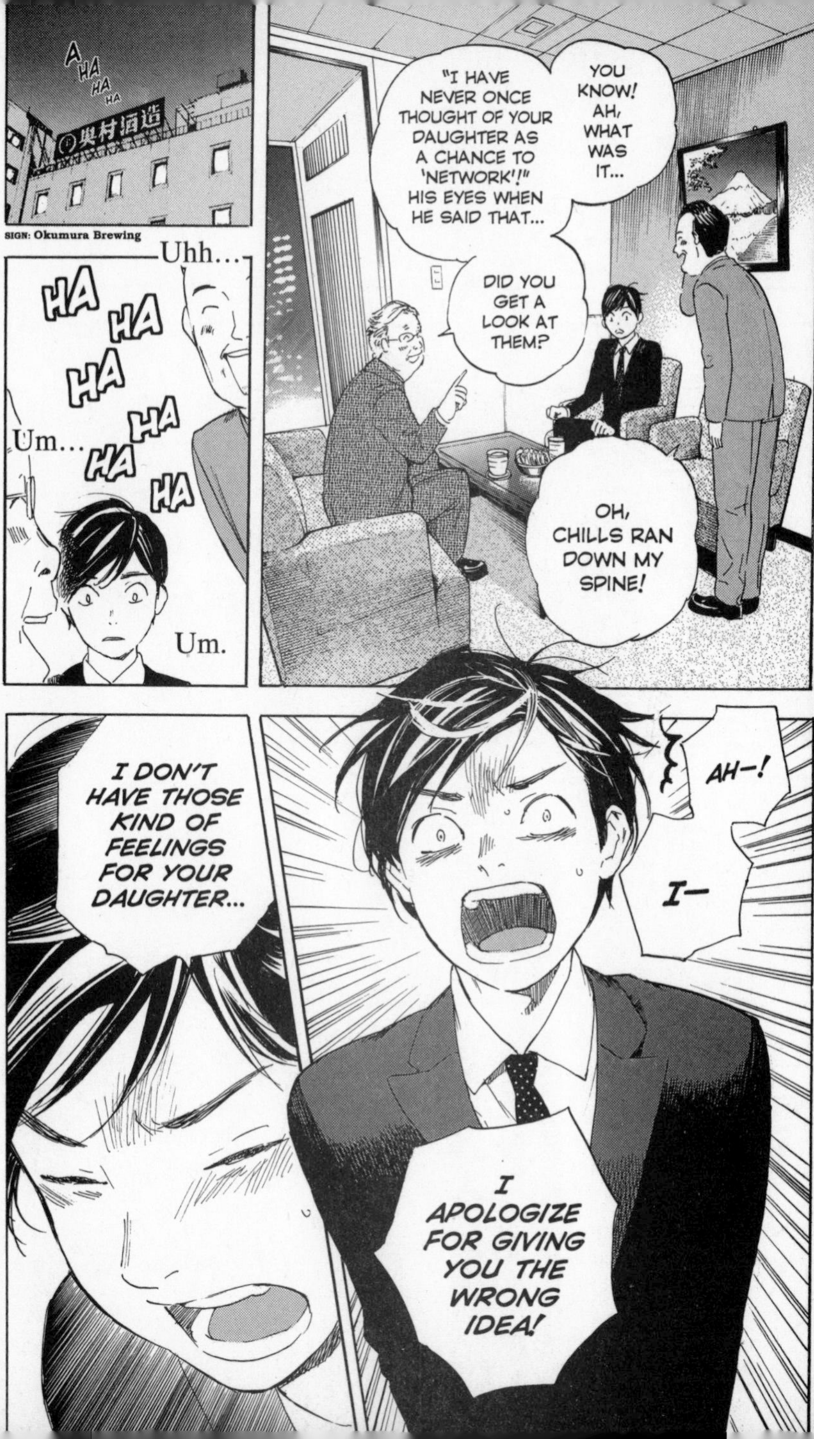
YOU KNOW! AH, WHAT WAS IT...
"I HAVE NEVER ONCE THOUGHT OF YOUR DAUGHTER AS A CHANCE TO 'NETWORK'!" HIS EYES WHEN HE SAID THAT...
DID YOU GET A LOOK AT THEM?
OH, CHILLS RAN DOWN MY SPINE!
A HA HA HA
奥村酒造
SIGN: Okumura Brewing
Uhh...
HA HA HA HA HA HA
Um...
Um.
AH—!
I—
I DON'T HAVE THOSE KIND OF FEELINGS FOR YOUR DAUGHTER...
I APOLOGIZE FOR GIVING YOU THE WRONG IDEA!

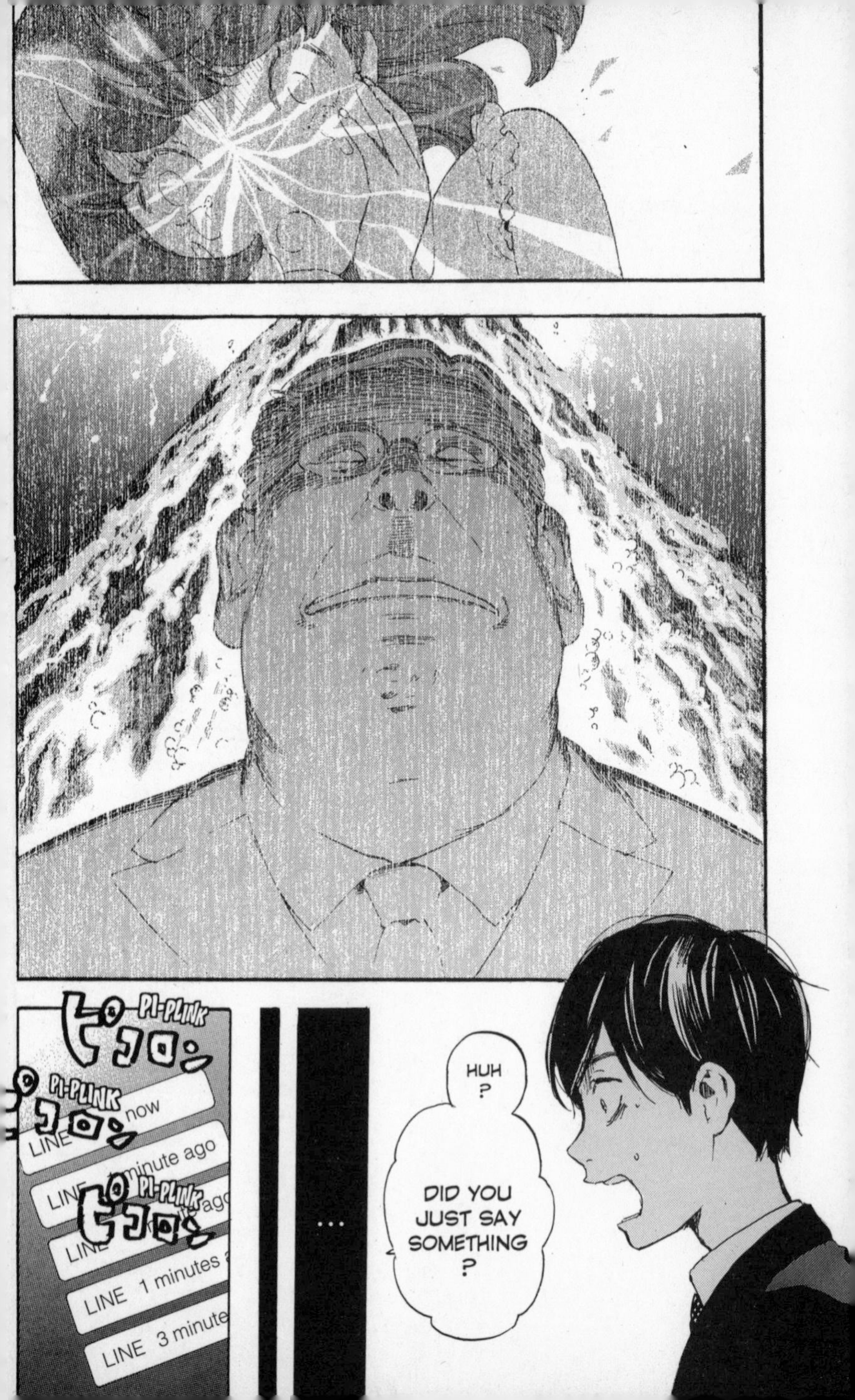
HUH?
DID YOU JUST SAY SOMETHING?
...
PI-PLINK
PI-PLINK
LINE now
LINE 1 minute ago
PI-PLINK
LINE 1 minutes
LINE 3 minute

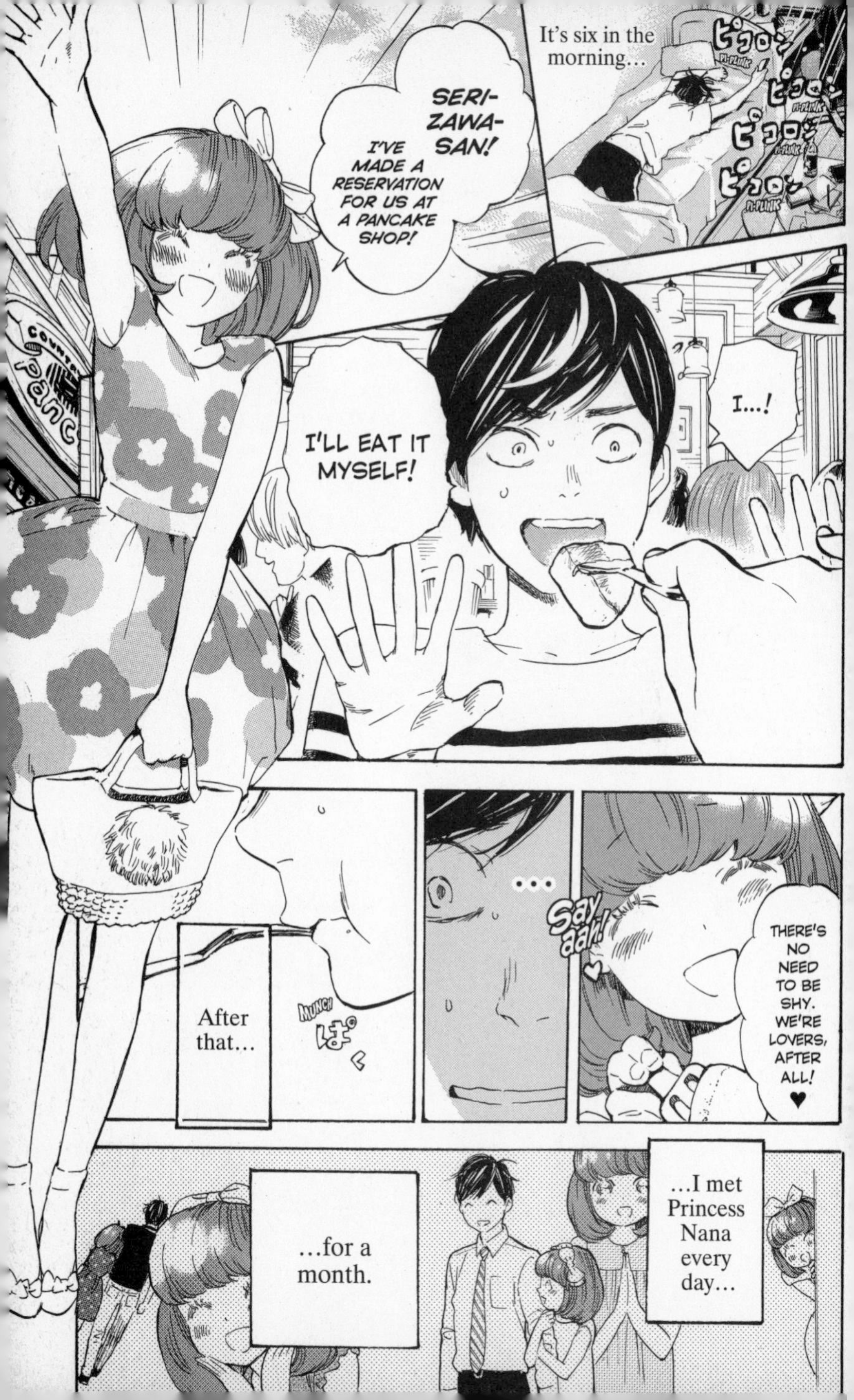
It's six in the morning…
PI-PLINK
PI-PLINK
PI-PLINK
PI-PLINK
SERI-ZAWA-SAN!
I'VE MADE A RESERVATION FOR US AT A PANCAKE SHOP!
I…!
I'LL EAT IT MYSELF!
THERE'S NO NEED TO BE SHY. WE'RE LOVERS, AFTER ALL! ♥
Say aah! ♥
…
MUNCH
After that…
…I met Princess Nana every day…
…for a month.

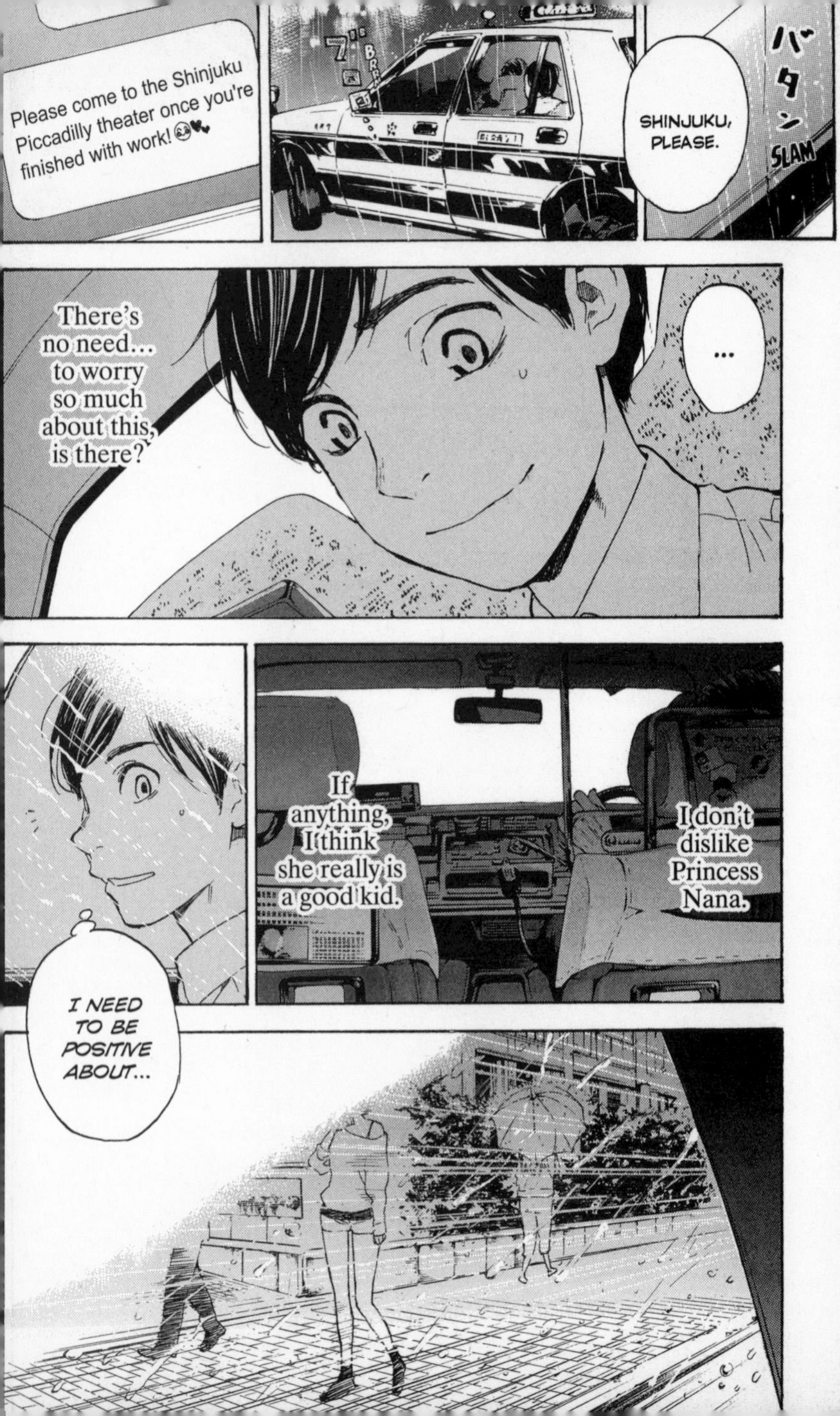
バタン
SLAM
SHINJUKU, PLEASE.
BRR
Please come to the Shinjuku Piccadilly theater once you're finished with work!
...
There's no need... to worry so much about this, is there?
I don't dislike Princess Nana.
If anything, I think she really is a good kid.
I NEED TO BE POSITIVE ABOUT...

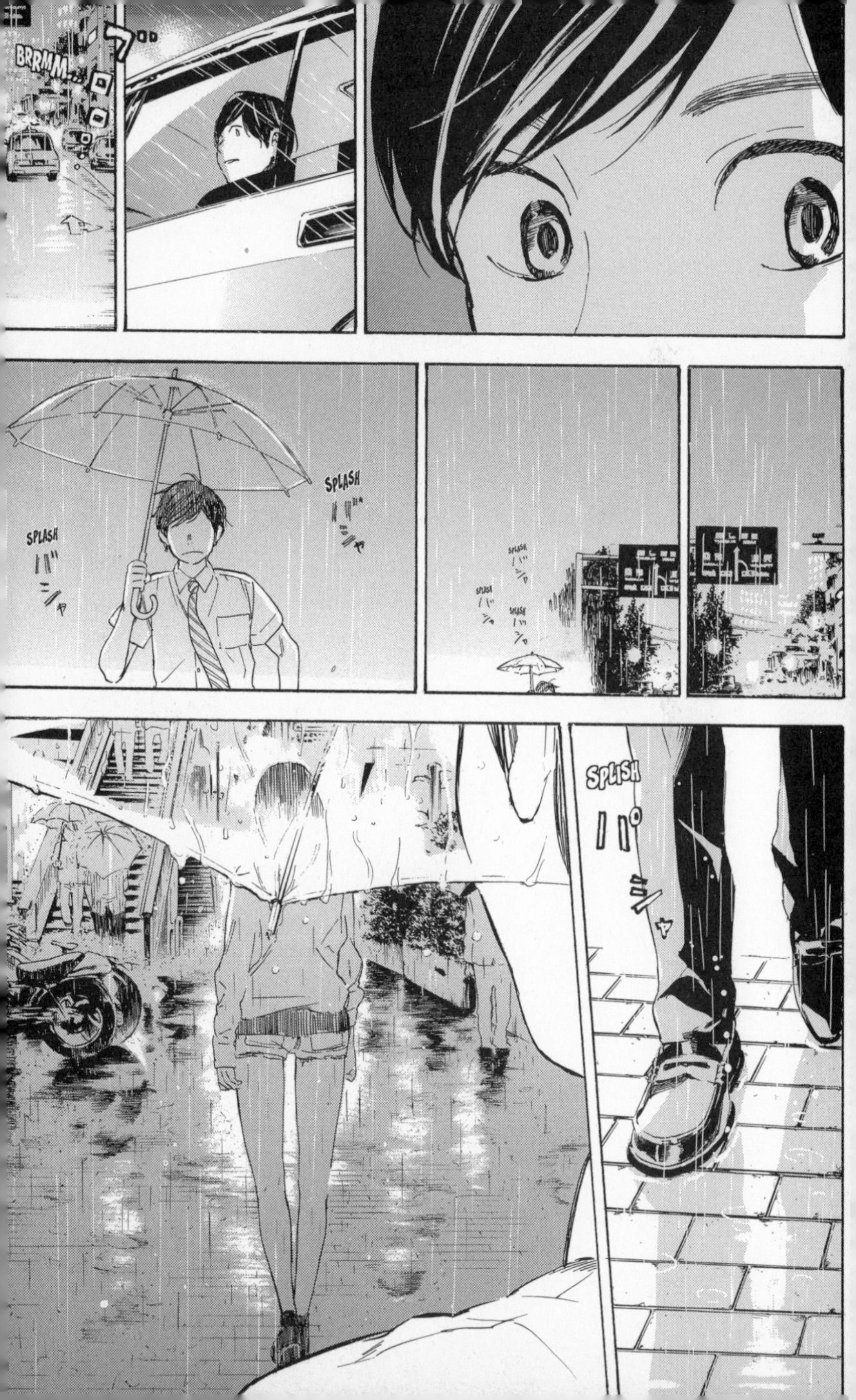
BRRMM...
SPLASH
SPLASH
SPLASH
SPLASH
SPLASH
SPLISH

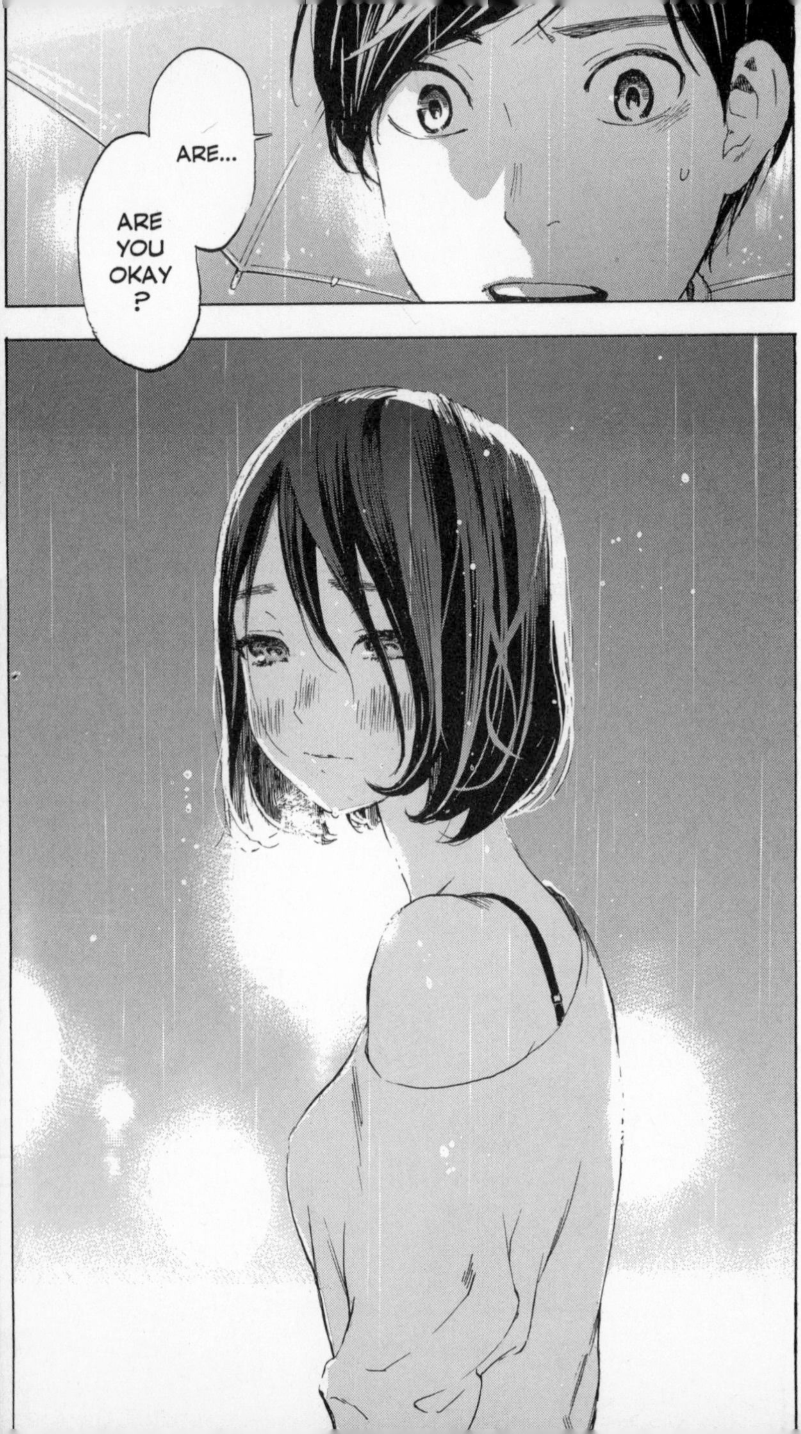
ARE...
ARE YOU OKAY?

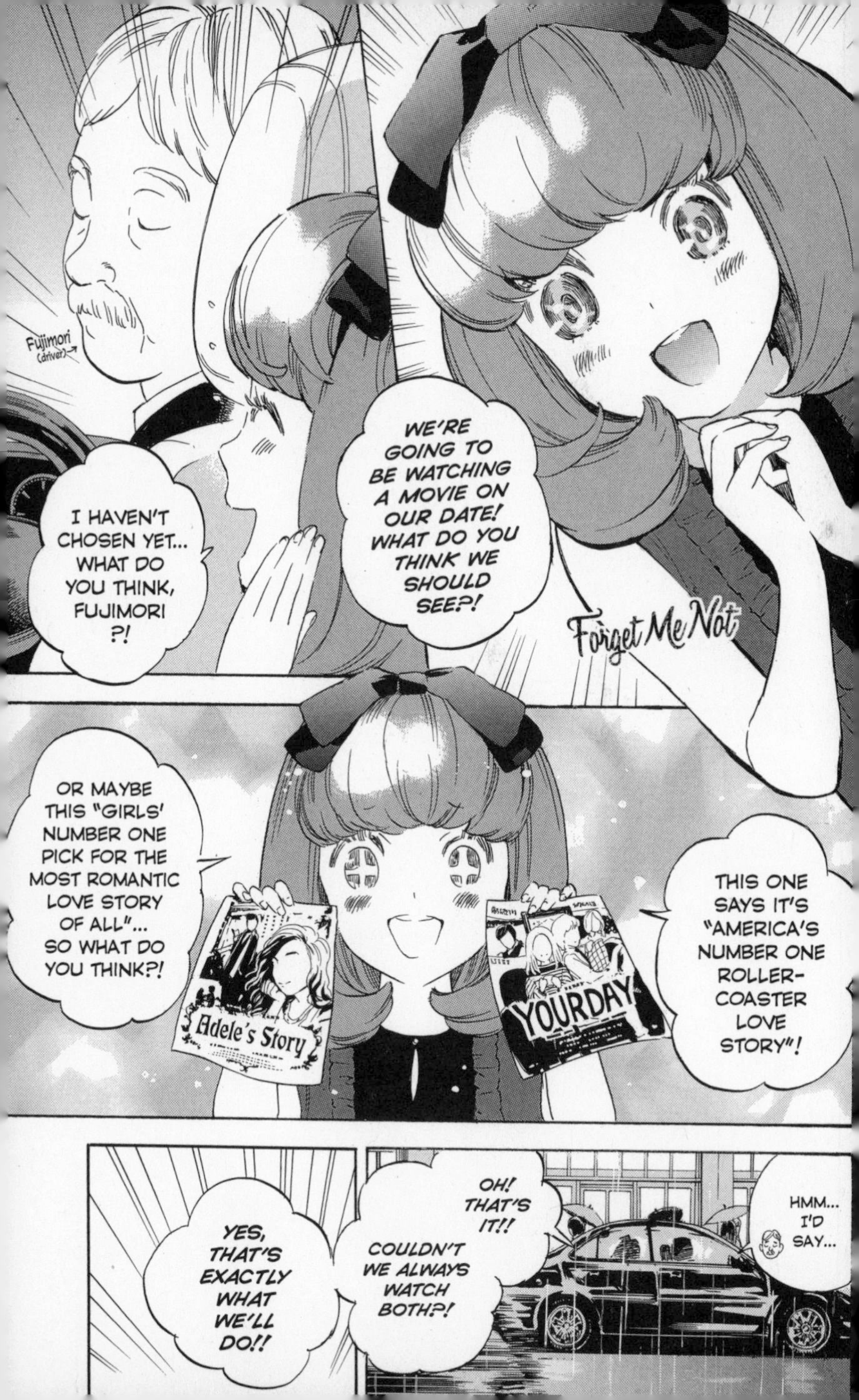
WE'RE GOING TO BE WATCHING A MOVIE ON OUR DATE! WHAT DO YOU THINK WE SHOULD SEE?!
Forget Me Not
Fujimori (driver)
I HAVEN'T CHOSEN YET... WHAT DO YOU THINK, FUJIMORI ?!
THIS ONE SAYS IT'S "AMERICA'S NUMBER ONE ROLLER-COASTER LOVE STORY"!
YOURDAY
Adele's Story
OR MAYBE THIS "GIRLS' NUMBER ONE PICK FOR THE MOST ROMANTIC LOVE STORY OF ALL"... SO WHAT DO YOU THINK?!
HMM... I'D SAY...
OH! THAT'S IT!!
COULDN'T WE ALWAYS WATCH BOTH?!
YES, THAT'S EXACTLY WHAT WE'LL DO!!

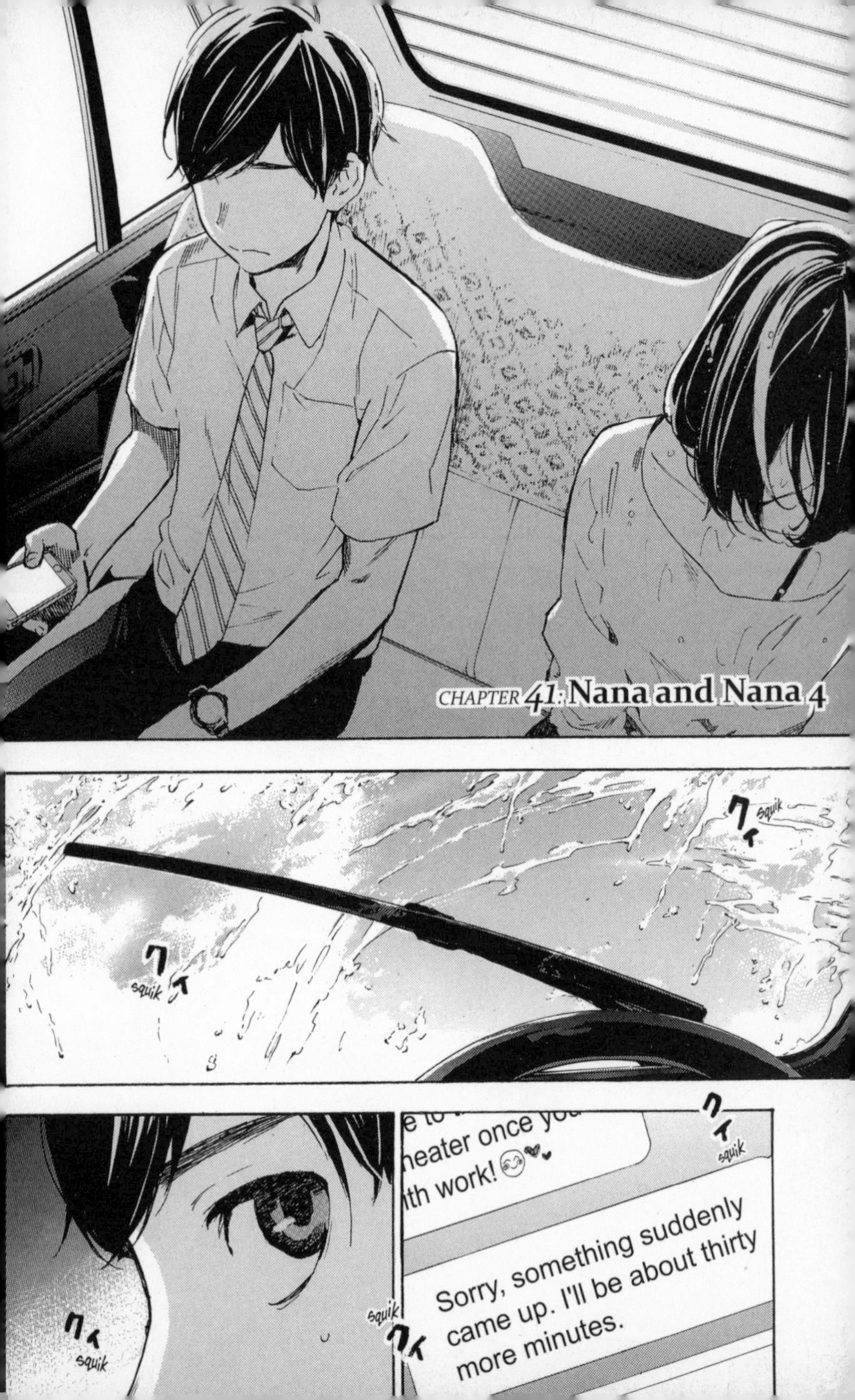
CHAPTER 41: Nana and Nana 4
squik
squik
squik
heater once you
ith work!
Sorry, something suddenly came up. I'll be about thirty more minutes.
squik
squik

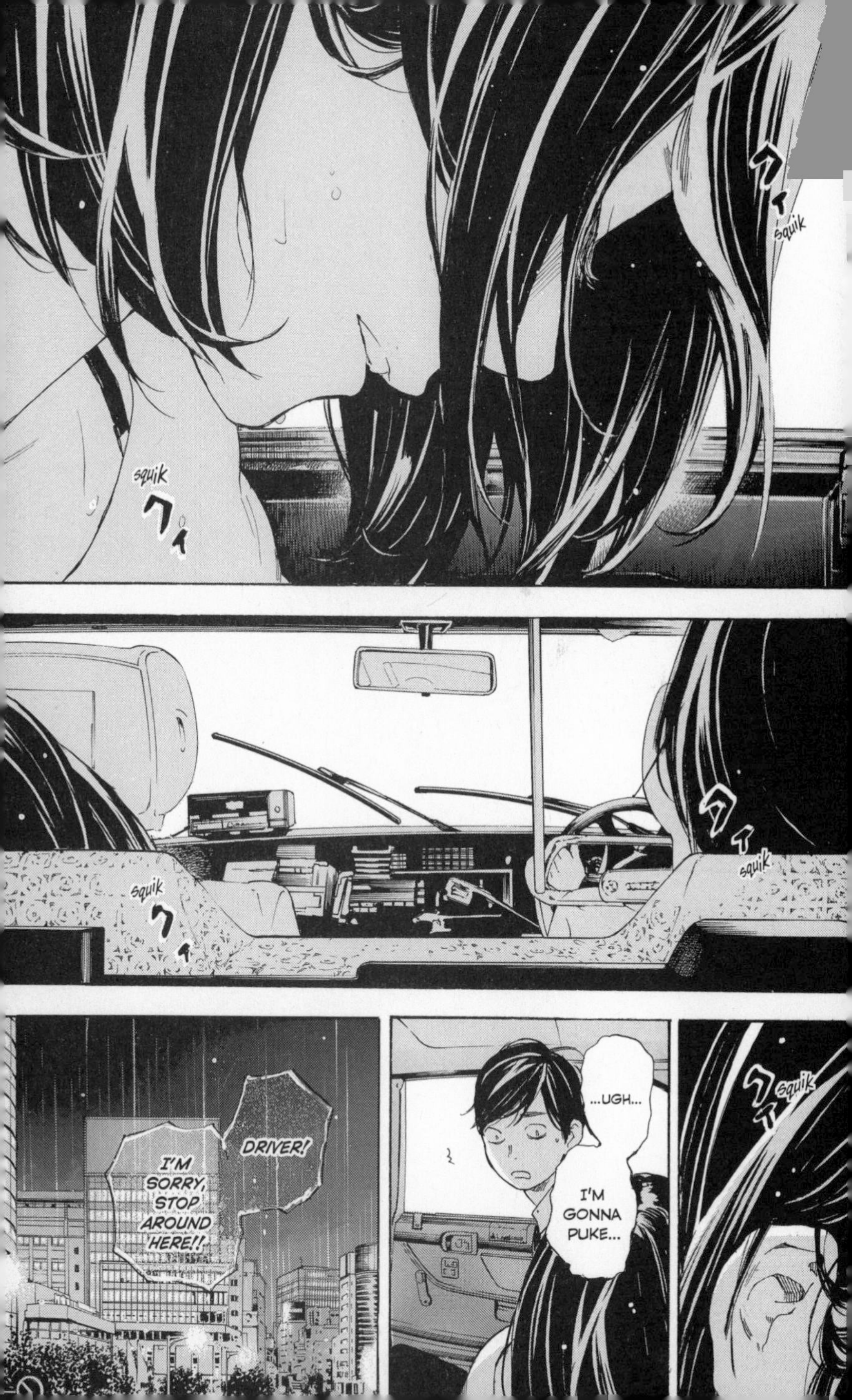
squik
squik
squik
squik
squik
...UGH...
I'M GONNA PUKE...
DRIVER!
I'M SORRY, STOP AROUND HERE!!

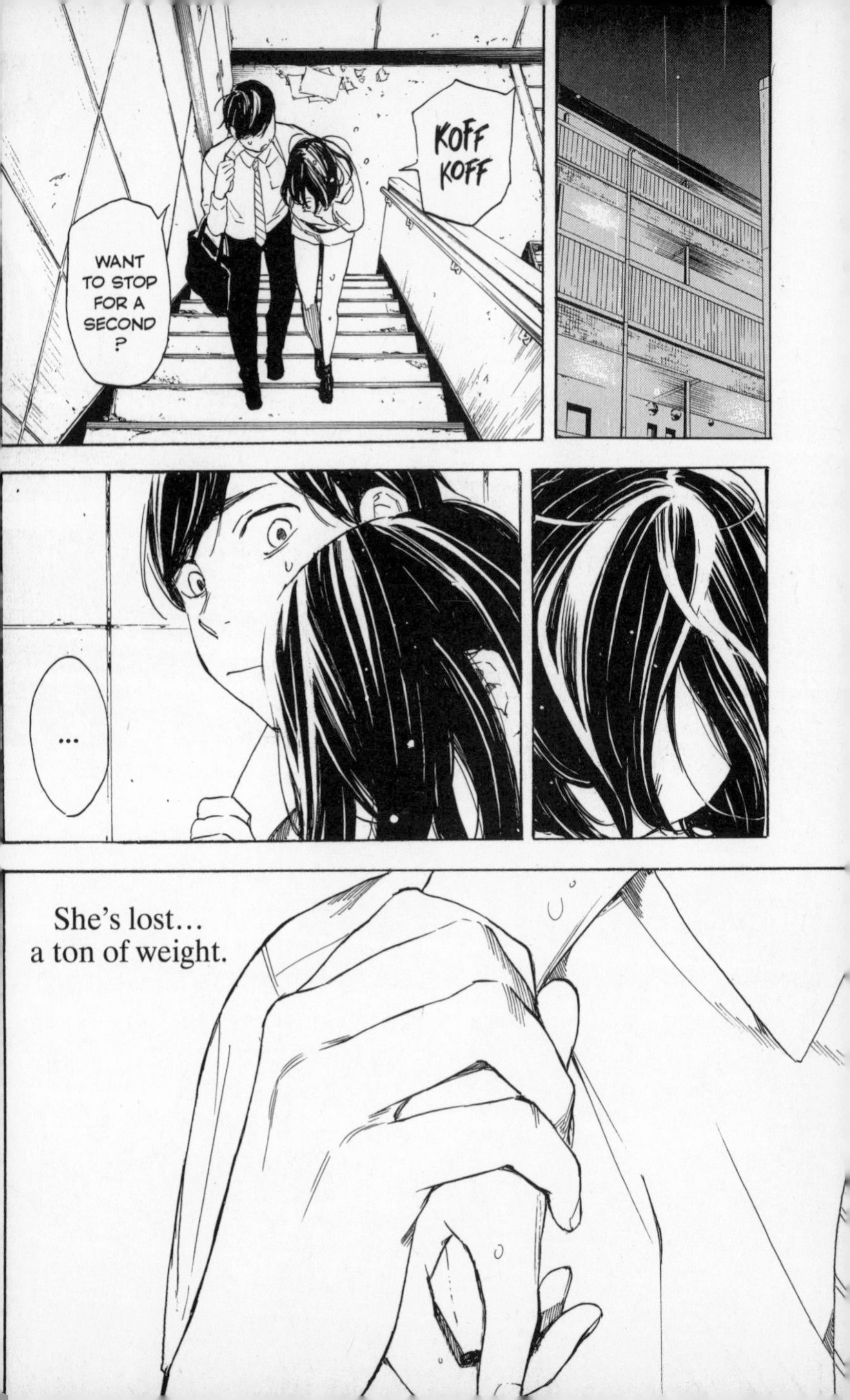
KOFF KOFF
WANT TO STOP FOR A SECOND?
...
She's lost… a ton of weight.

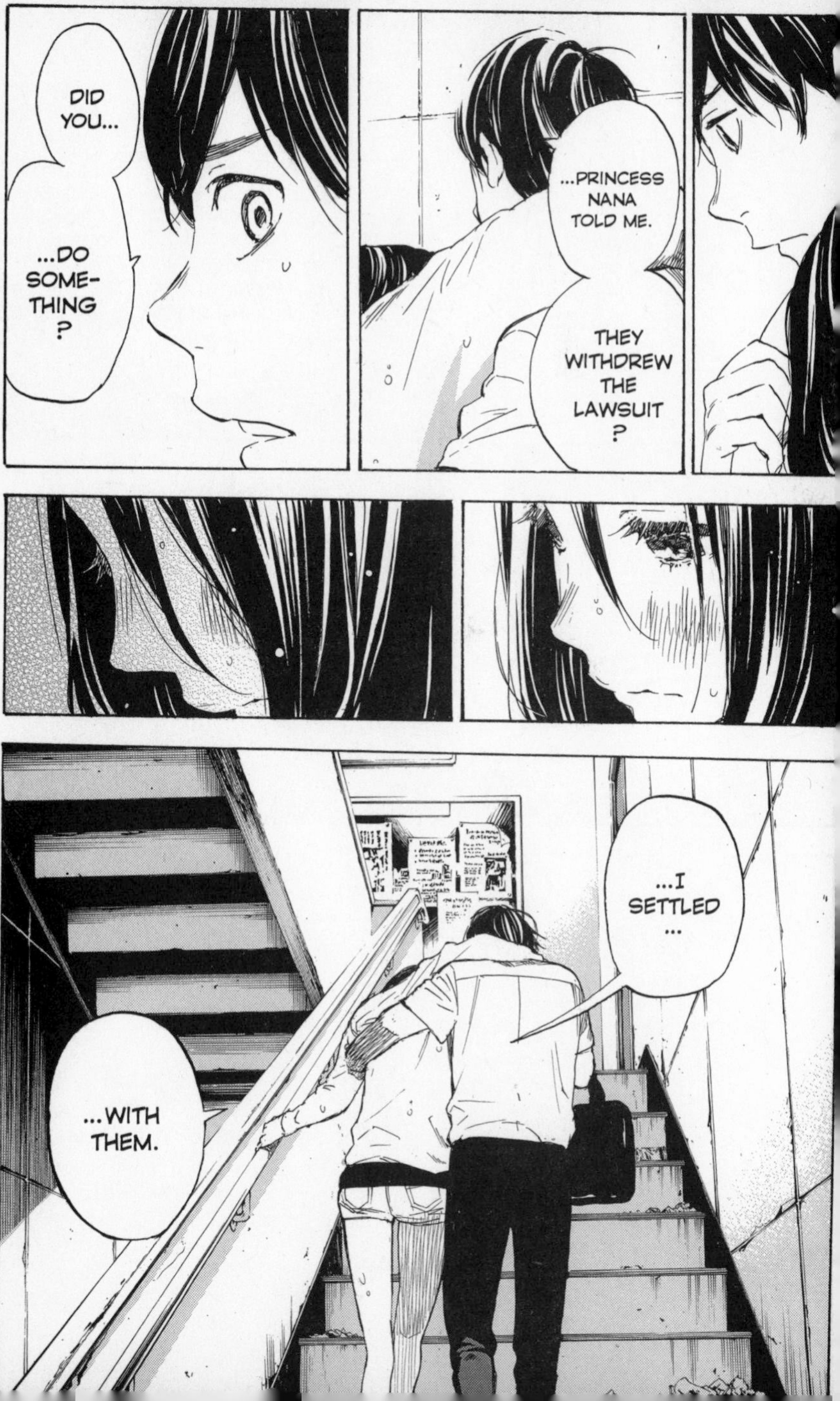
...PRINCESS NANA TOLD ME.
THEY WITHDREW THE LAWSUIT?
DID YOU...
...DO SOME-THING?
...I SETTLED...
...WITH THEM.

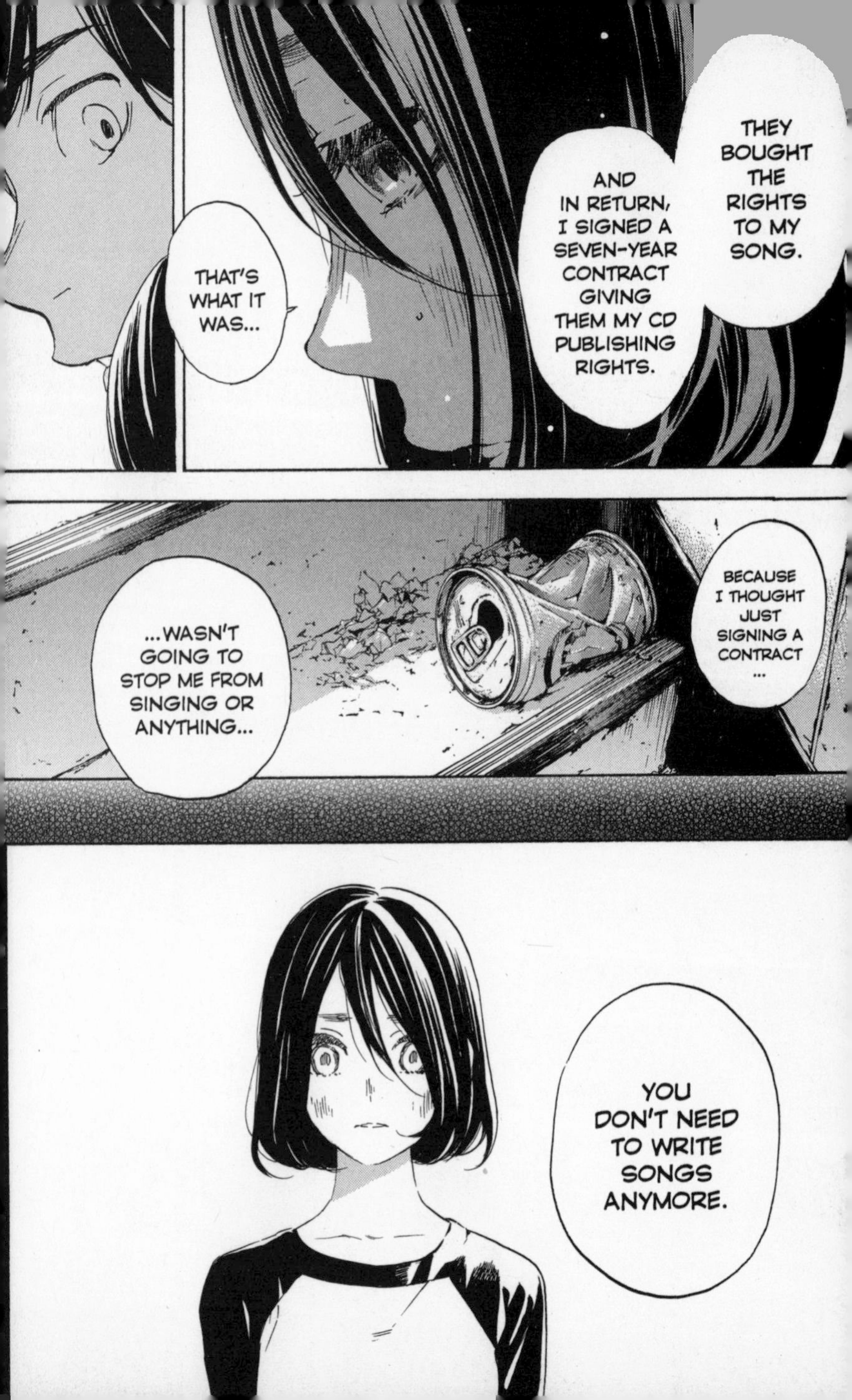
THEY BOUGHT THE RIGHTS TO MY SONG.
AND IN RETURN, I SIGNED A SEVEN-YEAR CONTRACT GIVING THEM MY CD PUBLISHING RIGHTS.
THAT'S WHAT IT WAS...
BECAUSE I THOUGHT JUST SIGNING A CONTRACT ...
...WASN'T GOING TO STOP ME FROM SINGING OR ANYTHING...
YOU DON'T NEED TO WRITE SONGS ANYMORE.

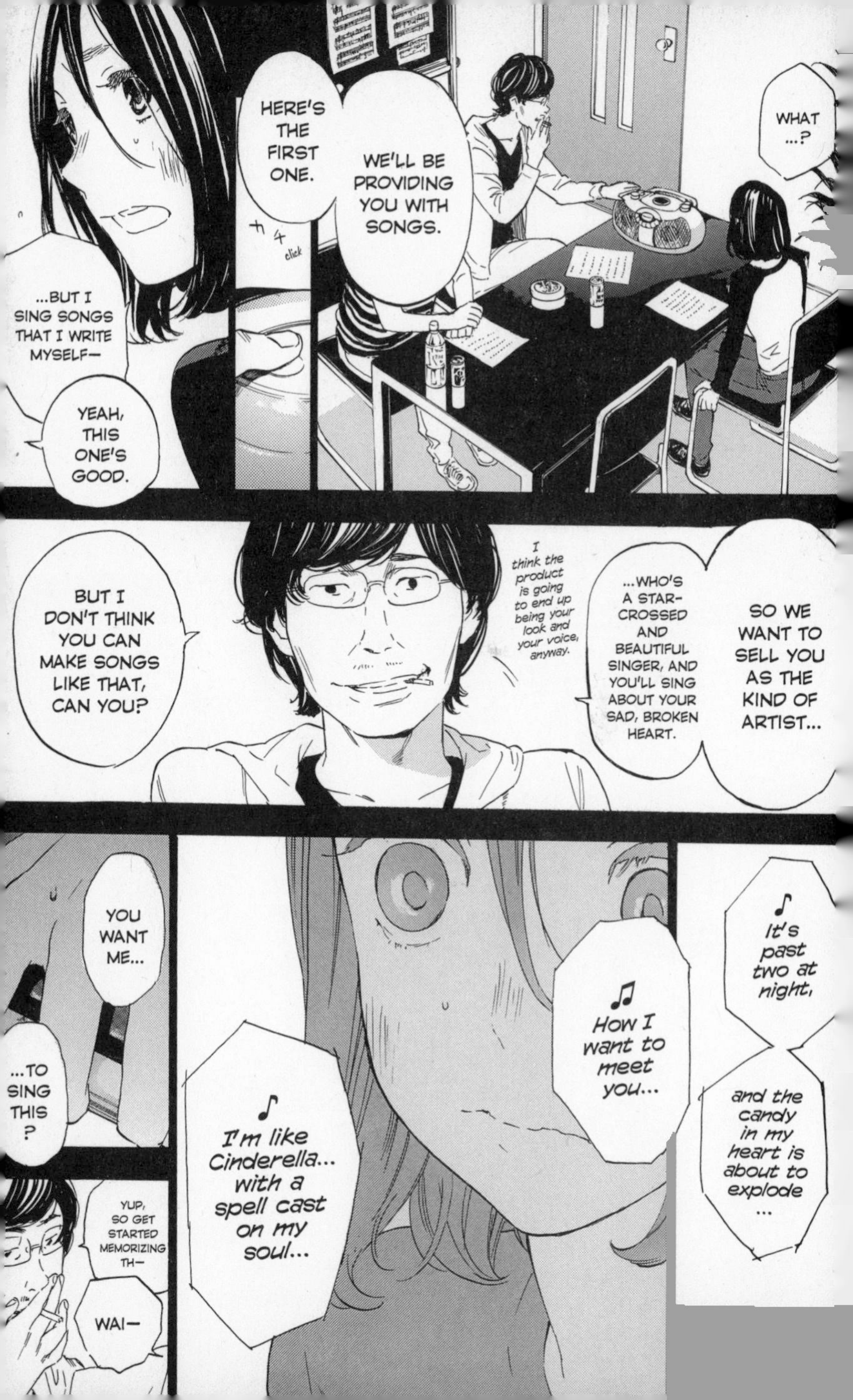
WHAT ...?
WE'LL BE PROVIDING YOU WITH SONGS.
HERE'S THE FIRST ONE.
click
...BUT I SING SONGS THAT I WRITE MYSELF—
YEAH, THIS ONE'S GOOD.
SO WE WANT TO SELL YOU AS THE KIND OF ARTIST...
...WHO'S A STAR-CROSSED AND BEAUTIFUL SINGER, AND YOU'LL SING ABOUT YOUR SAD, BROKEN HEART.
I think the product is going to end up being your look and your voice, anyway.
BUT I DON'T THINK YOU CAN MAKE SONGS LIKE THAT, CAN YOU?
♪ It's past two at night,
and the candy in my heart is about to explode ...
♫ How I want to meet you...
♪ I'm like Cinderella... with a spell cast on my soul...
YOU WANT ME...
...TO SING THIS ?
YUP, SO GET STARTED MEMORIZING TH—
WAI—

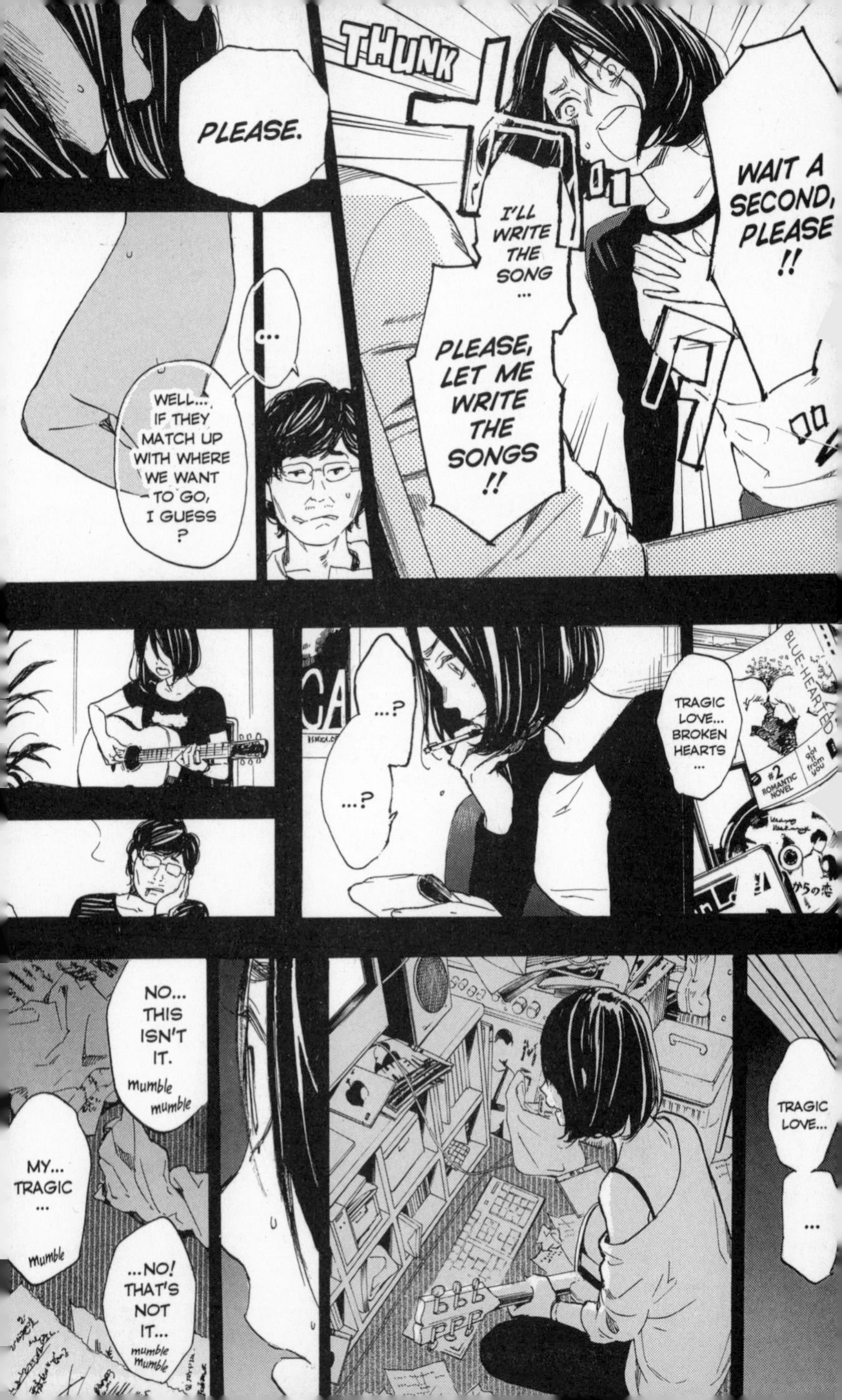
THUNK
WAIT A SECOND, PLEASE !!
I'LL WRITE THE SONG ...
PLEASE, LET ME WRITE THE SONGS !!
PLEASE.
...
WELL... IF THEY MATCH UP WITH WHERE WE WANT TO GO, I GUESS ?
TRAGIC LOVE... BROKEN HEARTS ...
BLUE-HEARTED
#2 ROMANTIC NOVEL
got it from you
からの恋
...?
...?
TRAGIC LOVE...
...
NO... THIS ISN'T IT.
mumble mumble
MY... TRAGIC ...
mumble
...NO! THAT'S NOT IT...
mumble mumble

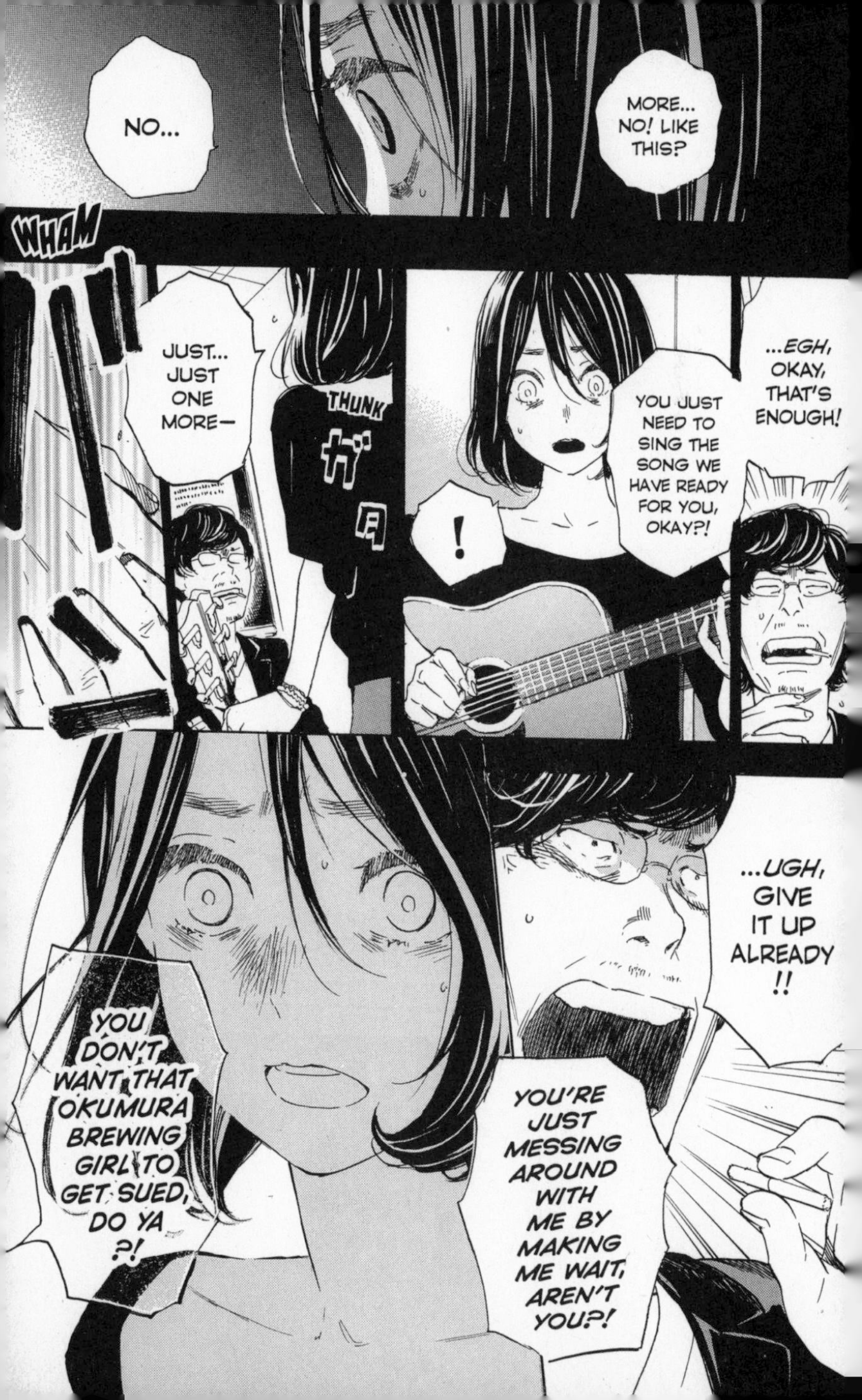
MORE... NO! LIKE THIS?
NO...
...EGH, OKAY, THAT'S ENOUGH!
YOU JUST NEED TO SING THE SONG WE HAVE READY FOR YOU, OKAY?!
!
WHAM
THUNK
ガタ
JUST... JUST ONE MORE—
...UGH, GIVE IT UP ALREADY!!
YOU'RE JUST MESSING AROUND WITH ME BY MAKING ME WAIT, AREN'T YOU?!
YOU DON'T WANT THAT OKUMURA BREWING GIRL TO GET SUED, DO YA?!

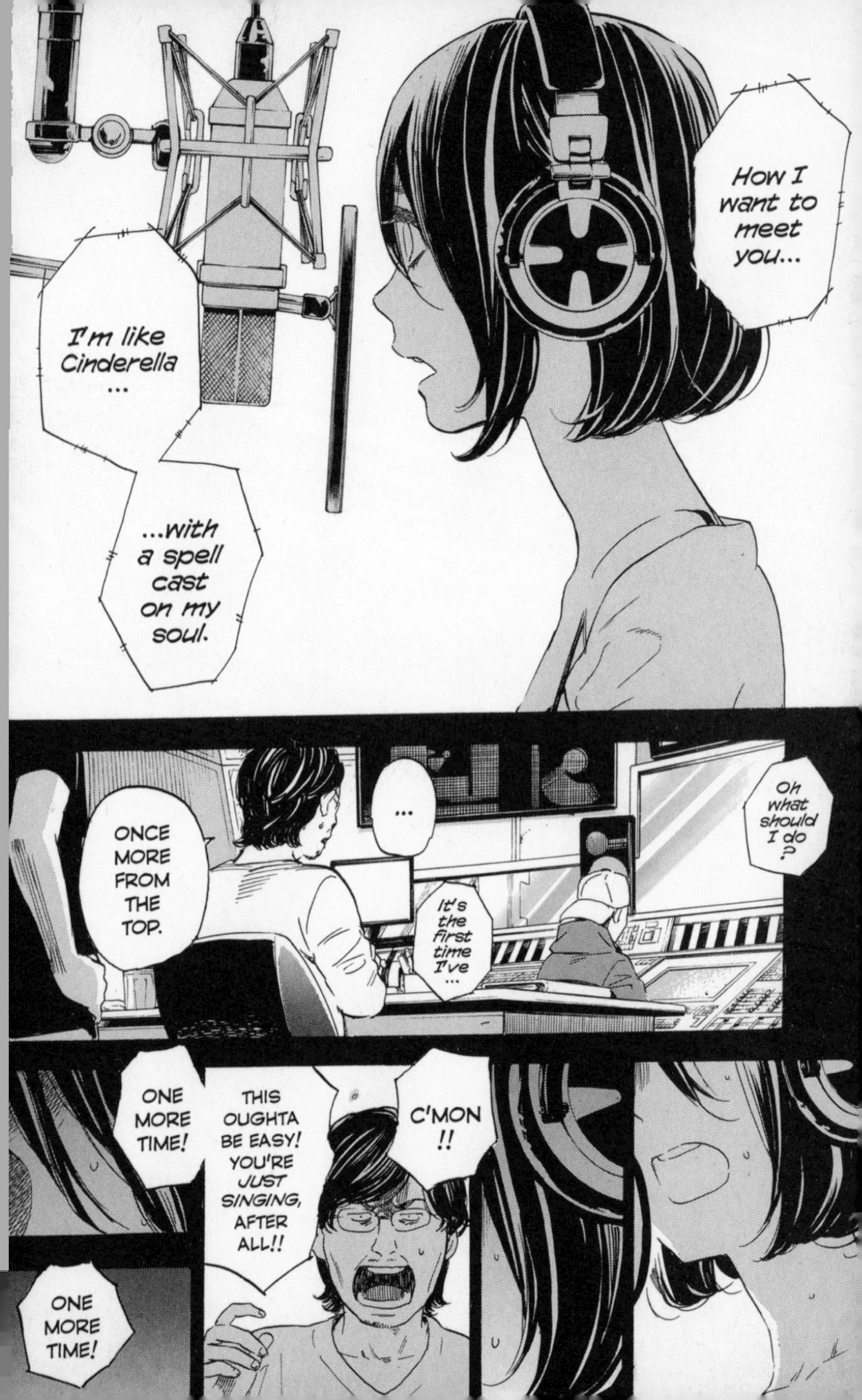
How I want to meet you...
I'm like Cinderella ...
...with a spell cast on my soul.
Oh what should I do?
It's the first time I've ...
...
ONCE MORE FROM THE TOP.
C'MON!!
THIS OUGHTA BE EASY! YOU'RE JUST SINGING, AFTER ALL!!
ONE MORE TIME!
ONE MORE TIME!

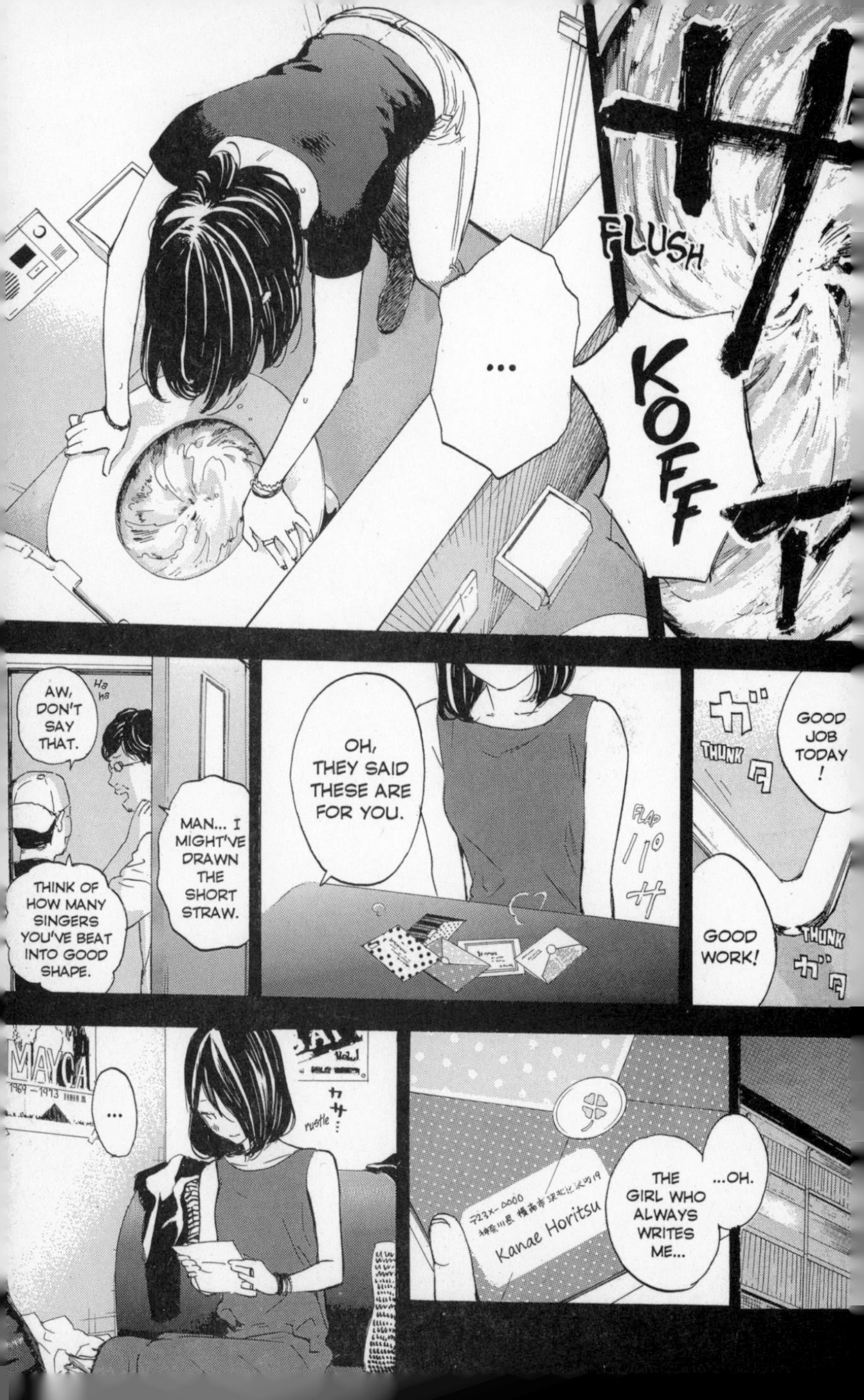
FLUSH
KOFF
...
GOOD JOB TODAY!
THUNK
GOOD WORK!
THUNK
OH, THEY SAID THESE ARE FOR YOU.
FLAP
MAN... I MIGHT'VE DRAWN THE SHORT STRAW.
AW, DON'T SAY THAT.
Ha ha
THINK OF HOW MANY SINGERS YOU'VE BEAT INTO GOOD SHAPE.
...OH.
THE GIRL WHO ALWAYS WRITES ME...
Kanae Horitsu
MAYCA
1969 — 1993
...
rustle

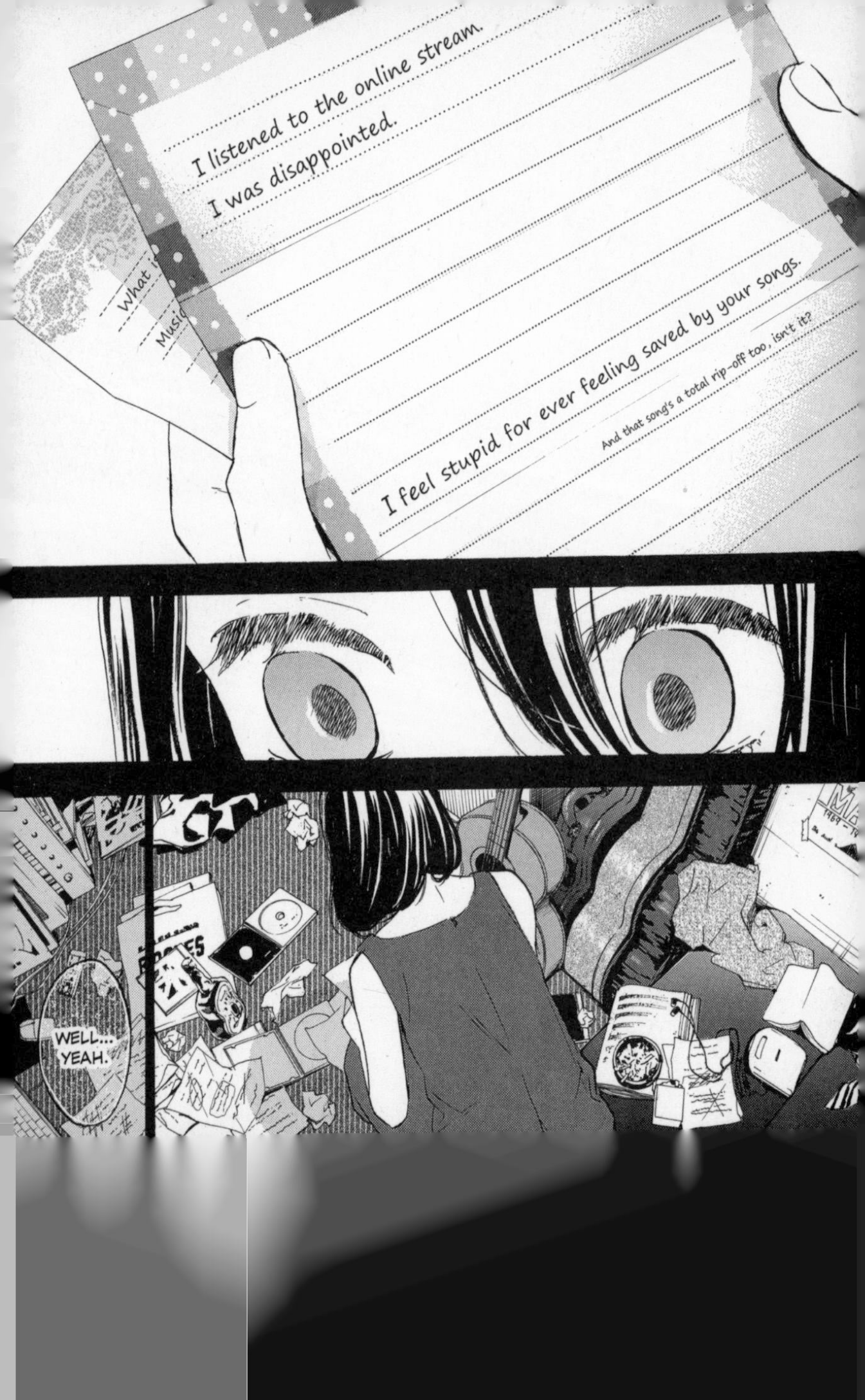
I listened to the online stream.
I was disappointed.
I feel stupid for ever feeling saved by your songs.
And that song's a total rip-off too, isn't it?
WELL... YEAH.

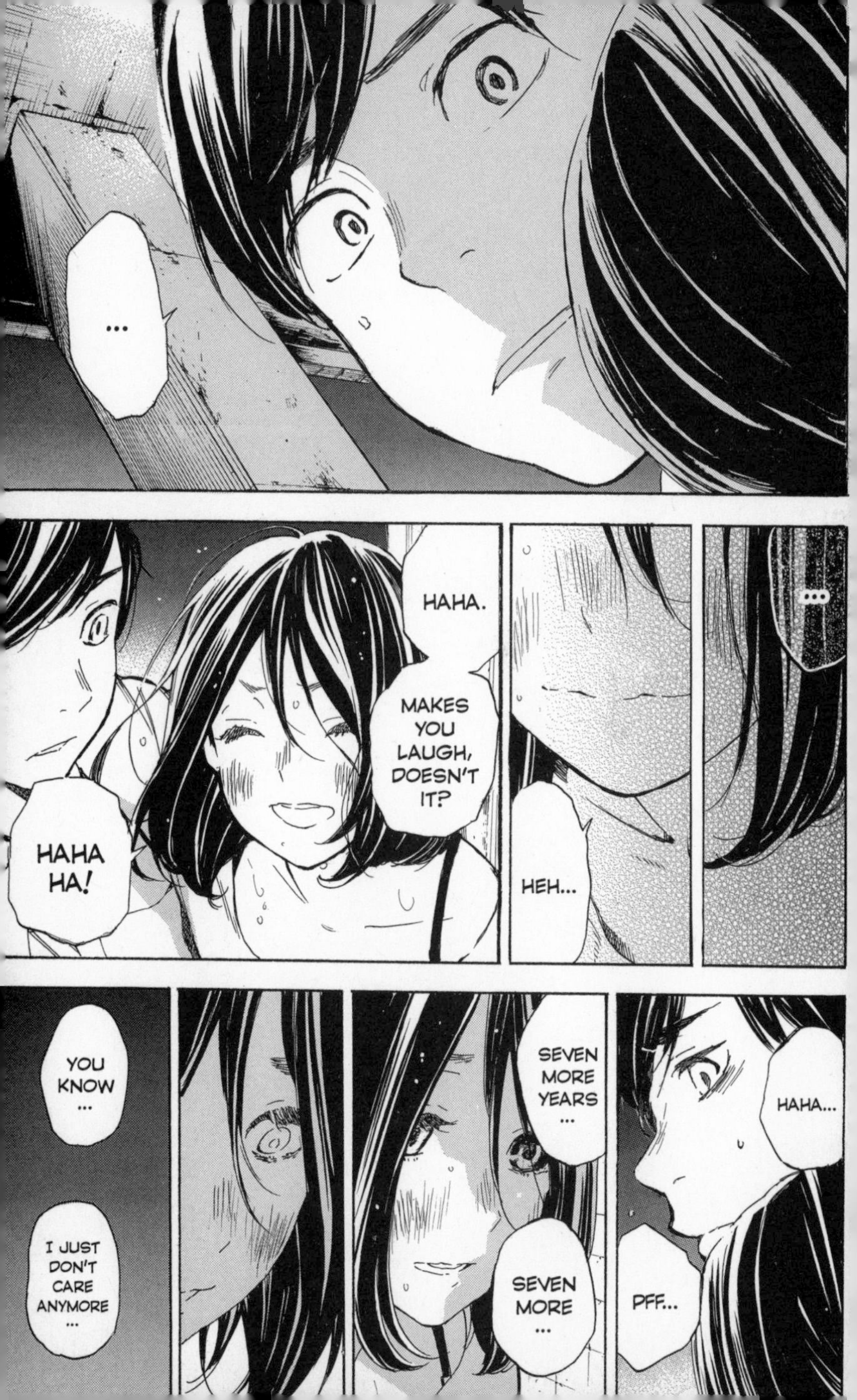
...
...
HEH...
HAHA.
MAKES YOU LAUGH, DOESN'T IT?
HAHA HA!
HAHA...
PFF...
SEVEN MORE YEARS ...
SEVEN MORE ...
YOU KNOW ...
I JUST DON'T CARE ANYMORE ...

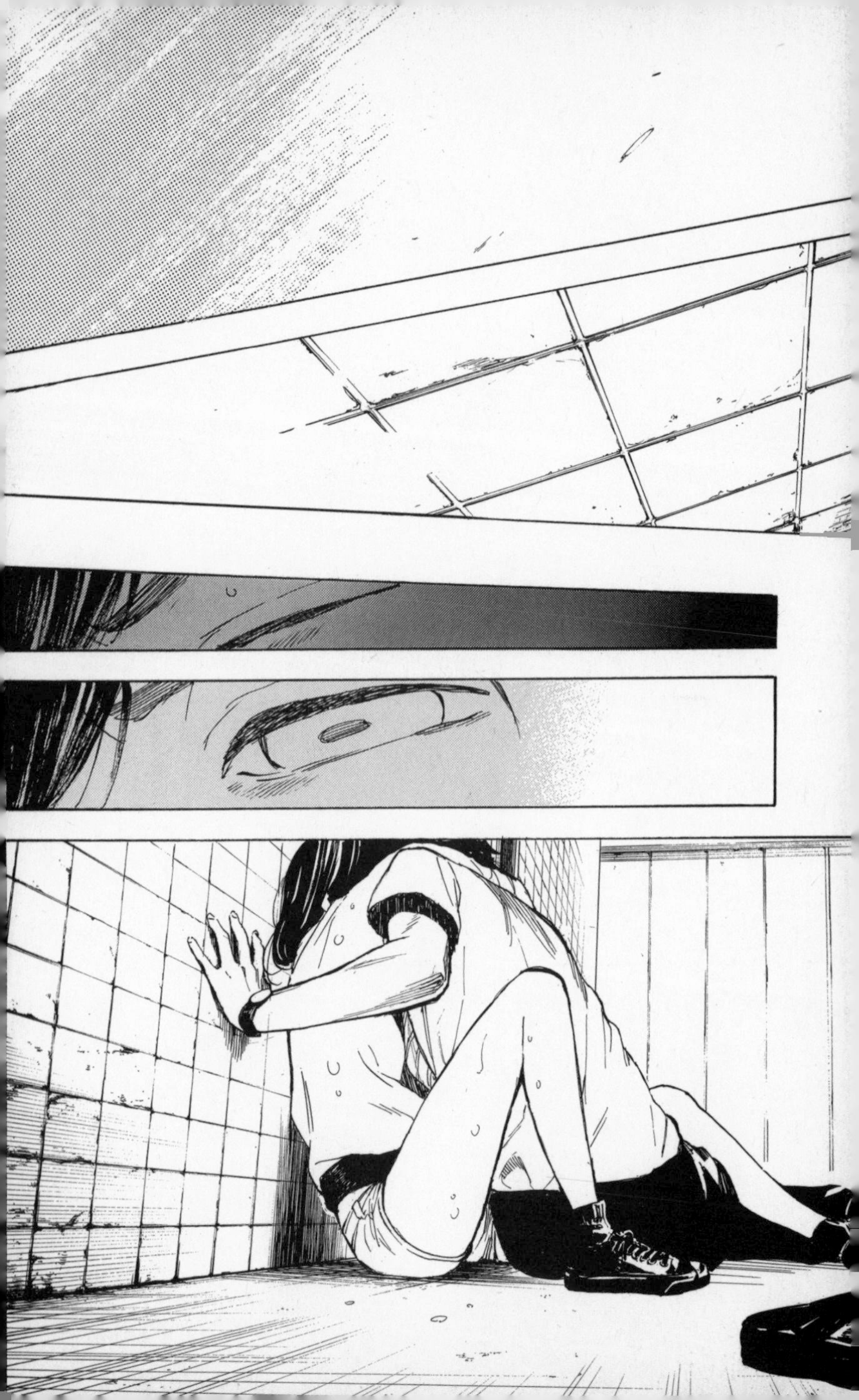

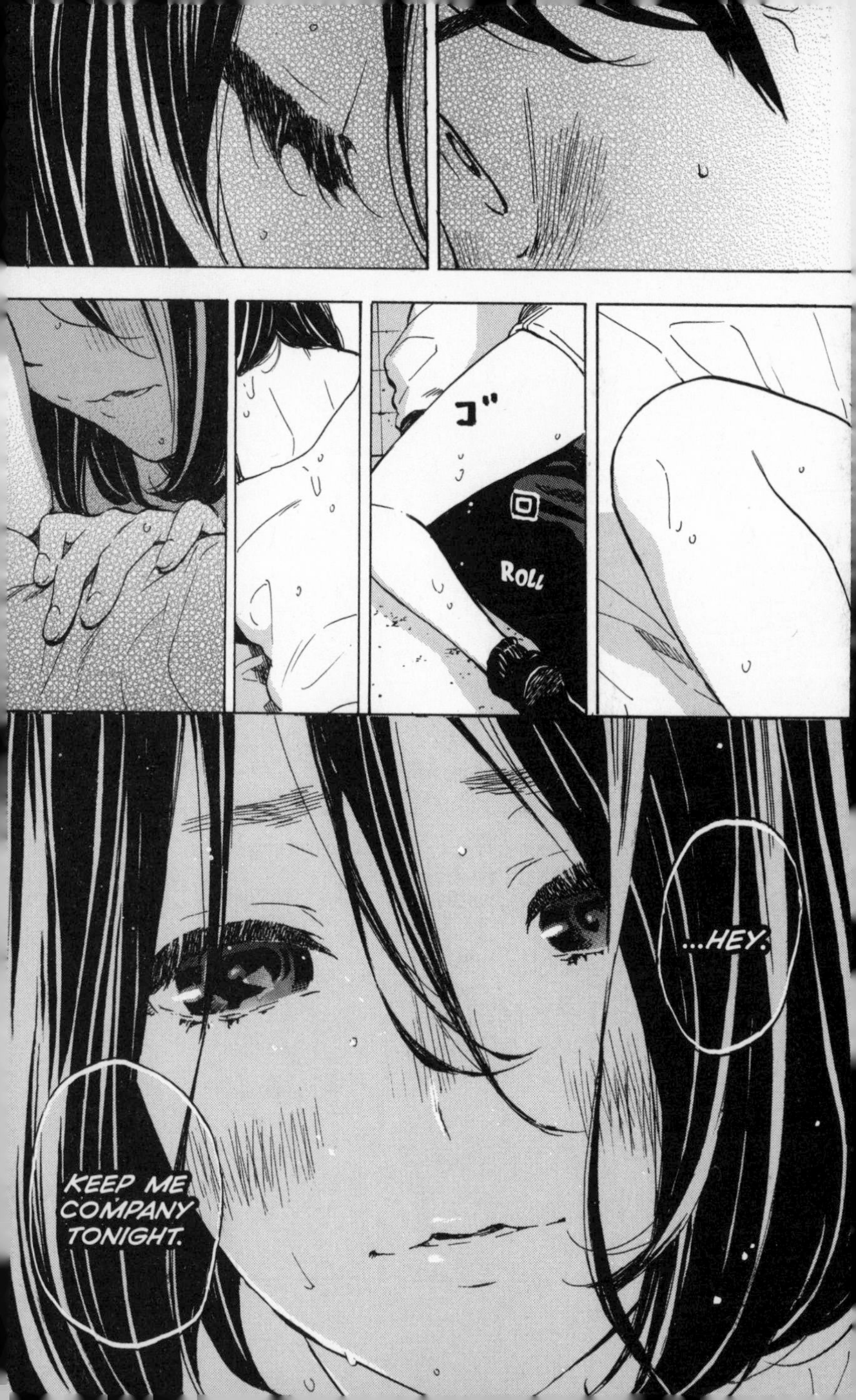

ゴ
ROLL
...HEY.
KEEP ME COMPANY TONIGHT.

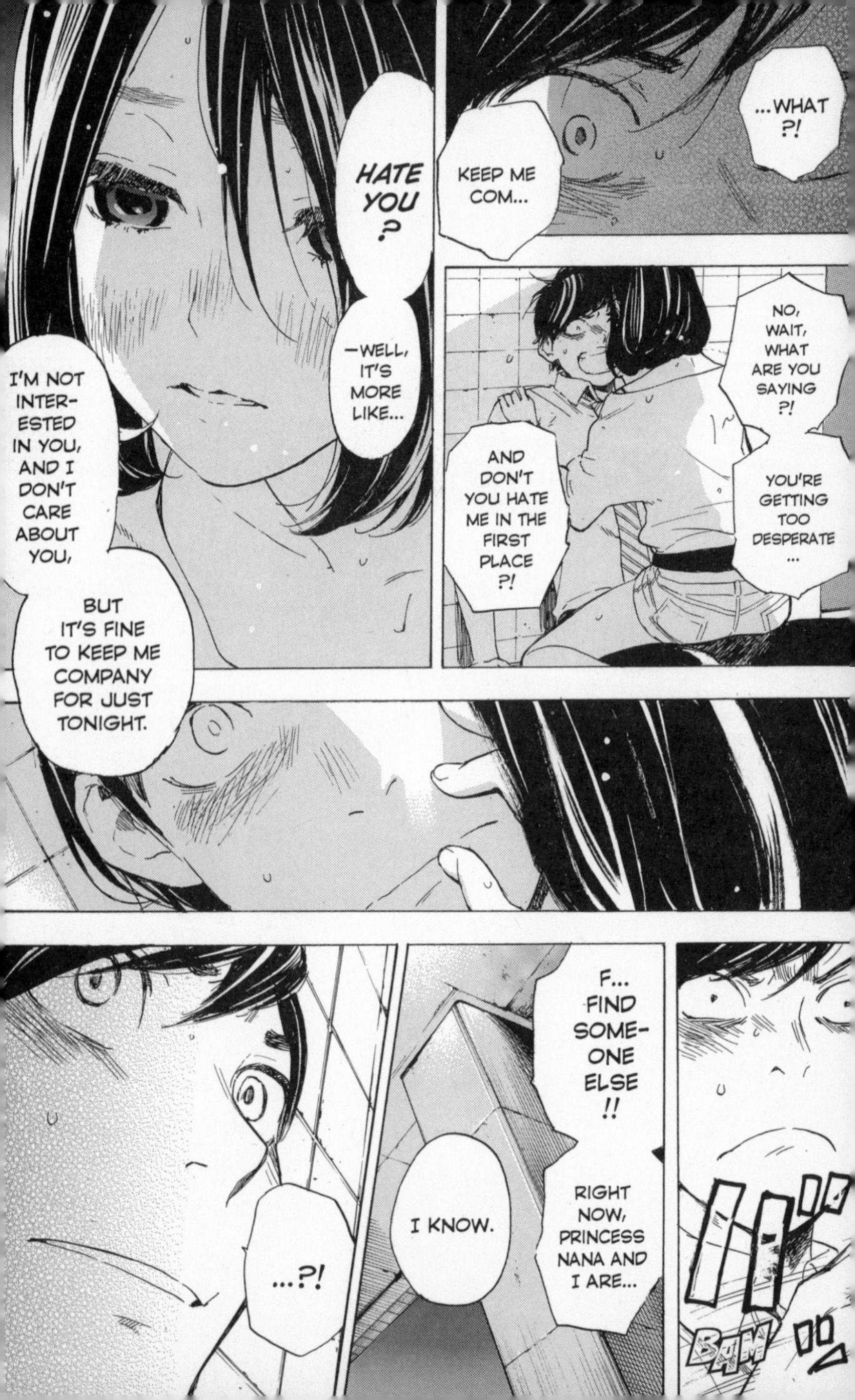
...WHAT ?!
KEEP ME COM...
NO, WAIT, WHAT ARE YOU SAYING ?!
YOU'RE GETTING TOO DESPERATE ...
AND DON'T YOU HATE ME IN THE FIRST PLACE ?!
HATE YOU ?
—WELL, IT'S MORE LIKE...
I'M NOT INTER-ESTED IN YOU, AND I DON'T CARE ABOUT YOU,
BUT IT'S FINE TO KEEP ME COMPANY FOR JUST TONIGHT.
BAM
F... FIND SOME-ONE ELSE !!
RIGHT NOW, PRINCESS NANA AND I ARE...
I KNOW.
...?!

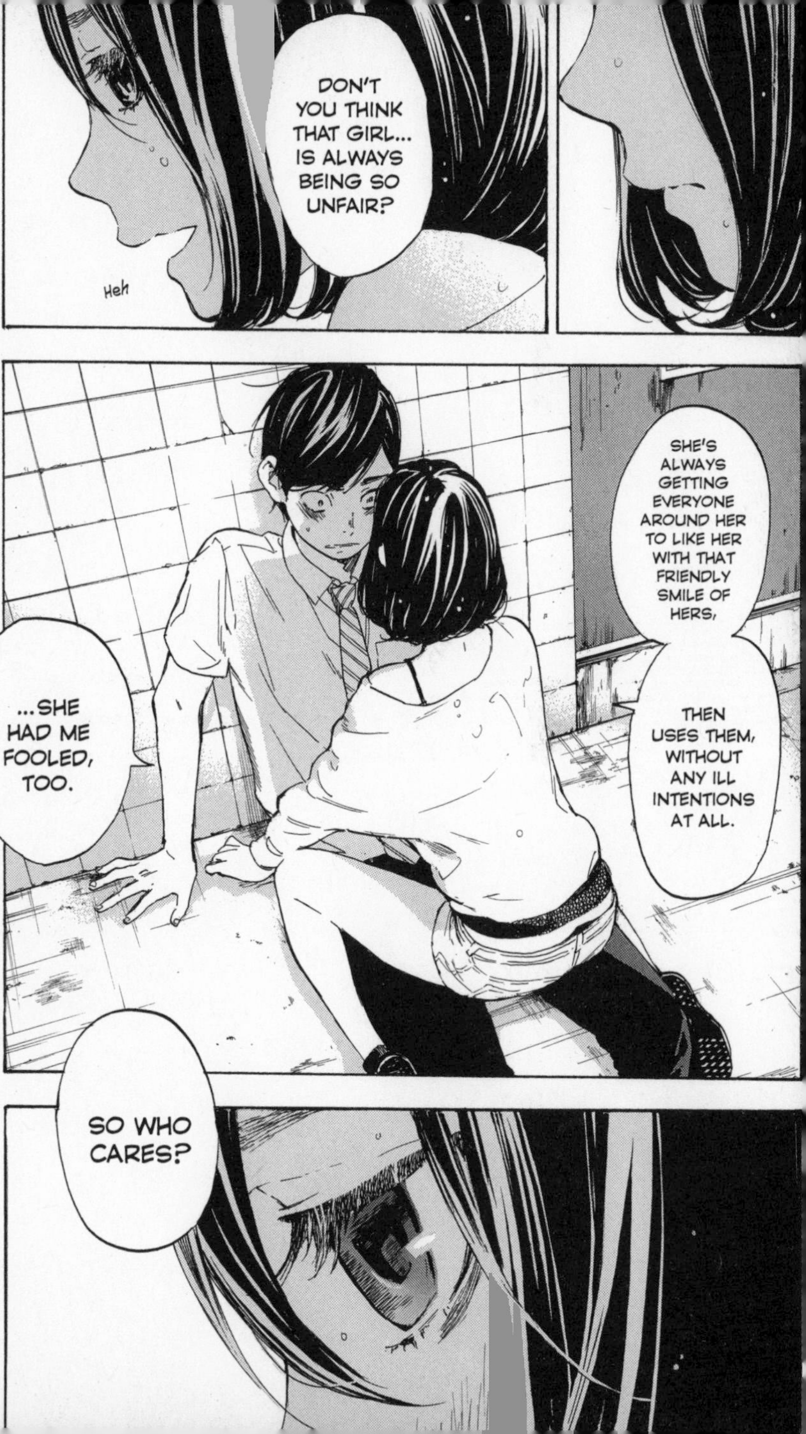
DON'T YOU THINK THAT GIRL... IS ALWAYS BEING SO UNFAIR?
Heh
SHE'S ALWAYS GETTING EVERYONE AROUND HER TO LIKE HER WITH THAT FRIENDLY SMILE OF HERS,
THEN USES THEM, WITHOUT ANY ILL INTENTIONS AT ALL.
...SHE HAD ME FOOLED, TOO.
SO WHO CARES?

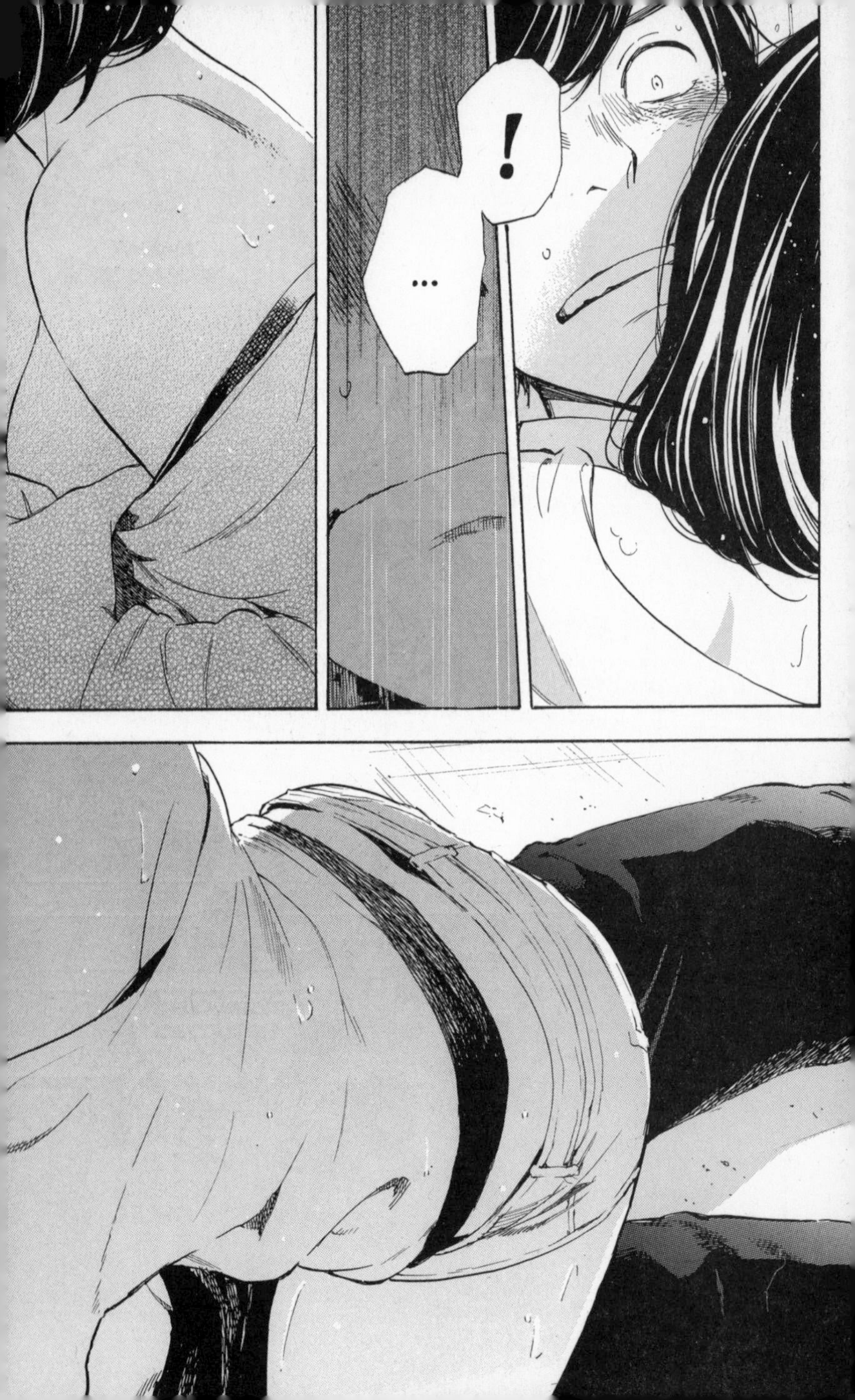
!
...

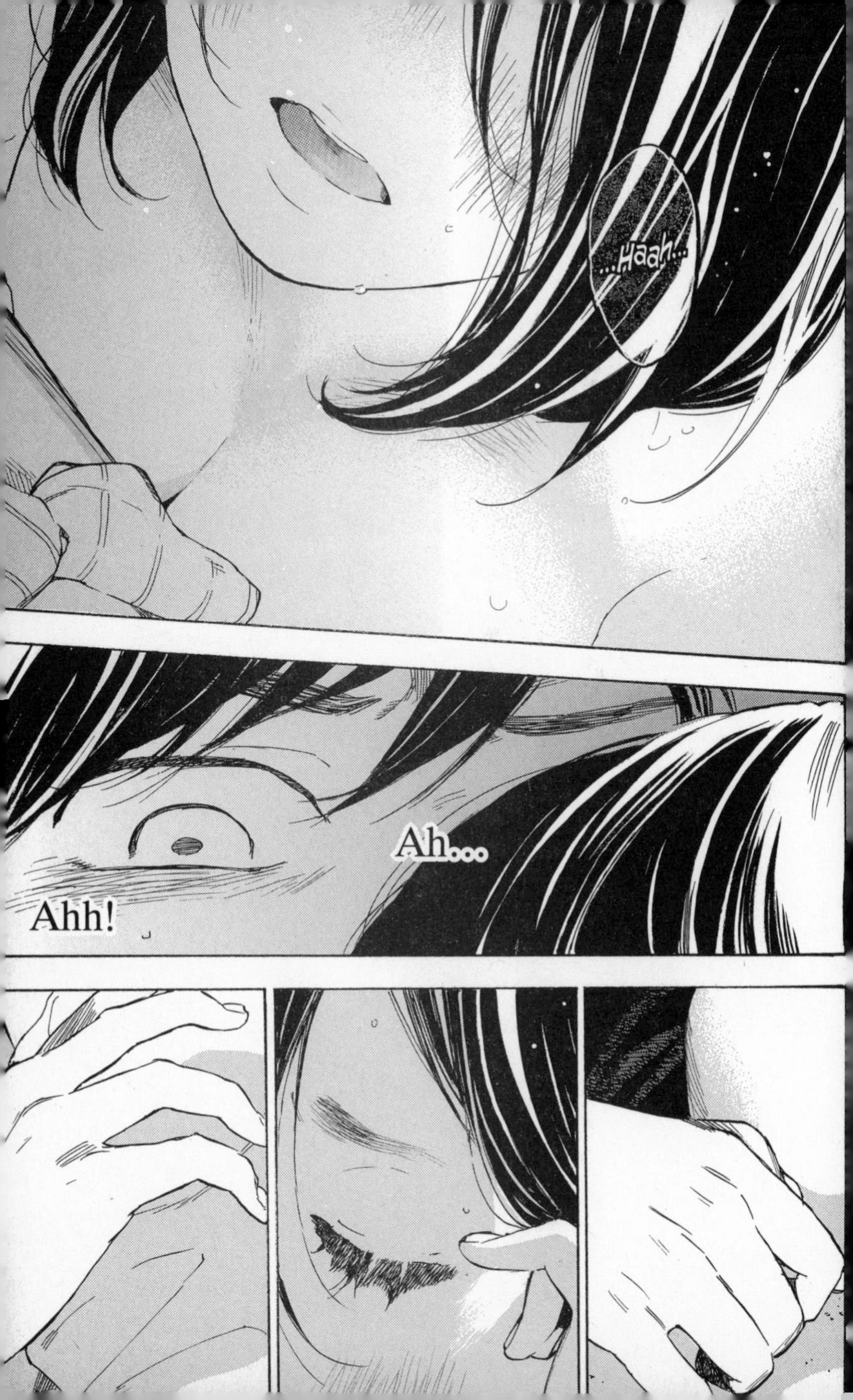
...Haah...
Ah...
Ahh!

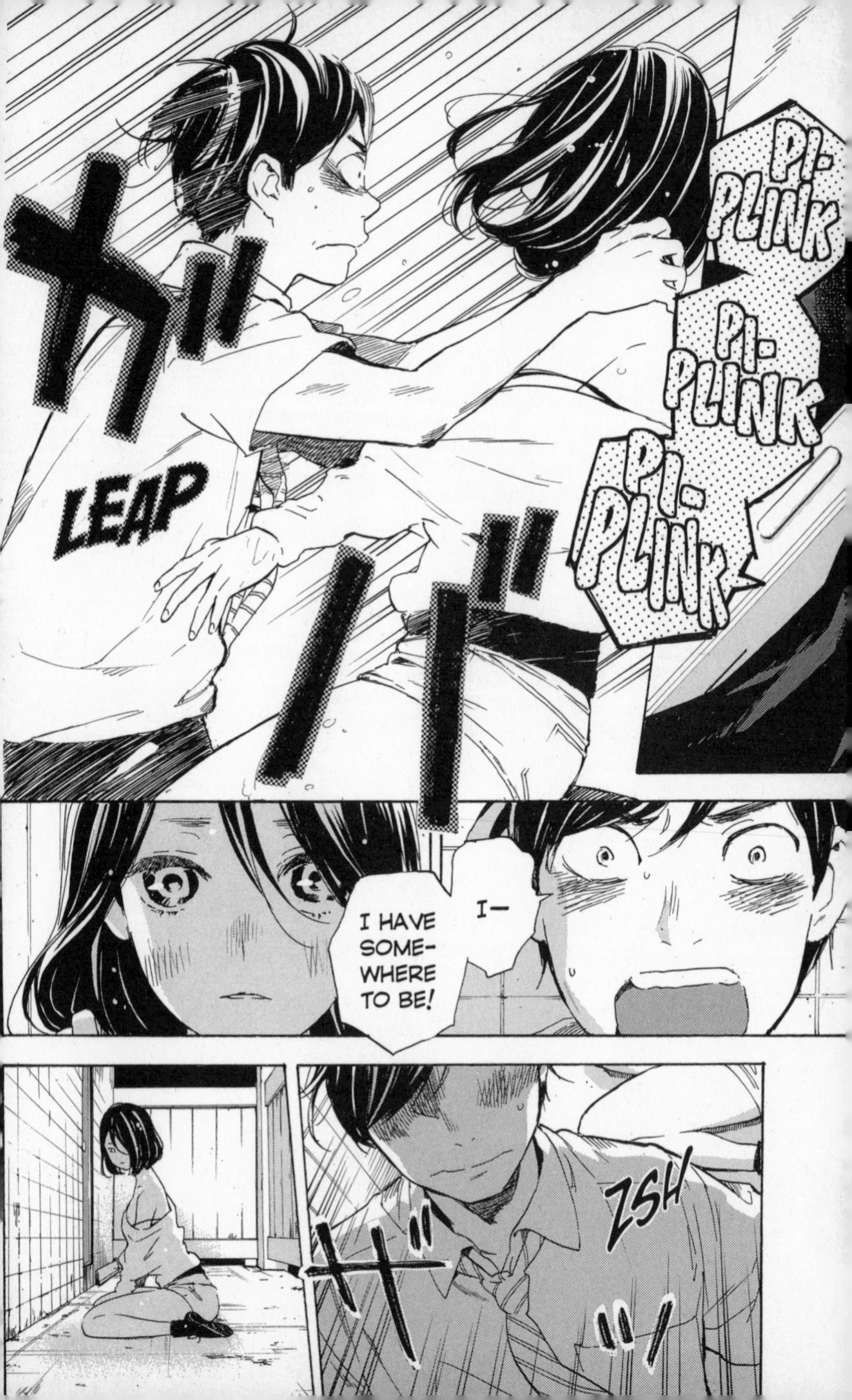
PI-PLINK
PI-PLINK
PI-PLINK
LEAP
I—
I HAVE SOME-WHERE TO BE!
ZSH

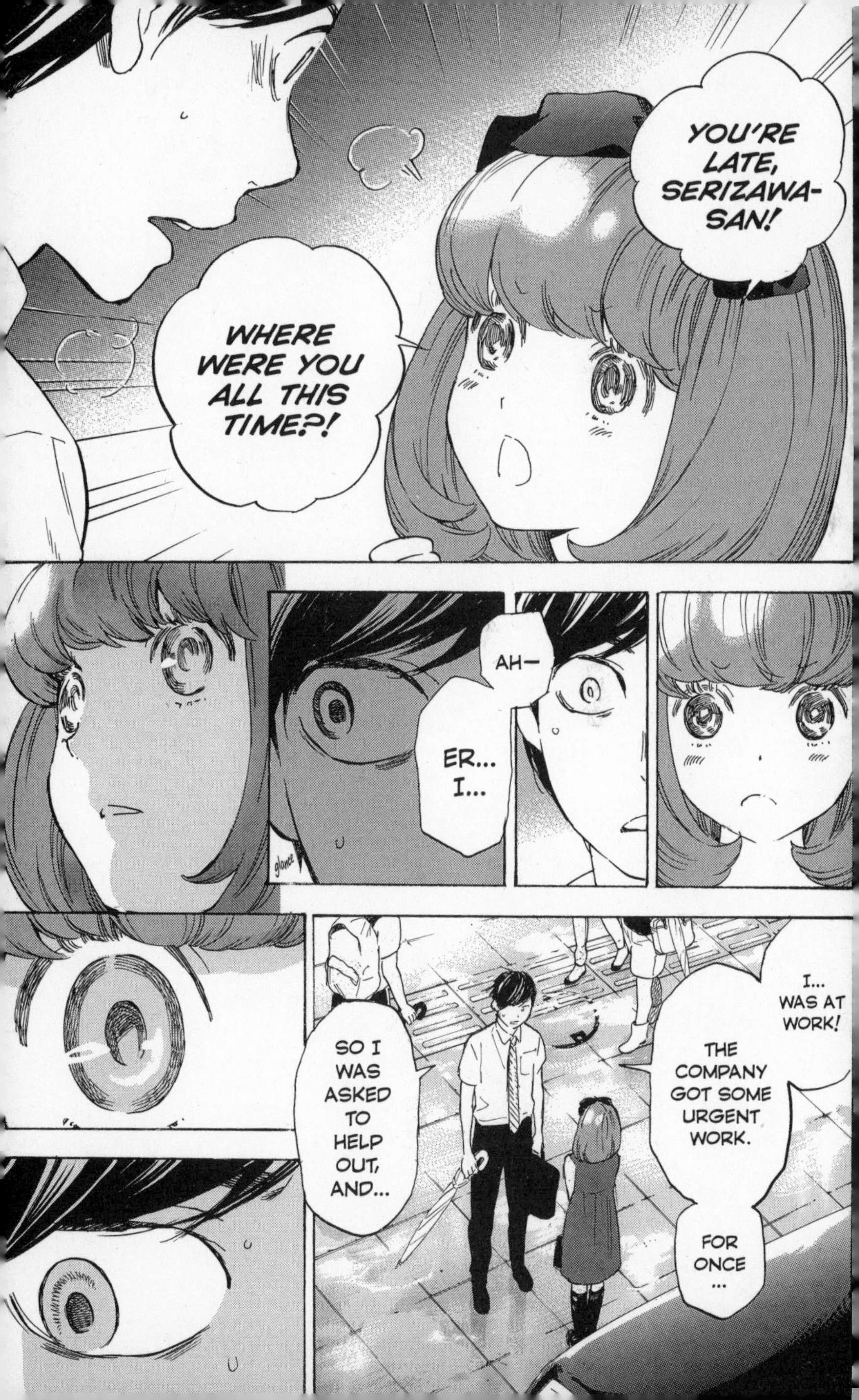
YOU'RE LATE, SERIZAWA-SAN!
WHERE WERE YOU ALL THIS TIME?!
AH—
ER... I...
glance
I... WAS AT WORK!
THE COMPANY GOT SOME URGENT WORK.
FOR ONCE ...
SO I WAS ASKED TO HELP OUT, AND...

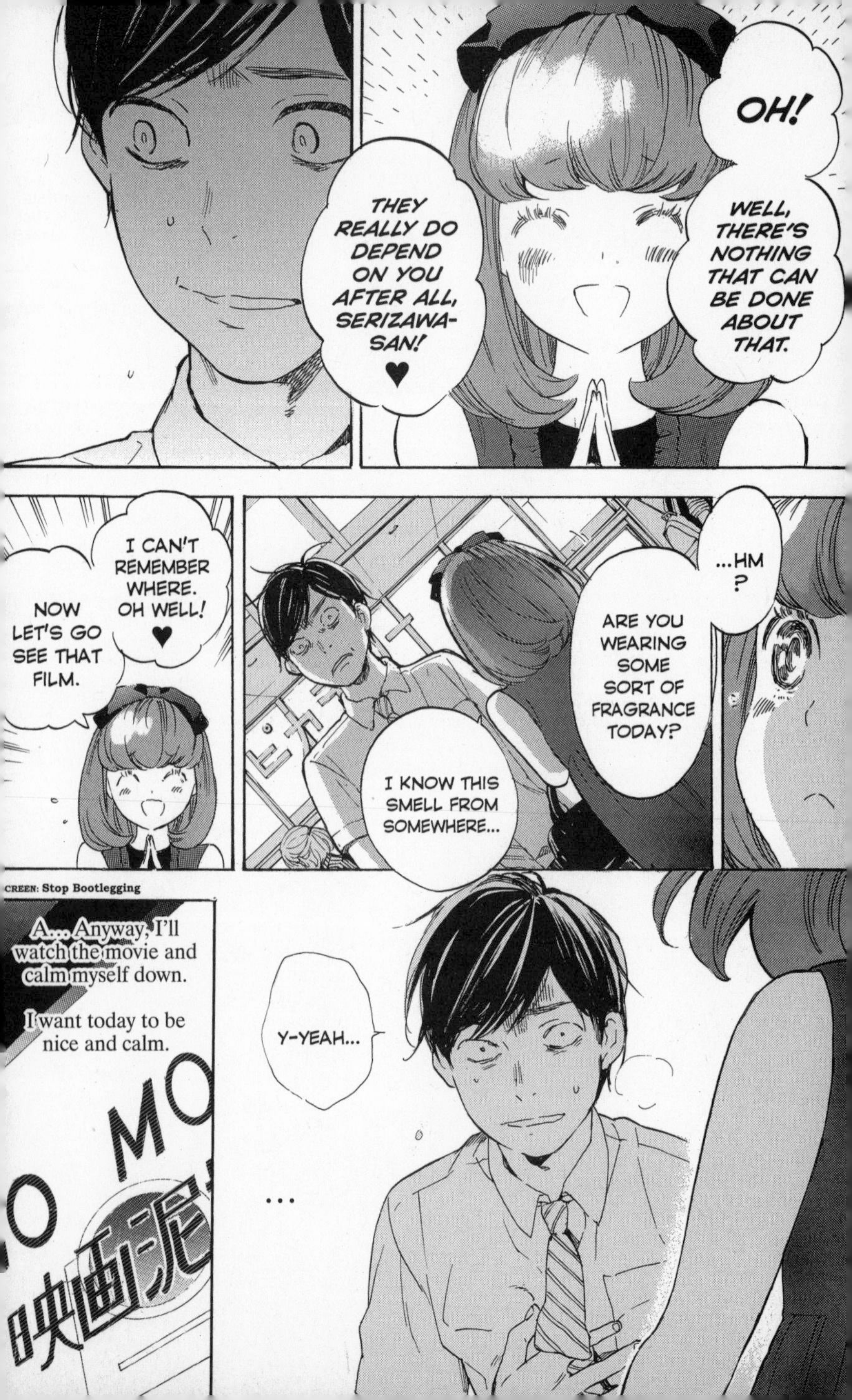
OH!
WELL, THERE'S NOTHING THAT CAN BE DONE ABOUT THAT.
THEY REALLY DO DEPEND ON YOU AFTER ALL, SERIZAWA-SAN! ♥
...HM?
ARE YOU WEARING SOME SORT OF FRAGRANCE TODAY?
I KNOW THIS SMELL FROM SOMEWHERE...
I CAN'T REMEMBER WHERE. OH WELL! ♥
NOW LET'S GO SEE THAT FILM.
Y-YEAH...
...
CREEN: Stop Bootlegging
A... Anyway, I'll watch the movie and calm myself down.
I want today to be nice and calm.

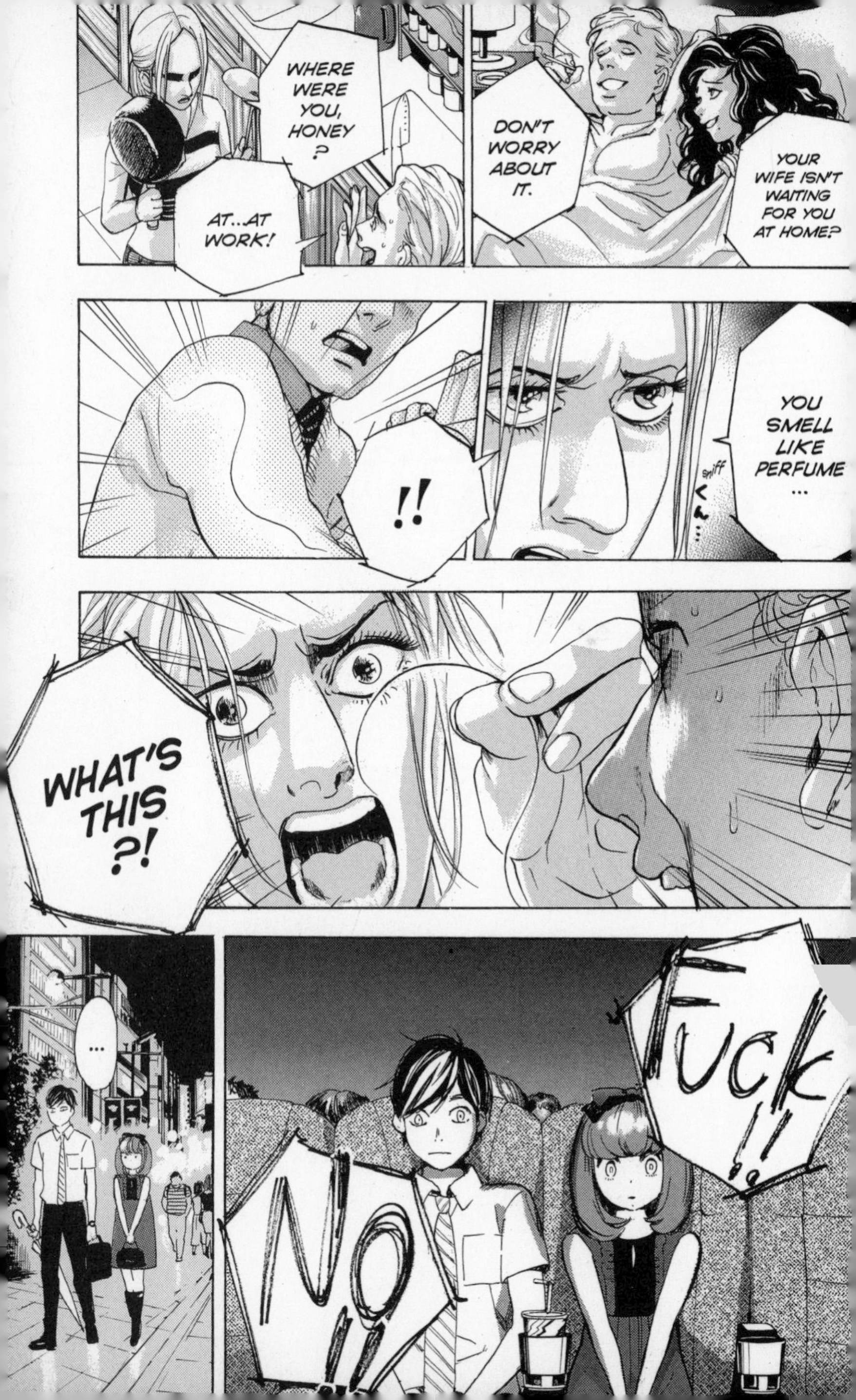
YOUR WIFE ISN'T WAITING FOR YOU AT HOME?
DON'T WORRY ABOUT IT.
WHERE WERE YOU, HONEY?
AT...AT WORK!
YOU SMELL LIKE PERFUME...
sniff
くん...
!!
WHAT'S THIS?!
FUCK!!
NO
...

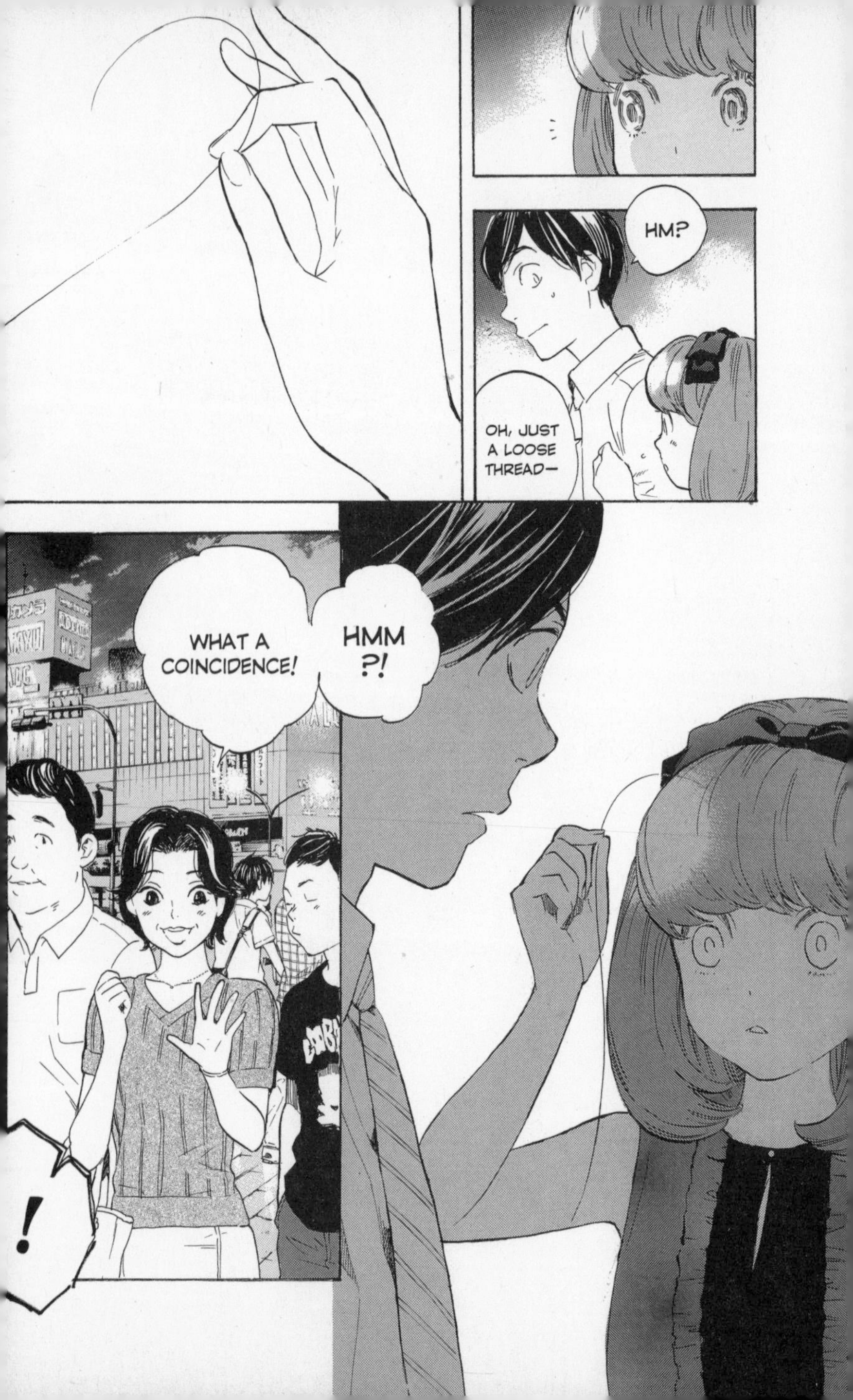
HM?
OH, JUST A LOOSE THREAD—
HMM ?!
WHAT A COINCIDENCE!
!

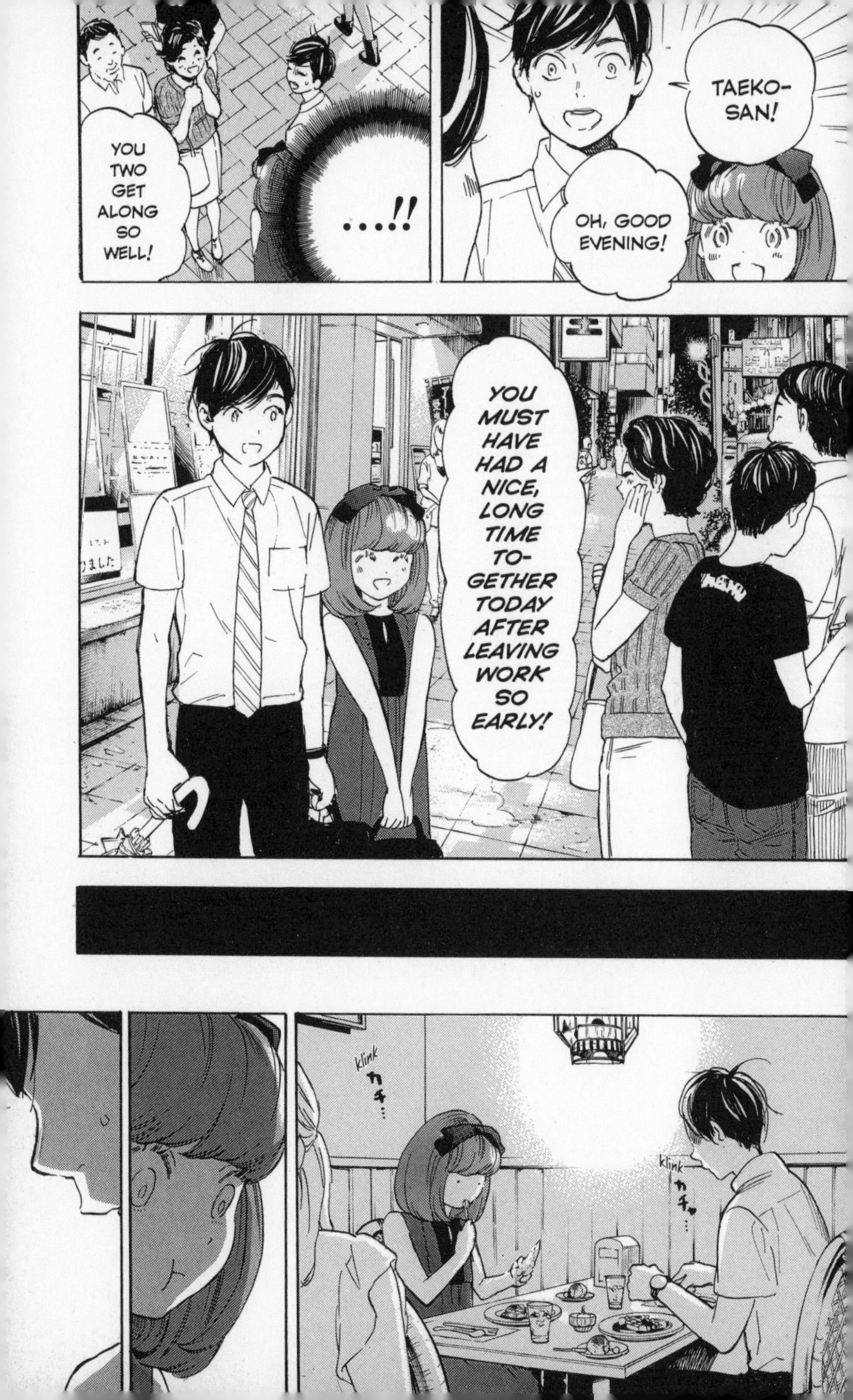

TAEKO-SAN!
OH, GOOD EVENING!
...!!
YOU TWO GET ALONG SO WELL!
YOU MUST HAVE HAD A NICE, LONG TIME TO-GETHER TODAY AFTER LEAVING WORK SO EARLY!
klink カチャ…
klink カチ…

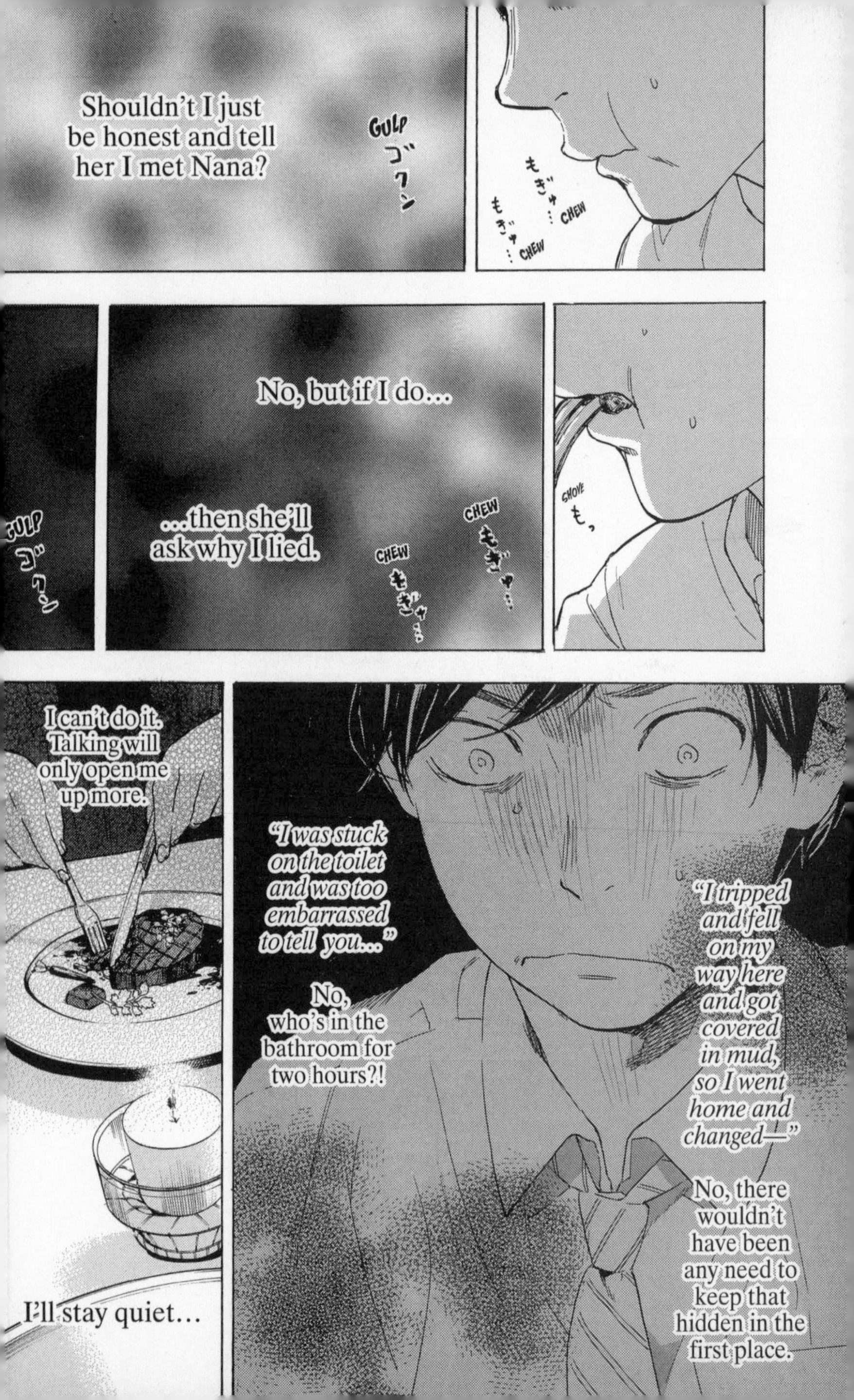

もぎゅ…
CHEW
もぎゅ…
CHEW
Shouldn't I just be honest and tell her I met Nana?
GULP
ゴクン
SHOVE
もっ
No, but if I do…
…then she'll ask why I lied.
CHEW
もぎゅ…
CHEW
もぎゅ…
GULP
ゴクン
"I tripped and fell on my way here and got covered in mud, so I went home and changed—"
No, there wouldn't have been any need to keep that hidden in the first place.
"I was stuck on the toilet and was too embarrassed to tell you…"
No, who's in the bathroom for two hours?!
I can't do it. Talking will only open me up more.
I'll stay quiet…

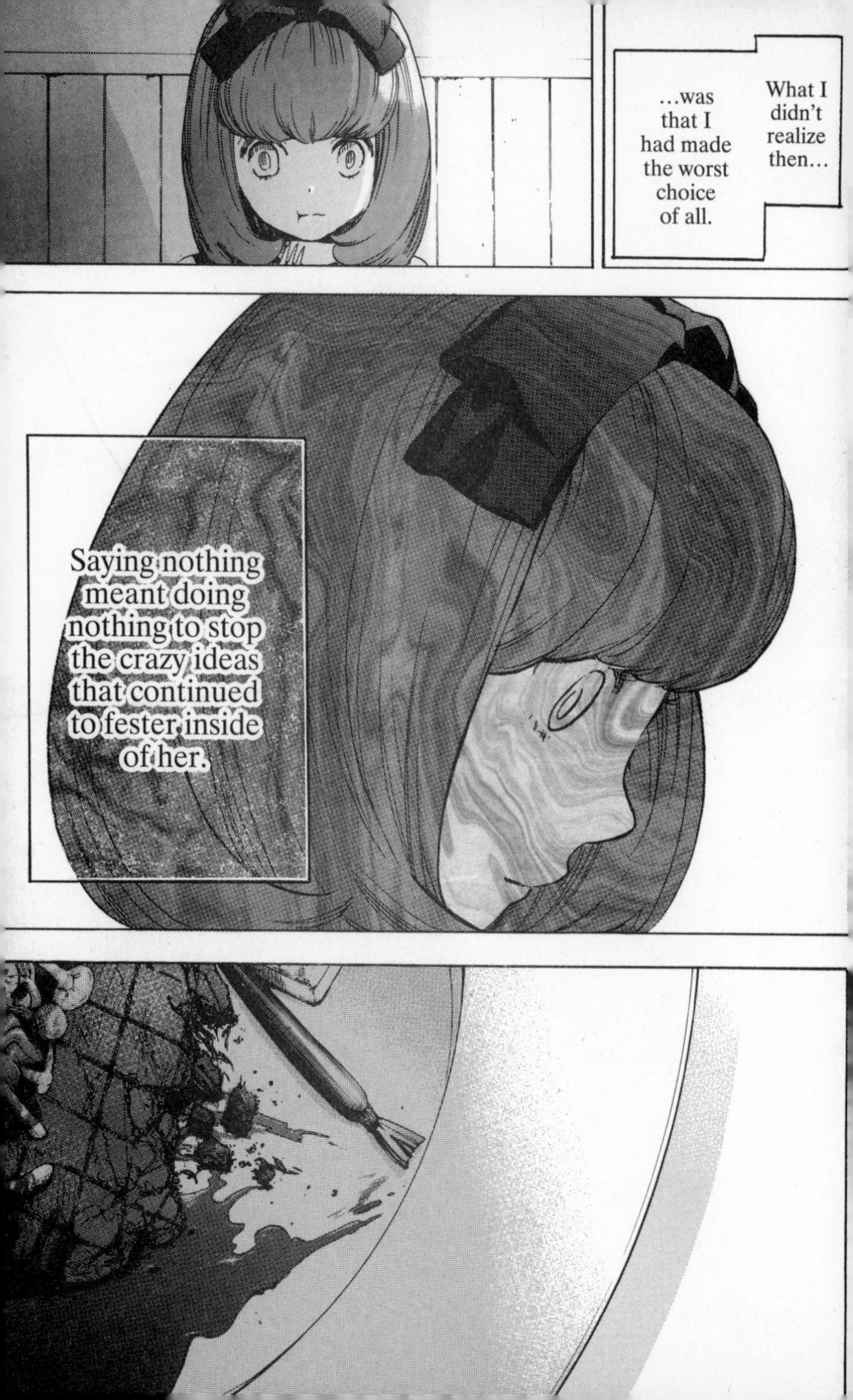
What I didn't realize then…
…was that I had made the worst choice of all.
Saying nothing meant doing nothing to stop the crazy ideas that continued to fester inside of her.

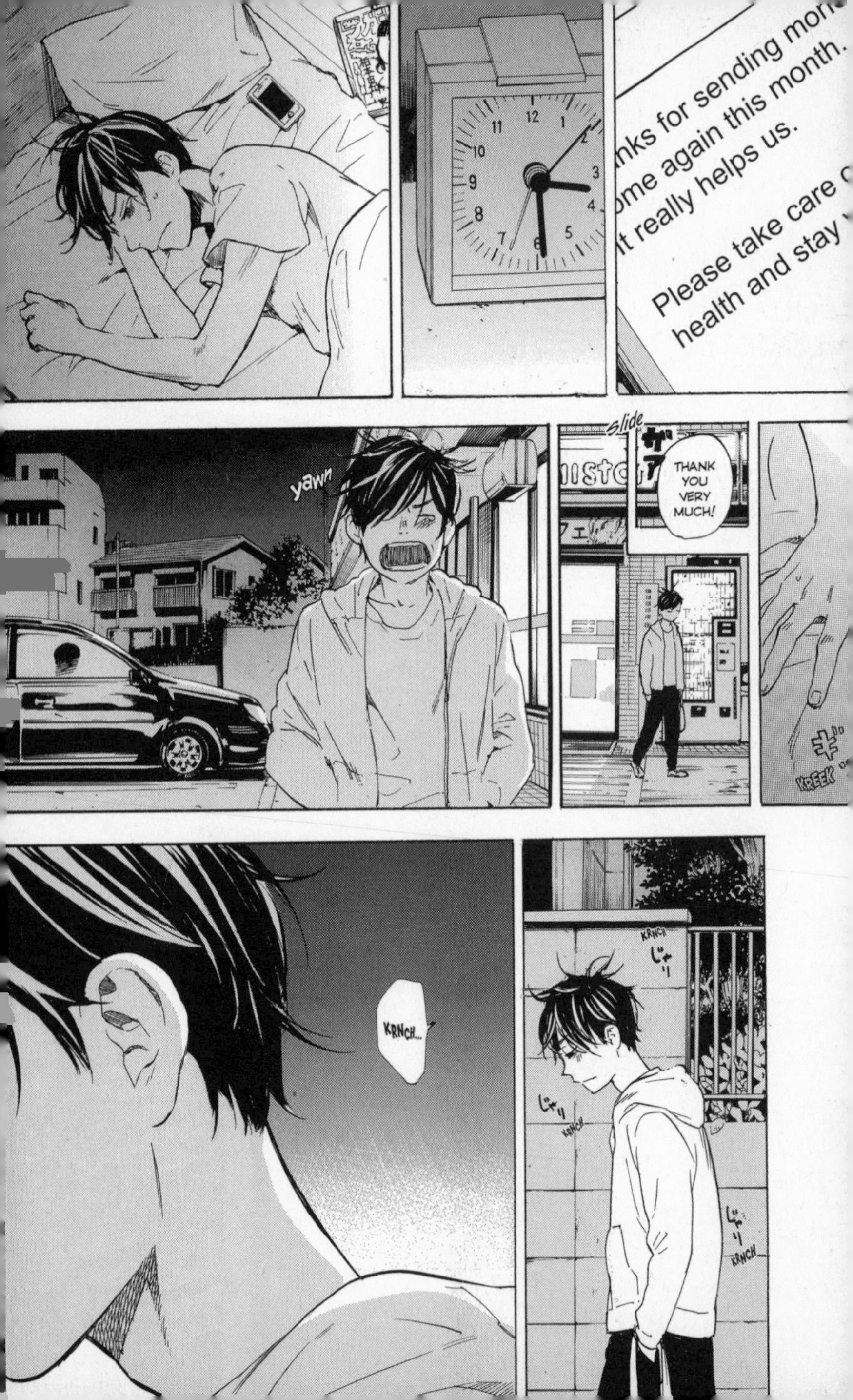
nks for sending mon
ome again this month.
It really helps us.
Please take care o
health and stay
ギ
KREEK
Slide
ガラ
THANK YOU VERY MUCH!
yawn
KRNCH
じゃり
じゃり
KRNCH
じゃり
KRNCH
KRNCH...

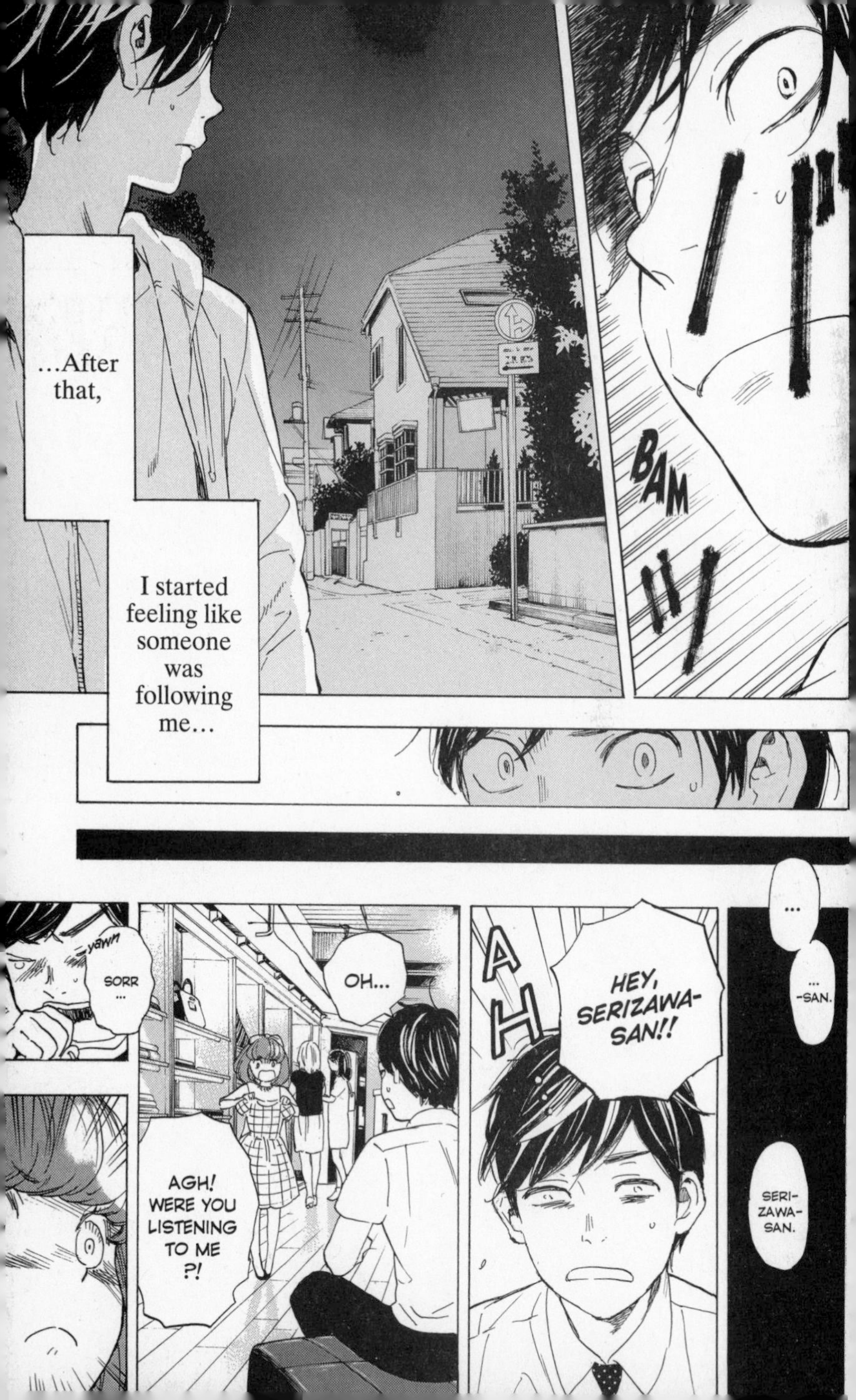
BAM
...After that,
I started feeling like someone was following me...
...
...-SAN.
SERI-ZAWA-SAN.
AH
HEY, SERIZAWA-SAN!!
OH...
AGH! WERE YOU LISTENING TO ME ?!
yawn
SORR ...

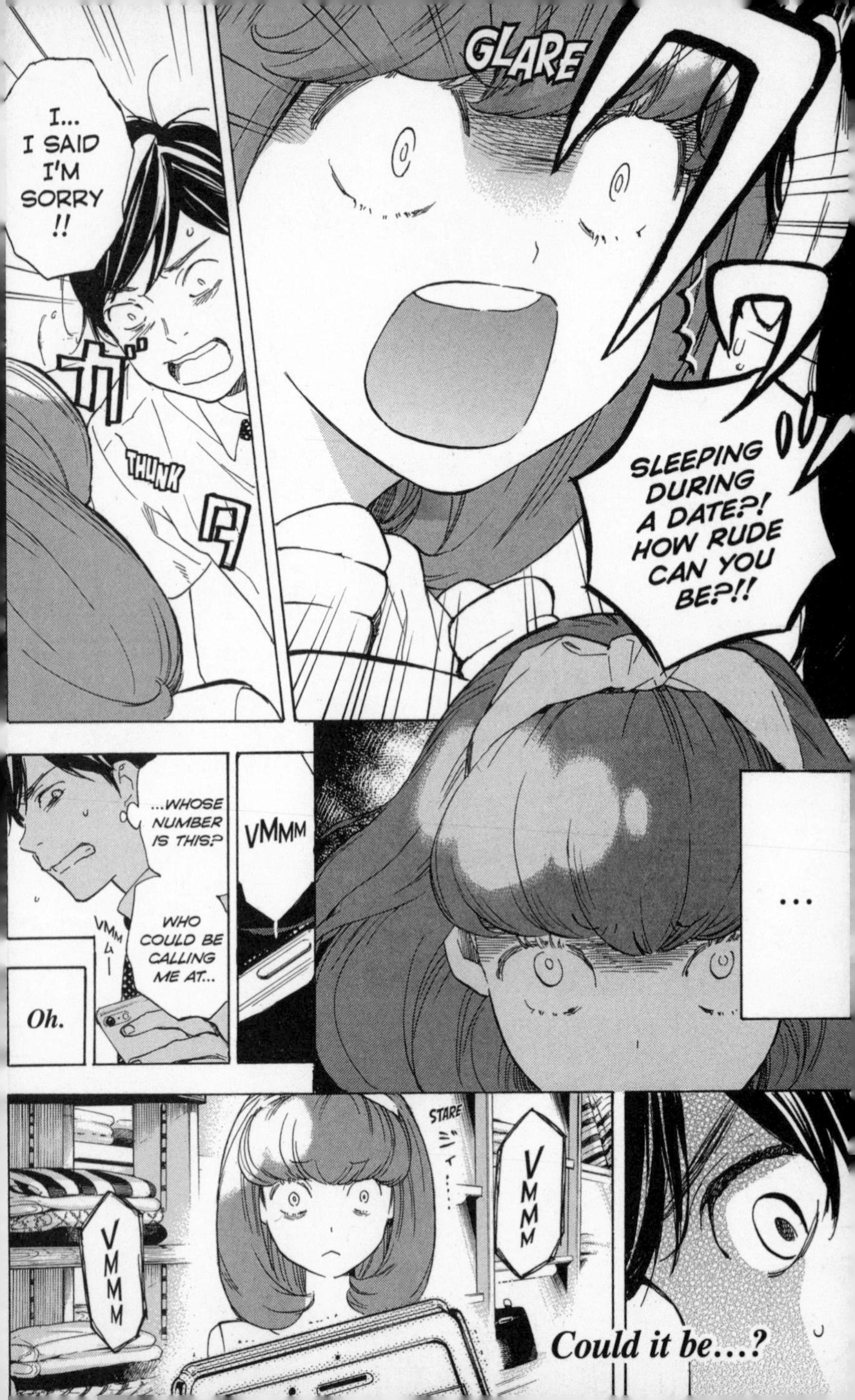

GLARE
SLEEPING DURING A DATE?! HOW RUDE CAN YOU BE?!!
THUNK
I... I SAID I'M SORRY!!
...
VMMM
...WHOSE NUMBER IS THIS?
WHO COULD BE CALLING ME AT...
VMMM
Oh.
Could it be...?
VMMM
STARE
VMMM

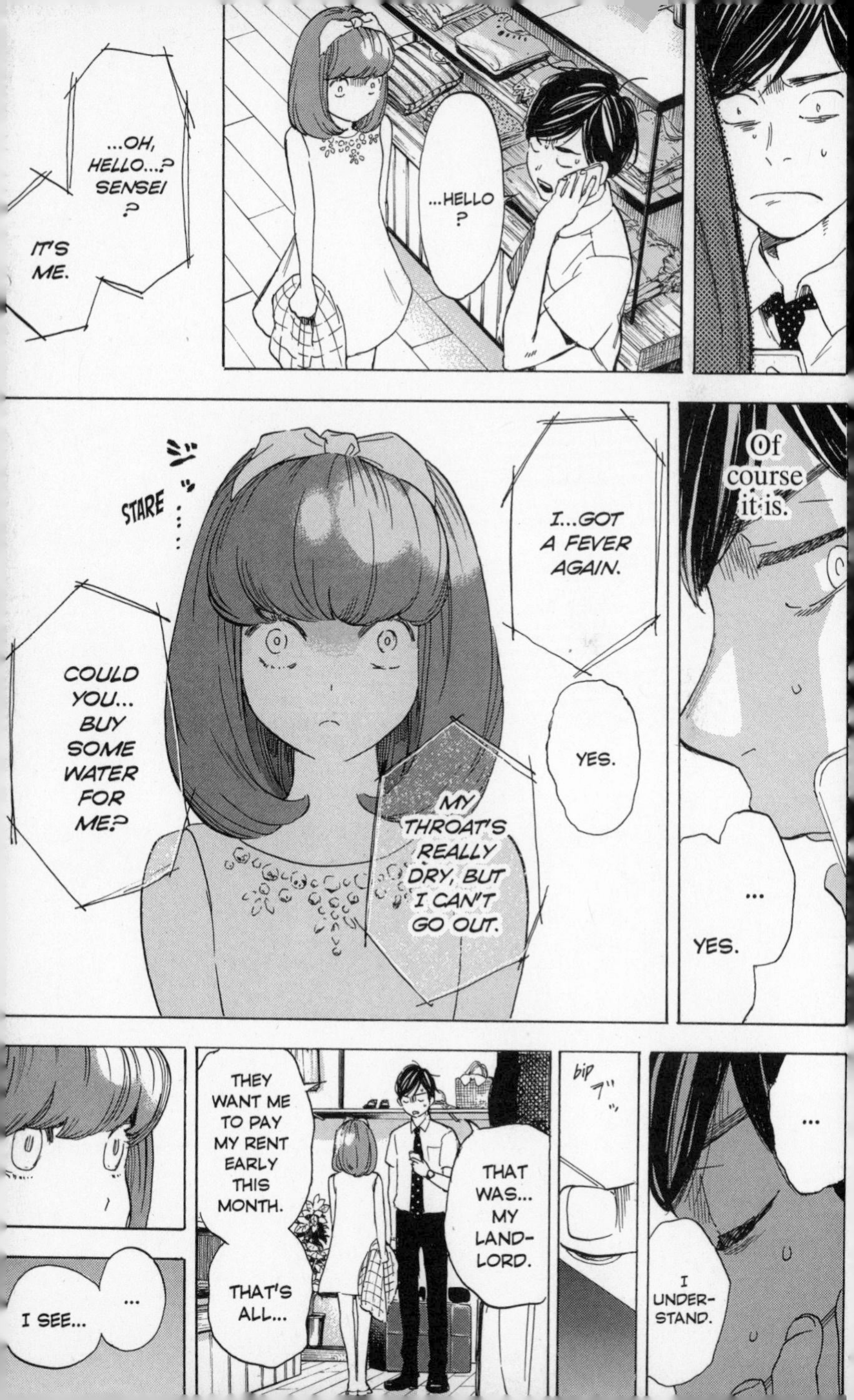
...HELLO ?
...OH, HELLO...? SENSEI ?
IT'S ME.
Of course it is.
...
YES.
I...GOT A FEVER AGAIN.
YES.
STARE
MY THROAT'S REALLY DRY, BUT I CAN'T GO OUT.
COULD YOU... BUY SOME WATER FOR ME?
...
I UNDERSTAND.
bip
THAT WAS... MY LANDLORD.
THEY WANT ME TO PAY MY RENT EARLY THIS MONTH.
THAT'S ALL...
...
I SEE...

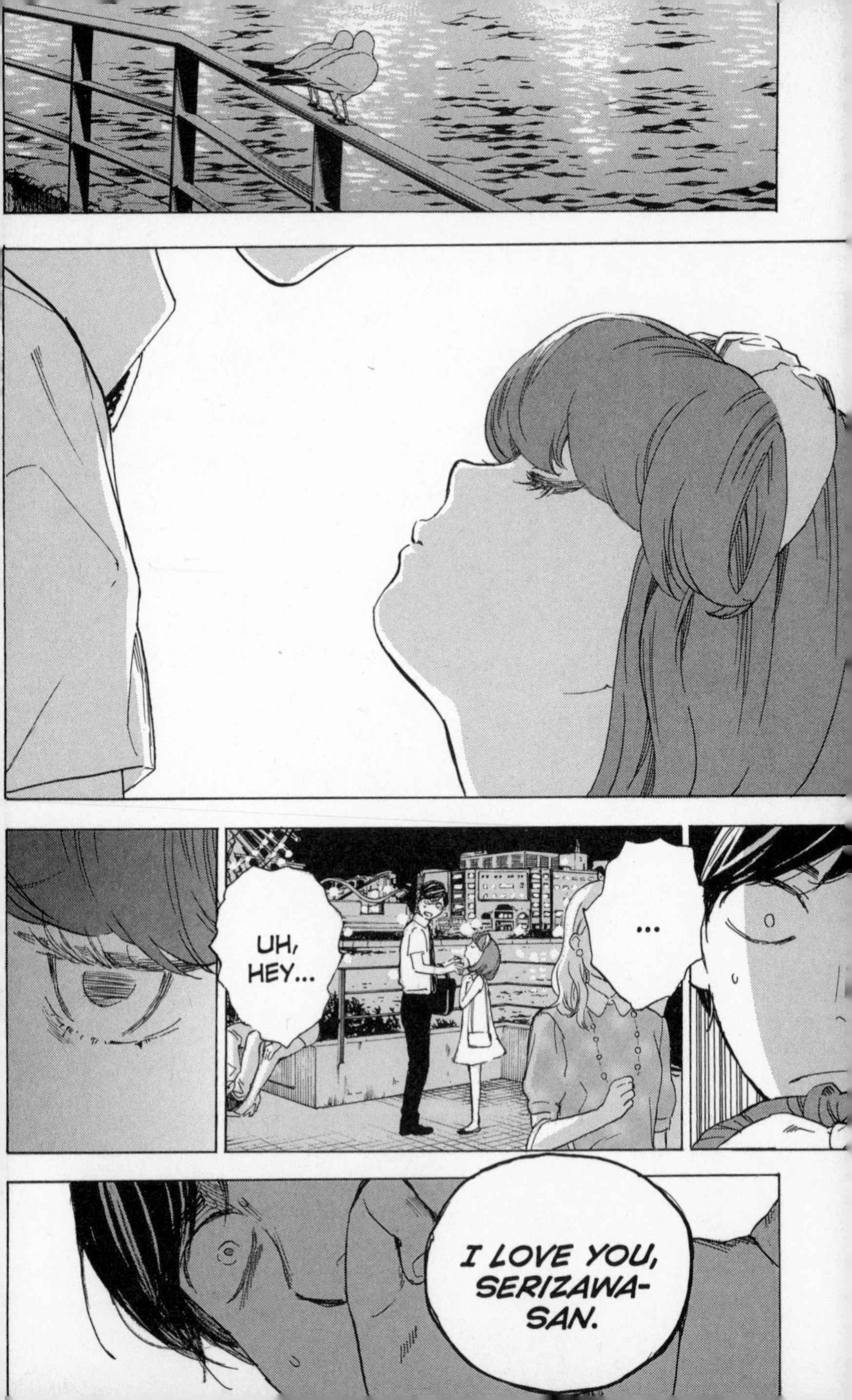
...
UH, HEY...
I LOVE YOU, SERIZAWA-SAN.

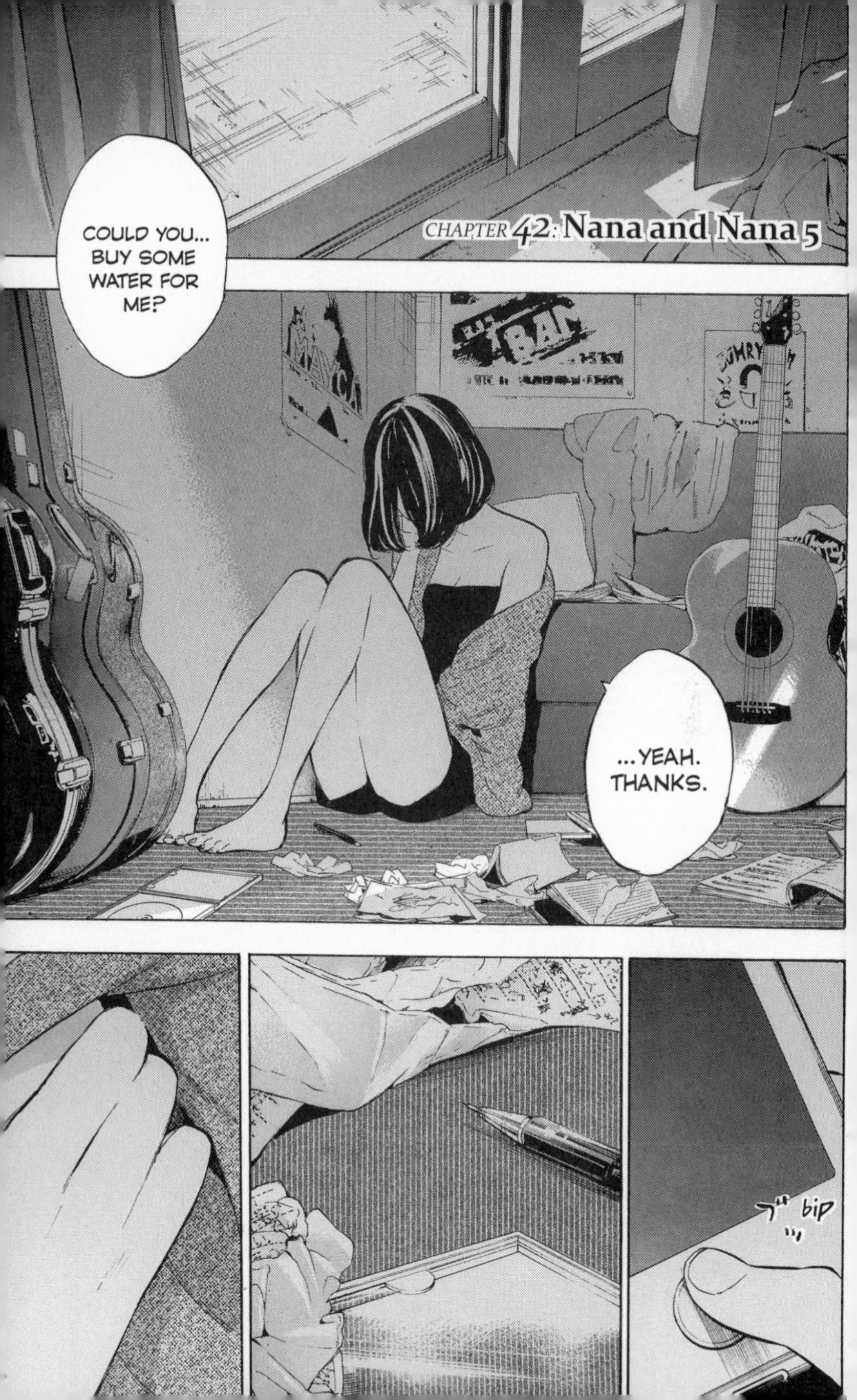
CHAPTER 42: Nana and Nana 5
COULD YOU... BUY SOME WATER FOR ME?
...YEAH. THANKS.
ブッ bip

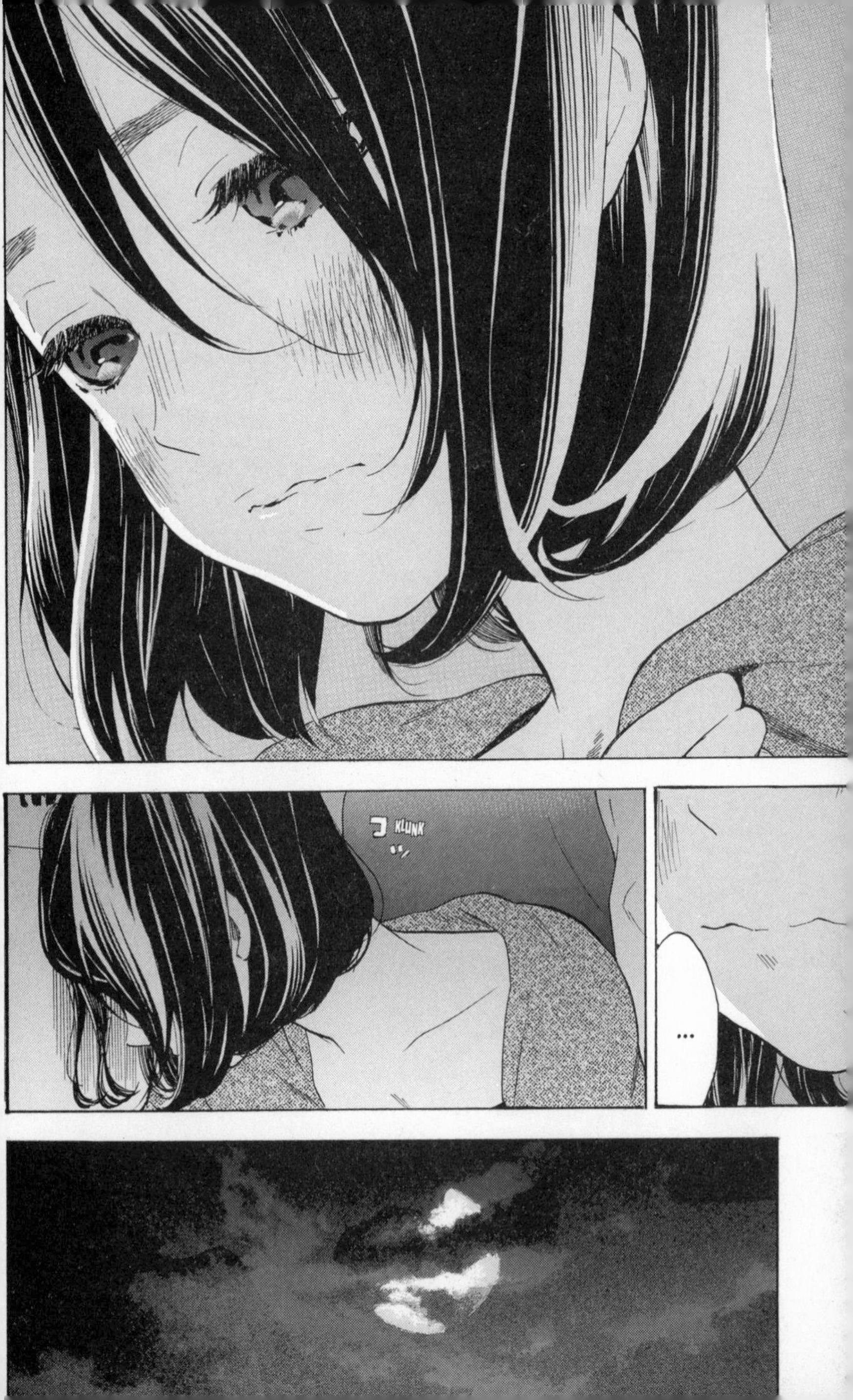
...
コ KLUNK

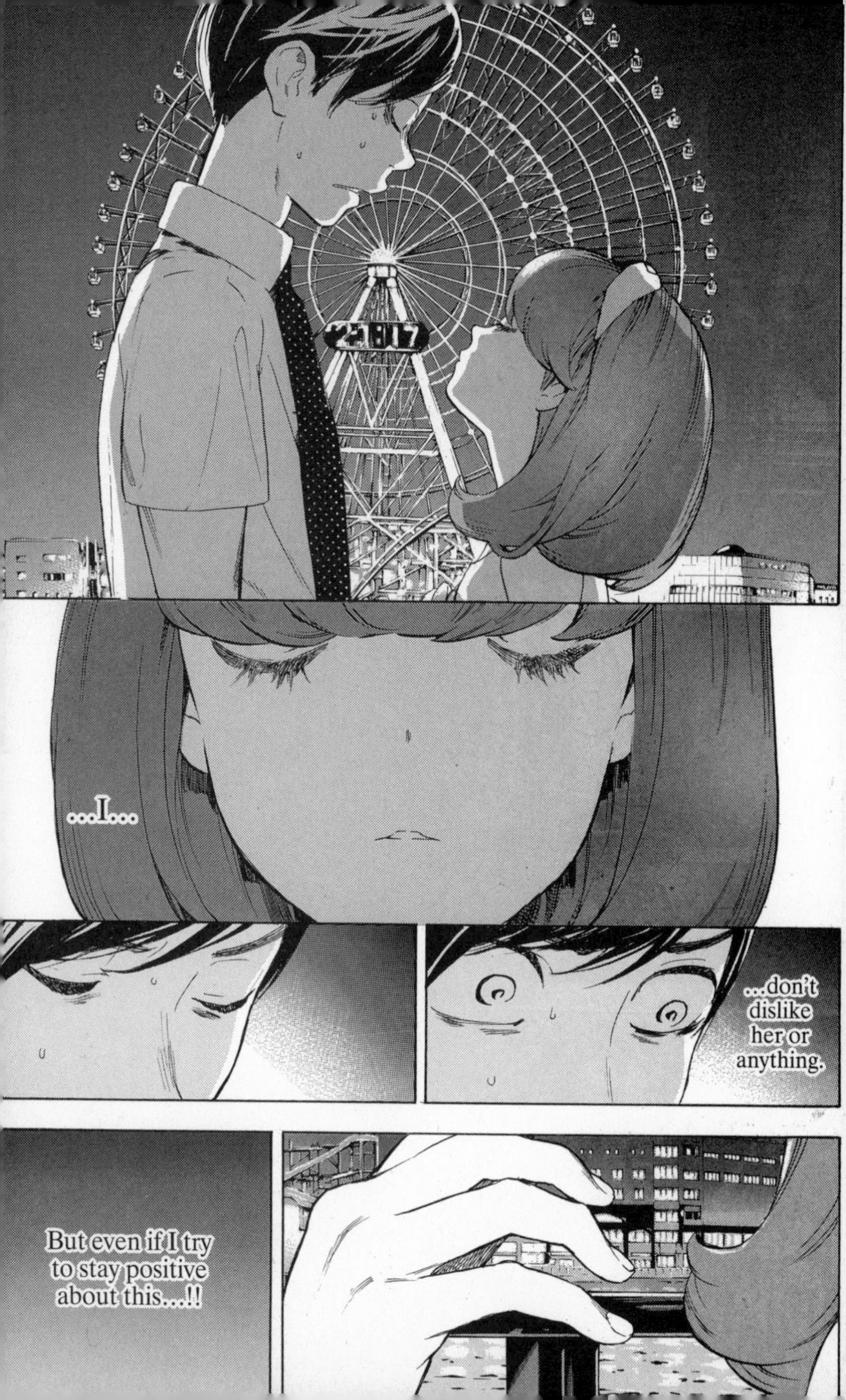
...I...
...don't dislike her or anything.
But even if I try to stay positive about this...!!

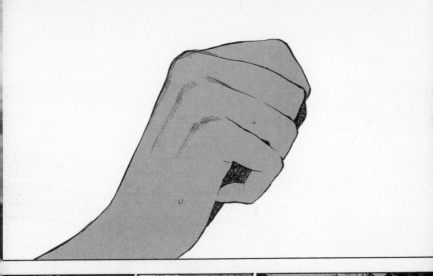

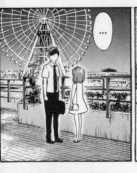

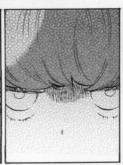

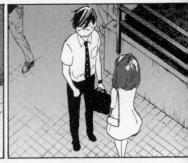

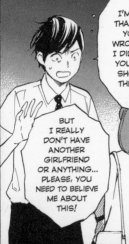

...
WE...
WE DON'T HAVE TO RUSH THINGS, YOU KNOW!
I'M SORRY THAT I GAVE YOU THE WRONG IDEA. I DIDN'T TELL YOU WHEN I SHOULD'VE THE OTHER DAY.
BUT I REALLY DON'T HAVE ANOTHER GIRLFRIEND OR ANYTHING... PLEASE, YOU NEED TO BELIEVE ME ABOUT THIS!

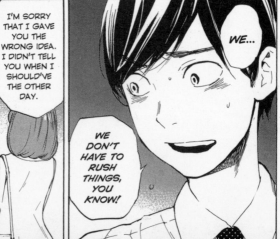

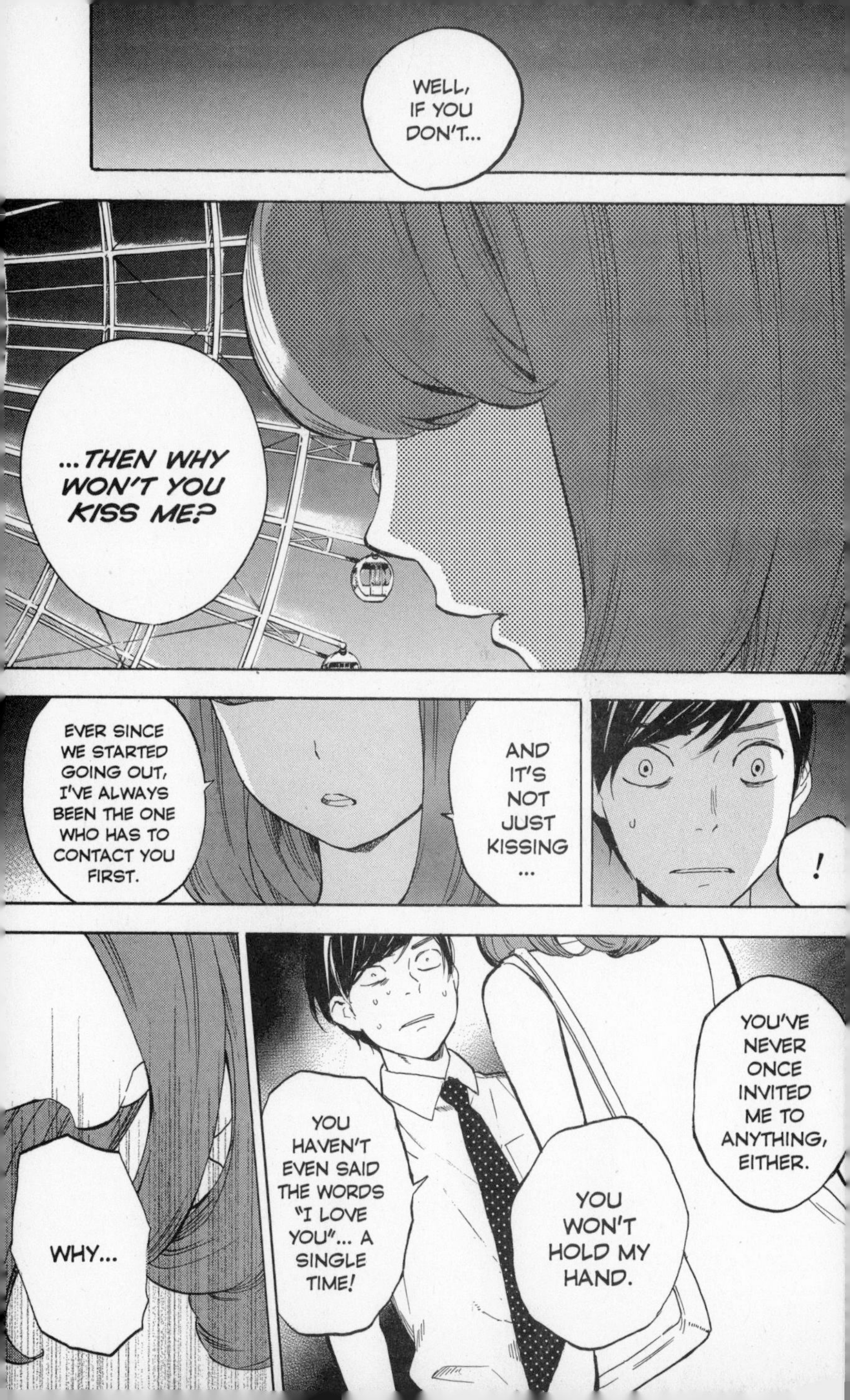
WELL, IF YOU DON'T...
...THEN WHY WON'T YOU KISS ME?
!
AND IT'S NOT JUST KISSING...
EVER SINCE WE STARTED GOING OUT, I'VE ALWAYS BEEN THE ONE WHO HAS TO CONTACT YOU FIRST.
YOU'VE NEVER ONCE INVITED ME TO ANYTHING, EITHER.
YOU WON'T HOLD MY HAND.
YOU HAVEN'T EVEN SAID THE WORDS "I LOVE YOU"... A SINGLE TIME!
WHY...

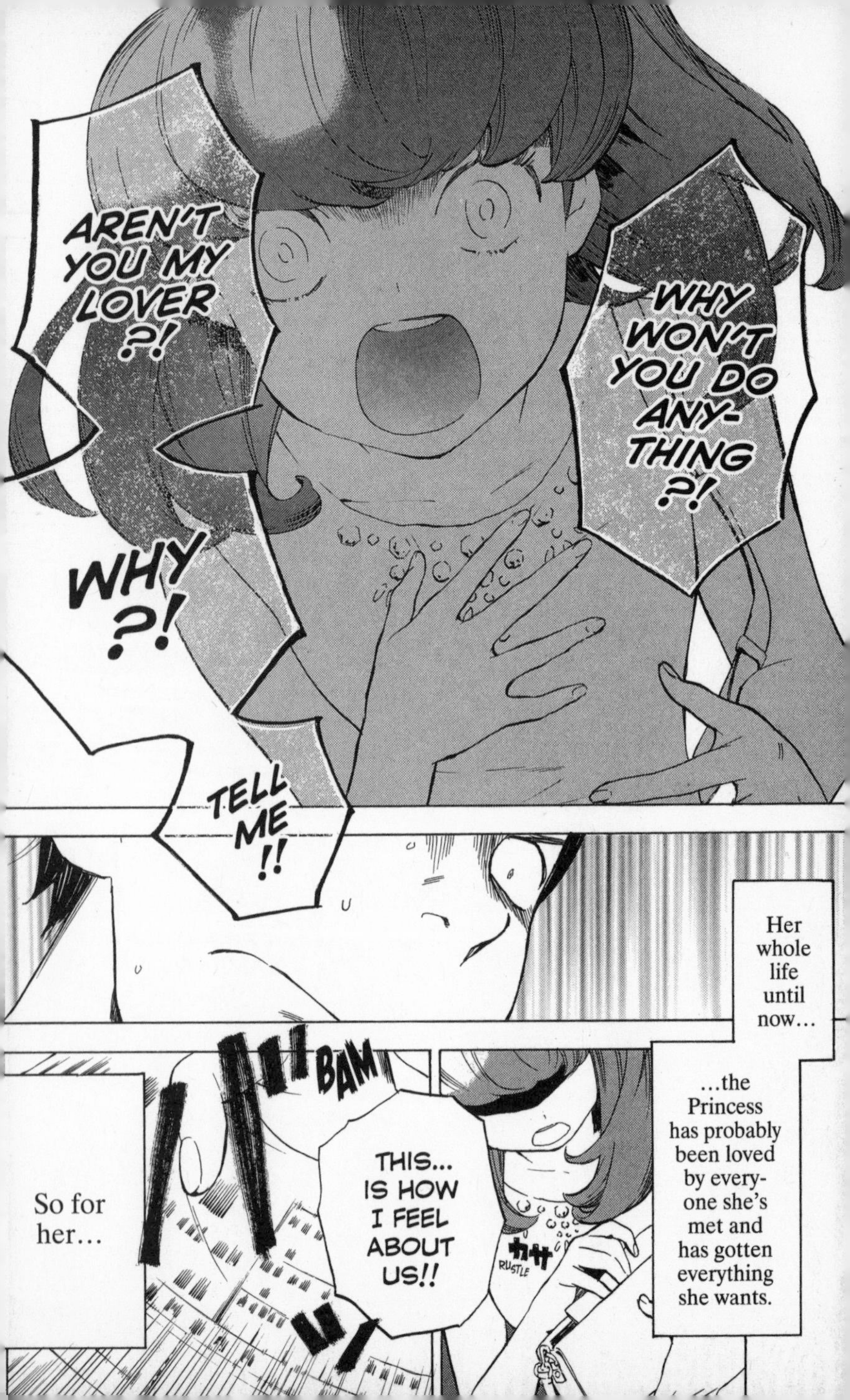
AREN'T YOU MY LOVER ?!
WHY WON'T YOU DO ANY-THING ?!
WHY ?!
TELL ME !!
Her whole life until now…
…the Princess has probably been loved by every-one she's met and has gotten everything she wants.
THIS… IS HOW I FEEL ABOUT US!!
カサ
RUSTLE
BAM
So for her…

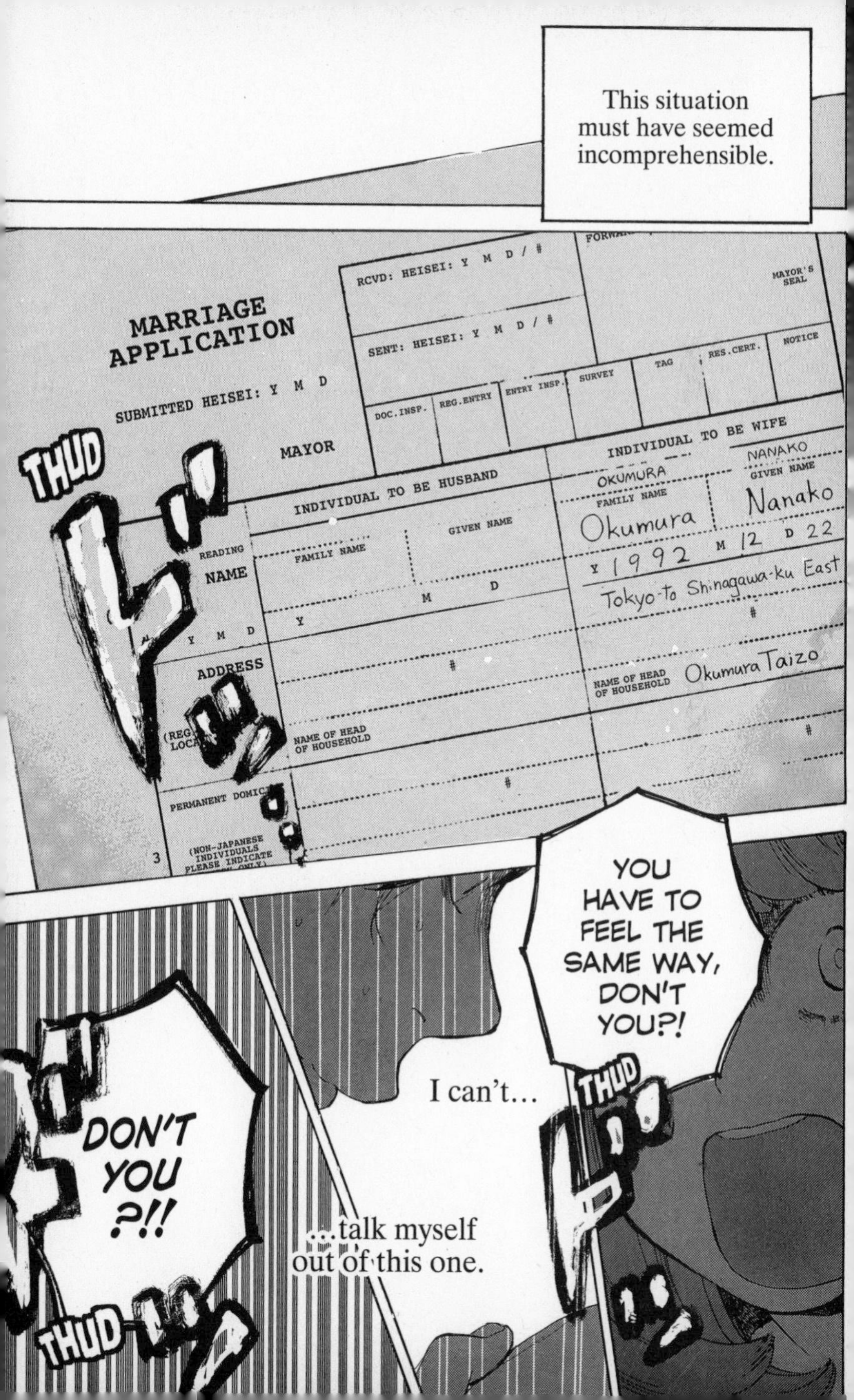
This situation must have seemed incomprehensible.
MARRIAGE APPLICATION
SUBMITTED HEISEI: Y M D
MAYOR
RCVD: HEISEI: Y M D / #
SENT: HEISEI: Y M D / #
MAYOR'S SEAL
DOC.INSP.
REG.ENTRY
ENTRY INSP.
SURVEY
TAG
RES.CERT.
NOTICE
INDIVIDUAL TO BE HUSBAND
INDIVIDUAL TO BE WIFE
READING
NAME
FAMILY NAME
GIVEN NAME
OKUMURA
NANAKO
Okumura
Nanako
Y 1992 M 12 D 22
Tokyo-to Shinagawa-ku East
ADDRESS
NAME OF HEAD OF HOUSEHOLD
Okumura Taizo
PERMANENT DOMIC
THUD
YOU HAVE TO FEEL THE SAME WAY, DON'T YOU?!
THUD
I can't…
DON'T YOU ?!!
THUD
…talk myself out of this one.

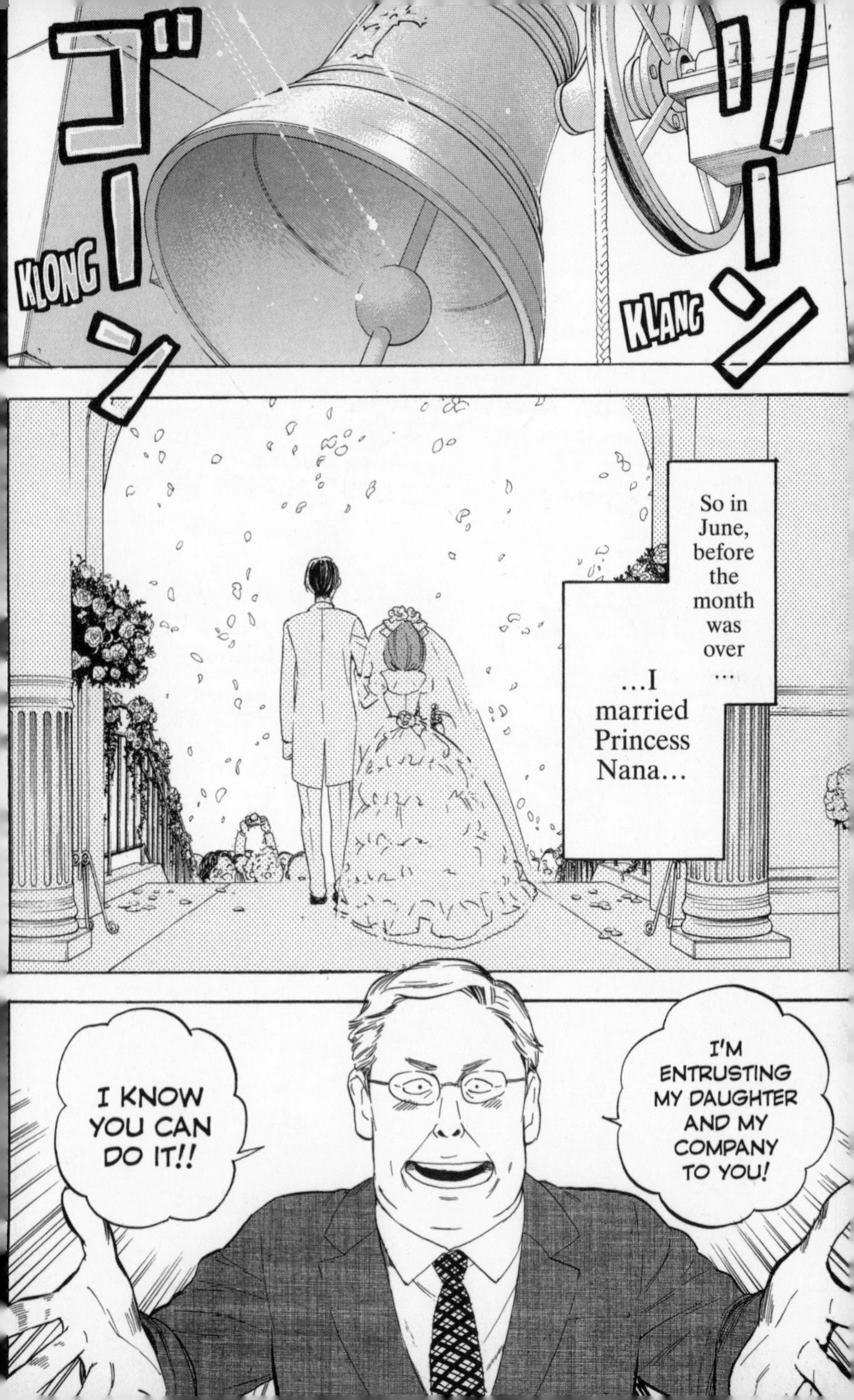
ゴーーン
KLONG
ゴーーン
KLANG
So in June, before the month was over…
…I married Princess Nana…
I'M ENTRUSTING MY DAUGHTER AND MY COMPANY TO YOU!
I KNOW YOU CAN DO IT!!

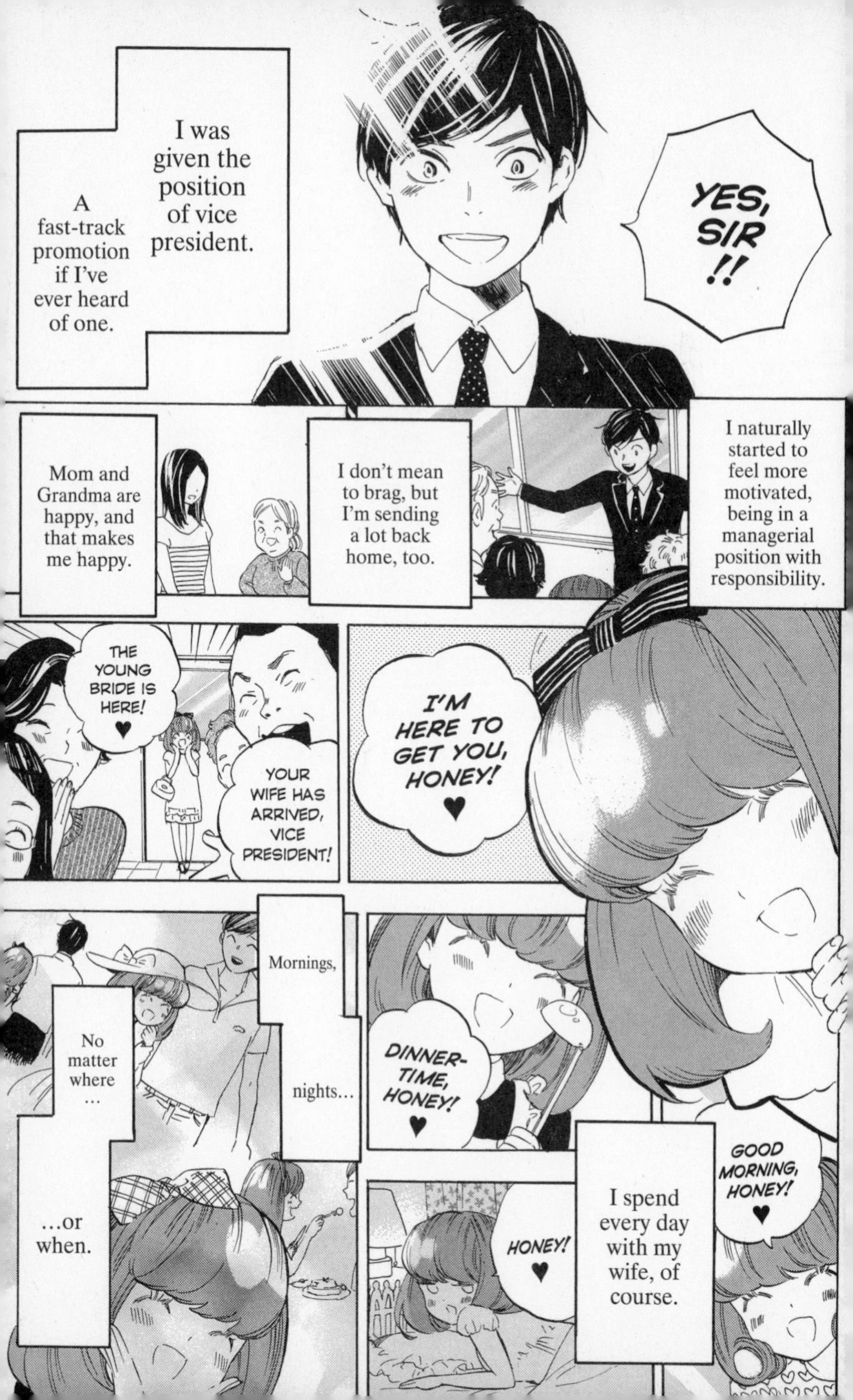
YES, SIR!!
I was given the position of vice president.
A fast-track promotion if I've ever heard of one.
I naturally started to feel more motivated, being in a managerial position with responsibility.
I don't mean to brag, but I'm sending a lot back home, too.
Mom and Grandma are happy, and that makes me happy.
I'M HERE TO GET YOU, HONEY! ♥
THE YOUNG BRIDE IS HERE! ♥
YOUR WIFE HAS ARRIVED, VICE PRESIDENT!
GOOD MORNING, HONEY! ♥
I spend every day with my wife, of course.
HONEY! ♥
DINNER-TIME, HONEY! ♥
Mornings,
nights…
No matter where…
…or when.

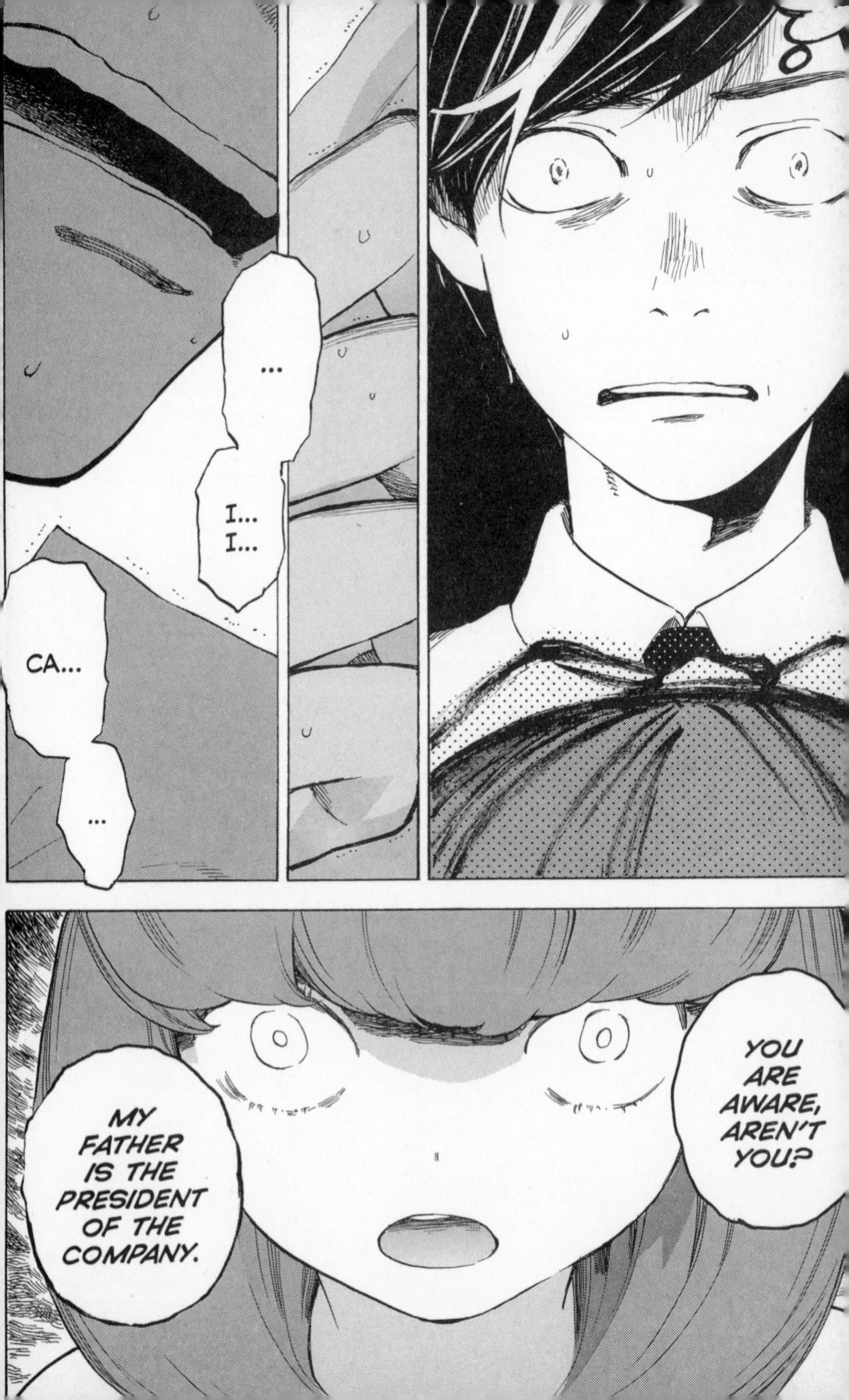
...
I... I...
CA...
...
YOU ARE AWARE, AREN'T YOU?
MY FATHER IS THE PRESIDENT OF THE COMPANY.

I'LL BE WAITING FOR YOU TOMORROW!!

ZSH

Marriage…

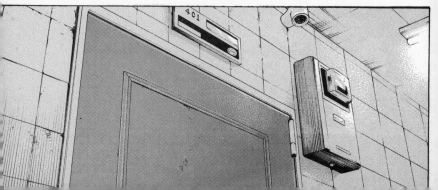

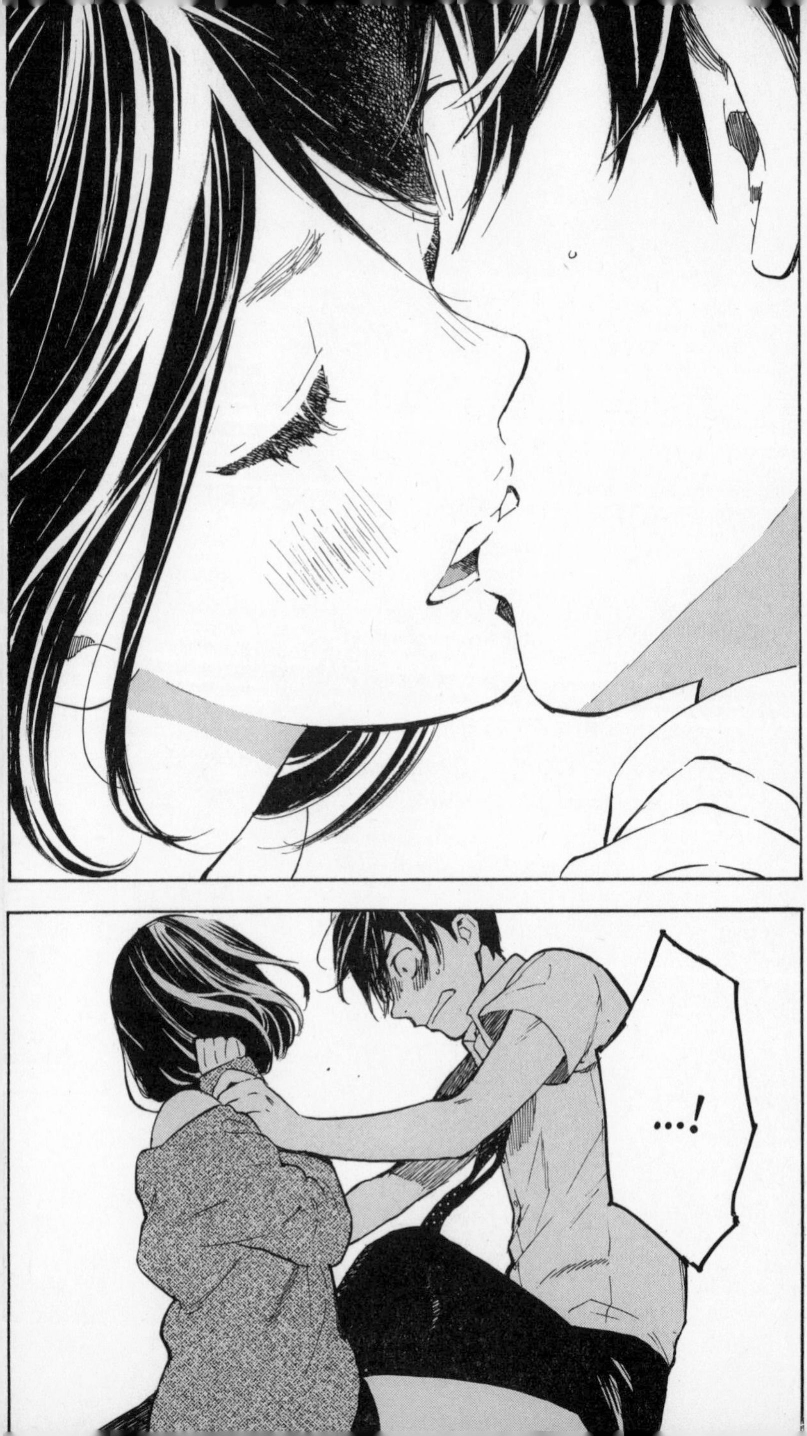
...!

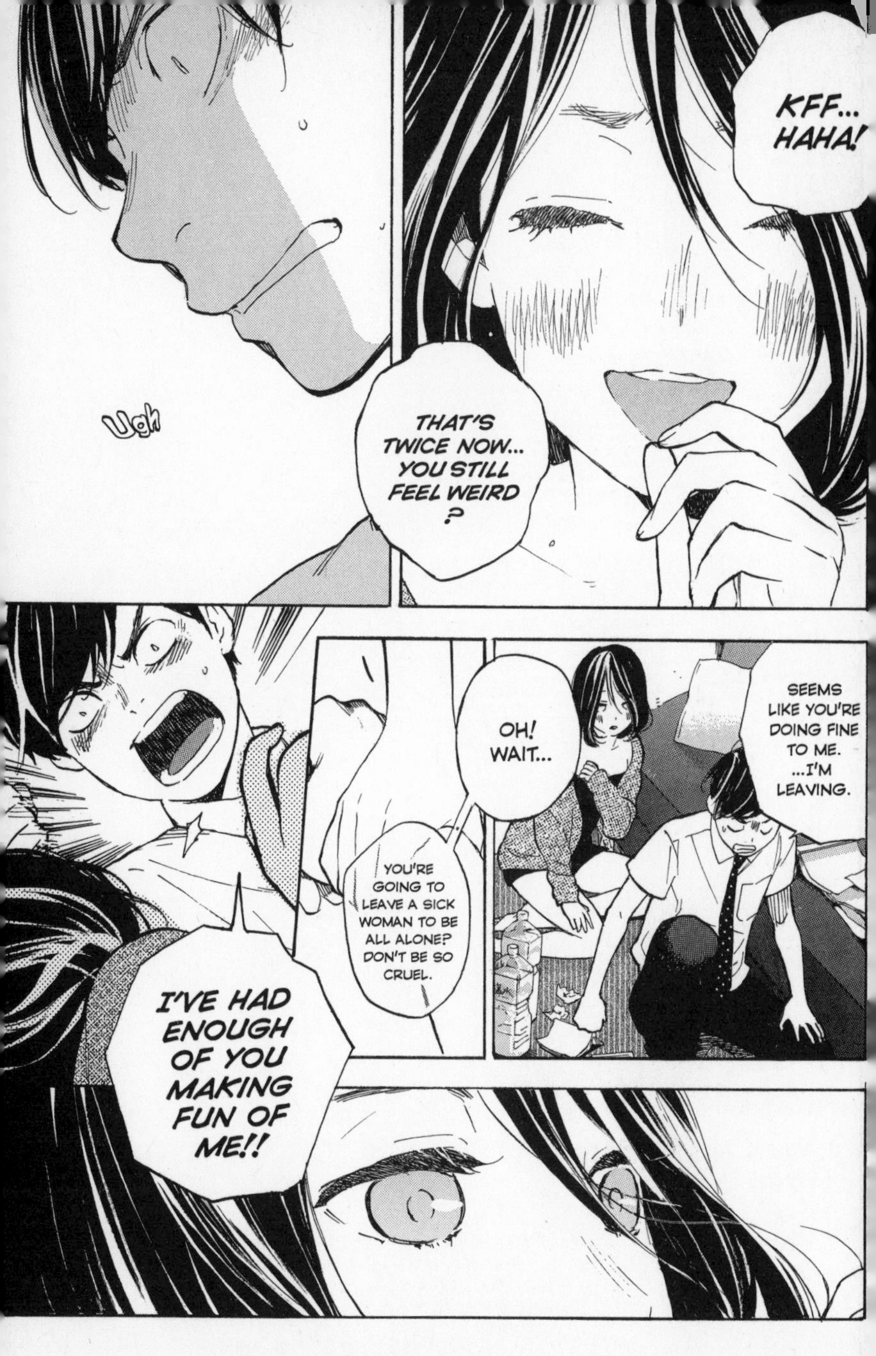
KFF... HAHA!
THAT'S TWICE NOW... YOU STILL FEEL WEIRD?
Ugh
SEEMS LIKE YOU'RE DOING FINE TO ME. ...I'M LEAVING.
OH! WAIT...
YOU'RE GOING TO LEAVE A SICK WOMAN TO BE ALL ALONE? DON'T BE SO CRUEL.
I'VE HAD ENOUGH OF YOU MAKING FUN OF ME!!

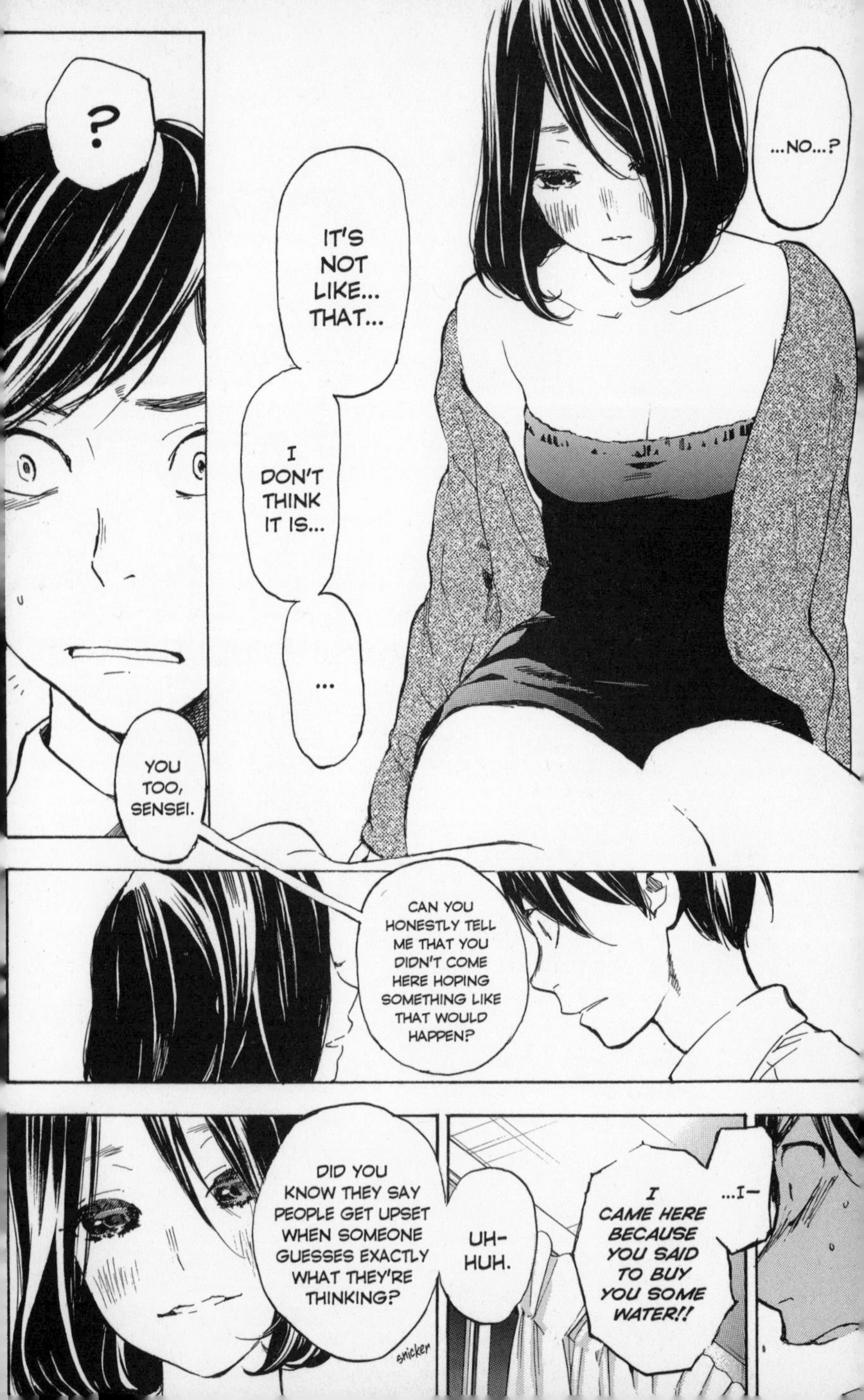
...NO...?
IT'S NOT LIKE... THAT...
I DON'T THINK IT IS...
...
?
YOU TOO, SENSEI.
CAN YOU HONESTLY TELL ME THAT YOU DIDN'T COME HERE HOPING SOMETHING LIKE THAT WOULD HAPPEN?
...I—
I CAME HERE BECAUSE YOU SAID TO BUY YOU SOME WATER!!
UH-HUH.
DID YOU KNOW THEY SAY PEOPLE GET UPSET WHEN SOMEONE GUESSES EXACTLY WHAT THEY'RE THINKING?
snicker

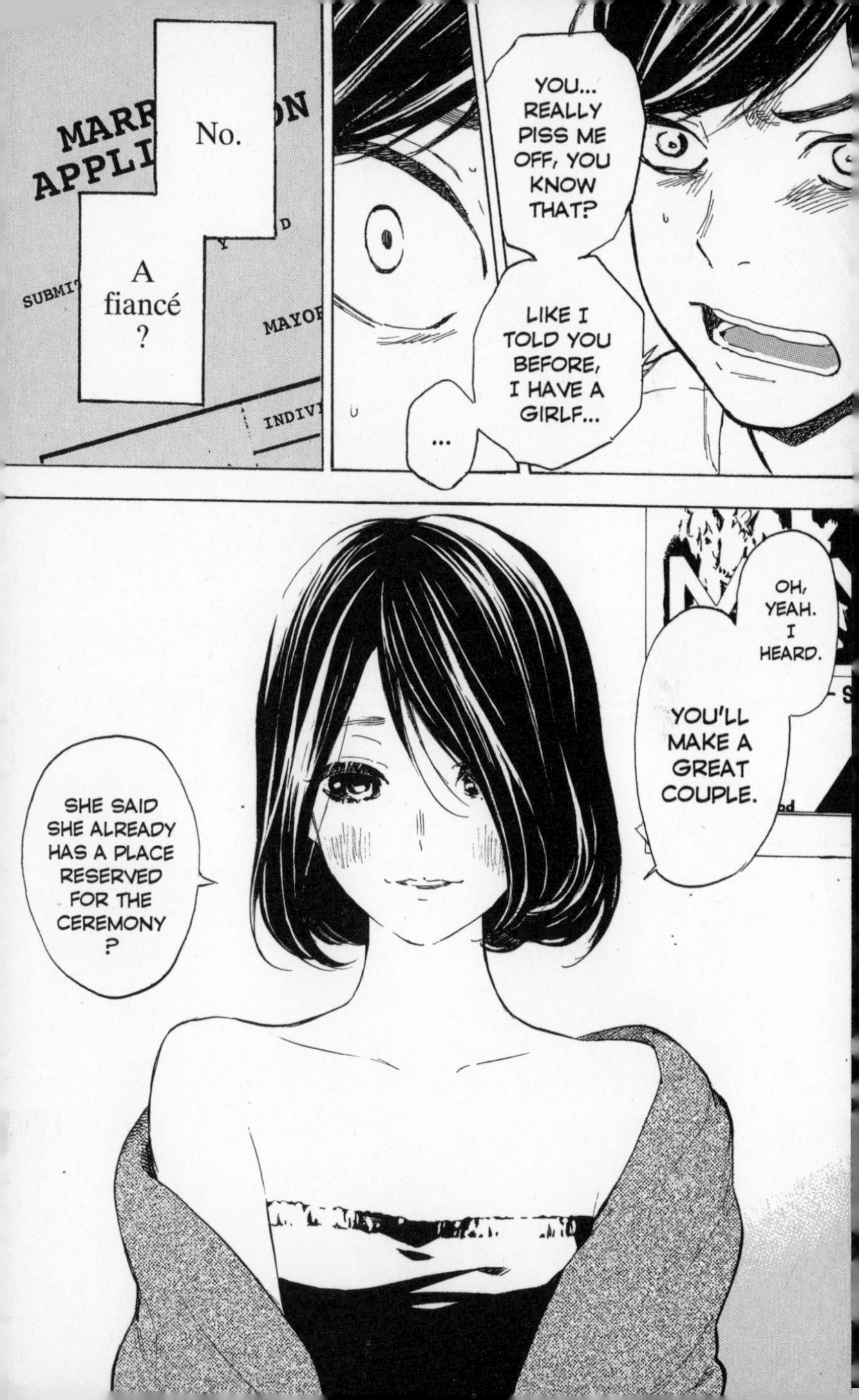

YOU... REALLY PISS ME OFF, YOU KNOW THAT?
LIKE I TOLD YOU BEFORE, I HAVE A GIRLF...
...
No.
A fiancé?
OH, YEAH. I HEARD.
YOU'LL MAKE A GREAT COUPLE.
SHE SAID SHE ALREADY HAS A PLACE RESERVED FOR THE CEREMONY?

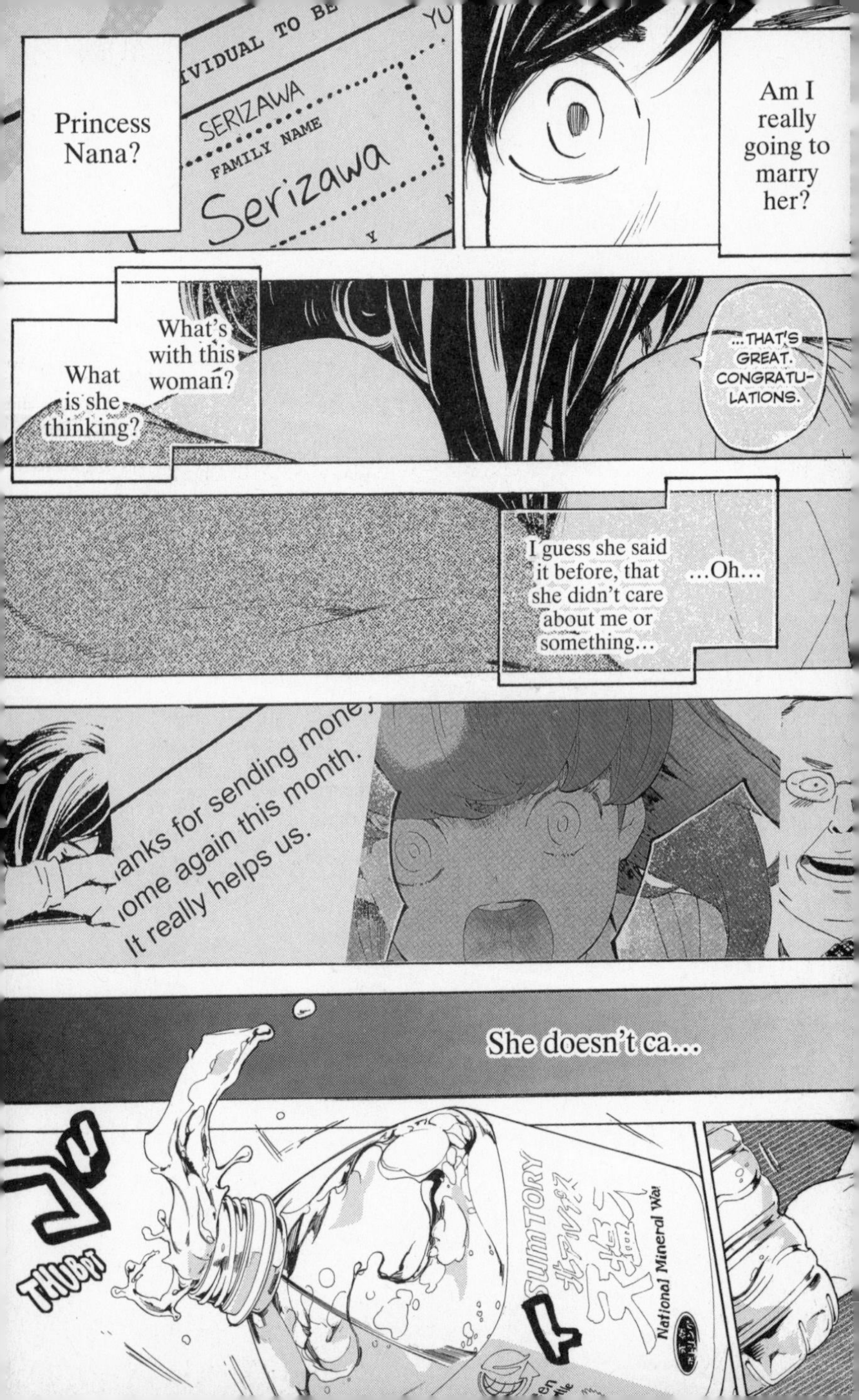
Am I really going to marry her?
IVIDUAL TO BE
SERIZAWA
FAMILY NAME
Serizawa
Princess Nana?
...THAT'S GREAT. CONGRATULATIONS.
What's with this woman?
What is she thinking?
...Oh...
I guess she said it before, that she didn't care about me or something...
anks for sending mone
ome again this month.
It really helps us.
She doesn't ca...
THUBP!
National Mineral Wat

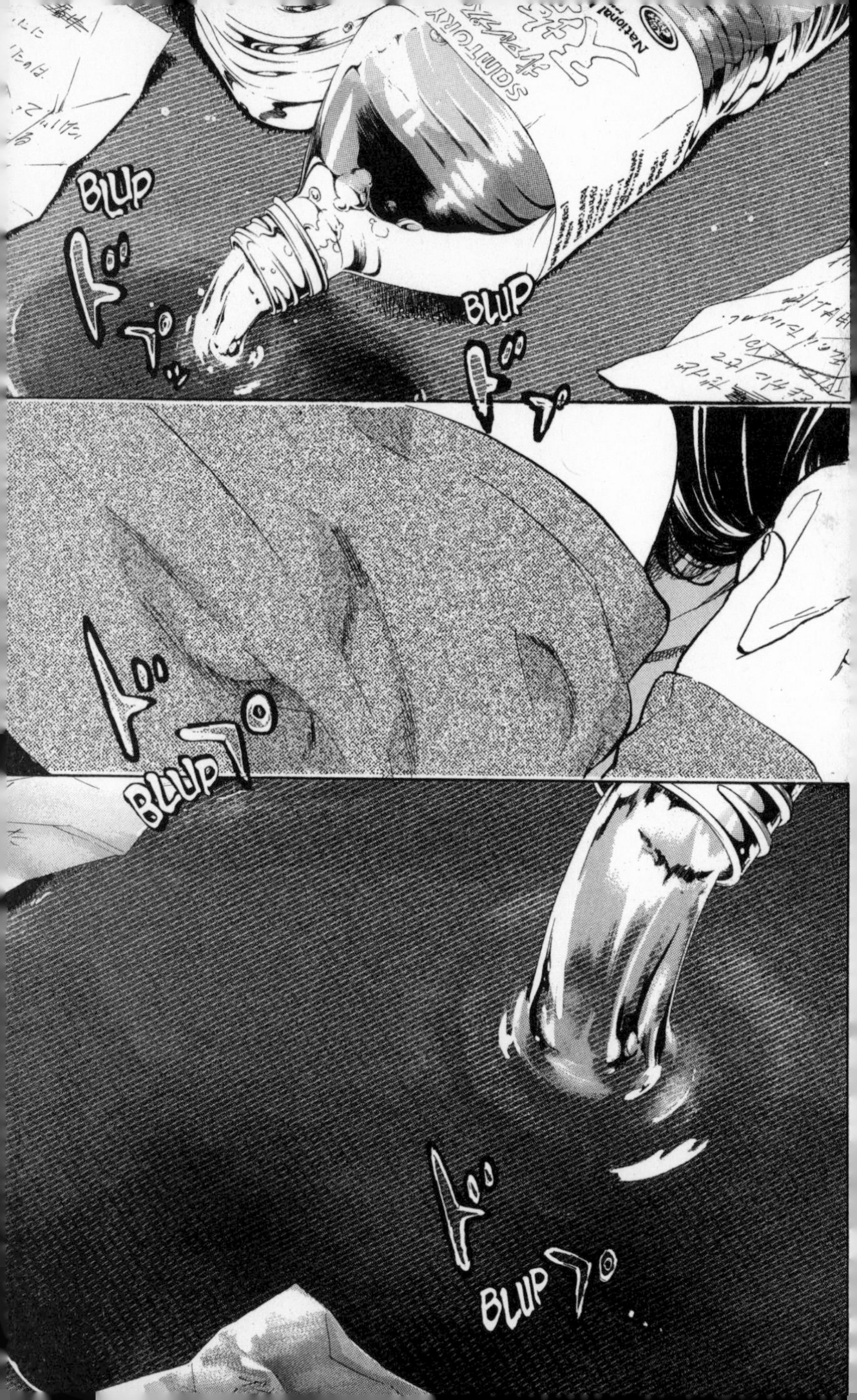

BLUP
ドプ
BLUP
ドプッ
ドプ
BLUP
ドプ
BLUP

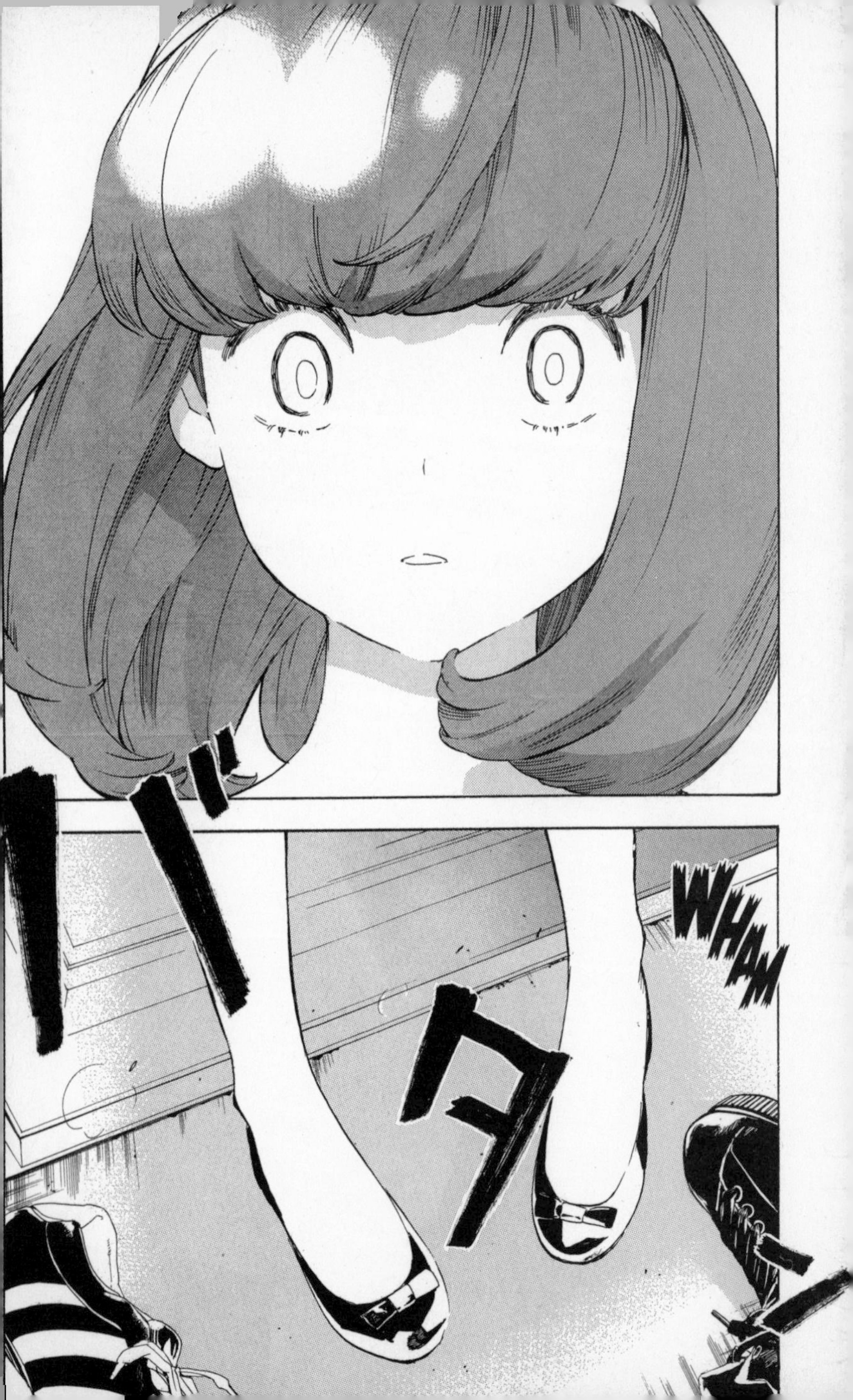
ガタ
WHAM

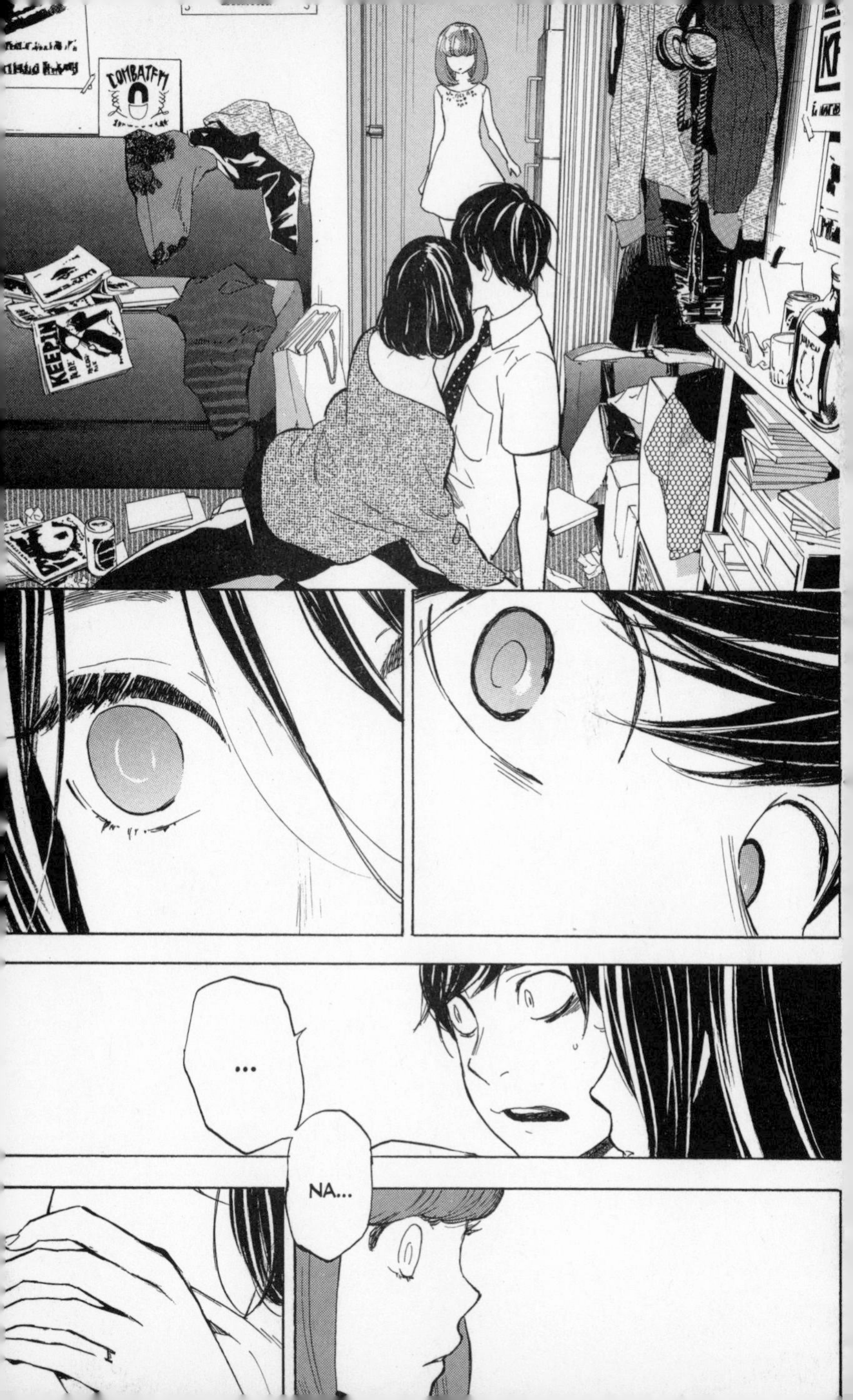
...
NA...

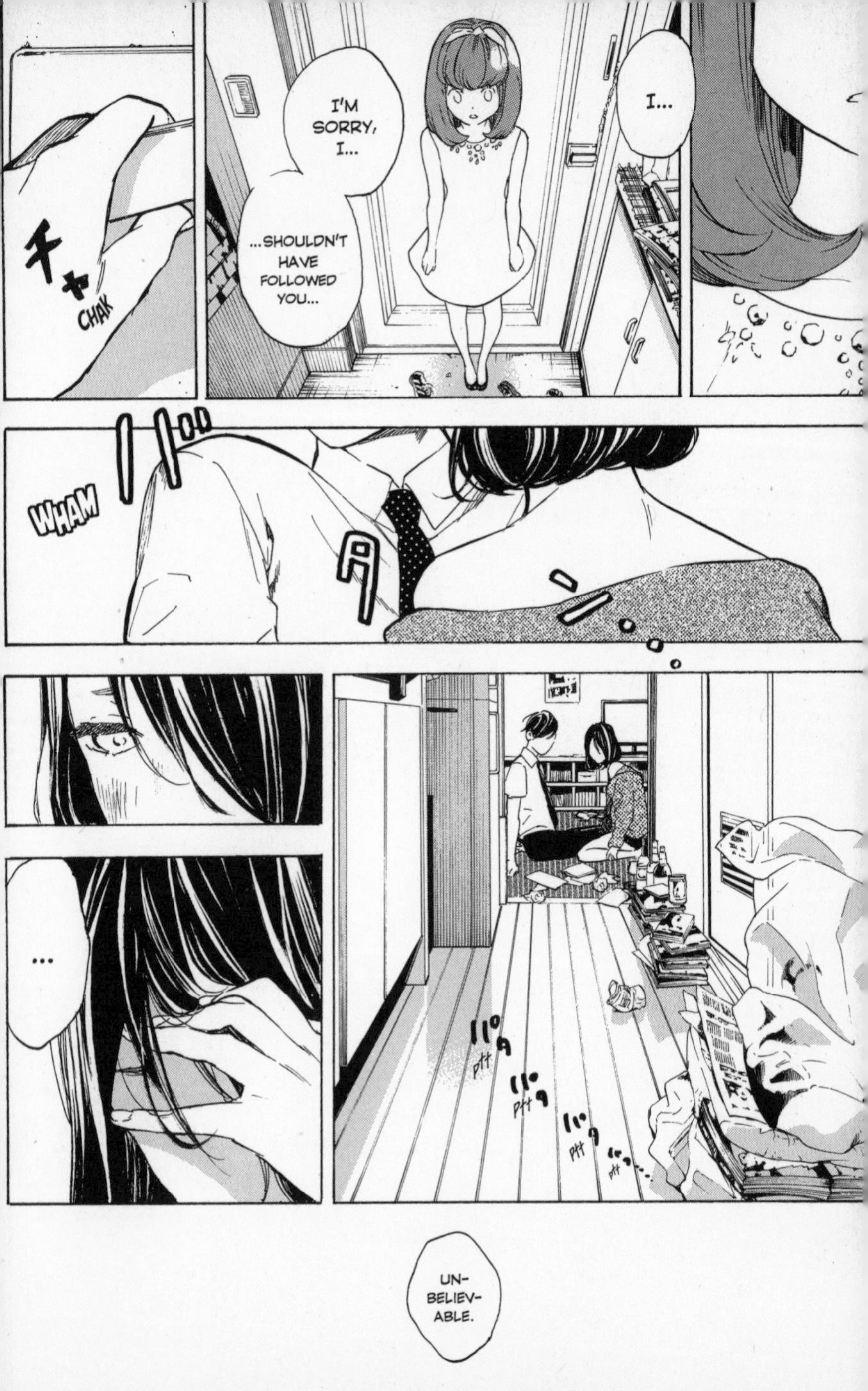
I...
I'M SORRY, I...
...SHOULDN'T HAVE FOLLOWED YOU...
チャ
CHAK
WHAM
ptt
ptt
ptt
ptt
...
UN-BELIEVABLE.

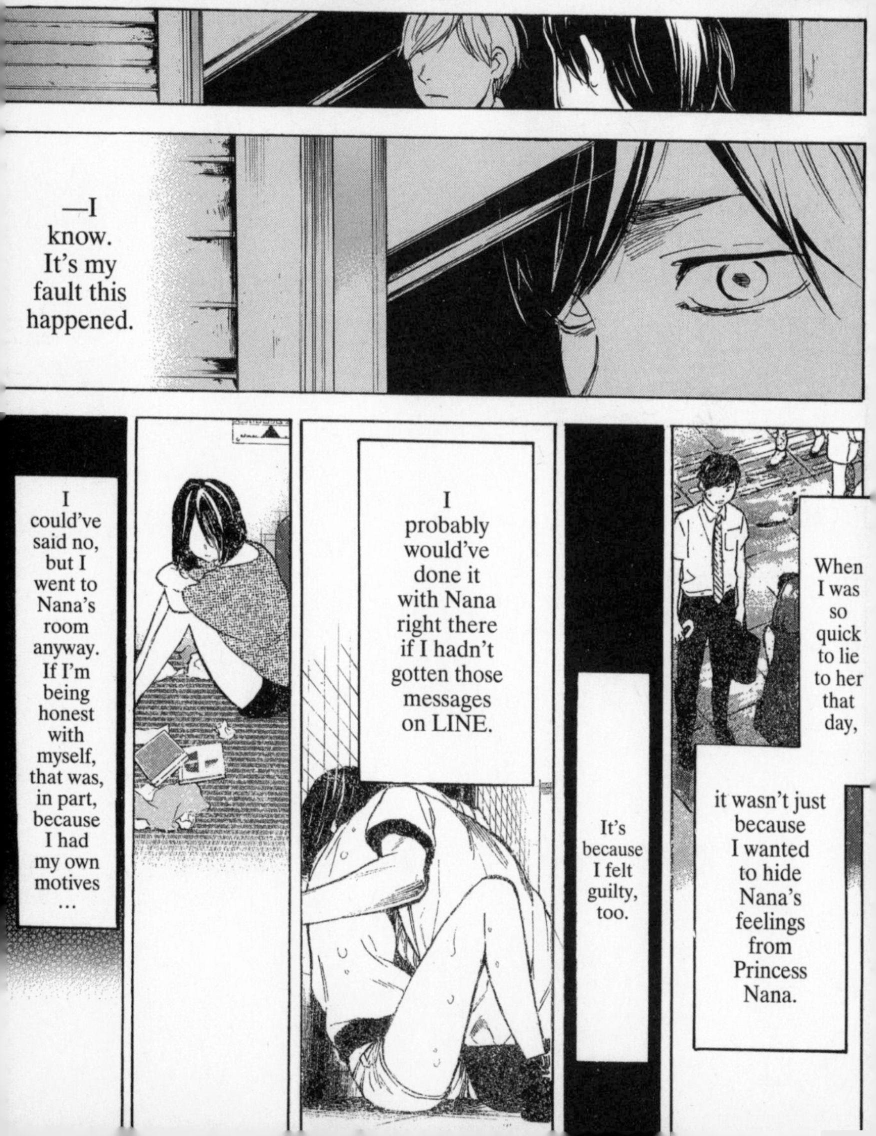
—I know. It's my fault this happened.
When I was so quick to lie to her that day,
it wasn't just because I wanted to hide Nana's feelings from Princess Nana.
It's because I felt guilty, too.
I probably would've done it with Nana right there if I hadn't gotten those messages on LINE.
I could've said no, but I went to Nana's room anyway. If I'm being honest with myself, that was, in part, because I had my own motives…

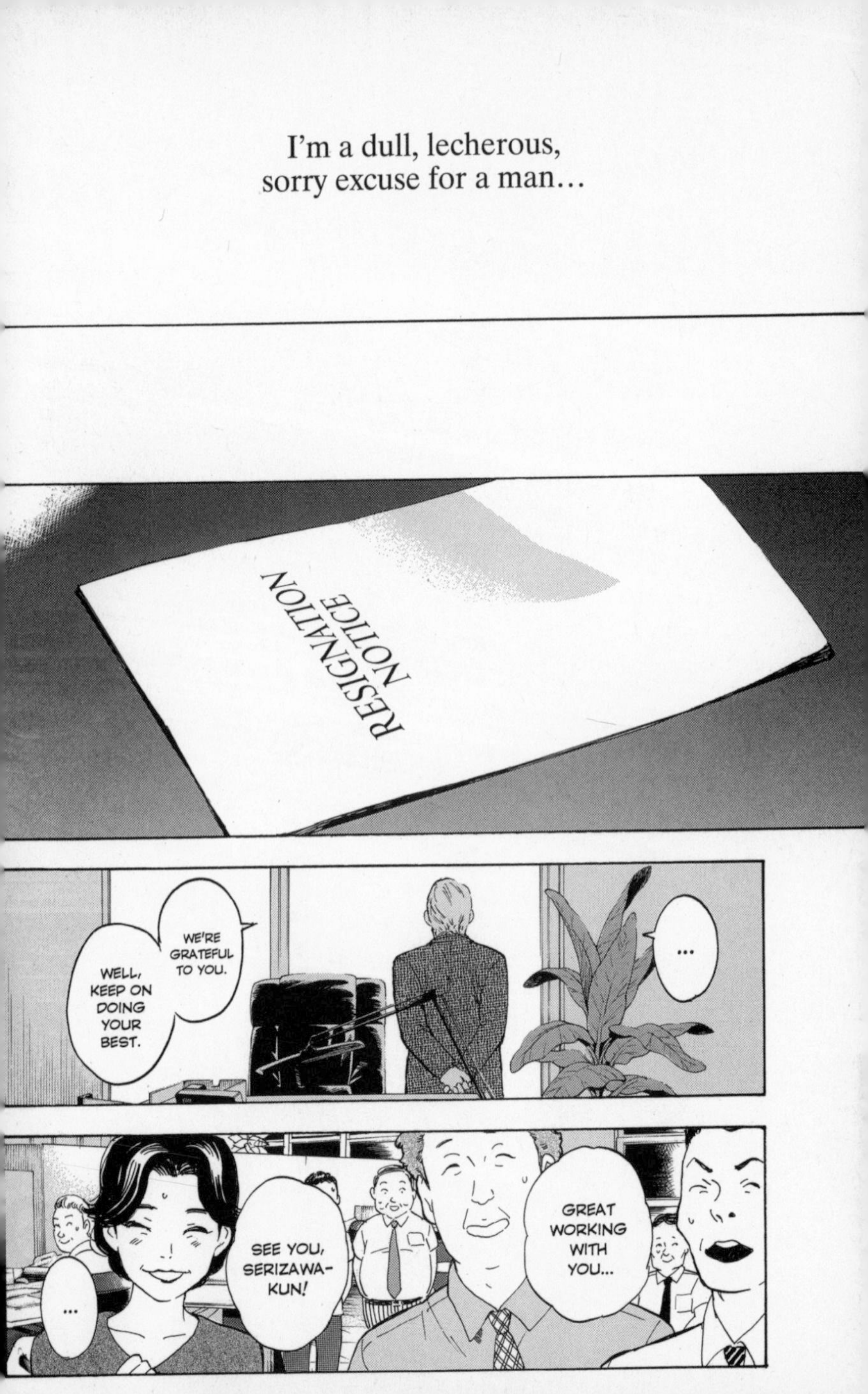
I'm a dull, lecherous, sorry excuse for a man…
RESIGNATION NOTICE
...
WE'RE GRATEFUL TO YOU.
WELL, KEEP ON DOING YOUR BEST.
GREAT WORKING WITH YOU...
SEE YOU, SERIZAWA-KUN!
...

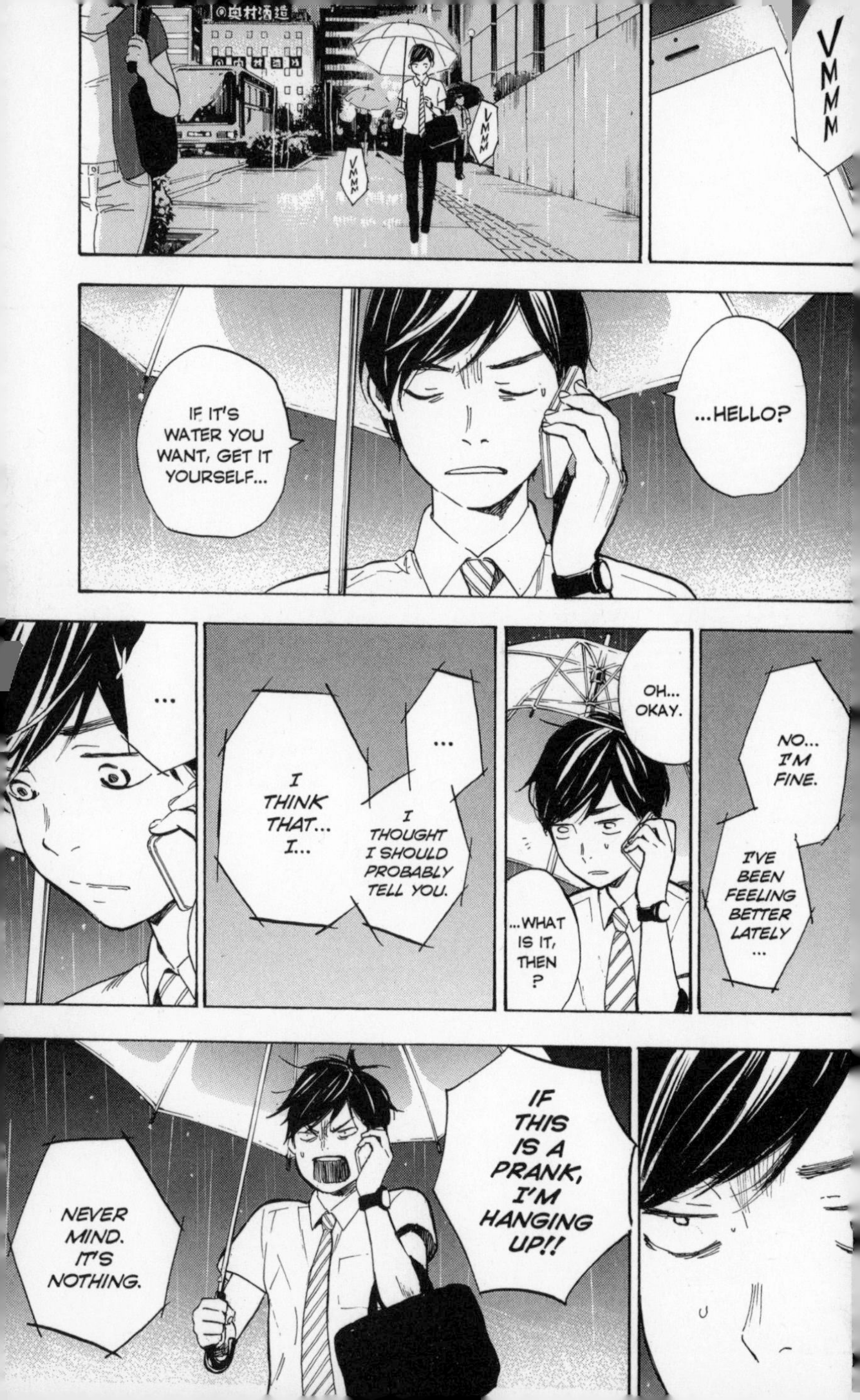
VMMM
奥村酒造
VMMM
VMMM
...HELLO?
IF IT'S WATER YOU WANT, GET IT YOURSELF...
NO... I'M FINE.
I'VE BEEN FEELING BETTER LATELY...
OH... OKAY.
...WHAT IS IT, THEN?
...
I THINK THAT... I...
I THOUGHT I SHOULD PROBABLY TELL YOU.
...
IF THIS IS A PRANK, I'M HANGING UP!!
NEVER MIND. IT'S NOTHING.

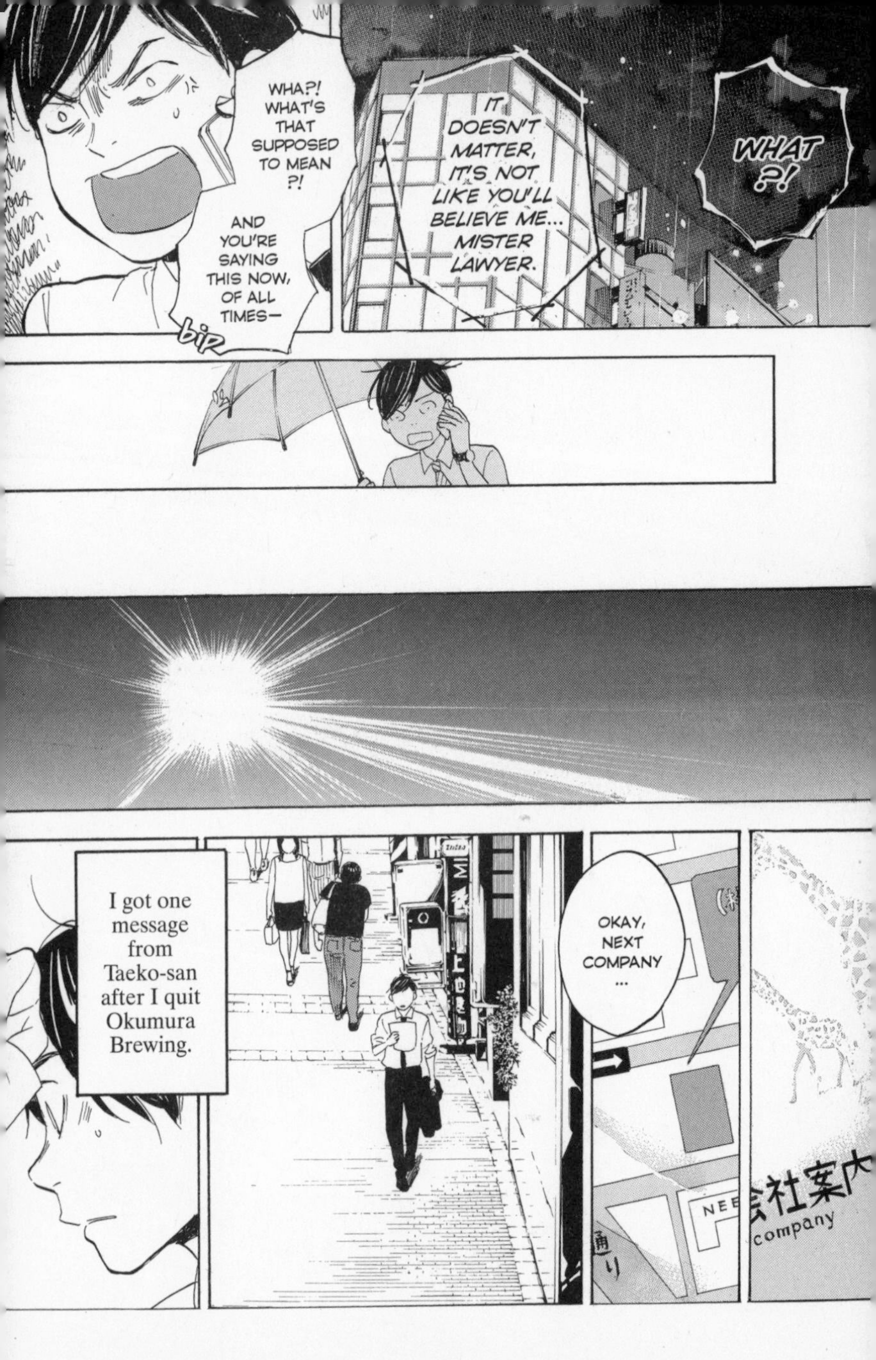
WHAT ?!
IT DOESN'T MATTER, IT'S NOT LIKE YOU'LL BELIEVE ME... MISTER LAWYER.
WHA?! WHAT'S THAT SUPPOSED TO MEAN ?!
AND YOU'RE SAYING THIS NOW, OF ALL TIMES—
bip
会社案内
company
通り
OKAY, NEXT COMPANY ...
I got one message from Taeko-san after I quit Okumura Brewing.

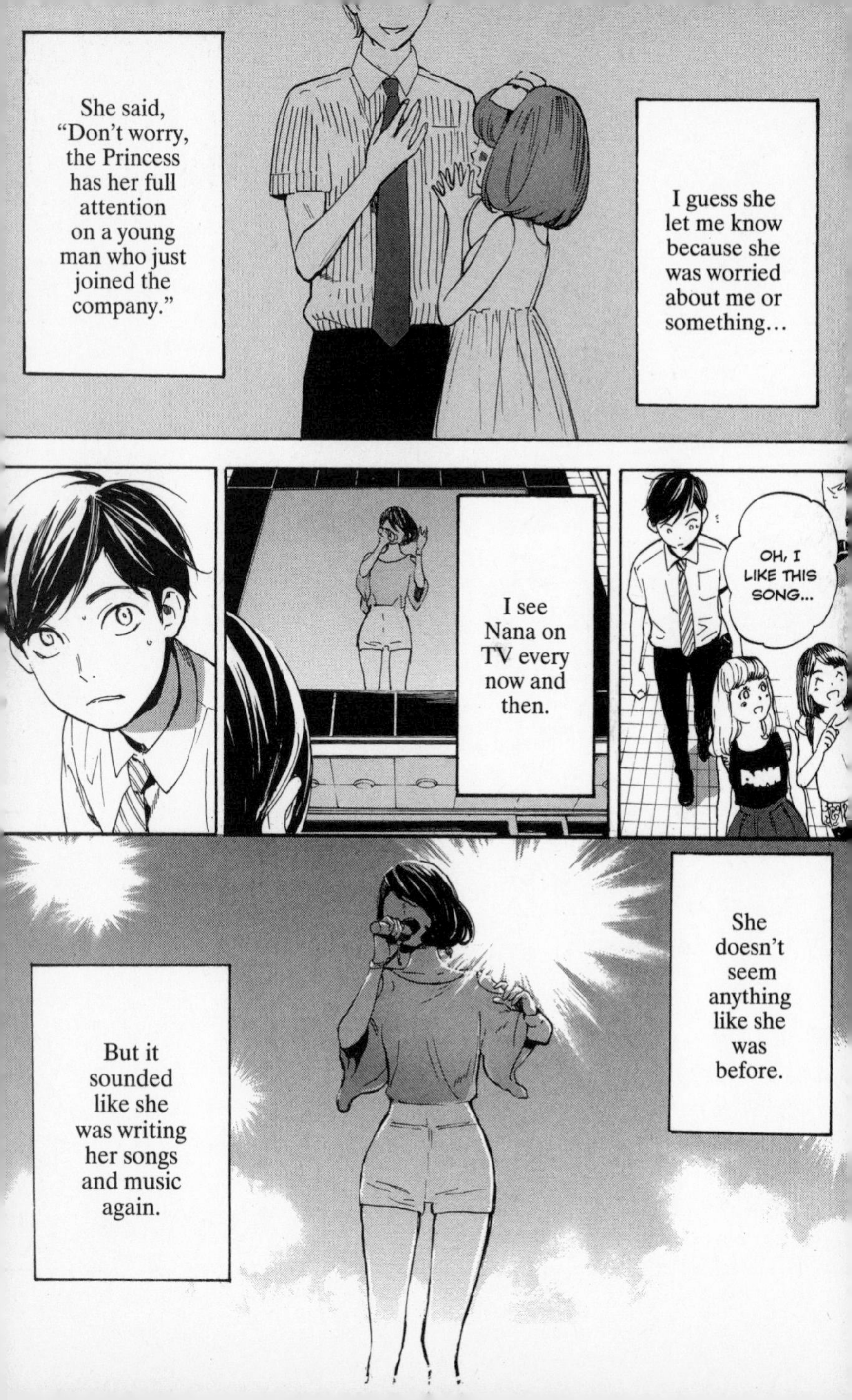
She said, "Don't worry, the Princess has her full attention on a young man who just joined the company."
I guess she let me know because she was worried about me or something…
OH, I LIKE THIS SONG...
I see Nana on TV every now and then.
She doesn't seem anything like she was before.
But it sounded like she was writing her songs and music again.

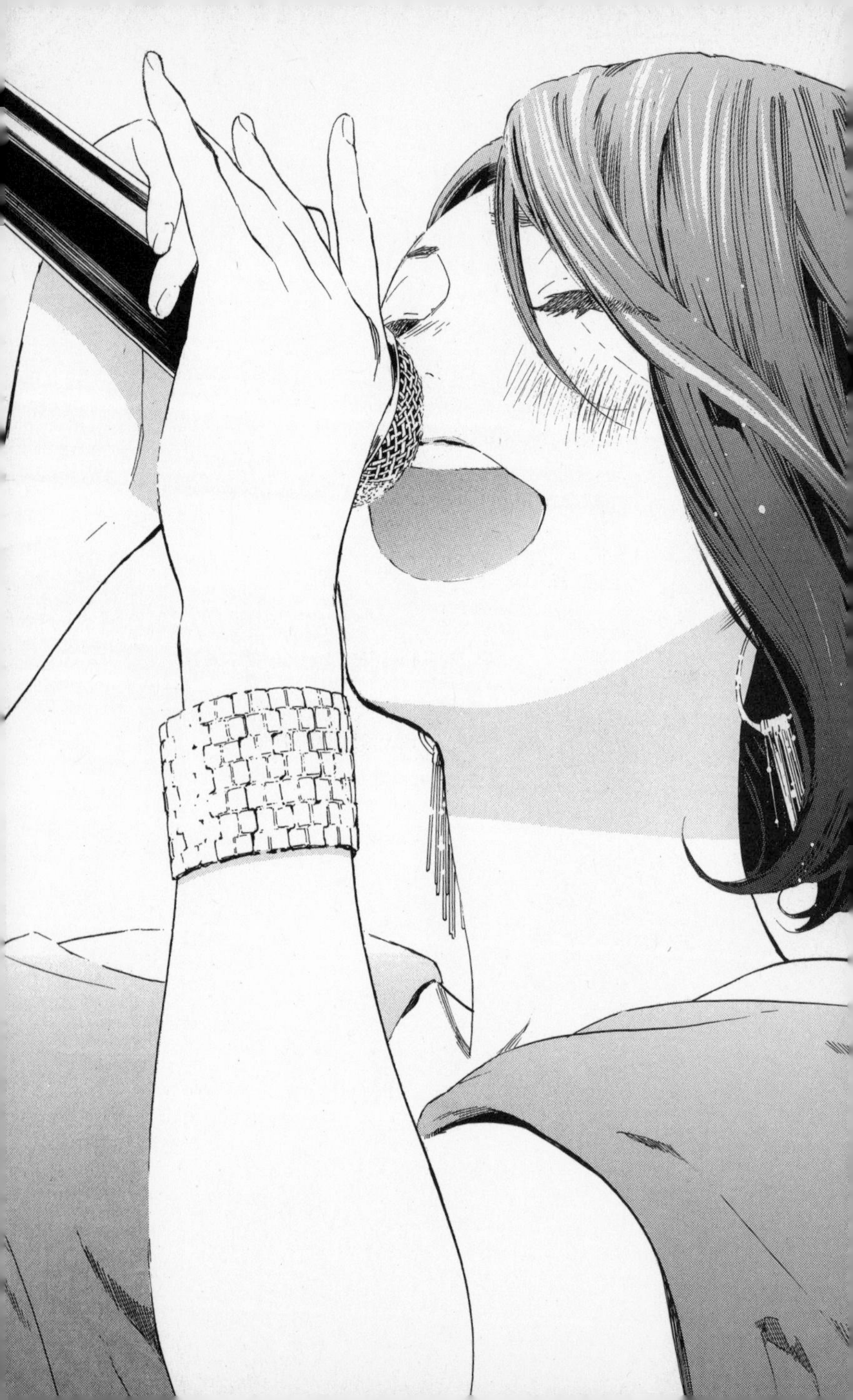

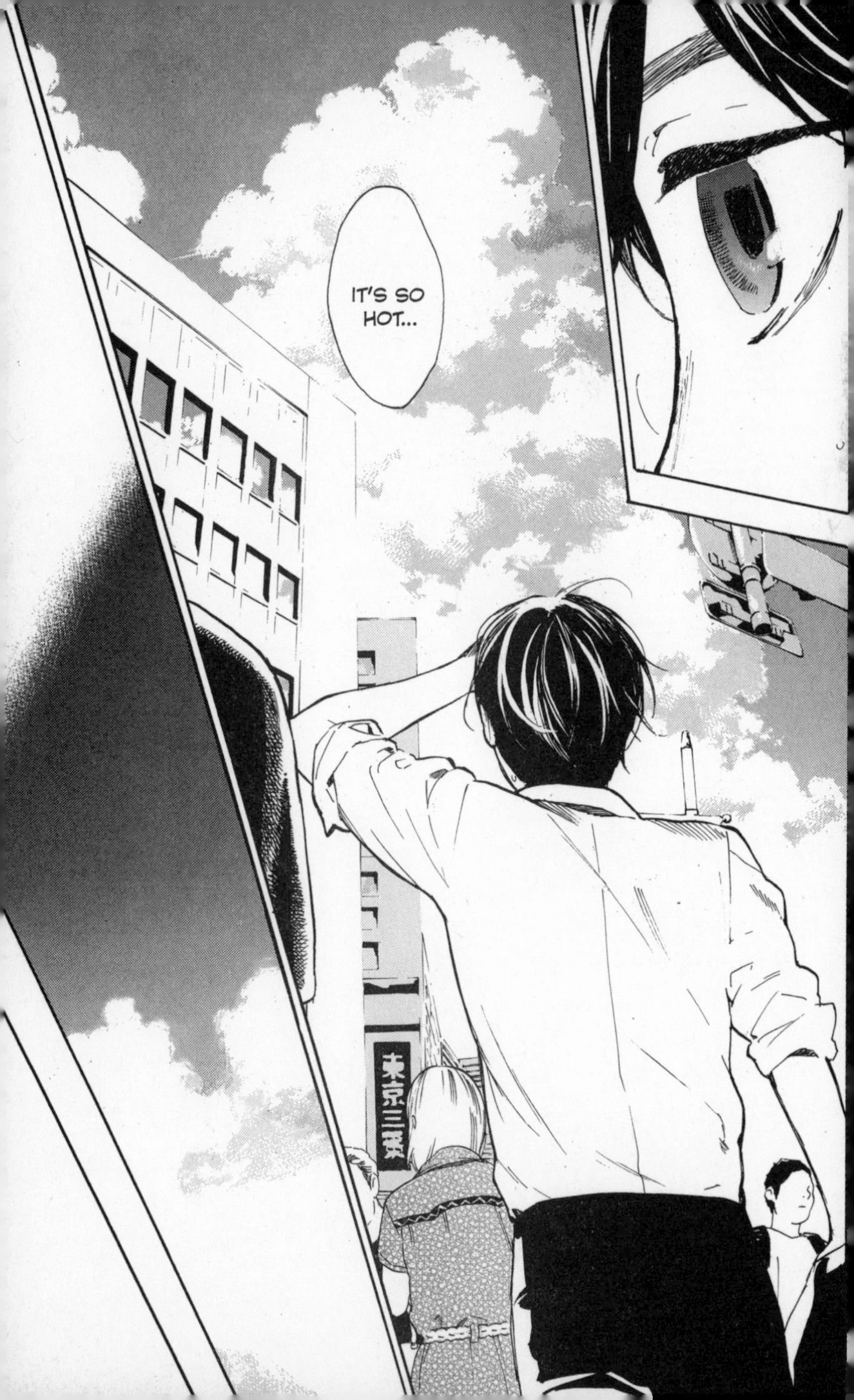
IT'S SO HOT...
東京三菱

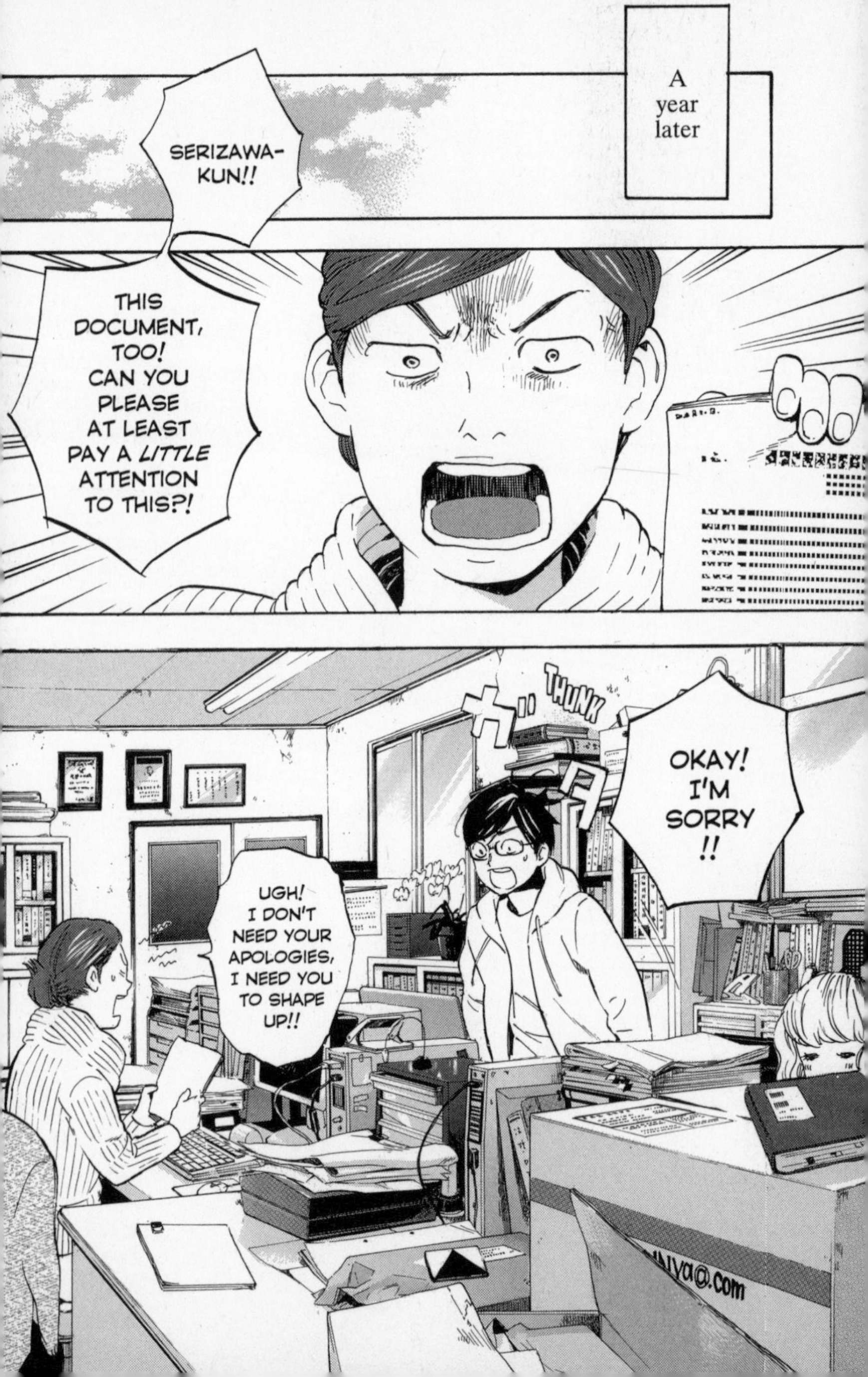
A year later
SERIZAWA-KUN!!
THIS DOCUMENT, TOO! CAN YOU PLEASE AT LEAST PAY A *LITTLE* ATTENTION TO THIS?!
THUNK
OKAY! I'M SORRY !!
UGH! I DON'T NEED YOUR APOLOGIES, I NEED YOU TO SHAPE UP!!

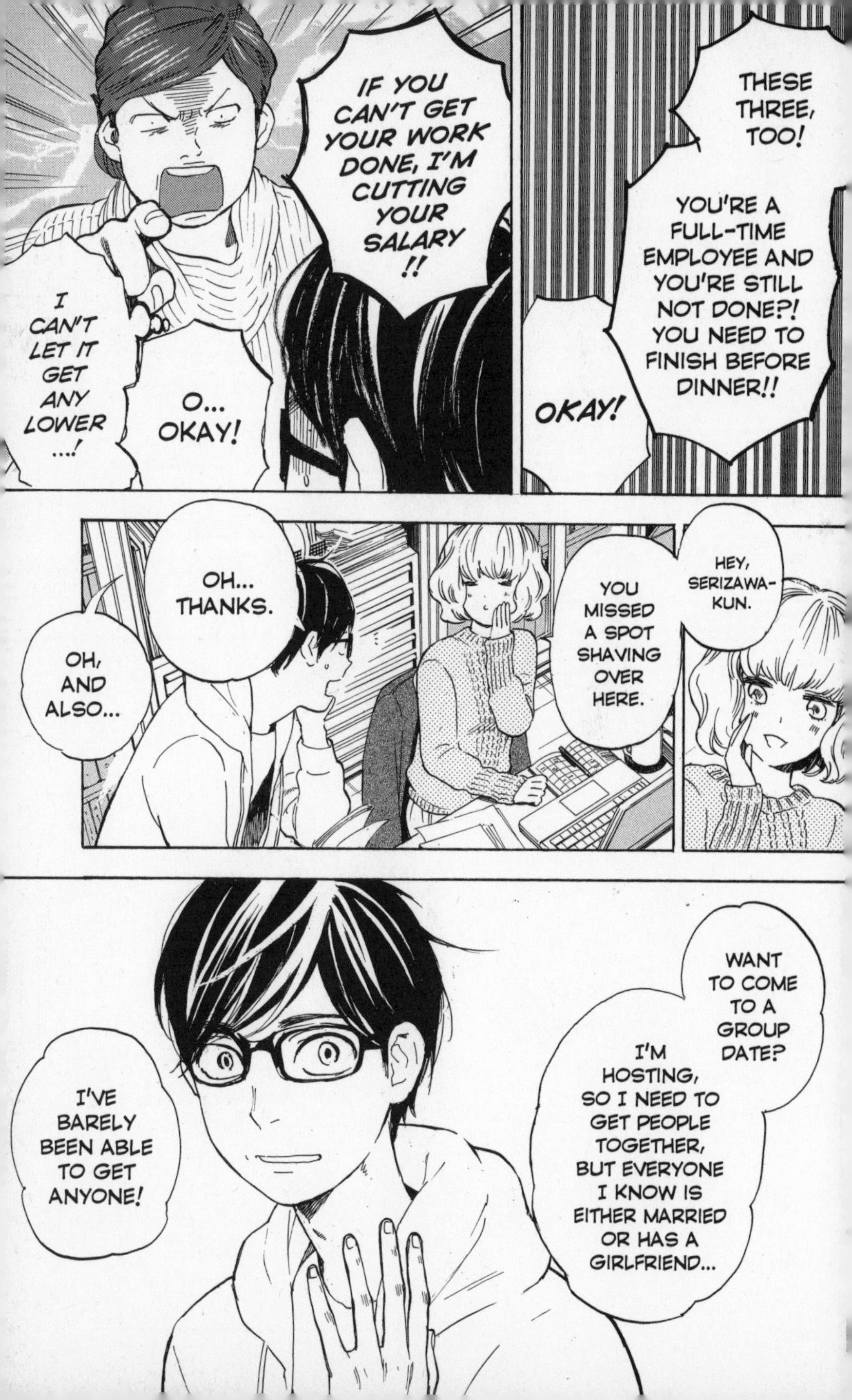
THESE THREE, TOO!
YOU'RE A FULL-TIME EMPLOYEE AND YOU'RE STILL NOT DONE?! YOU NEED TO FINISH BEFORE DINNER!!
OKAY!
IF YOU CAN'T GET YOUR WORK DONE, I'M CUTTING YOUR SALARY!!
O... OKAY!
I CAN'T LET IT GET ANY LOWER ...!
HEY, SERIZAWA-KUN.
YOU MISSED A SPOT SHAVING OVER HERE.
OH... THANKS.
OH, AND ALSO...
WANT TO COME TO A GROUP DATE?
I'M HOSTING, SO I NEED TO GET PEOPLE TOGETHER, BUT EVERYONE I KNOW IS EITHER MARRIED OR HAS A GIRLFRIEND...
I'VE BARELY BEEN ABLE TO GET ANYONE!

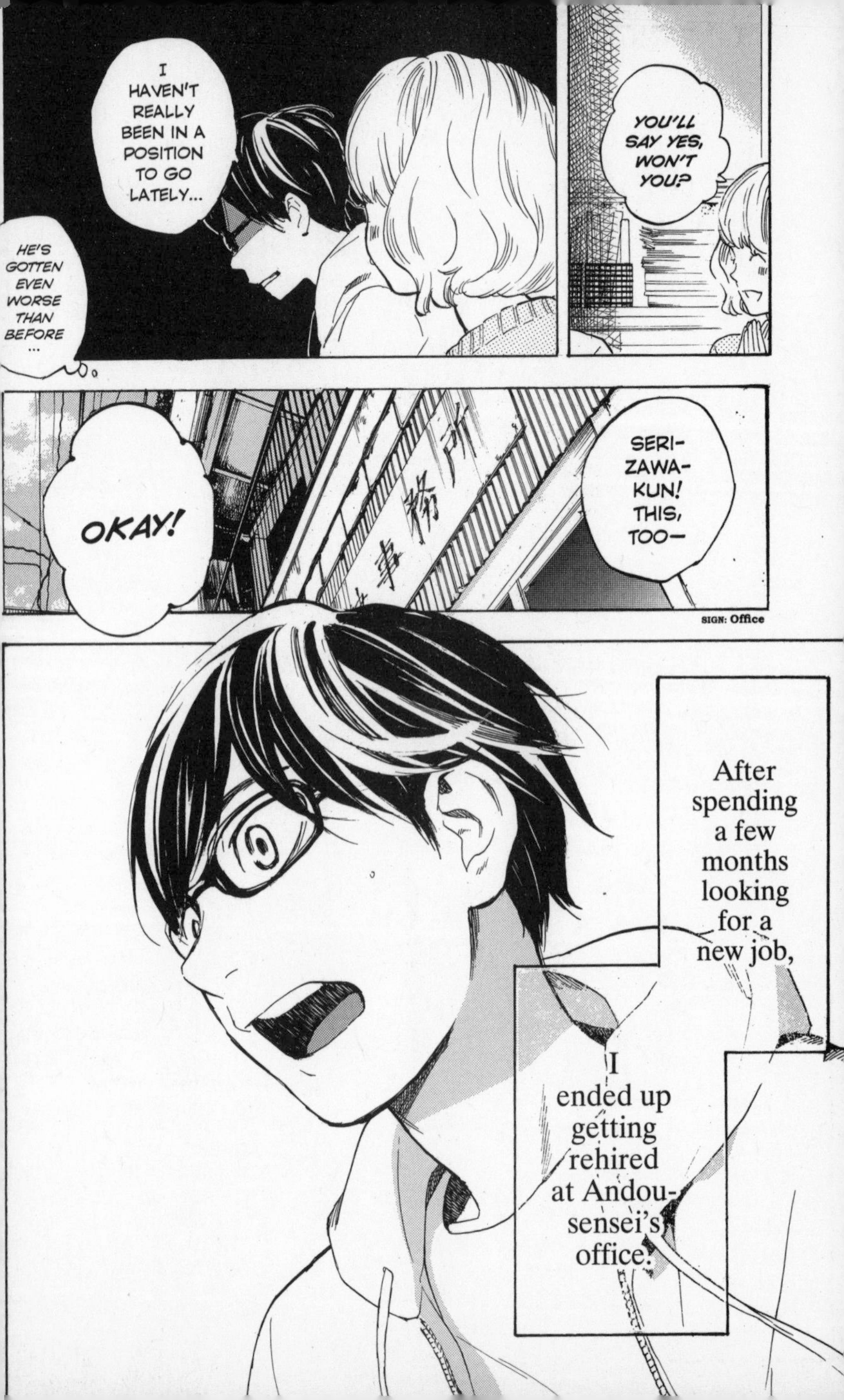
YOU'LL SAY YES, WON'T YOU?
I HAVEN'T REALLY BEEN IN A POSITION TO GO LATELY...
HE'S GOTTEN EVEN WORSE THAN BEFORE...
SERI-ZAWA-KUN! THIS, TOO—
OKAY!
SIGN: Office
After spending a few months looking for a new job,
I ended up getting rehired at Andou-sensei's office.

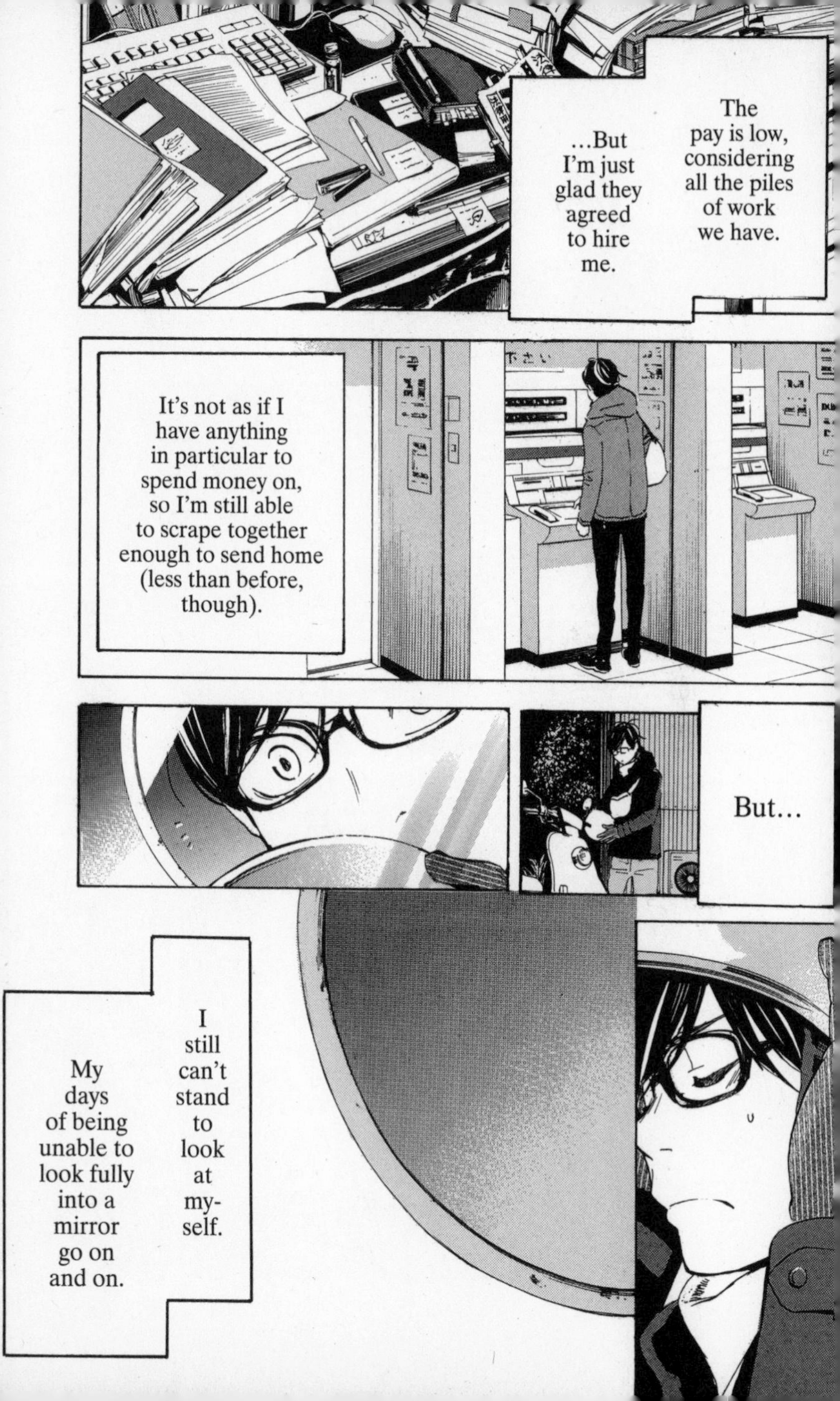
The pay is low, considering all the piles of work we have.
...But I'm just glad they agreed to hire me.
It's not as if I have anything in particular to spend money on, so I'm still able to scrape together enough to send home (less than before, though).
But...
I still can't stand to look at my-self.
My days of being unable to look fully into a mirror go on and on.

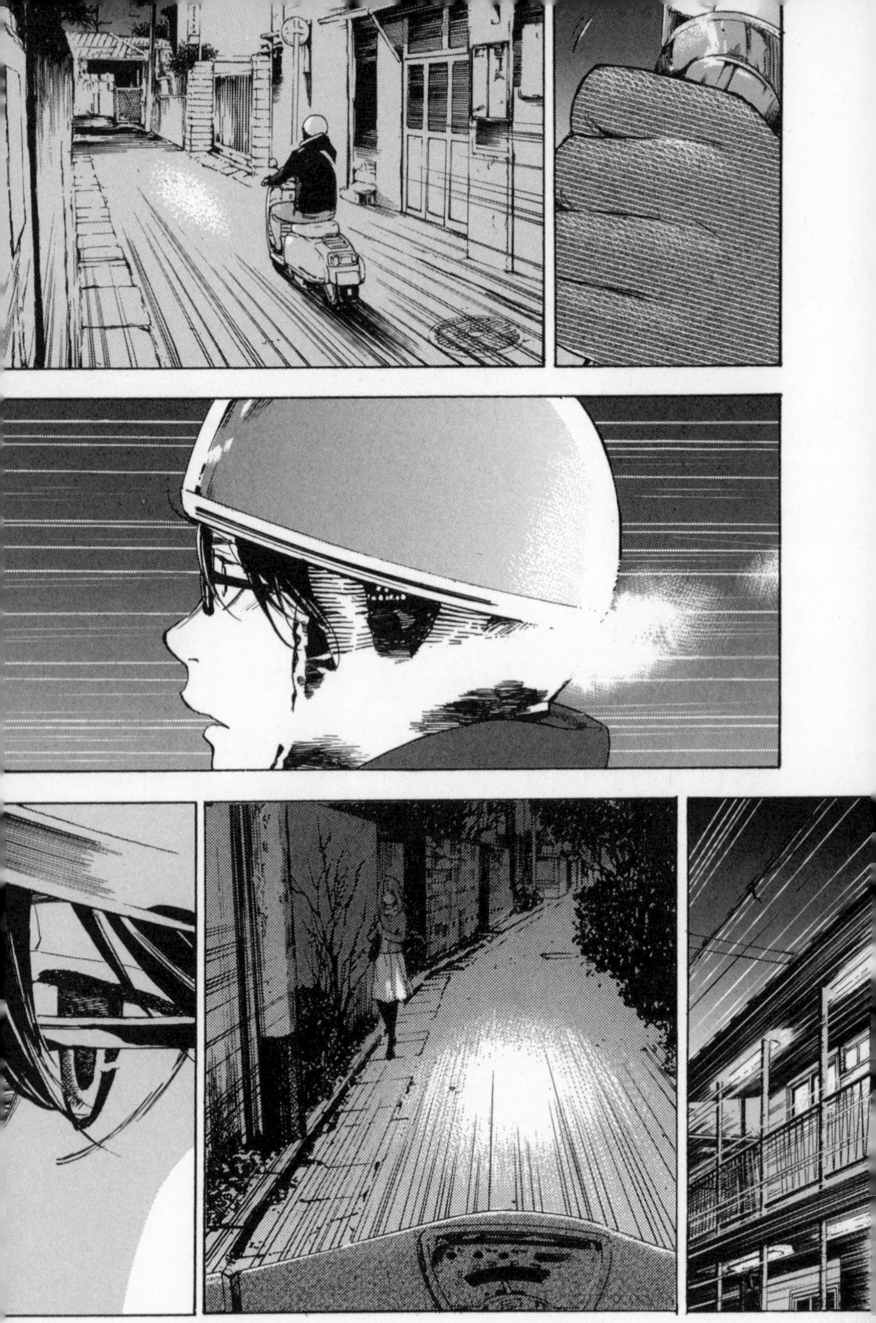

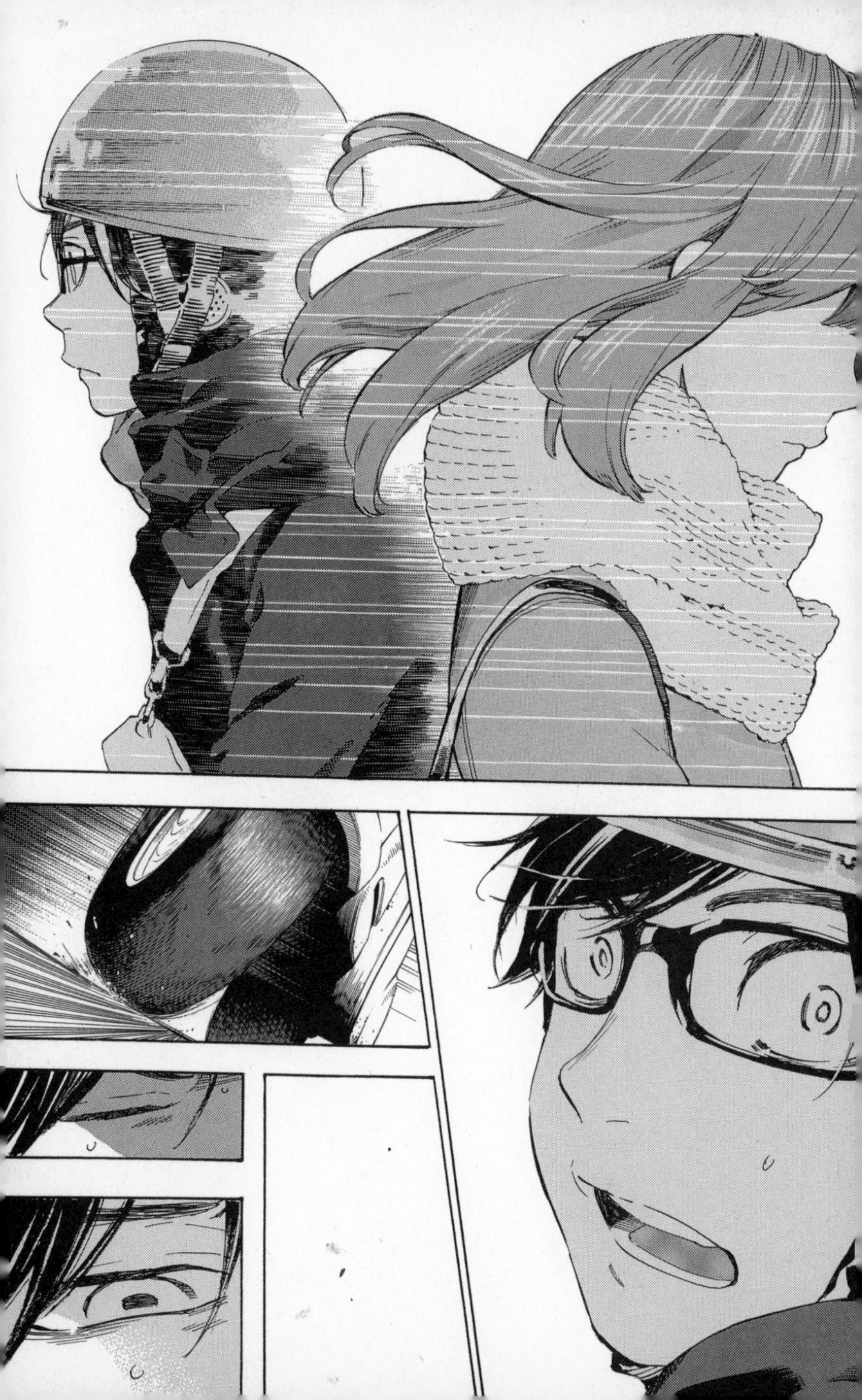

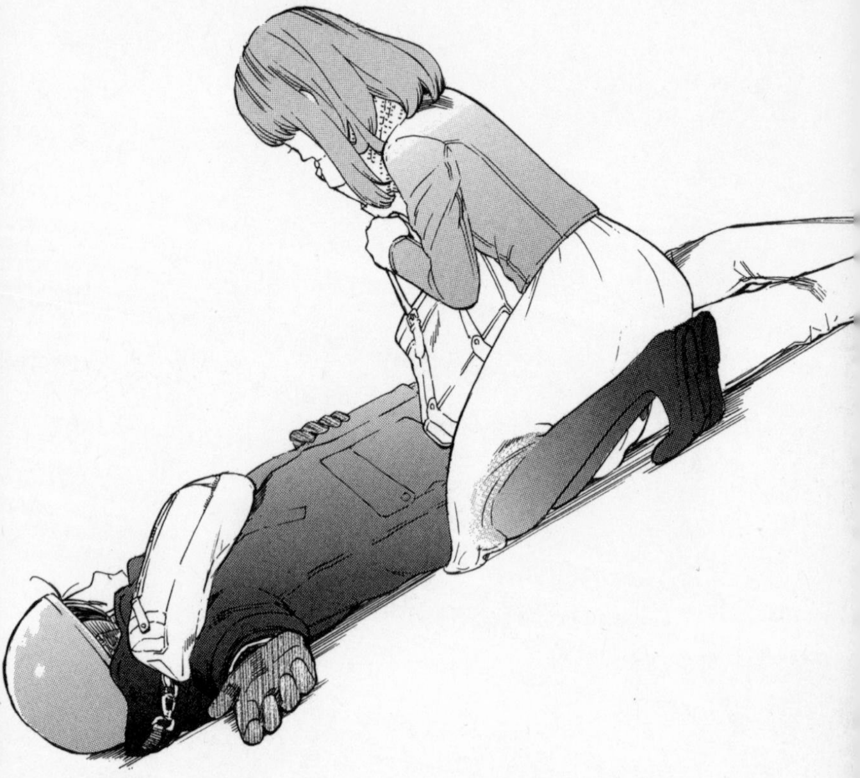

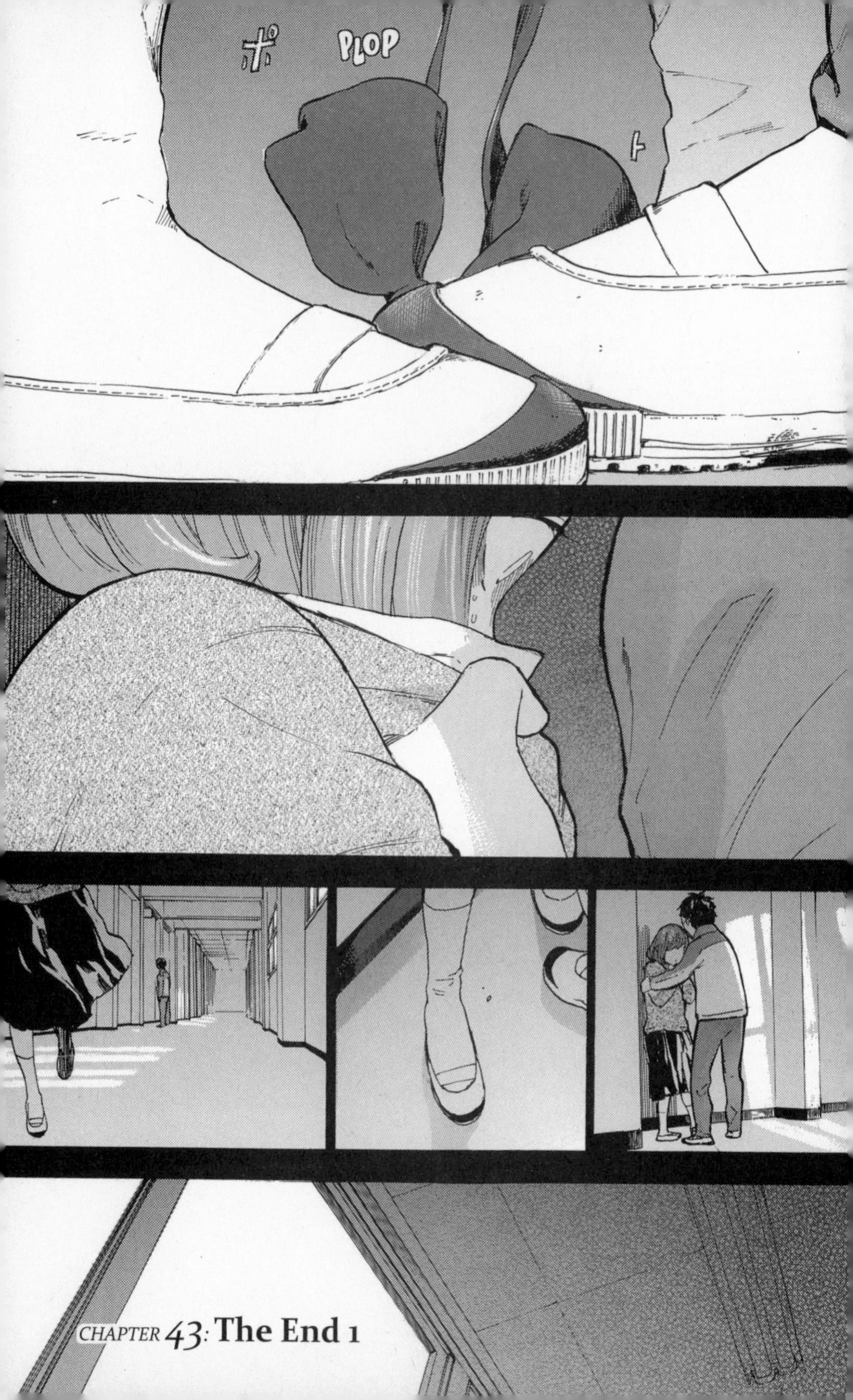
ポ
PLOP
ト
CHAPTER 43: The End 1

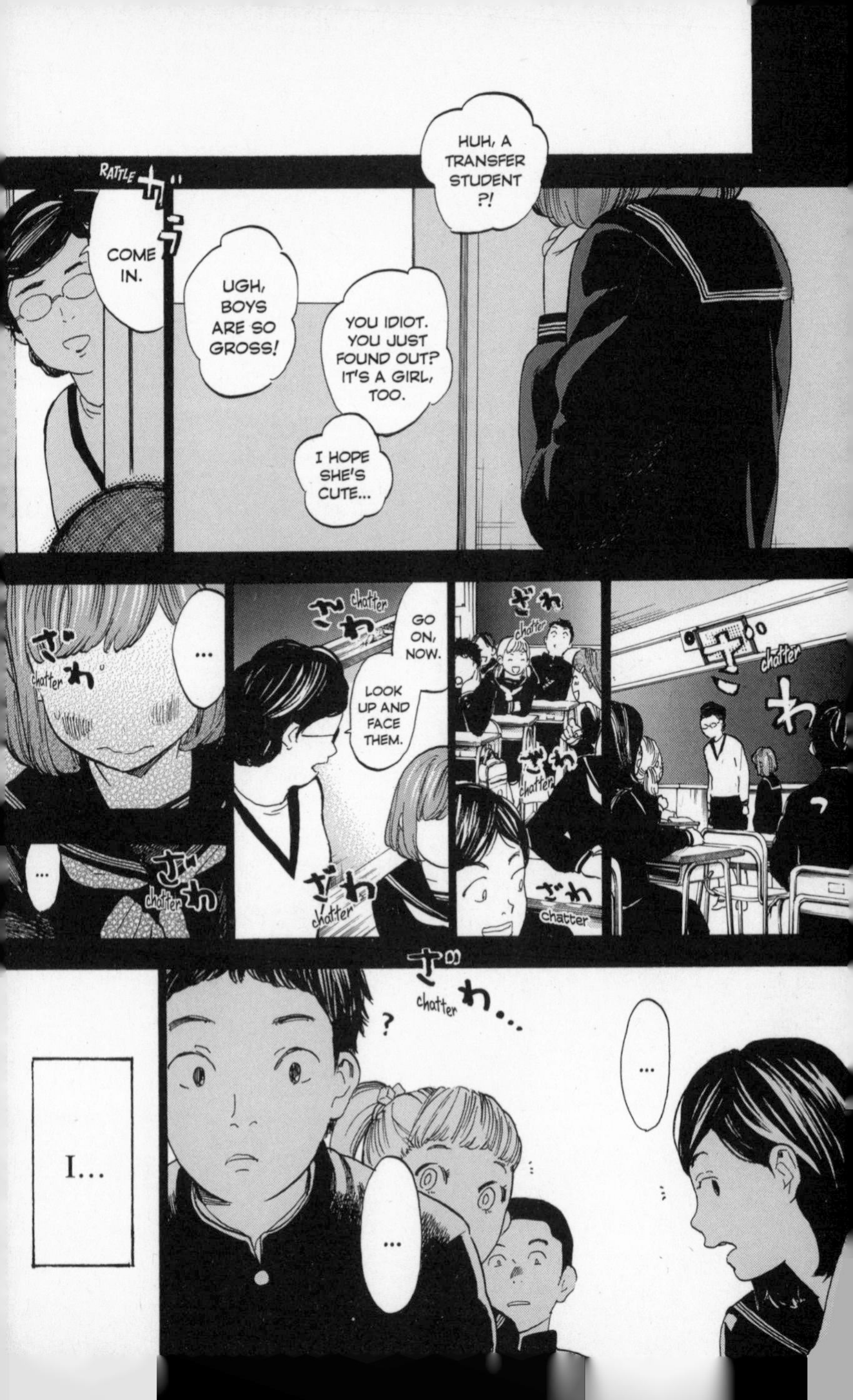
HUH, A TRANSFER STUDENT ?!
UGH, BOYS ARE SO GROSS!
YOU IDIOT. YOU JUST FOUND OUT? IT'S A GIRL, TOO.
I HOPE SHE'S CUTE...
RATTLE
COME IN.
chatter
chatter
chatter
chatter
GO ON, NOW.
LOOK UP AND FACE THEM.
chatter
...
chatter
...
chatter
chatter...
?
...
...
I...

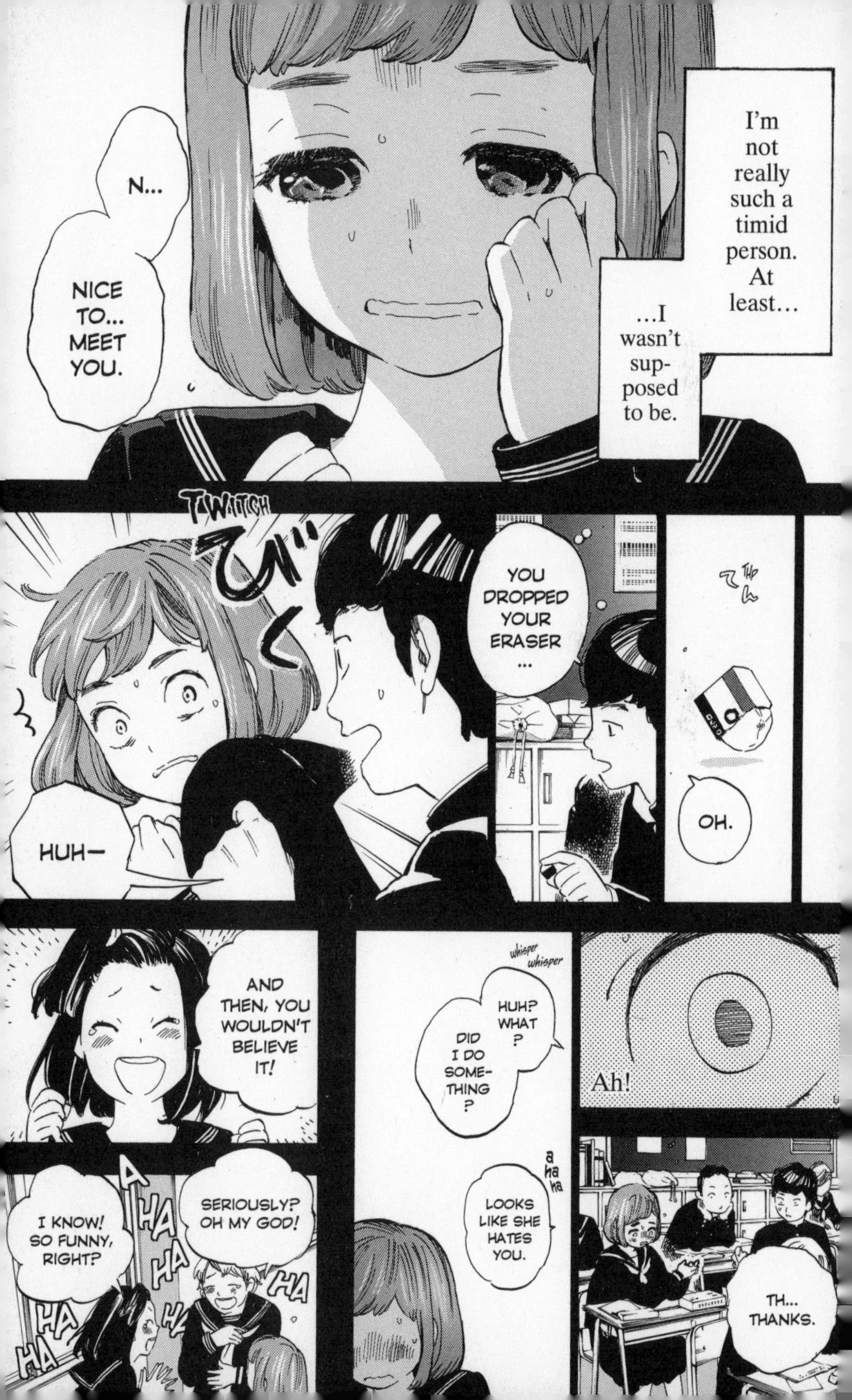
I'm not really such a timid person. At least…
…I wasn't sup-posed to be.
N…
NICE TO… MEET YOU.
THP
OH.
YOU DROPPED YOUR ERASER …
TWITCH
HUH—
Ah!
TH… THANKS.
whisper whisper
HUH? WHAT?
DID I DO SOME-THING?
a ha ha
LOOKS LIKE SHE HATES YOU.
AND THEN, YOU WOULDN'T BELIEVE IT!
SERIOUSLY? OH MY GOD!
A HA HA HA
I KNOW! SO FUNNY, RIGHT?
HA HA HA

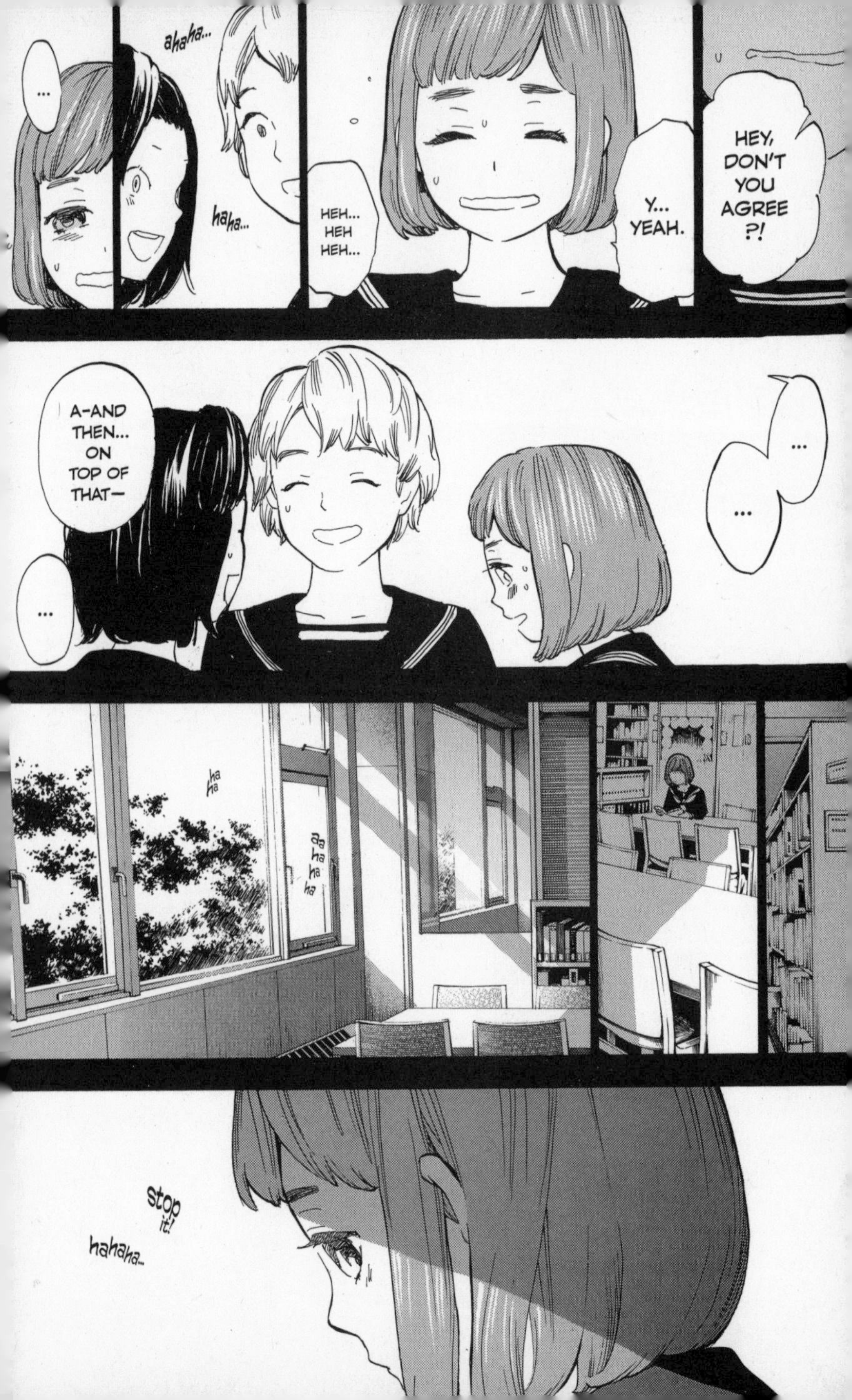
HEY, DON'T YOU AGREE ?!
Y... YEAH.
HEH... HEH HEH...
ahaha...
haha...
...
...
...
A-AND THEN... ON TOP OF THAT—
...
ha ha
aa ha ha ha
stop it!
hahaha...

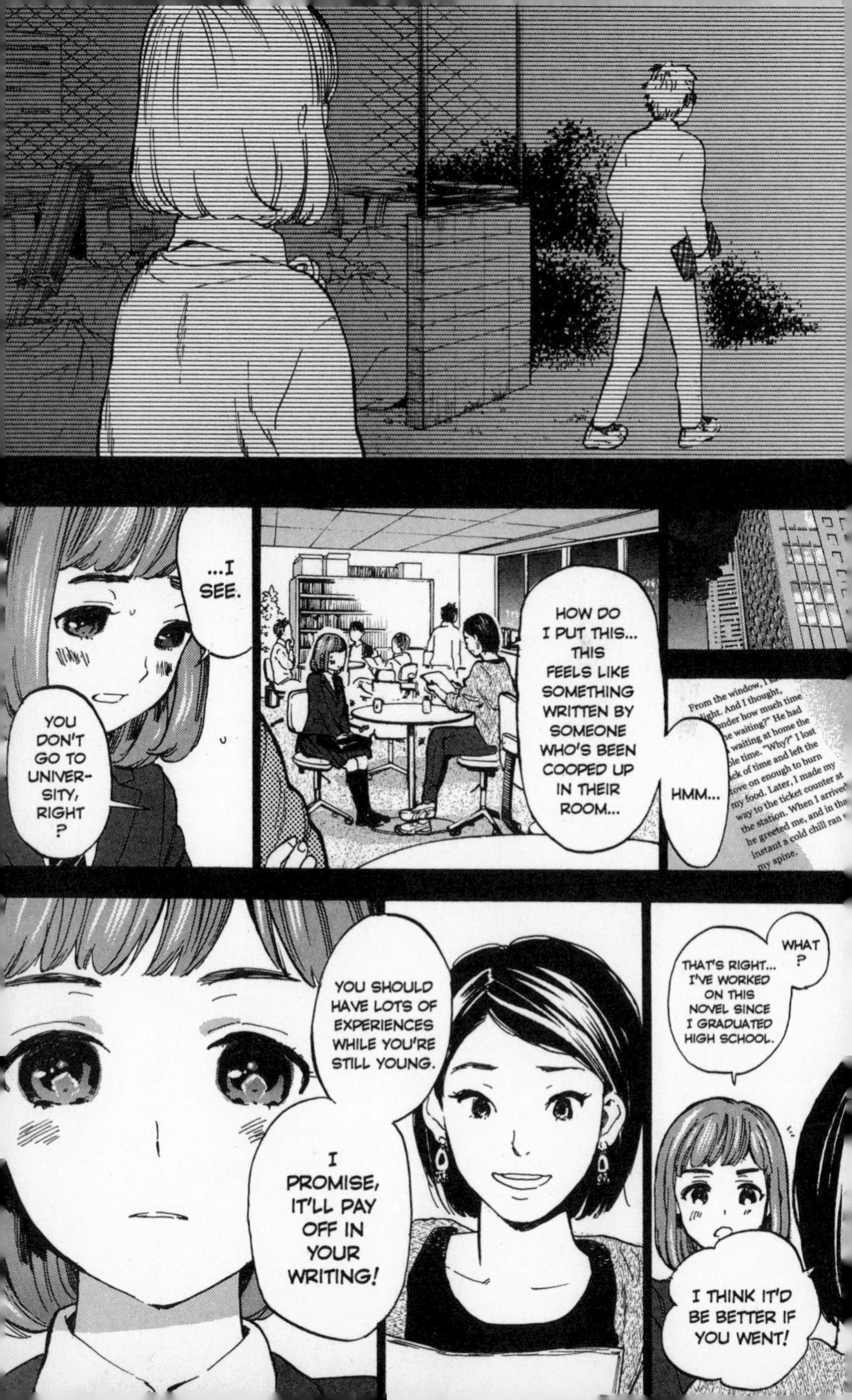
From the window, I sa
light. And I thought,
onder how much time
he waiting?" He had
waiting at home the
ble time. "Why?" I lost
ack of time and left the
tove on enough to burn
my food. Later, I made my
way to the ticket counter at
the station. When I arrived
he greeted me, and in the
instant a cold chill ran
my spine.
HMM...
HOW DO I PUT THIS... THIS FEELS LIKE SOMETHING WRITTEN BY SOMEONE WHO'S BEEN COOPED UP IN THEIR ROOM...
...I SEE.
YOU DON'T GO TO UNIVER-SITY, RIGHT?
WHAT?
THAT'S RIGHT... I'VE WORKED ON THIS NOVEL SINCE I GRADUATED HIGH SCHOOL.
I THINK IT'D BE BETTER IF YOU WENT!
YOU SHOULD HAVE LOTS OF EXPERIENCES WHILE YOU'RE STILL YOUNG.
I PROMISE, IT'LL PAY OFF IN YOUR WRITING!

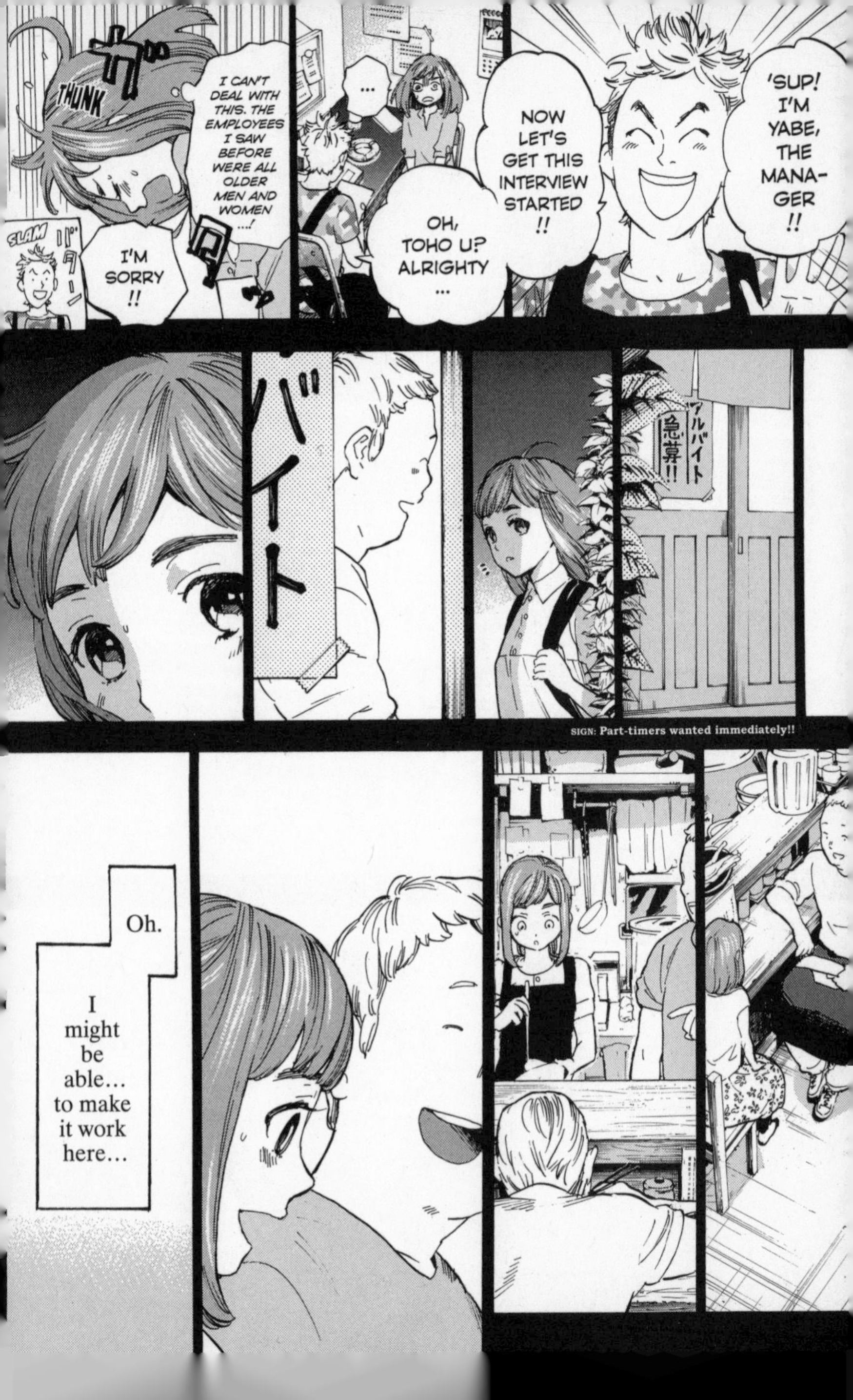
'SUP! I'M YABE, THE MANA-GER!!
NOW LET'S GET THIS INTERVIEW STARTED!!
...
OH, TOHO U? ALRIGHTY...
I CAN'T DEAL WITH THIS. THE EMPLOYEES I SAW BEFORE WERE ALL OLDER MEN AND WOMEN...!
THUNK
I'M SORRY!!
SLAM
アルバイト急募!!
バイト
SIGN: Part-timers wanted immediately!!
Oh.
I might be able... to make it work here...

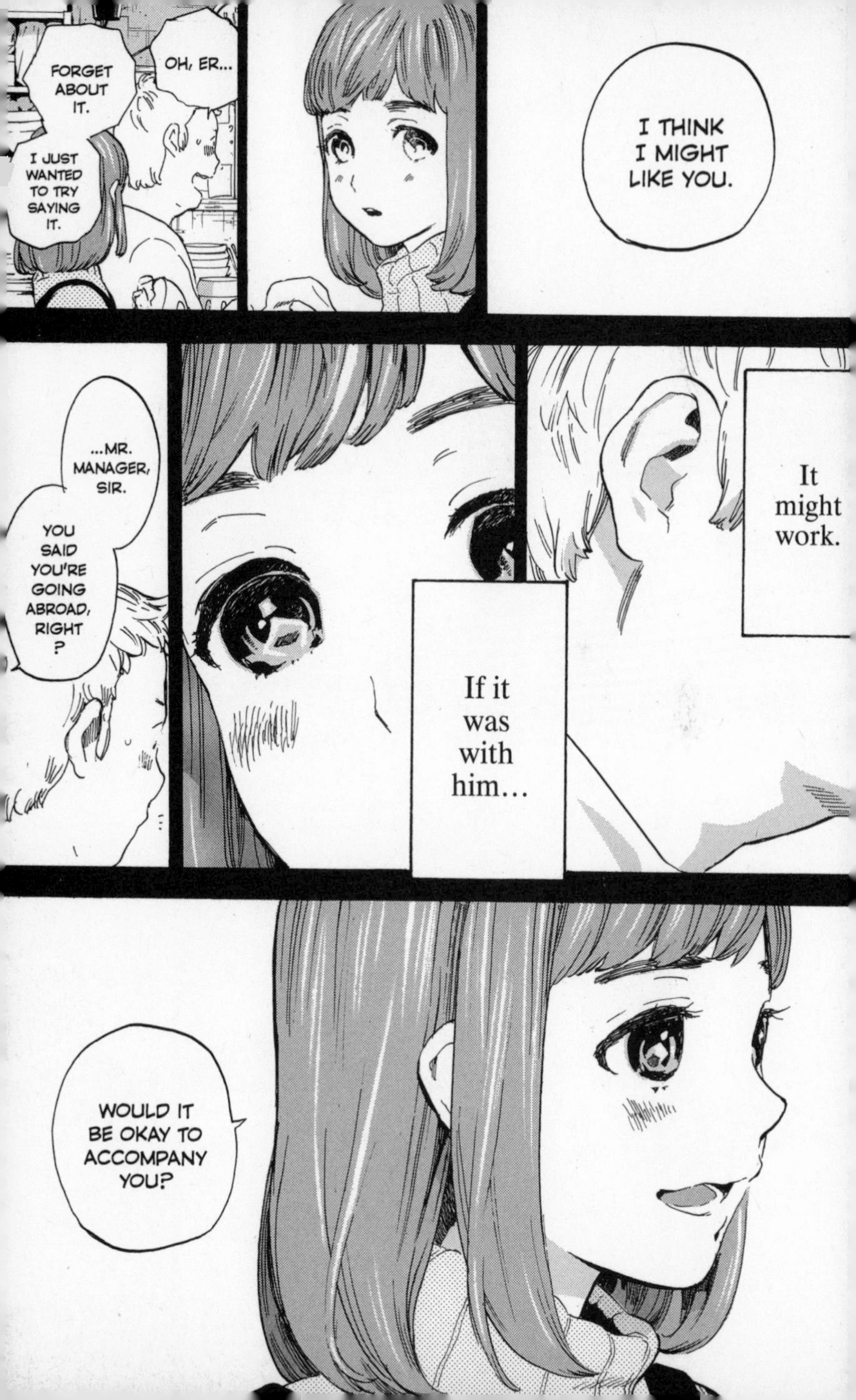
I THINK I MIGHT LIKE YOU.
OH, ER...
FORGET ABOUT IT.
I JUST WANTED TO TRY SAYING IT.
It might work.
If it was with him…
...MR. MANAGER, SIR.
YOU SAID YOU'RE GOING ABROAD, RIGHT?
WOULD IT BE OKAY TO ACCOMPANY YOU?

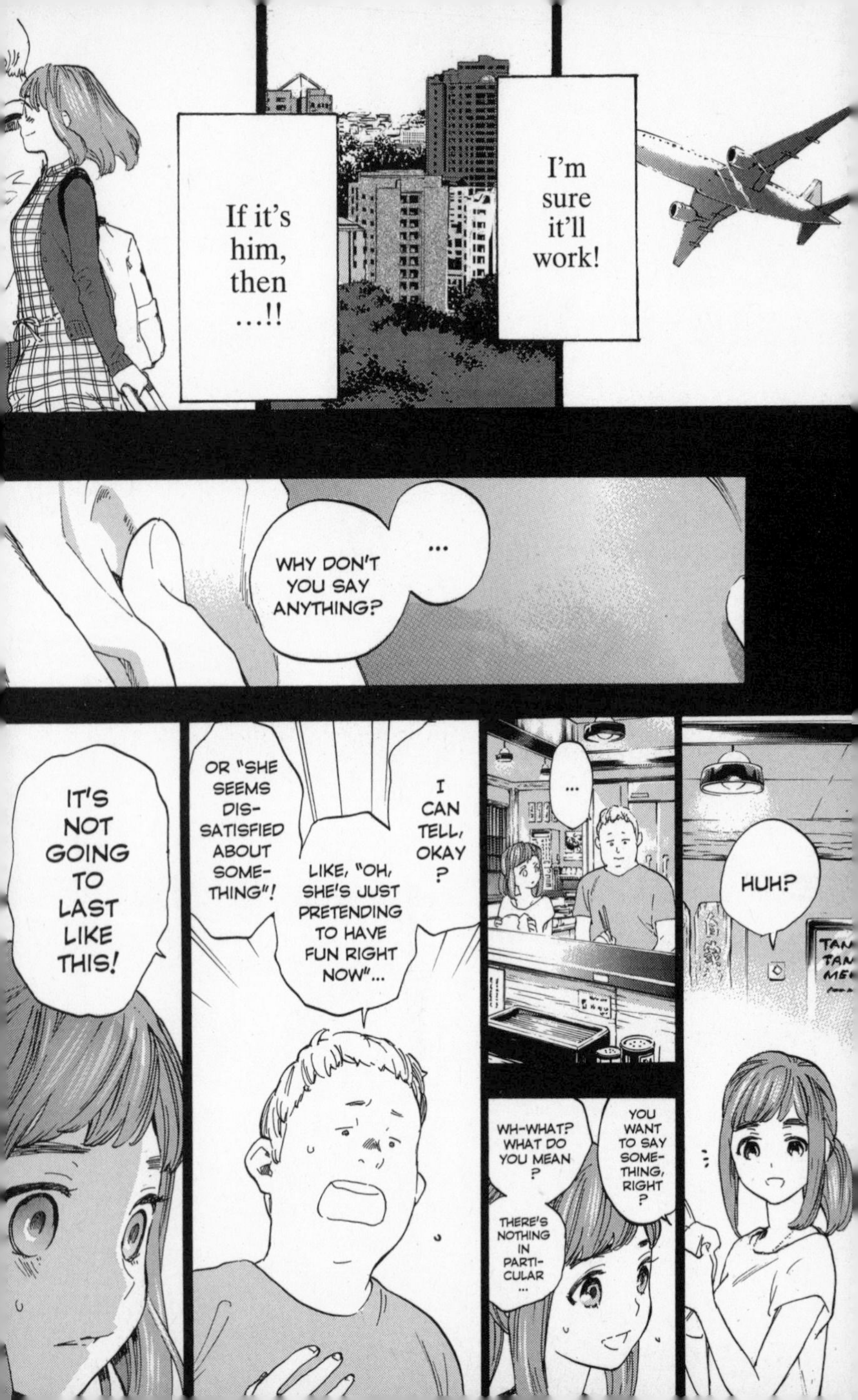
I'm sure it'll work!
If it's him, then ...!!
...
WHY DON'T YOU SAY ANYTHING?
HUH?
...
YOU WANT TO SAY SOMETHING, RIGHT?
WH-WHAT? WHAT DO YOU MEAN?
THERE'S NOTHING IN PARTICULAR...
I CAN TELL, OKAY?
LIKE, "OH, SHE'S JUST PRETENDING TO HAVE FUN RIGHT NOW"...
OR "SHE SEEMS DIS-SATISFIED ABOUT SOME-THING"!
IT'S NOT GOING TO LAST LIKE THIS!

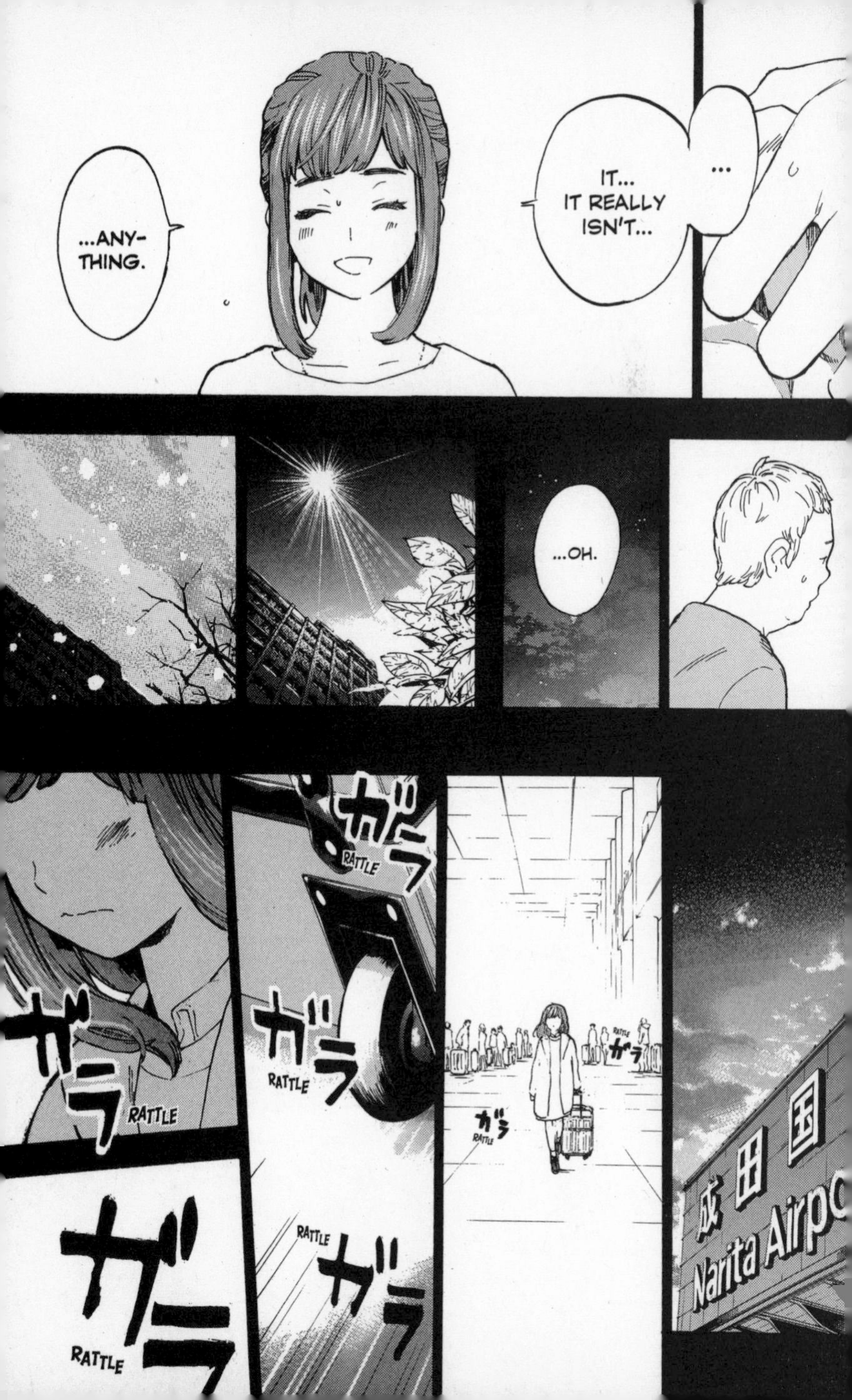
...
IT... IT REALLY ISN'T...
...ANY-THING.
...OH.
成田国
Narita Airpo
RATTLE ガラ
ガラ RATTLE
ガラ RATTLE
ガラ RATTLE
ガラ RATTLE
RATTLE ガラ
ガラ RATTLE
ガラ RATTLE

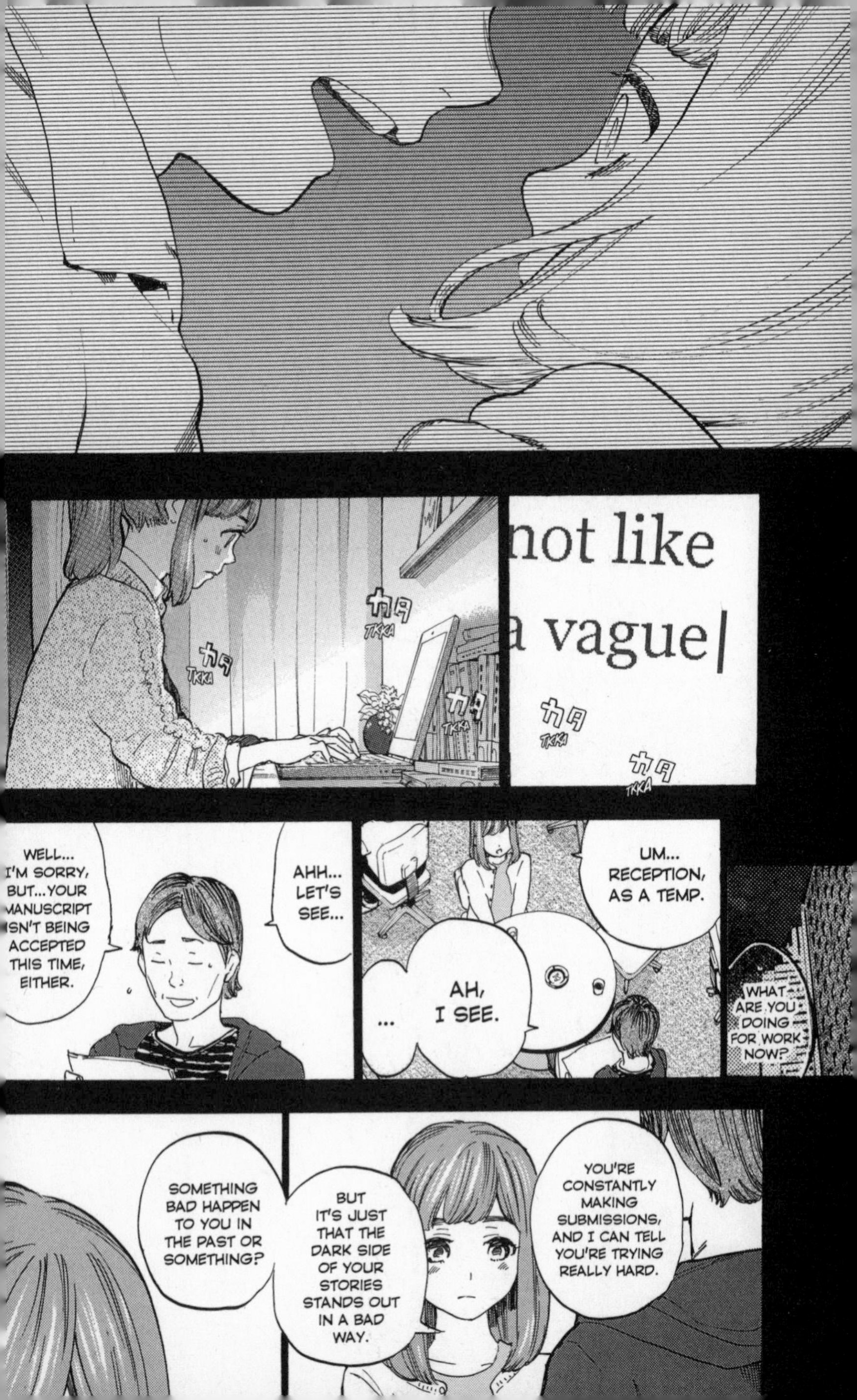
not like
a vague|
カタ TKKA
カタ TKKA
カタ TKKA
カタ TKKA
カタ TKKA
カタ TKKA
WHAT ARE YOU DOING FOR WORK NOW?
UM... RECEPTION, AS A TEMP.
AH, I SEE.
...
AHH... LET'S SEE...
WELL... I'M SORRY, BUT...YOUR MANUSCRIPT ISN'T BEING ACCEPTED THIS TIME, EITHER.
YOU'RE CONSTANTLY MAKING SUBMISSIONS, AND I CAN TELL YOU'RE TRYING REALLY HARD.
BUT IT'S JUST THAT THE DARK SIDE OF YOUR STORIES STANDS OUT IN A BAD WAY.
SOMETHING BAD HAPPEN TO YOU IN THE PAST OR SOMETHING?

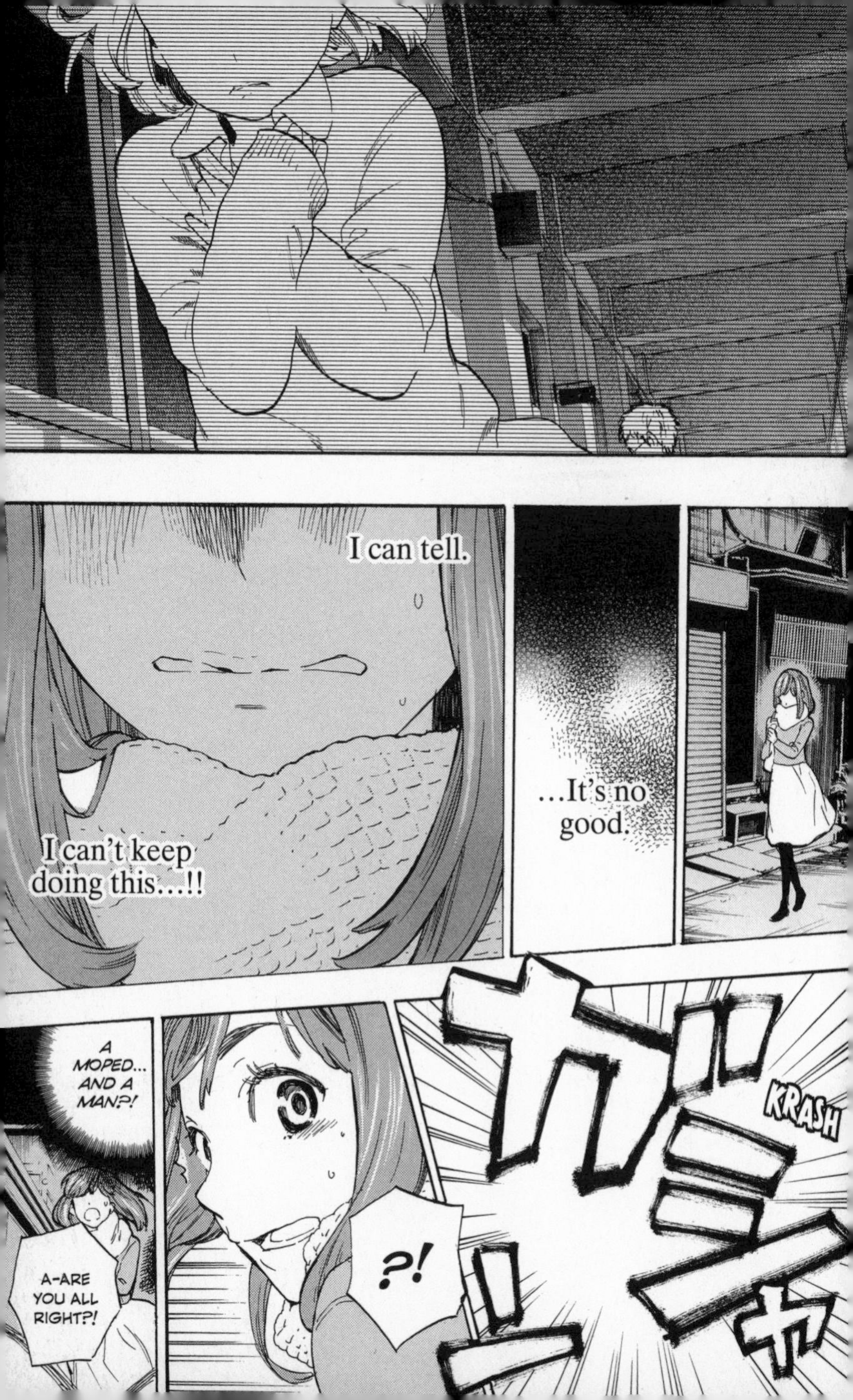
…It's no good.
I can tell.
I can't keep doing this…!!
KRASH
?!
A MOPED… AND A MAN?!
A-ARE YOU ALL RIGHT?!

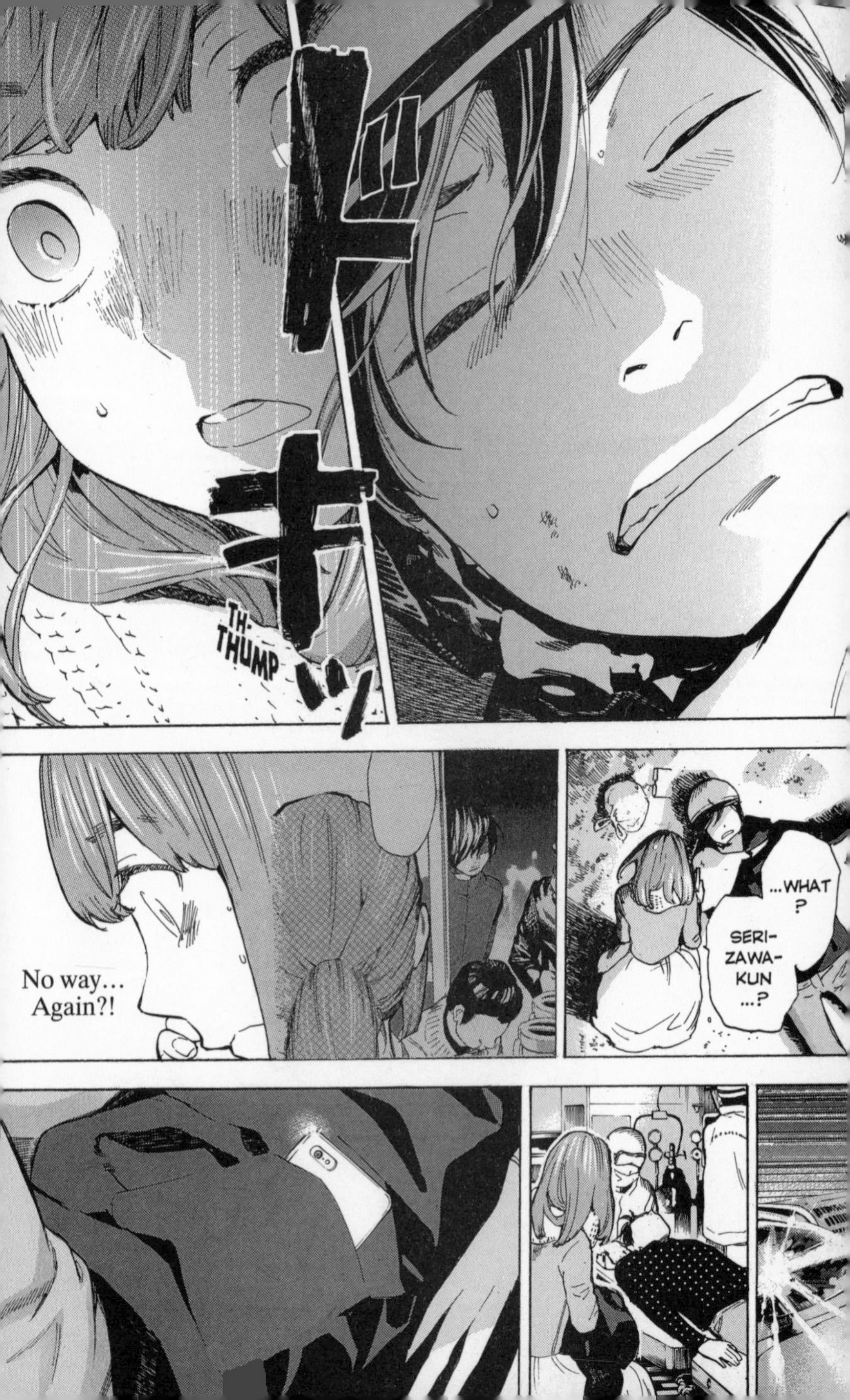
TH-THUMP
...WHAT?
SERI-ZAWA-KUN...?
No way… Again?!

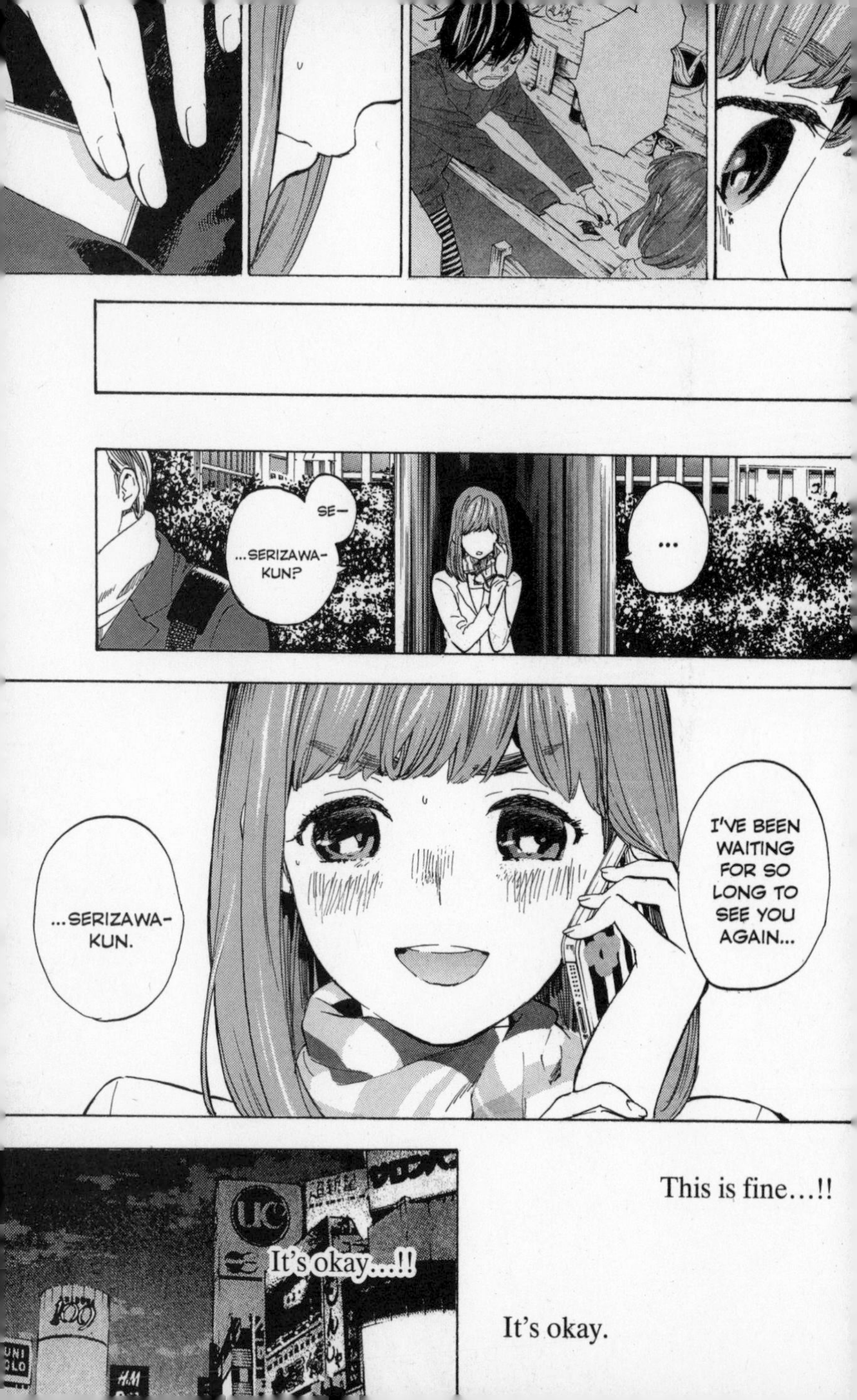
...
SE— ...SERIZAWA-KUN?
I'VE BEEN WAITING FOR SO LONG TO SEE YOU AGAIN...
...SERIZAWA-KUN.
This is fine…!!
It’s okay.
It’s okay…!!

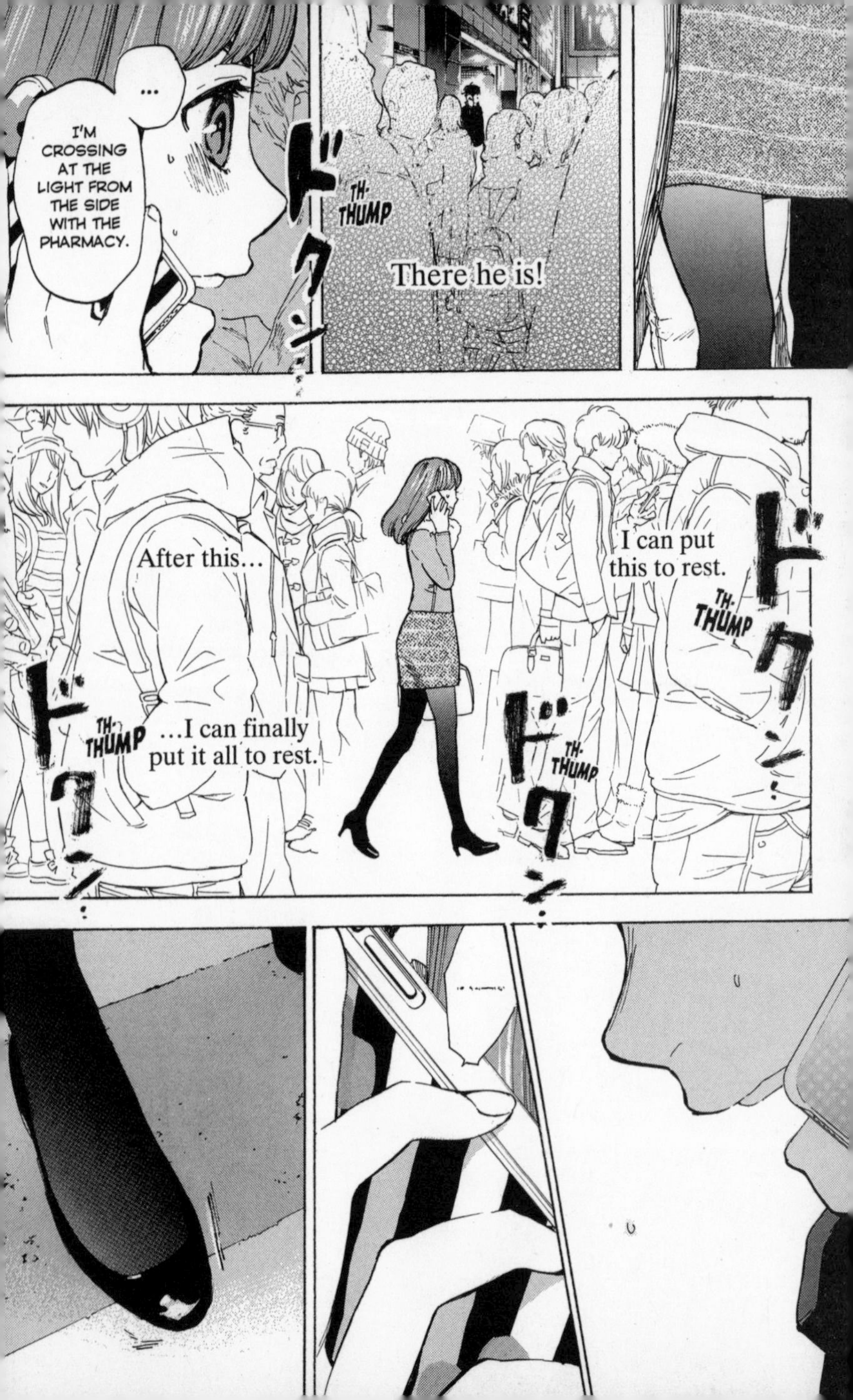
TH-THUMP
There he is!
...
I'M CROSSING AT THE LIGHT FROM THE SIDE WITH THE PHARMACY.
I can put this to rest.
TH-THUMP
After this…
TH-THUMP
…I can finally put it all to rest.
TH-THUMP

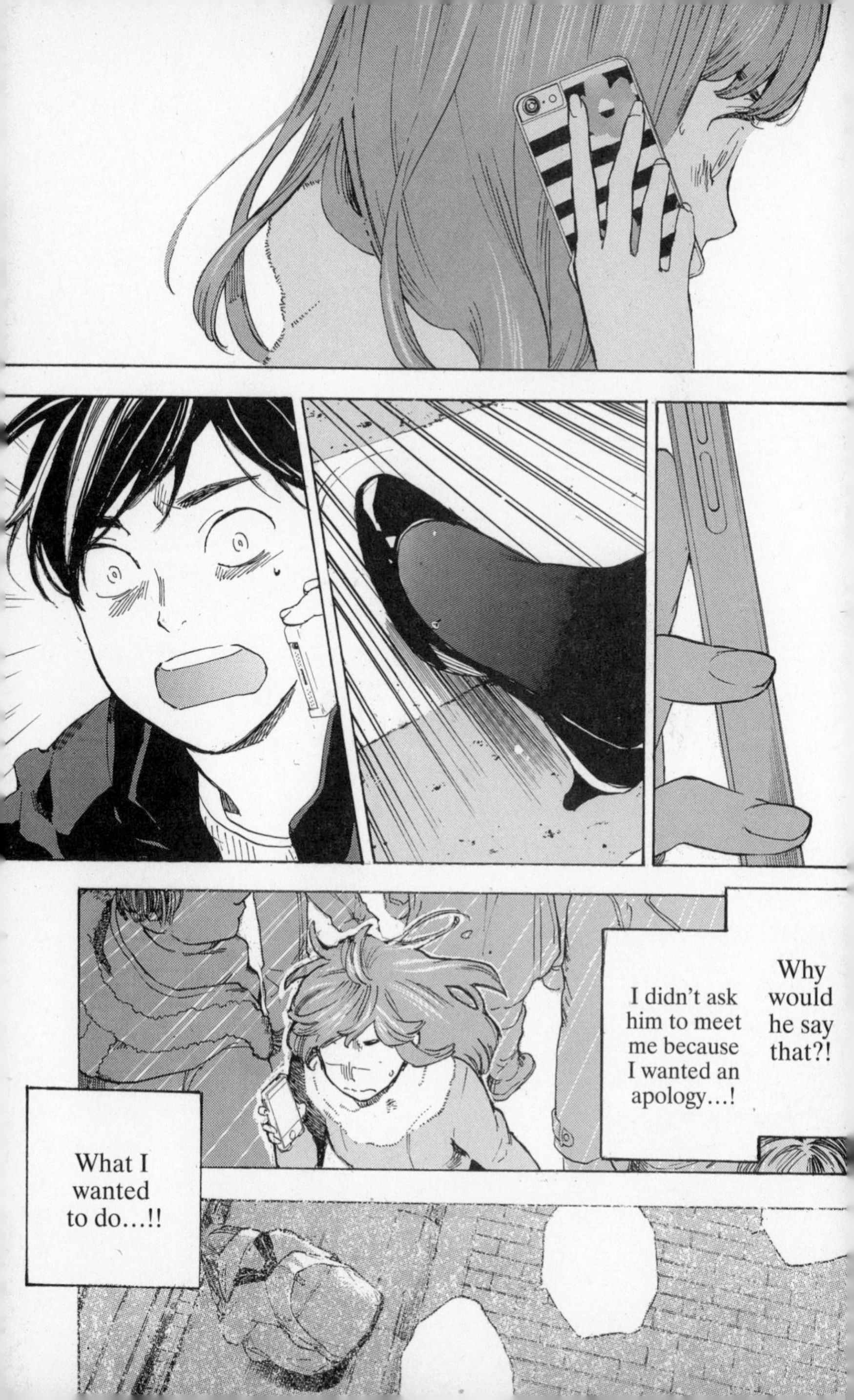
Why would he say that?!
I didn't ask him to meet me because I wanted an apology...!
What I wanted to do...!!

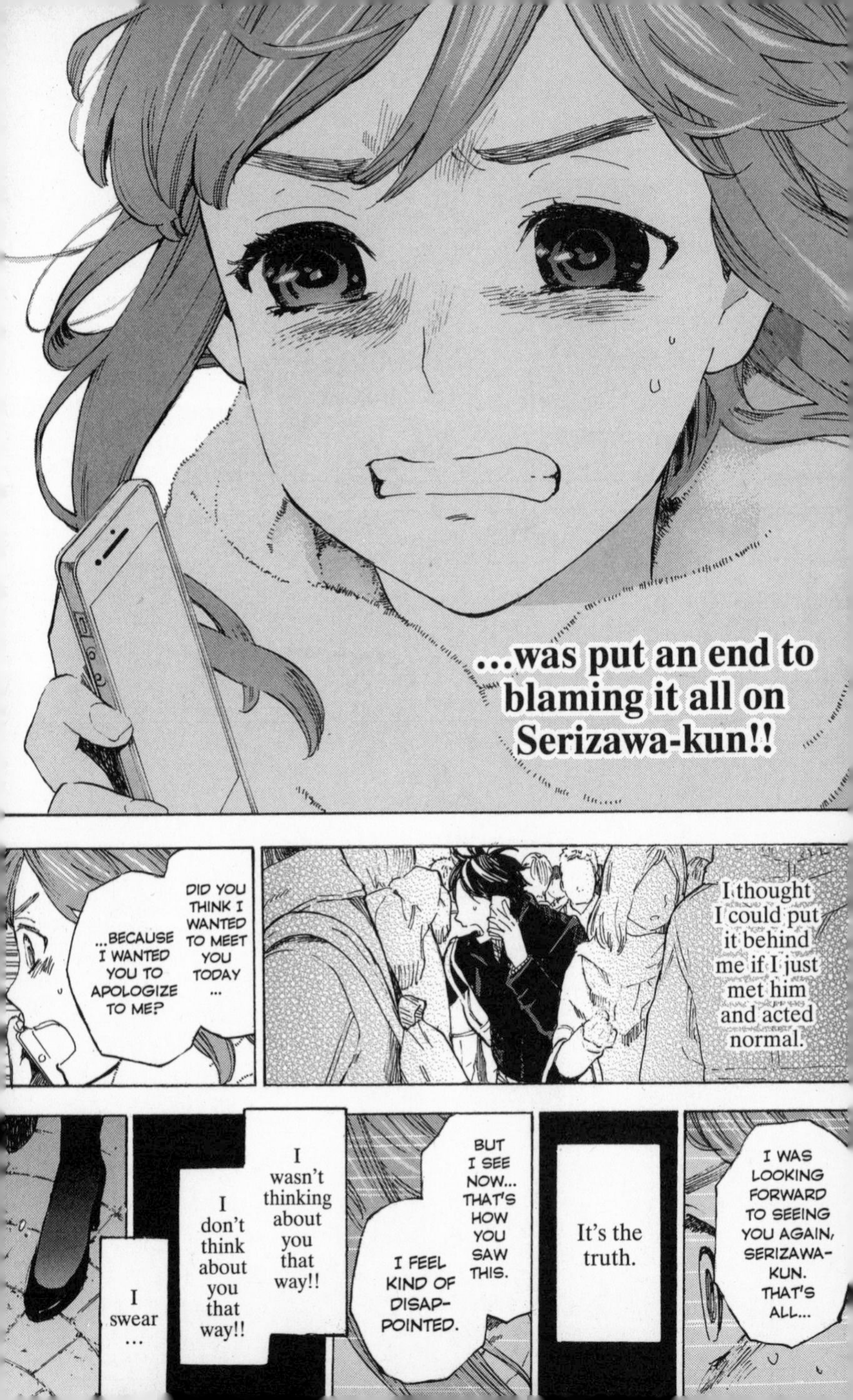
...was put an end to blaming it all on Serizawa-kun!!
I thought I could put it behind me if I just met him and acted normal.
DID YOU THINK I WANTED TO MEET YOU TODAY...
...BECAUSE I WANTED YOU TO APOLOGIZE TO ME?
I WAS LOOKING FORWARD TO SEEING YOU AGAIN, SERIZAWA-KUN. THAT'S ALL...
It's the truth.
BUT I SEE NOW... THAT'S HOW YOU SAW THIS.
I FEEL KIND OF DISAPPOINTED.
I wasn't thinking about you that way!!
I don't think about you that way!!
I swear...

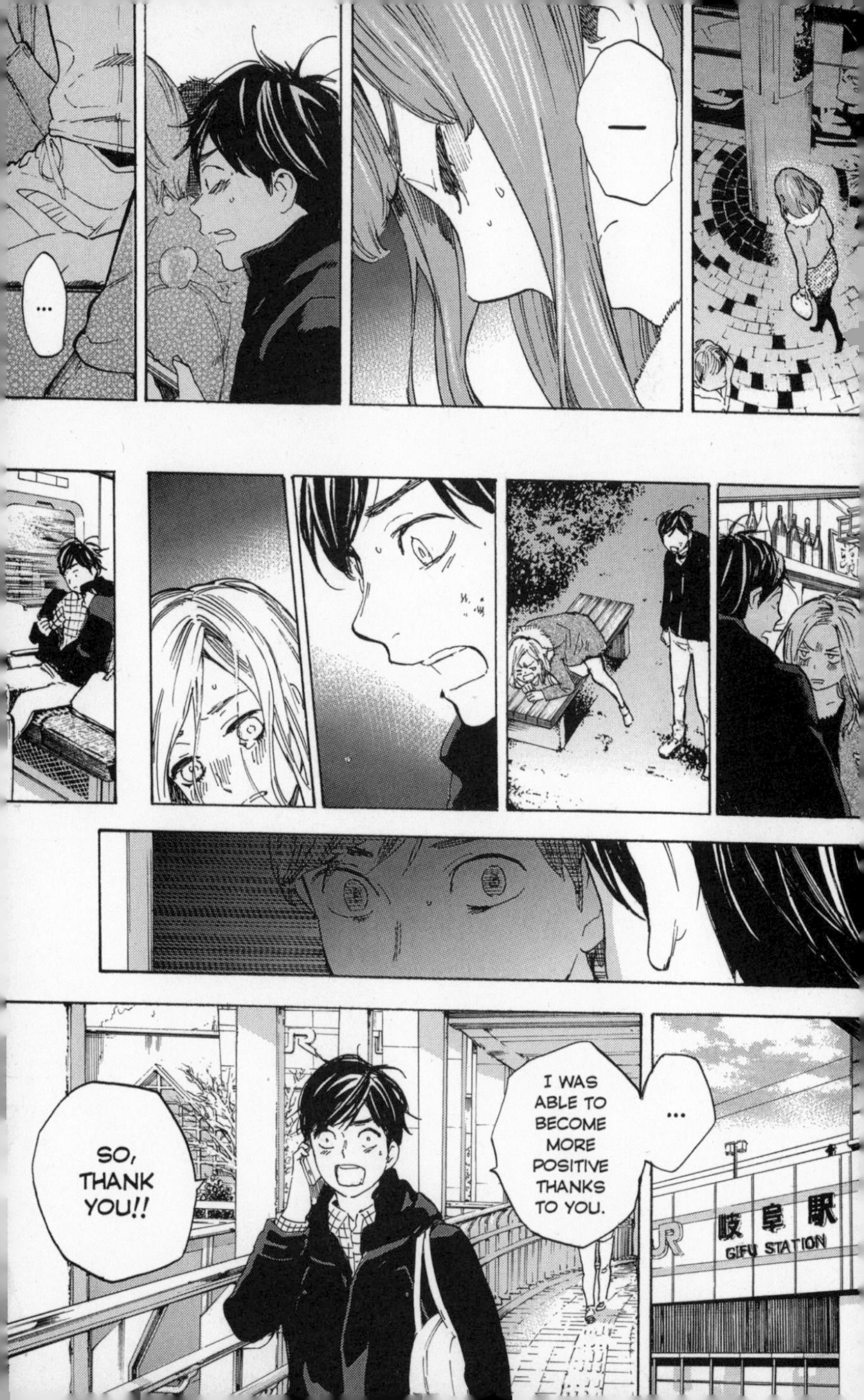
—
...
...
岐阜駅
GIFU STATION
I WAS ABLE TO BECOME MORE POSITIVE THANKS TO YOU.
SO, THANK YOU!!

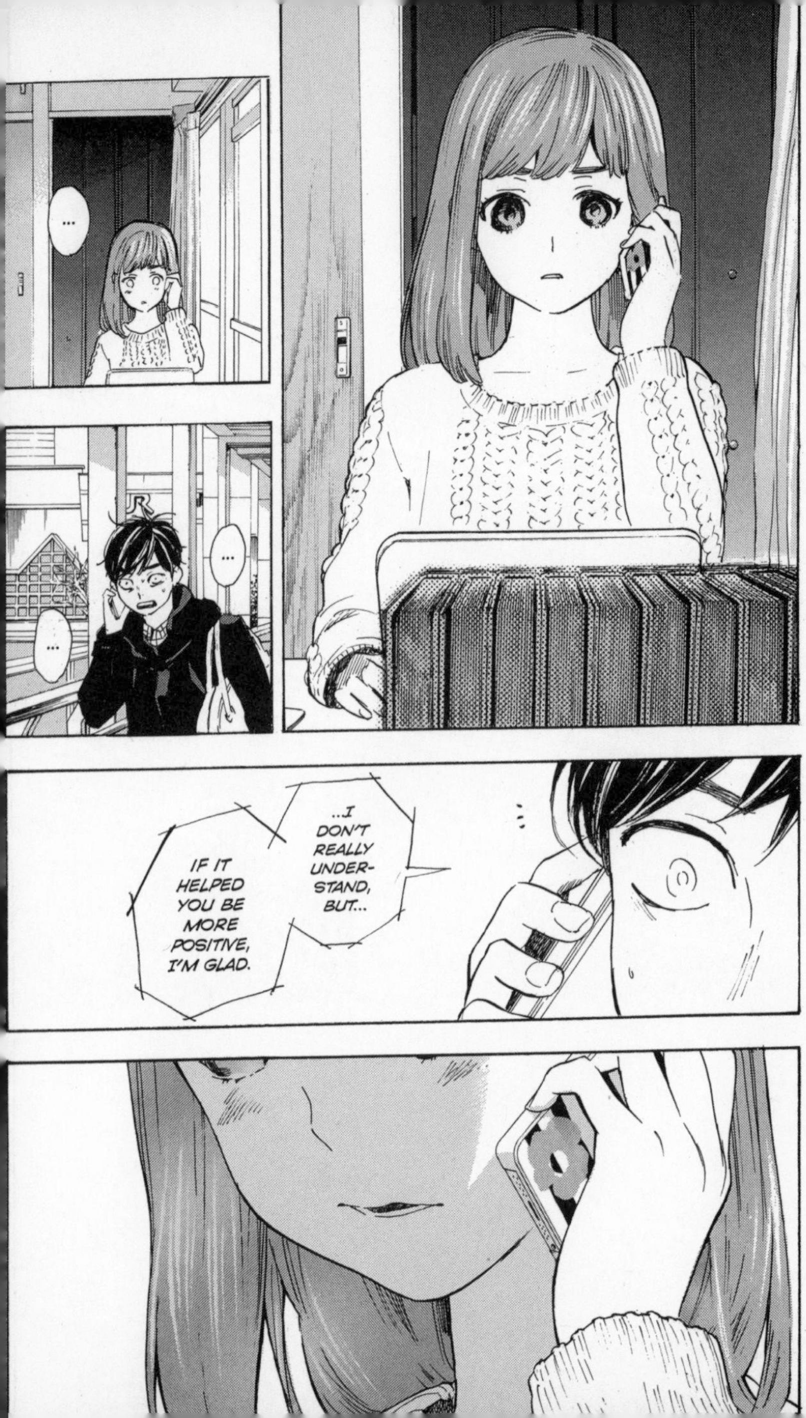
...
...
...
..I DON'T REALLY UNDER-STAND, BUT...
IF IT HELPED YOU BE MORE POSITIVE, I'M GLAD.

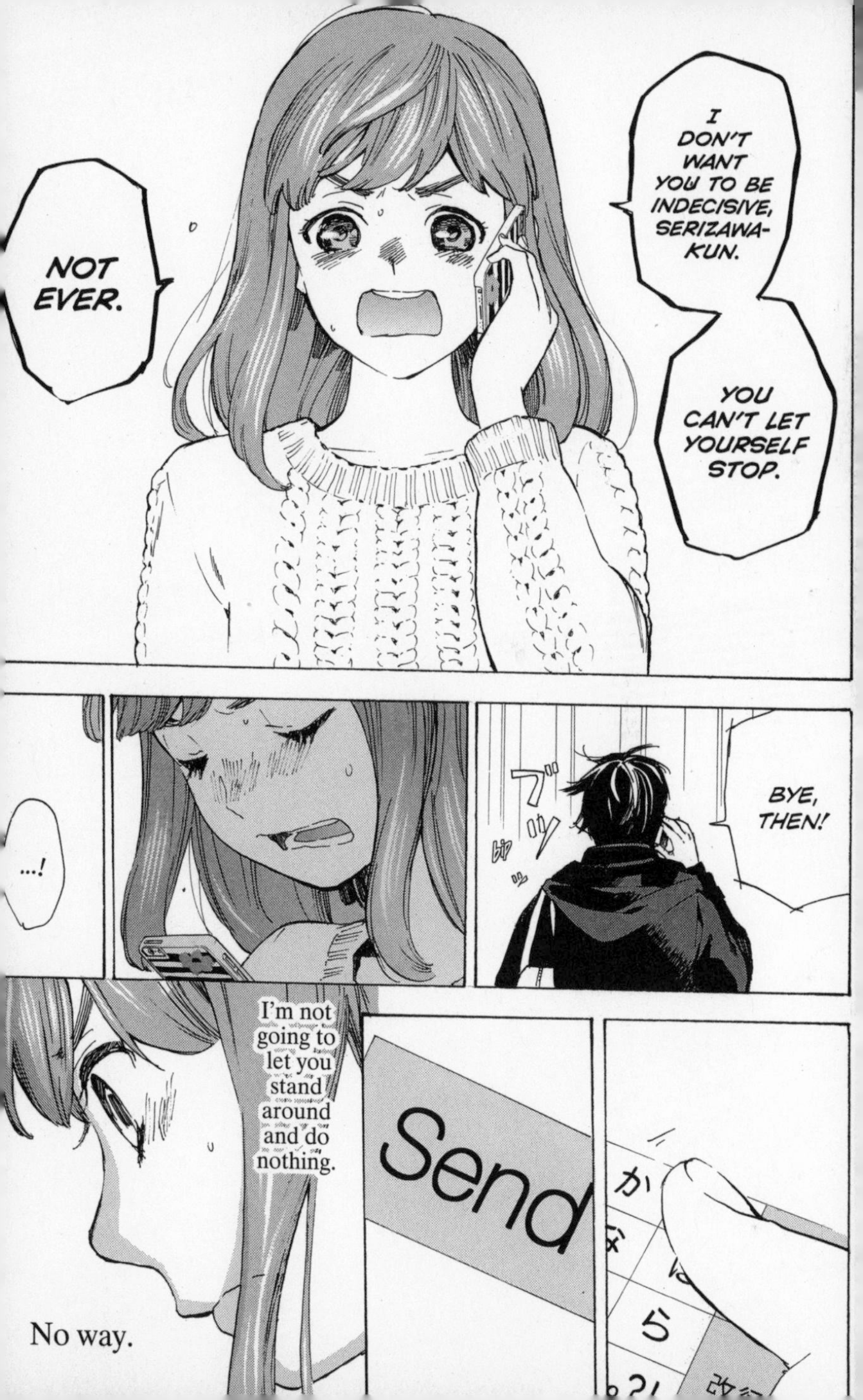
I DON'T WANT YOU TO BE INDECISIVE, SERIZAWA-KUN.
YOU CAN'T LET YOURSELF STOP.
NOT EVER.
BYE, THEN!
...!
Send
I'm not going to let you stand around and do nothing.
No way.

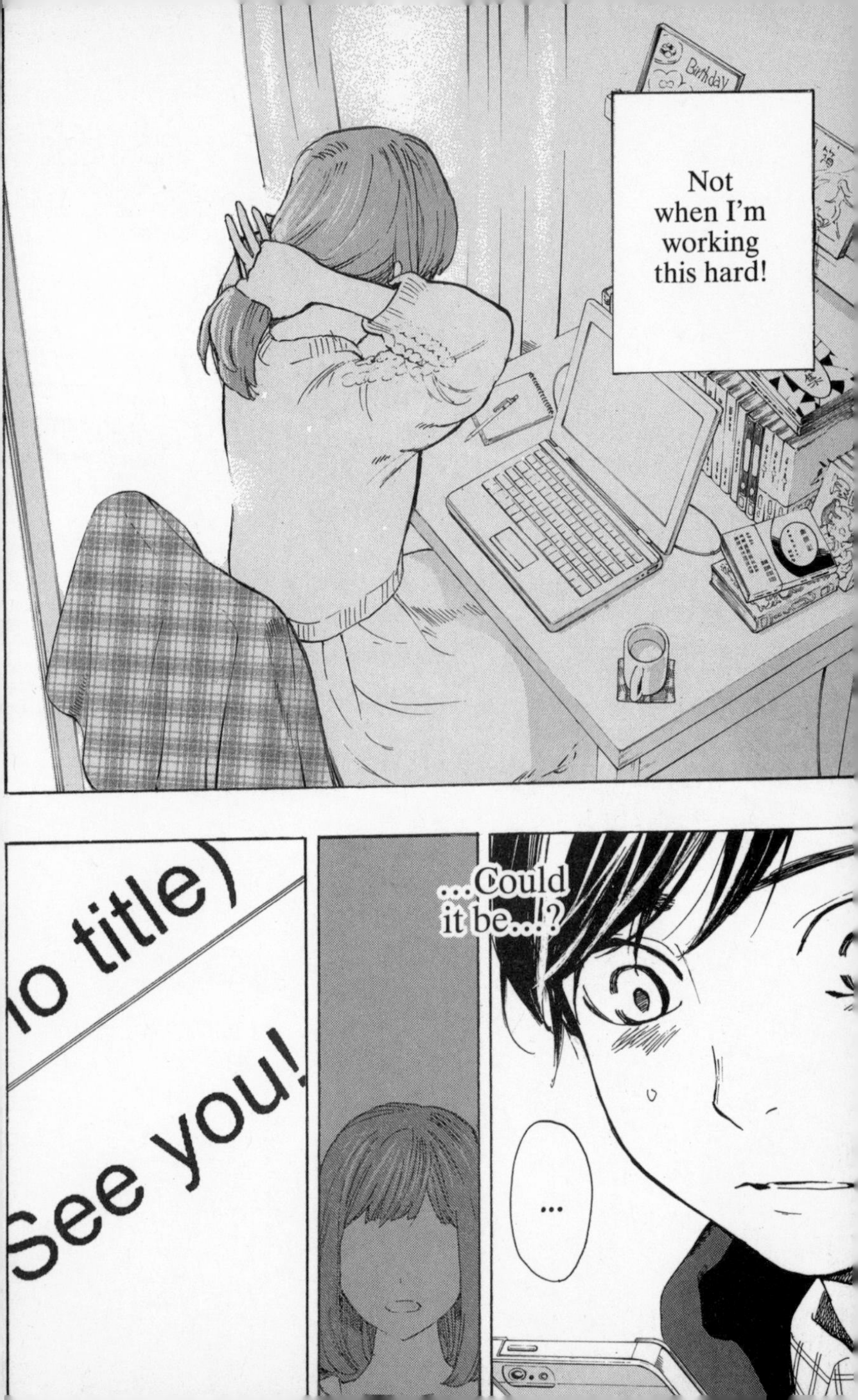

Birthday
Not when I'm working this hard!
...Could it be...?
...
o title)
See you!

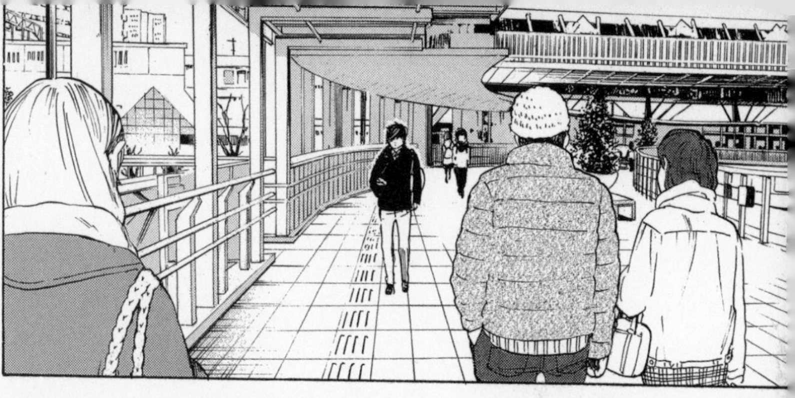
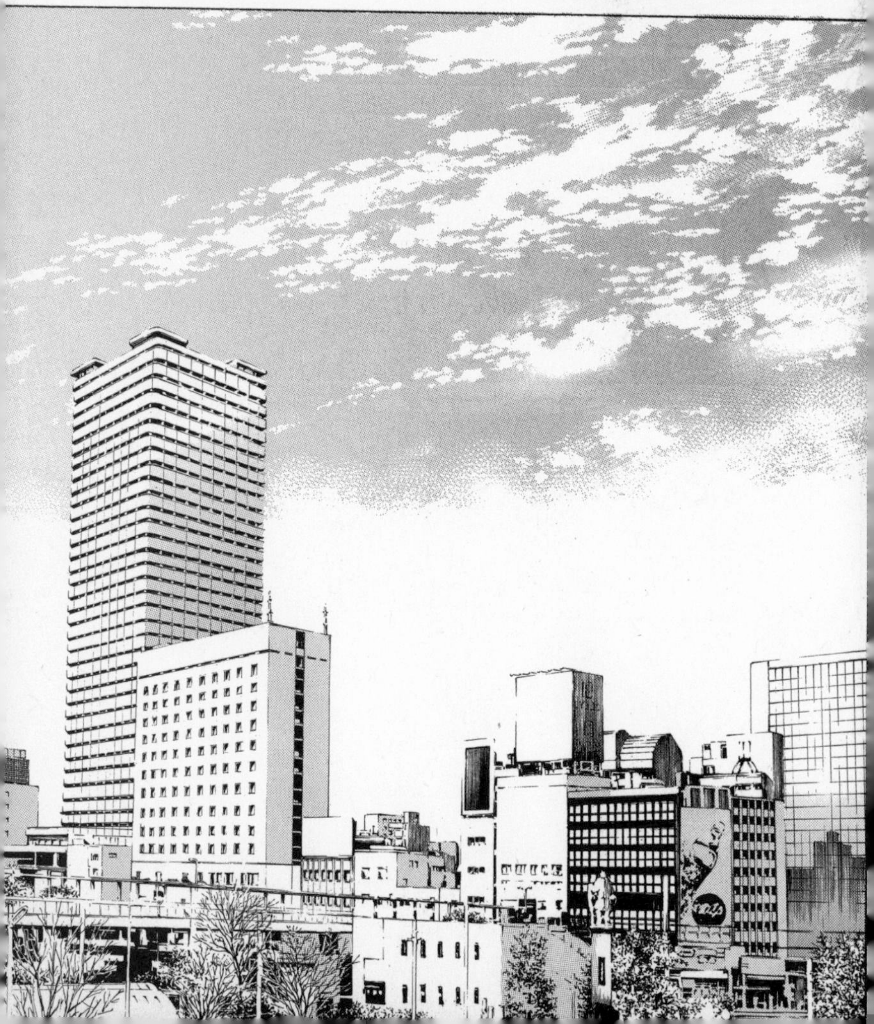

Forget Me Not

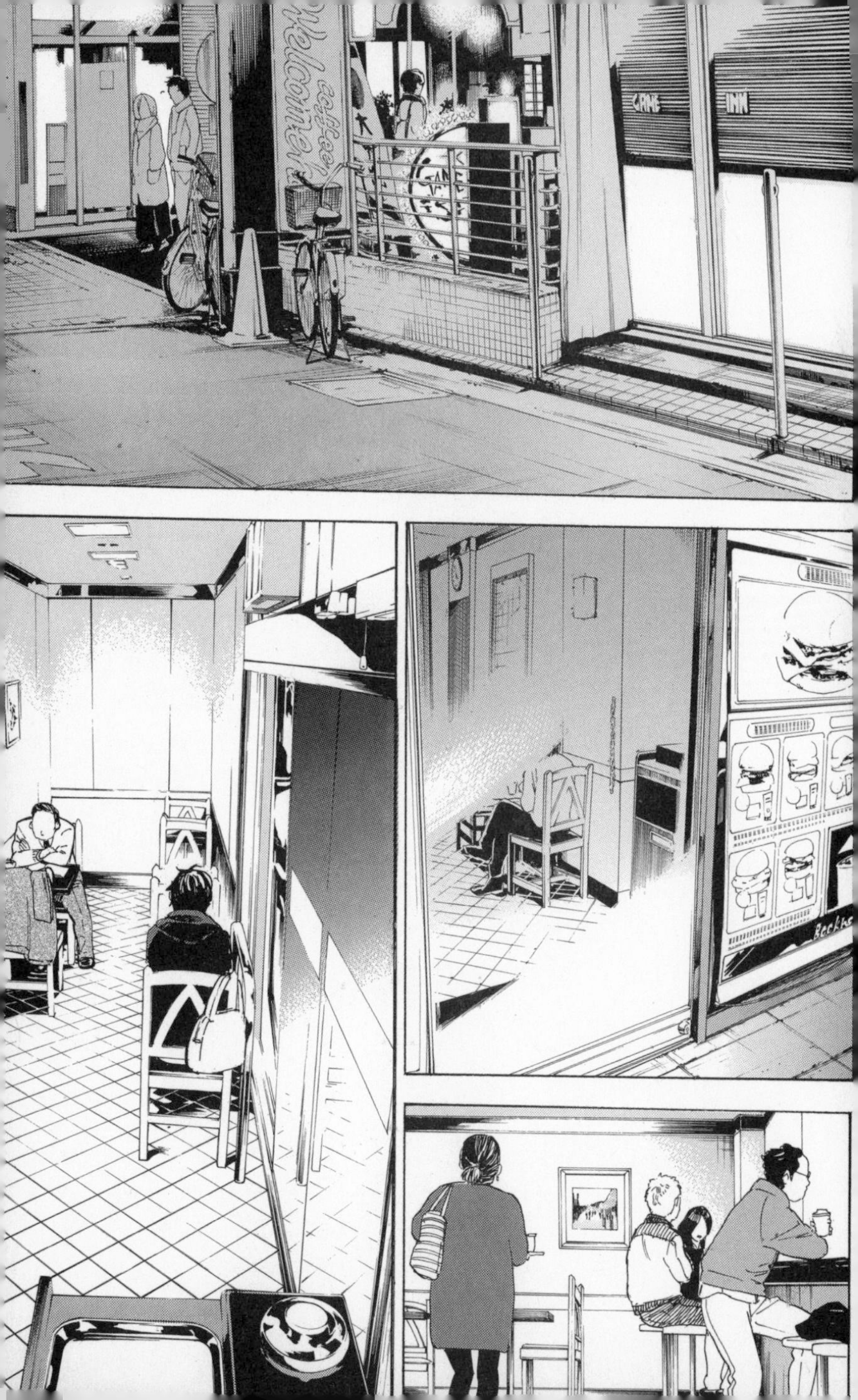
GAME
INN
coffee

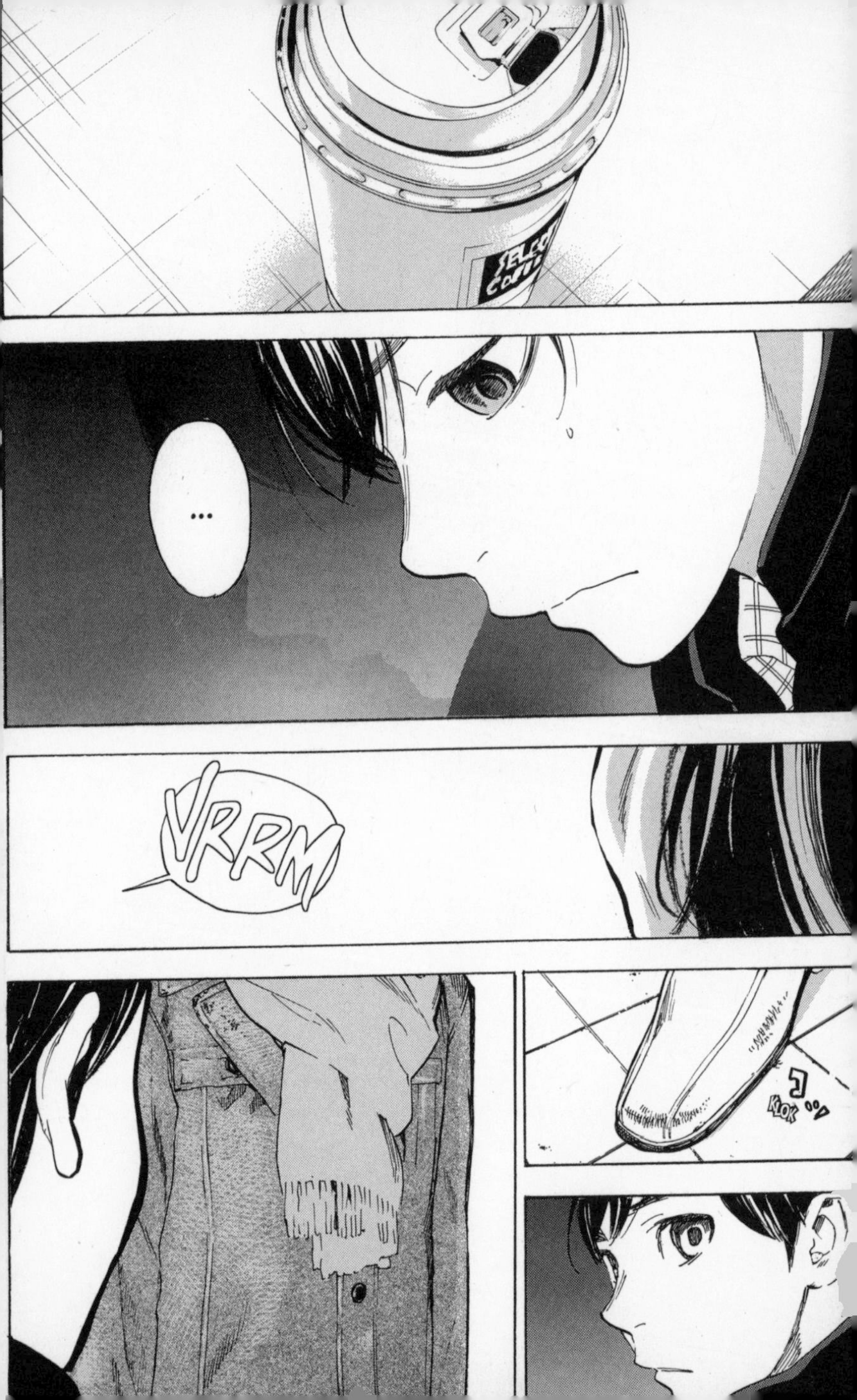
...
VRRM
KLOK

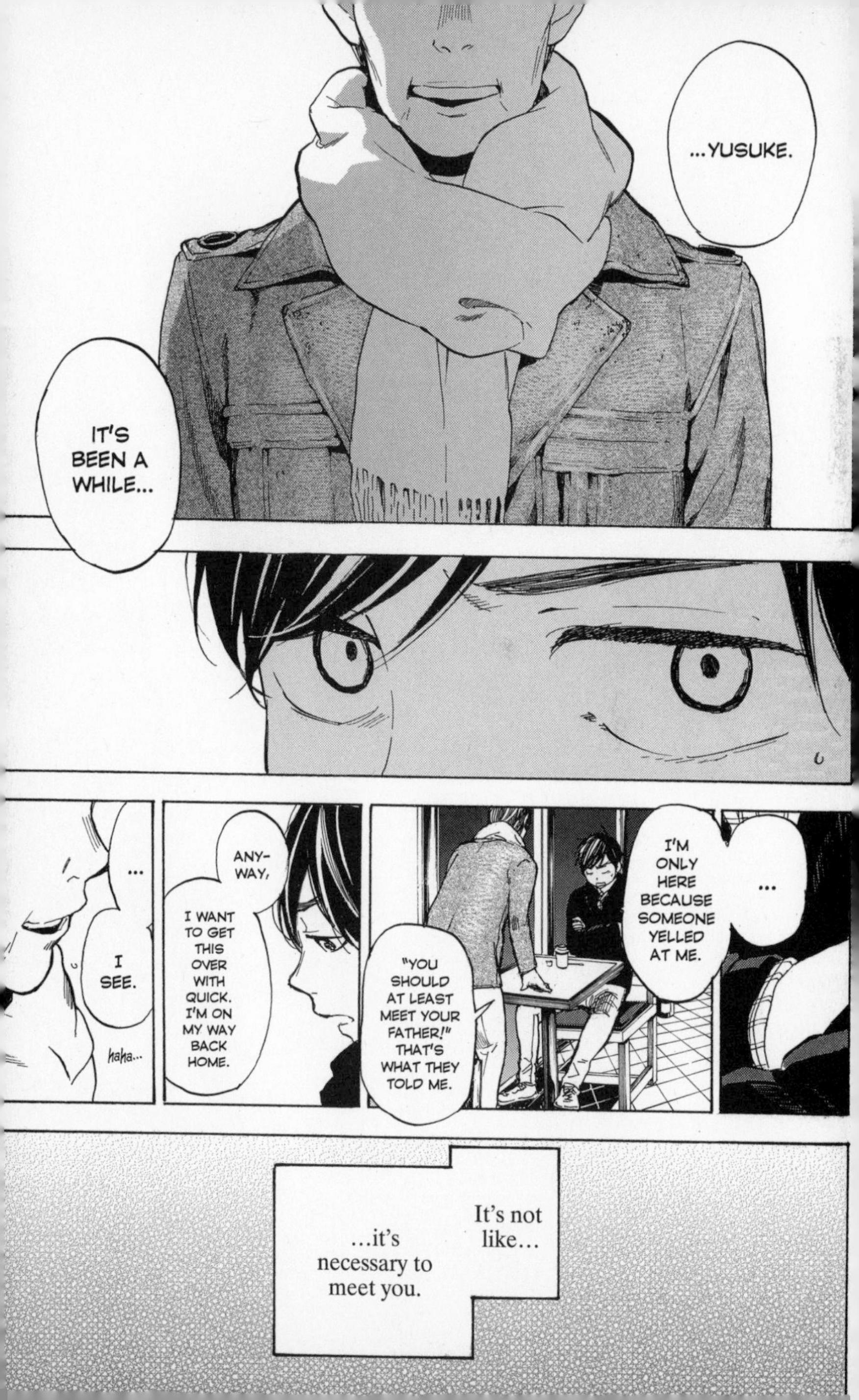
...YUSUKE.
IT'S BEEN A WHILE...
...
I'M ONLY HERE BECAUSE SOMEONE YELLED AT ME.
"YOU SHOULD AT LEAST MEET YOUR FATHER!" THAT'S WHAT THEY TOLD ME.
ANY-WAY,
I WANT TO GET THIS OVER WITH QUICK. I'M ON MY WAY BACK HOME.
...
I SEE.
haha...
It's not like...
...it's necessary to meet you.

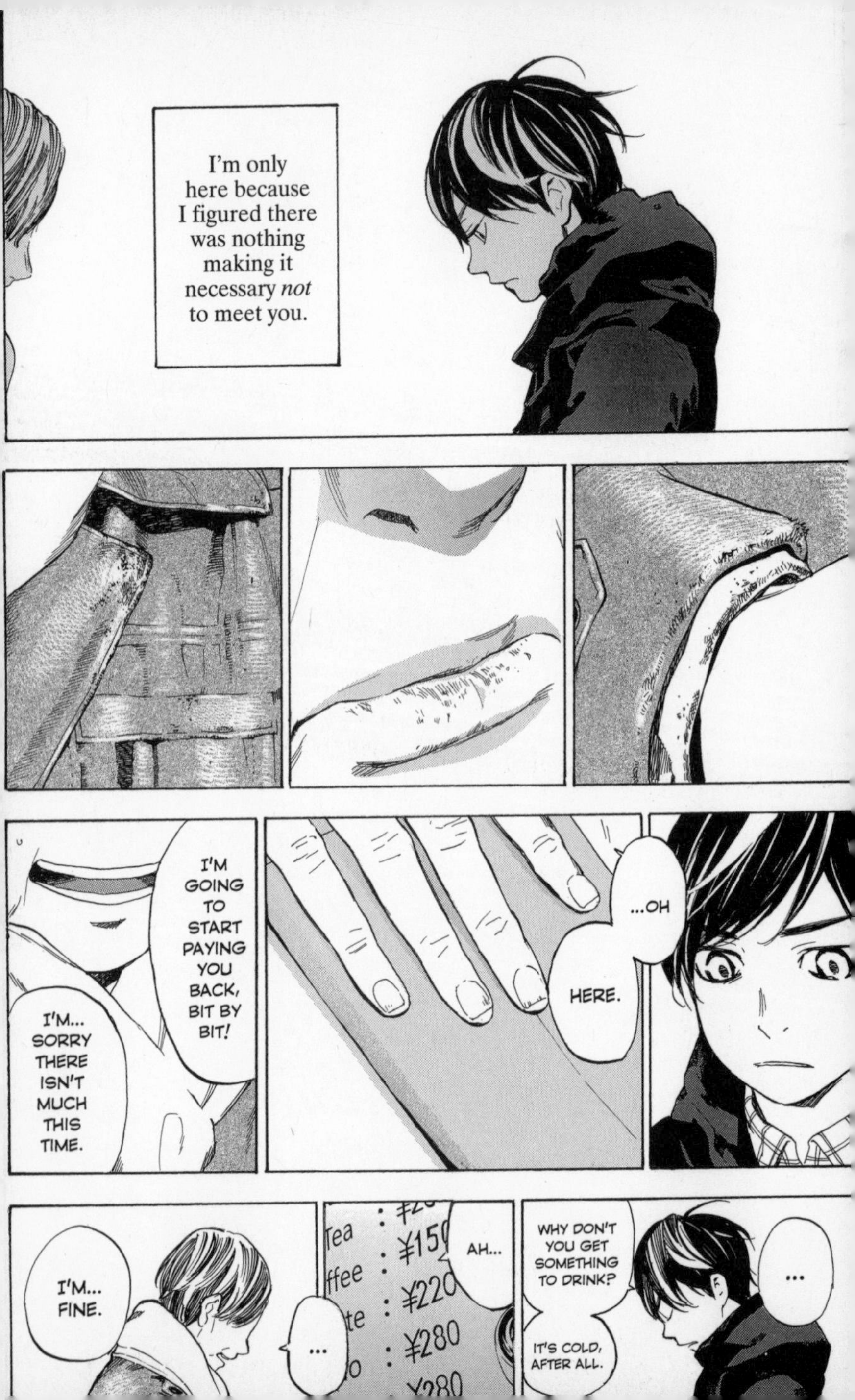
I'm only here because I figured there was nothing making it necessary *not* to meet you.
...OH
HERE.
I'M GOING TO START PAYING YOU BACK, BIT BY BIT!
I'M... SORRY THERE ISN'T MUCH THIS TIME.
...
WHY DON'T YOU GET SOMETHING TO DRINK?
IT'S COLD, AFTER ALL.
AH...
Tea
¥220
¥280
...
I'M... FINE.

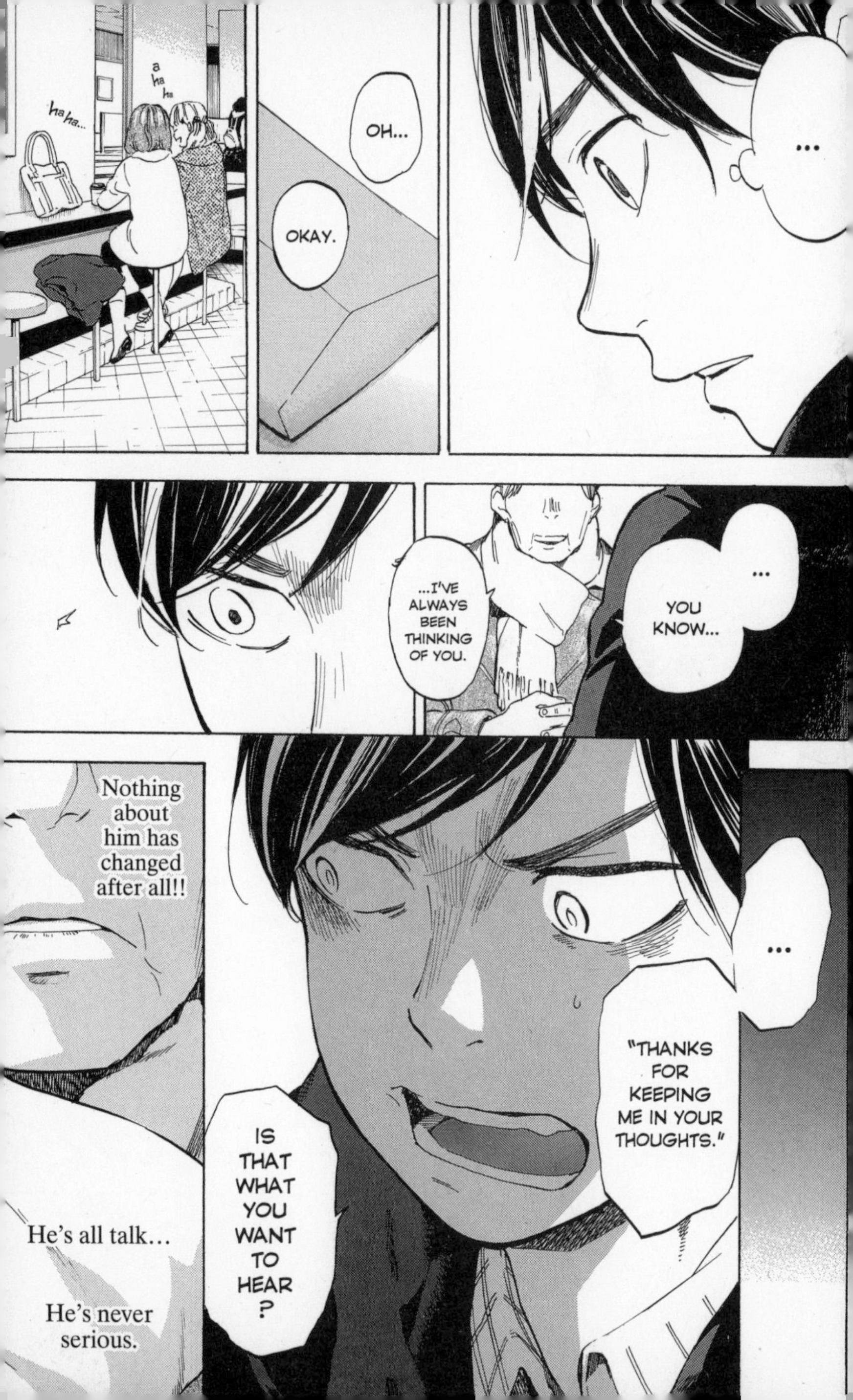
...
OH...
OKAY.
a ha ha
haha...
...
YOU KNOW...
...I'VE ALWAYS BEEN THINKING OF YOU.
...
"THANKS FOR KEEPING ME IN YOUR THOUGHTS."
IS THAT WHAT YOU WANT TO HEAR?
Nothing about him has changed after all!!
He's all talk...
He's never serious.

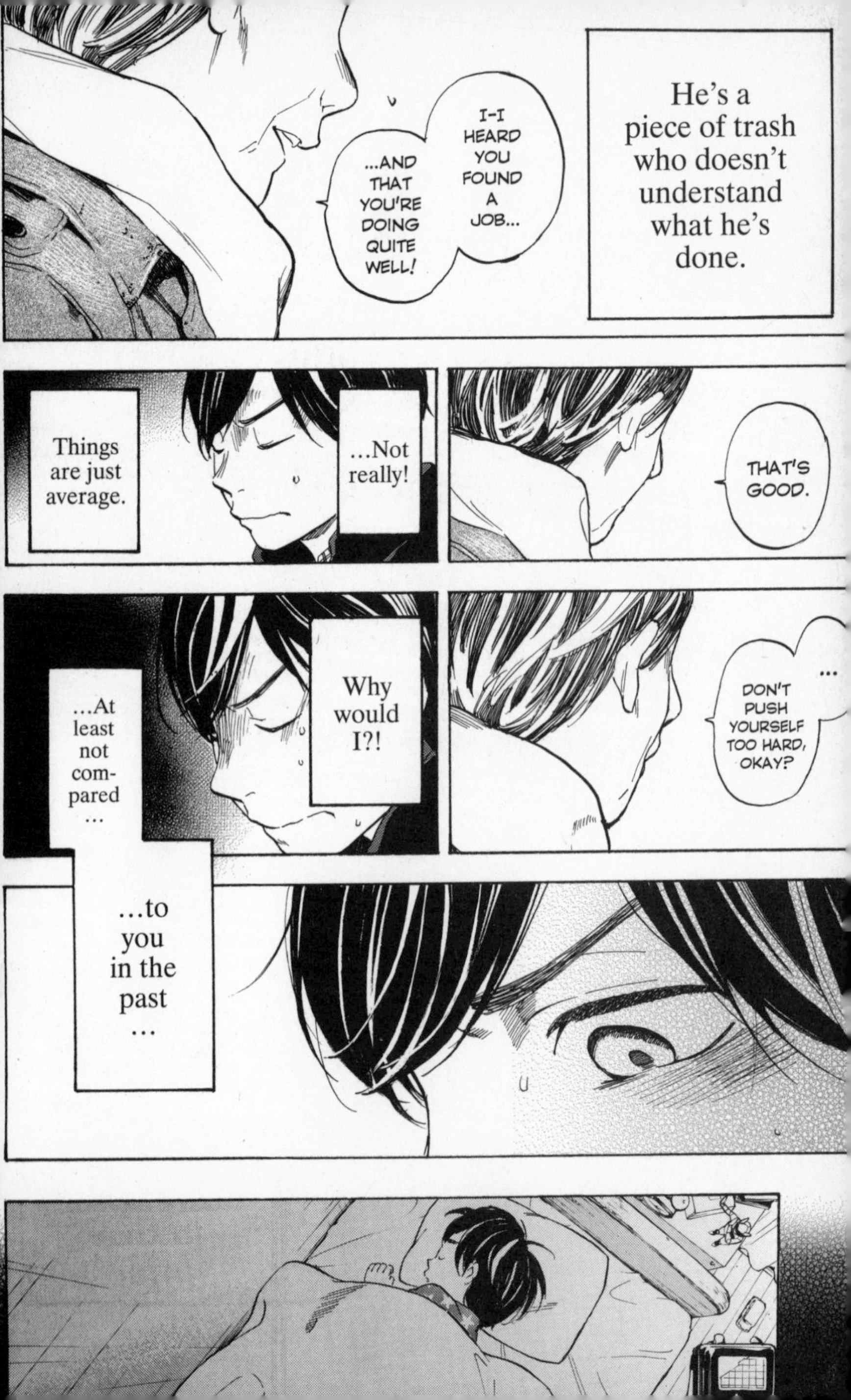
He's a piece of trash who doesn't understand what he's done.
I-I HEARD YOU FOUND A JOB...
...AND THAT YOU'RE DOING QUITE WELL!
THAT'S GOOD.
...Not really!
Things are just average.
...
DON'T PUSH YOURSELF TOO HARD, OKAY?
Why would I?!
...At least not com-pared...
...to you in the past...

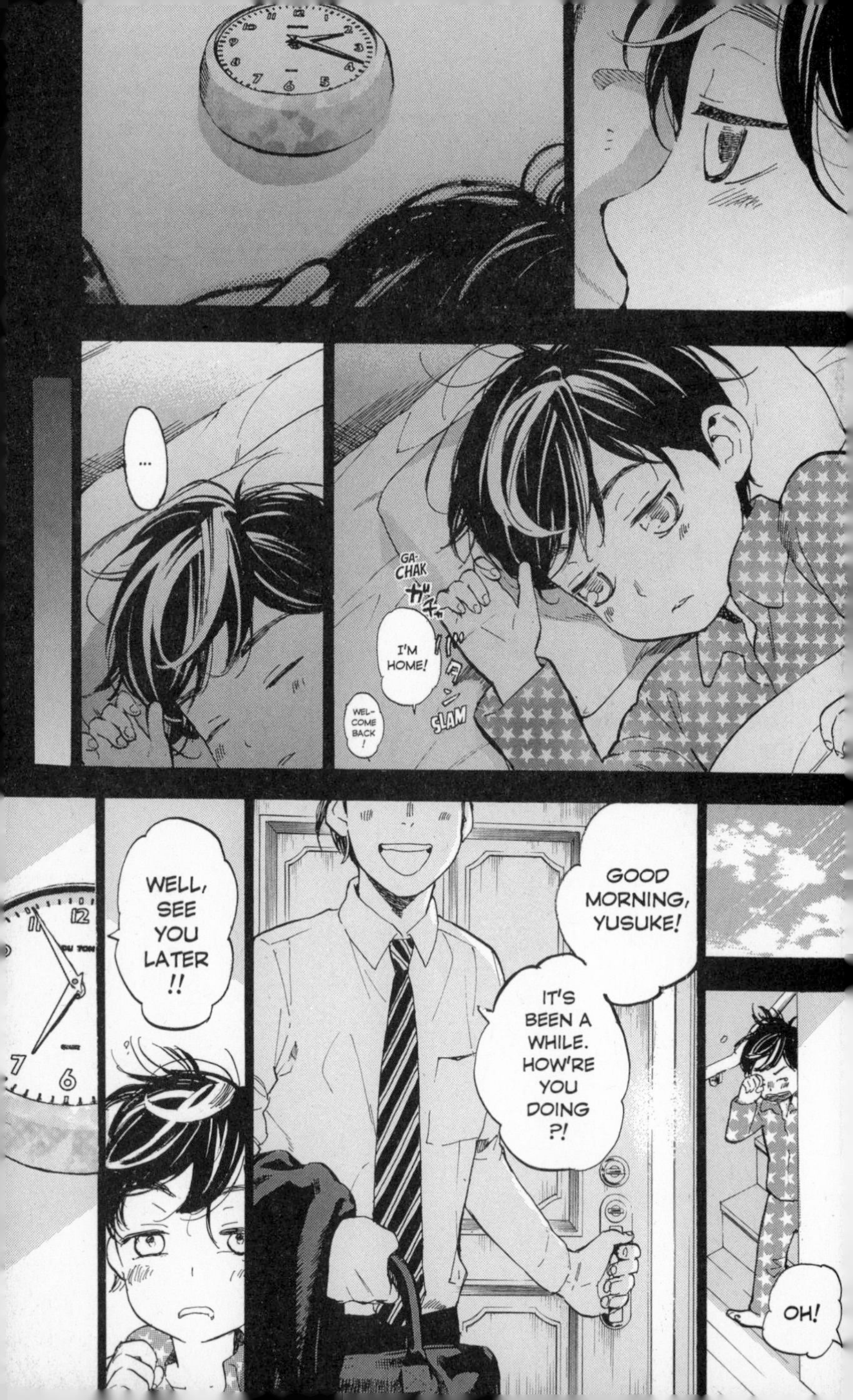
GA-CHAK
I'M HOME!
SLAM
WEL-COME BACK!
...
OH!
GOOD MORNING, YUSUKE!
IT'S BEEN A WHILE. HOW'RE YOU DOING?!
WELL, SEE YOU LATER!!

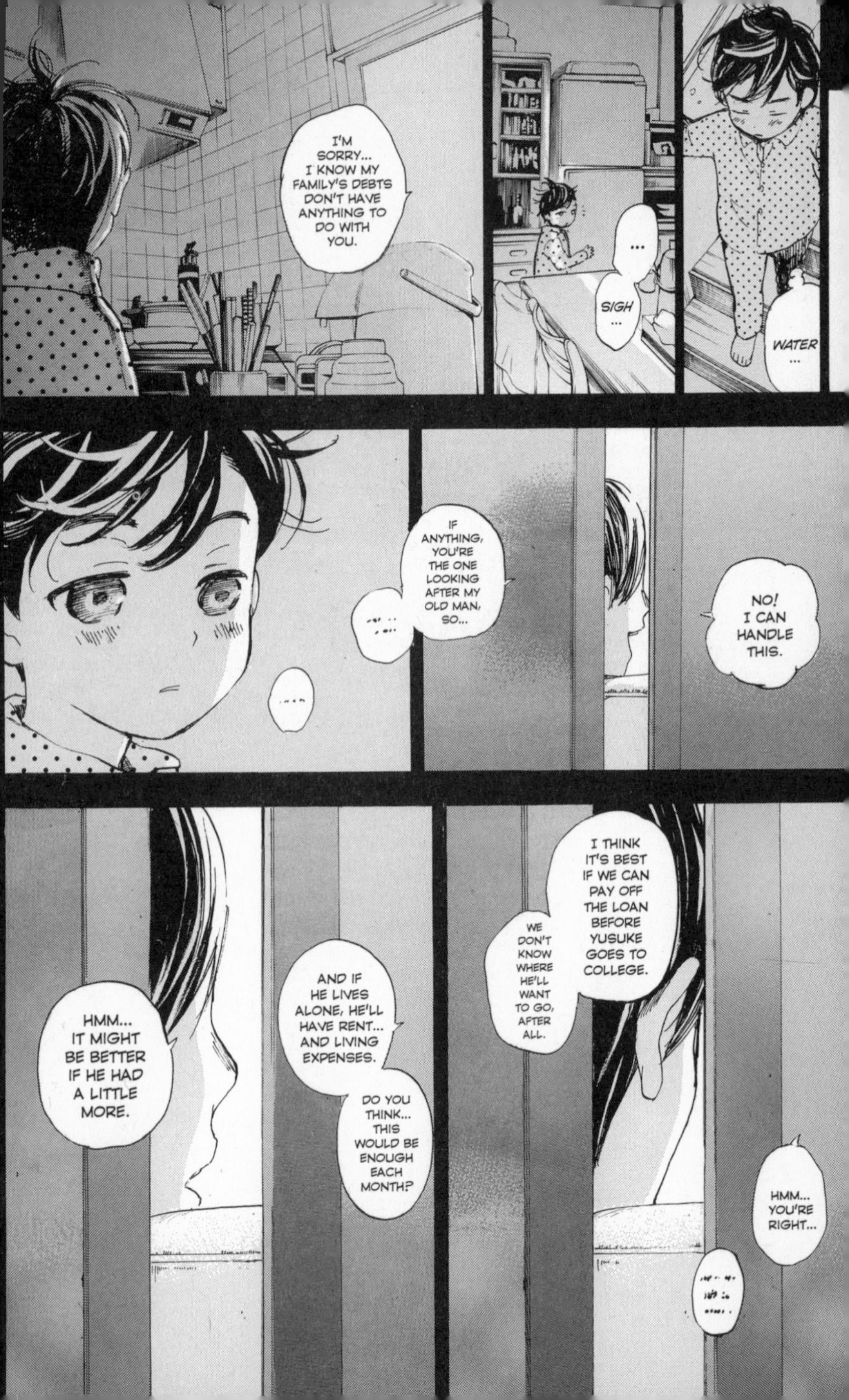
WATER...
...
SIGH...
I'M SORRY... I KNOW MY FAMILY'S DEBTS DON'T HAVE ANYTHING TO DO WITH YOU.
NO! I CAN HANDLE THIS.
IF ANYTHING, YOU'RE THE ONE LOOKING AFTER MY OLD MAN, SO...
I THINK IT'S BEST IF WE CAN PAY OFF THE LOAN BEFORE YUSUKE GOES TO COLLEGE.
WE DON'T KNOW WHERE HE'LL WANT TO GO, AFTER ALL.
HMM... YOU'RE RIGHT...
AND IF HE LIVES ALONE, HE'LL HAVE RENT... AND LIVING EXPENSES.
DO YOU THINK... THIS WOULD BE ENOUGH EACH MONTH?
HMM... IT MIGHT BE BETTER IF HE HAD A LITTLE MORE.

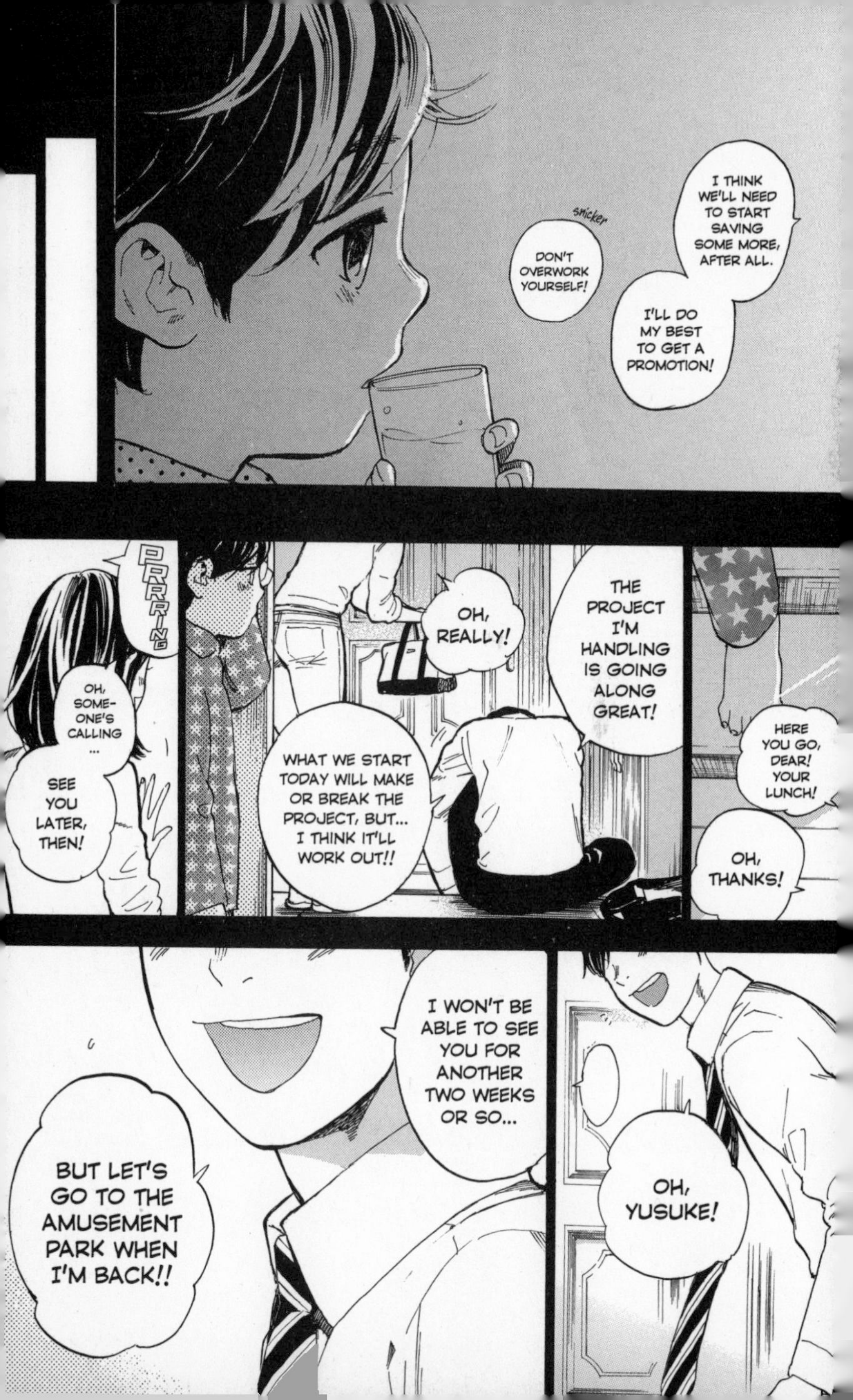

I THINK WE'LL NEED TO START SAVING SOME MORE, AFTER ALL.
I'LL DO MY BEST TO GET A PROMOTION!
snicker
DON'T OVERWORK YOURSELF!
HERE YOU GO, DEAR! YOUR LUNCH!
OH, THANKS!
THE PROJECT I'M HANDLING IS GOING ALONG GREAT!
OH, REALLY!
WHAT WE START TODAY WILL MAKE OR BREAK THE PROJECT, BUT... I THINK IT'LL WORK OUT!!
PRRRING
OH, SOMEONE'S CALLING ...
SEE YOU LATER, THEN!
OH, YUSUKE!
I WON'T BE ABLE TO SEE YOU FOR ANOTHER TWO WEEKS OR SO...
BUT LET'S GO TO THE AMUSEMENT PARK WHEN I'M BACK!!

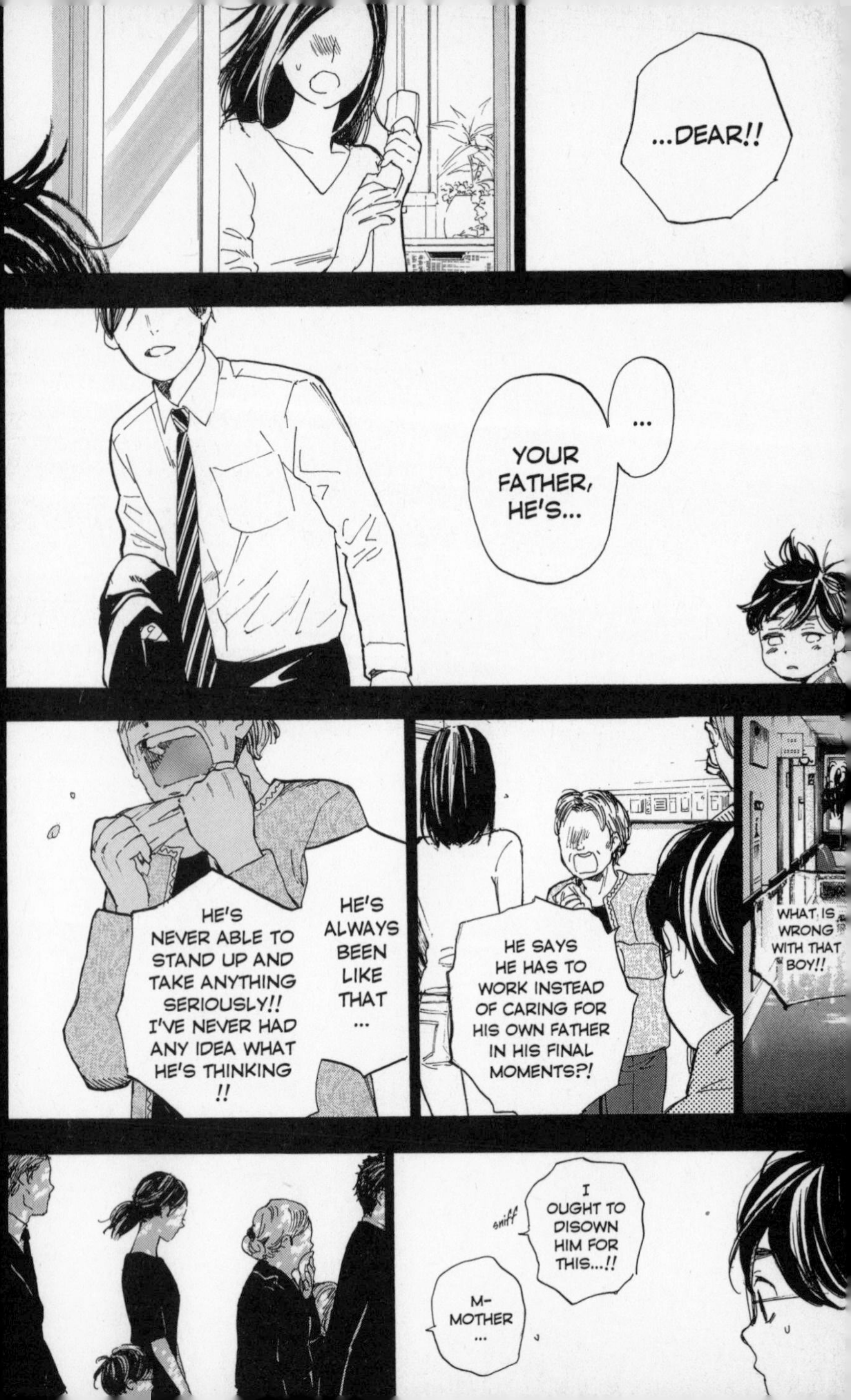
...DEAR!!
...
YOUR FATHER, HE'S...
WHAT IS WRONG WITH THAT BOY!!
HE SAYS HE HAS TO WORK INSTEAD OF CARING FOR HIS OWN FATHER IN HIS FINAL MOMENTS?!
HE'S ALWAYS BEEN LIKE THAT...
HE'S NEVER ABLE TO STAND UP AND TAKE ANYTHING SERIOUSLY!! I'VE NEVER HAD ANY IDEA WHAT HE'S THINKING!!
sniff
I OUGHT TO DISOWN HIM FOR THIS...!!
M-MOTHER...

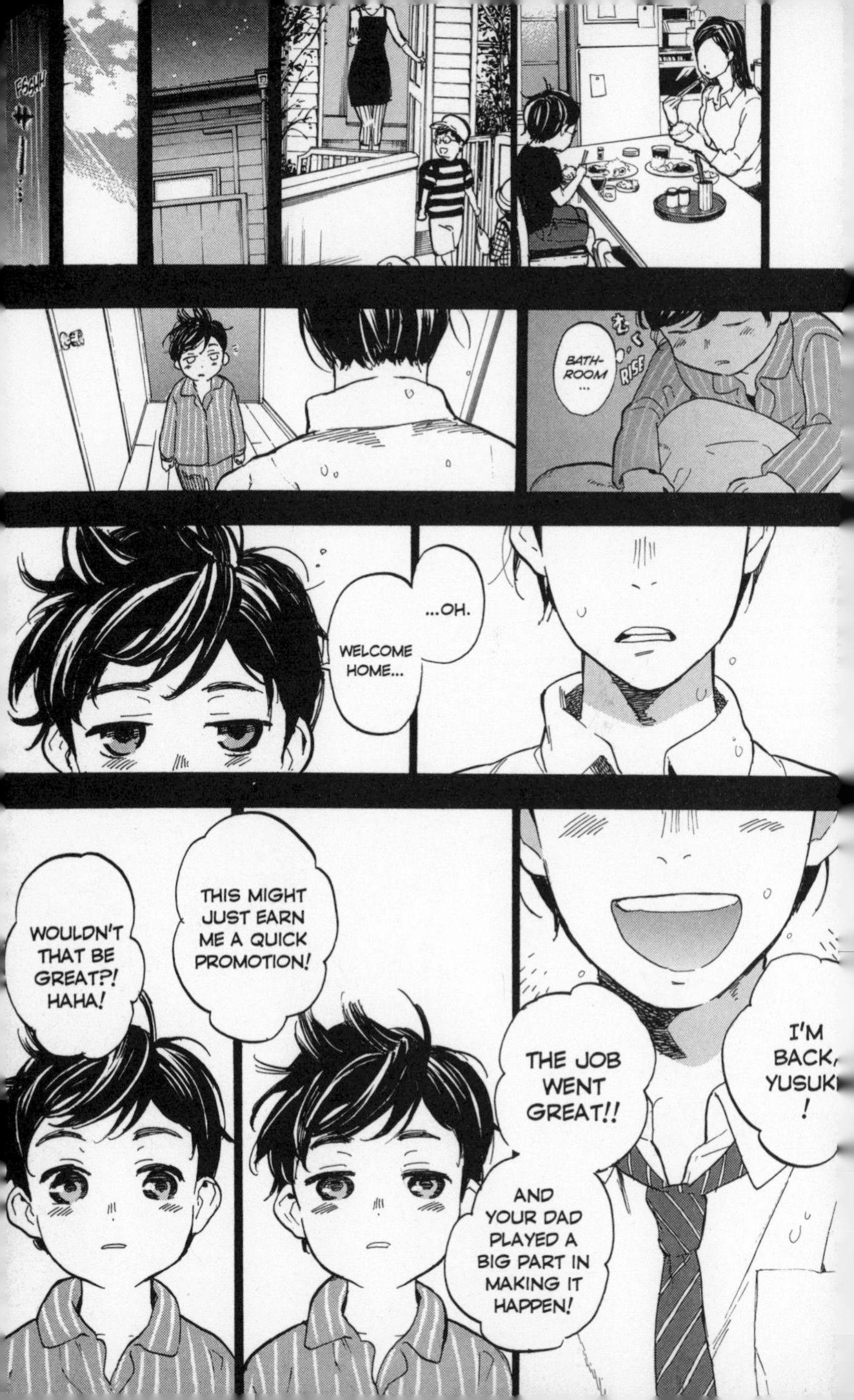
FSSHH
BATH-ROOM ...
RISE
...OH.
WELCOME HOME...
I'M BACK, YUSUK !
THE JOB WENT GREAT!!
AND YOUR DAD PLAYED A BIG PART IN MAKING IT HAPPEN!
THIS MIGHT JUST EARN ME A QUICK PROMOTION!
WOULDN'T THAT BE GREAT?! HAHA!

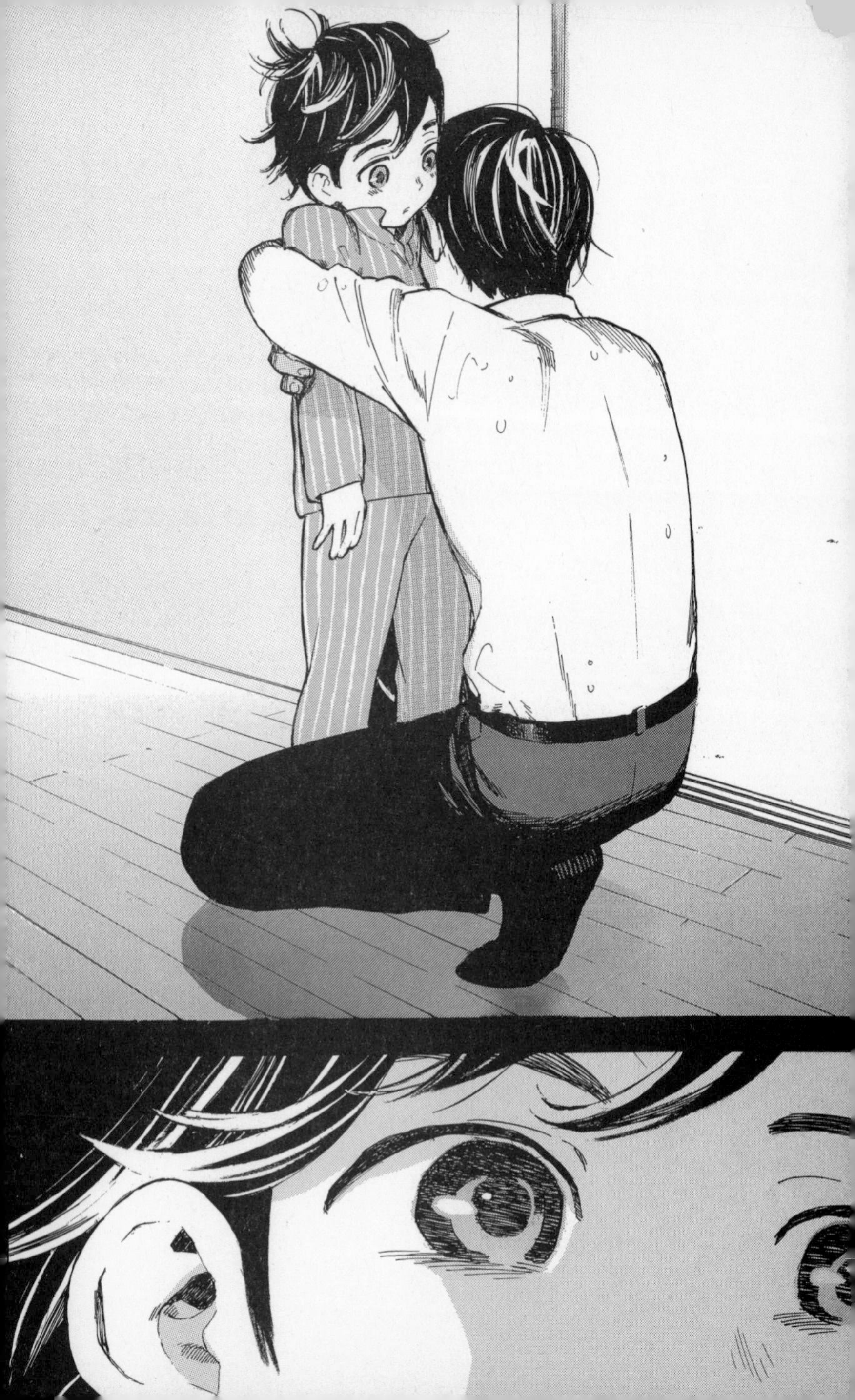

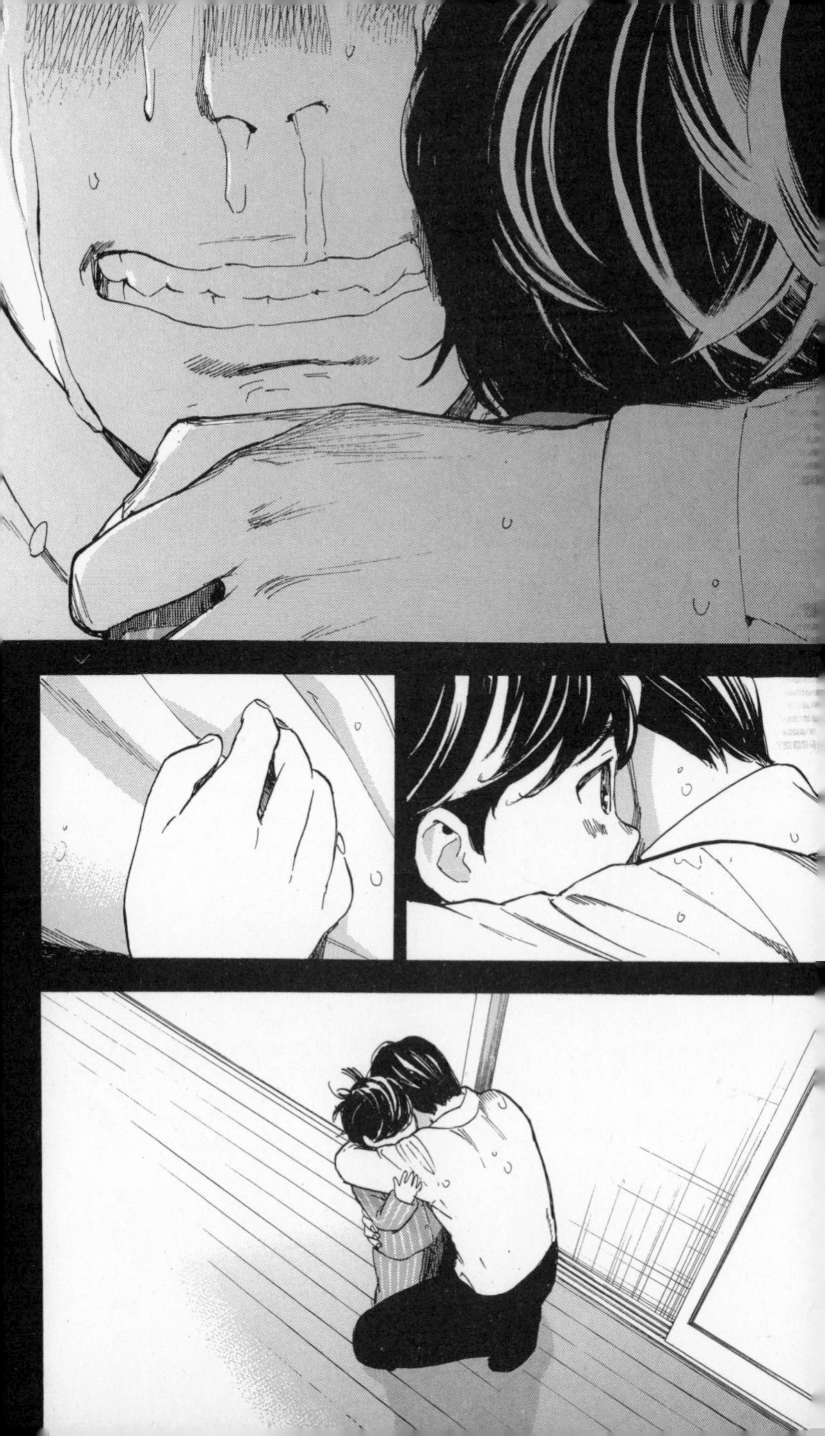

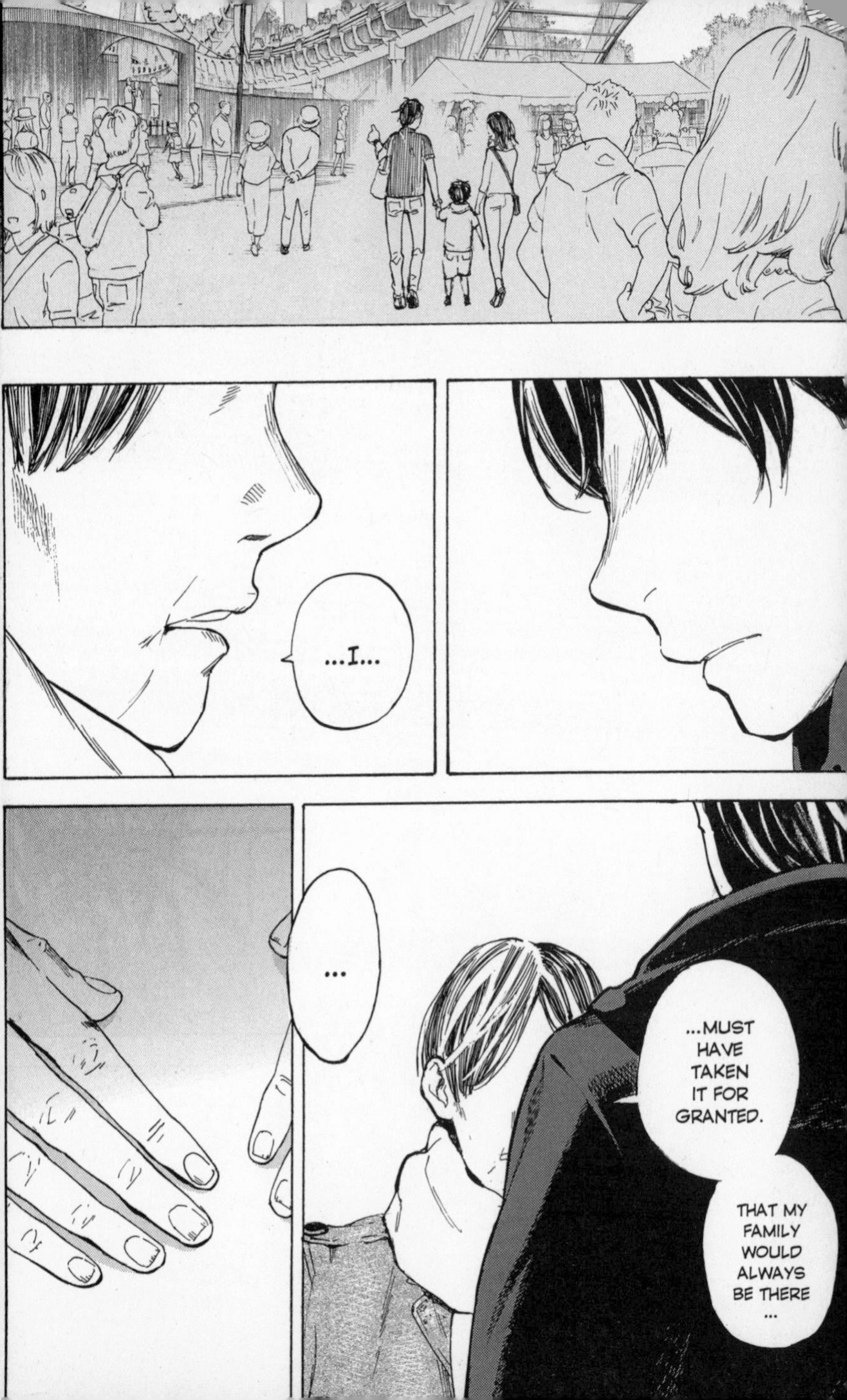
...I...
...MUST HAVE TAKEN IT FOR GRANTED.
THAT MY FAMILY WOULD ALWAYS BE THERE ...
...

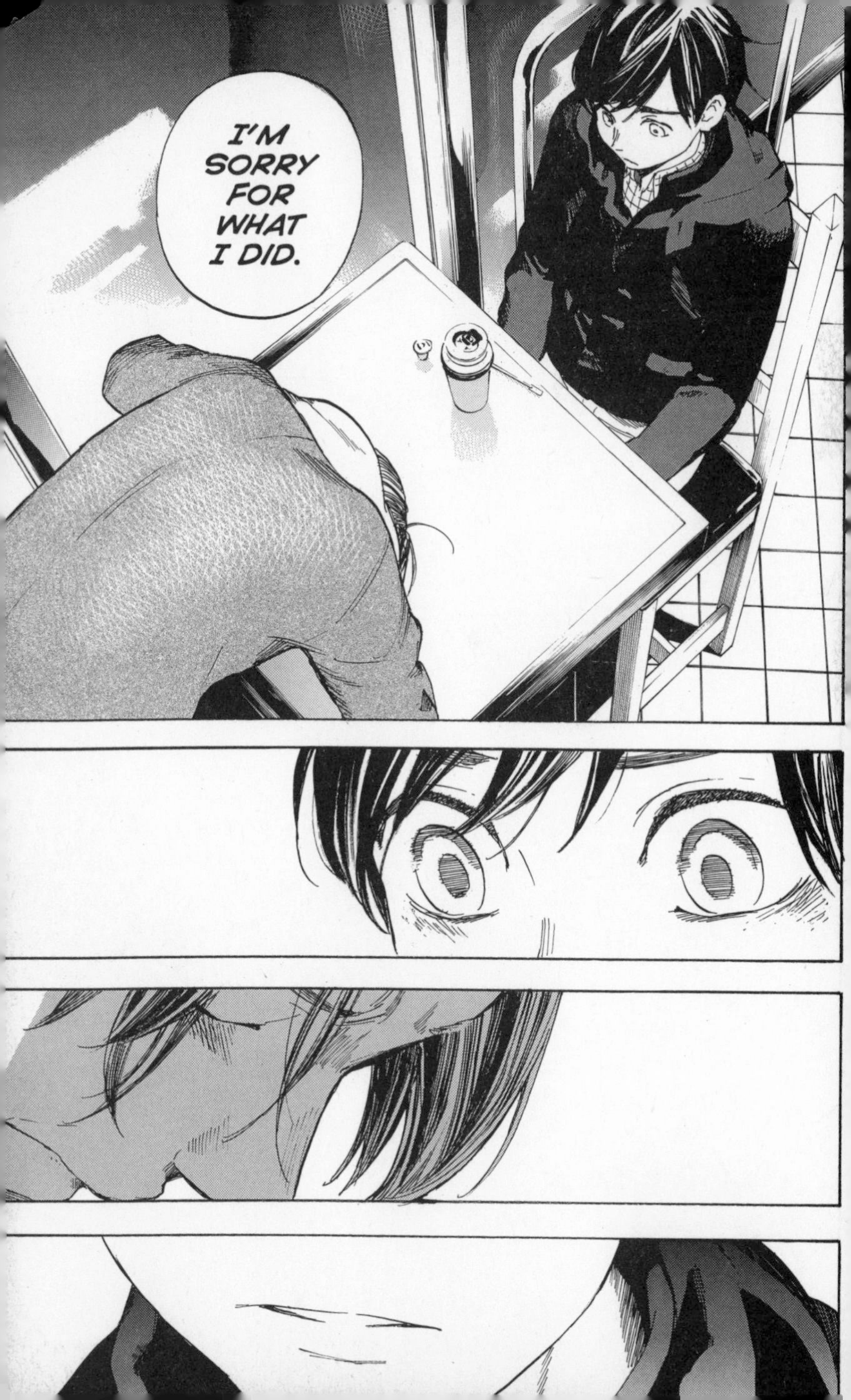
I'M SORRY FOR WHAT I DID.

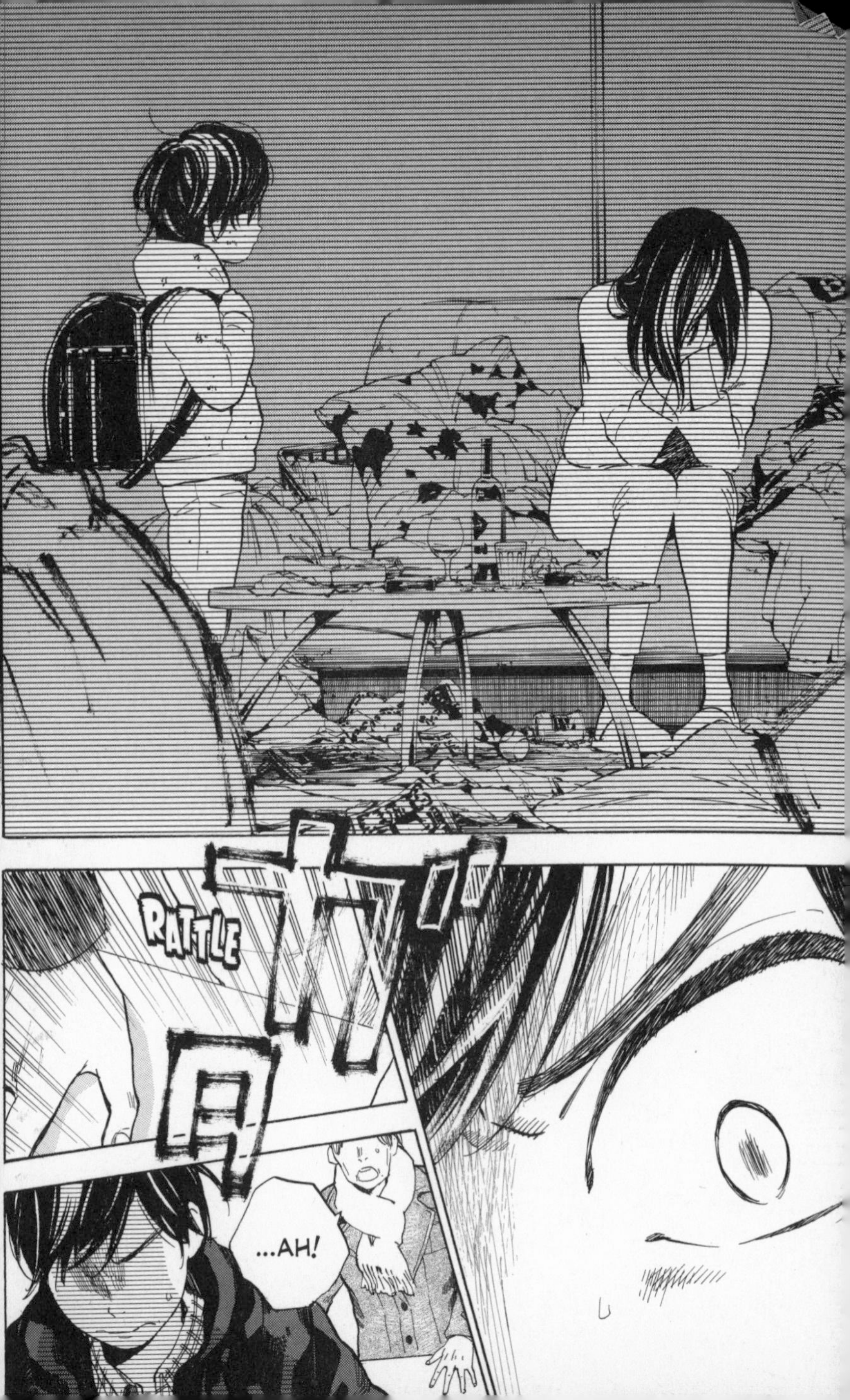
RATTLE
...AH!

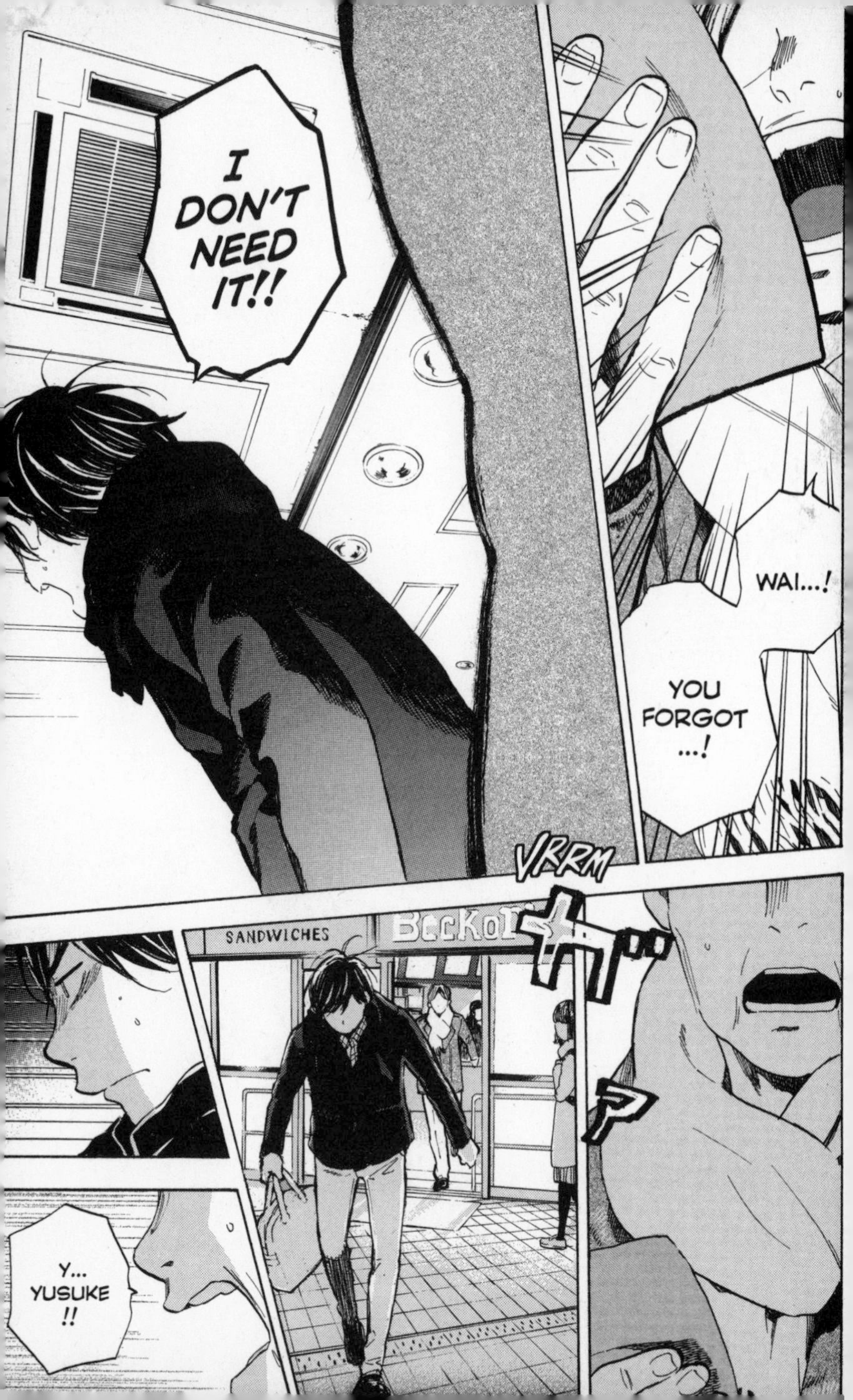
WAI...!
YOU FORGOT ...!
I DON'T NEED IT!!
VRRM
SANDWICHES
Y... YUSUKE !!

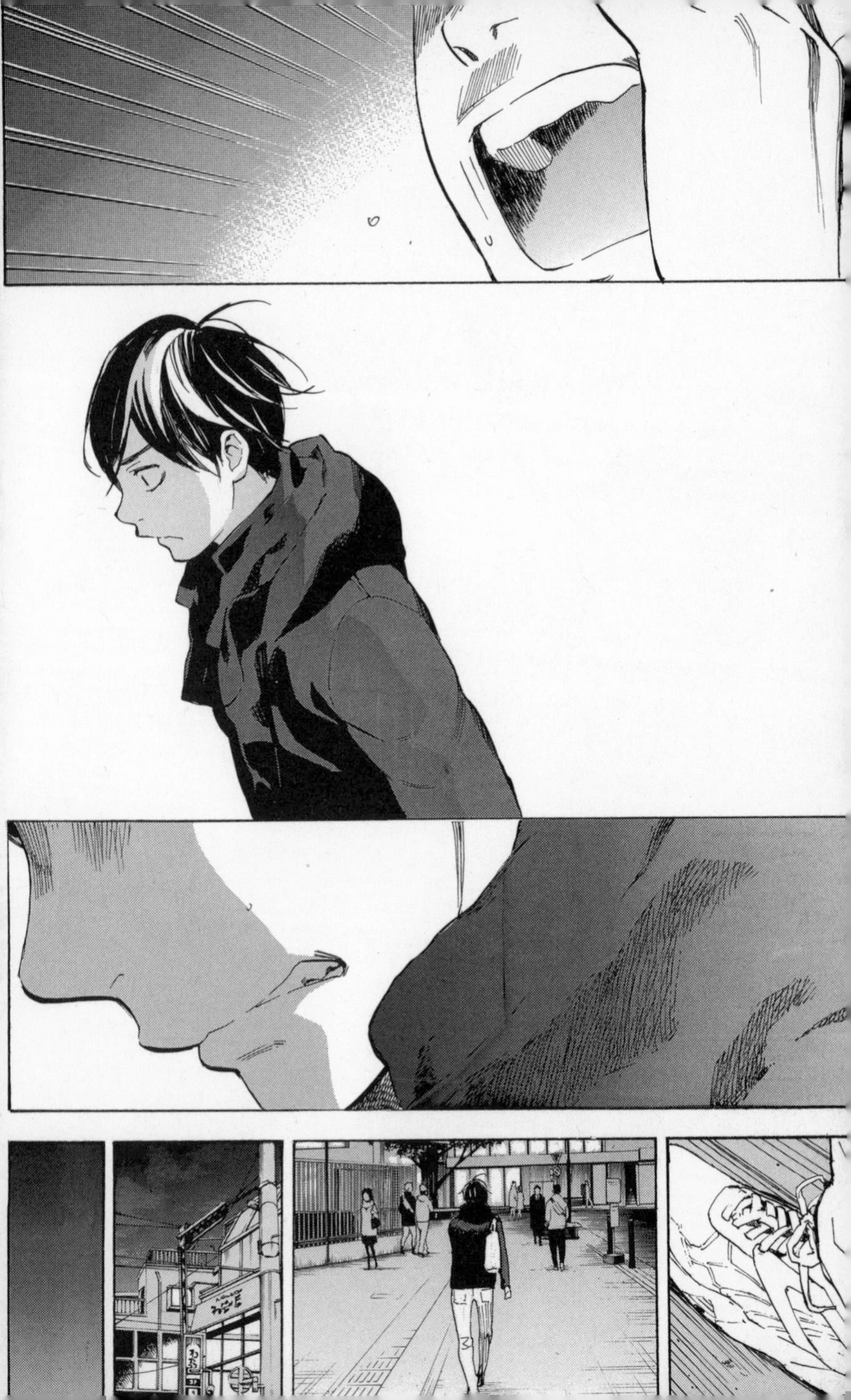

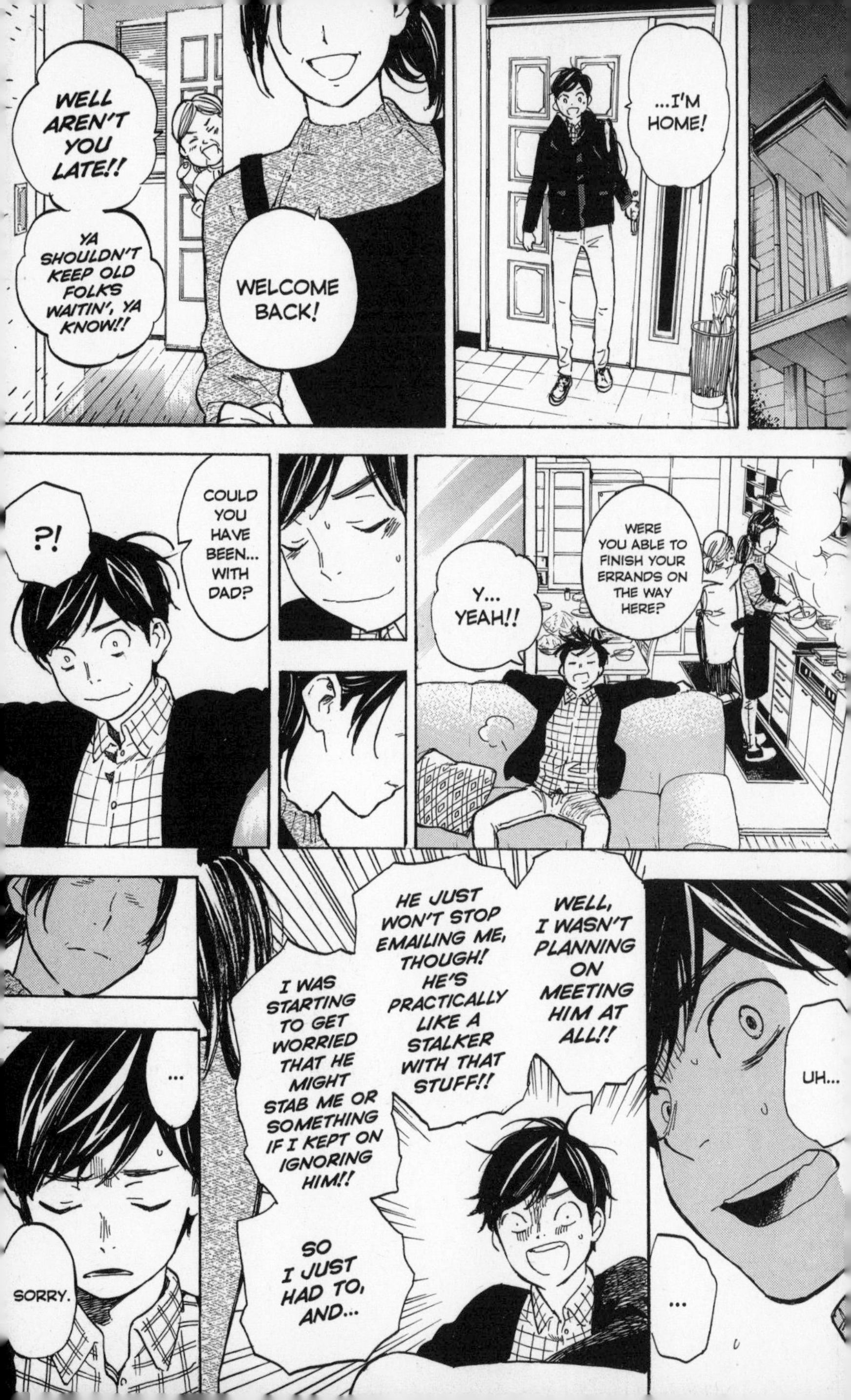
...I'M HOME!
WELCOME BACK!
WELL AREN'T YOU LATE!!
YA SHOULDN'T KEEP OLD FOLKS WAITIN', YA KNOW!!
WERE YOU ABLE TO FINISH YOUR ERRANDS ON THE WAY HERE?
Y... YEAH!!
COULD YOU HAVE BEEN... WITH DAD?
?!
UH...
...
WELL, I WASN'T PLANNING ON MEETING HIM AT ALL!!
HE JUST WON'T STOP EMAILING ME, THOUGH! HE'S PRACTICALLY LIKE A STALKER WITH THAT STUFF!!
I WAS STARTING TO GET WORRIED THAT HE MIGHT STAB ME OR SOMETHING IF I KEPT ON IGNORING HIM!!
SO I JUST HAD TO, AND...
...
SORRY.

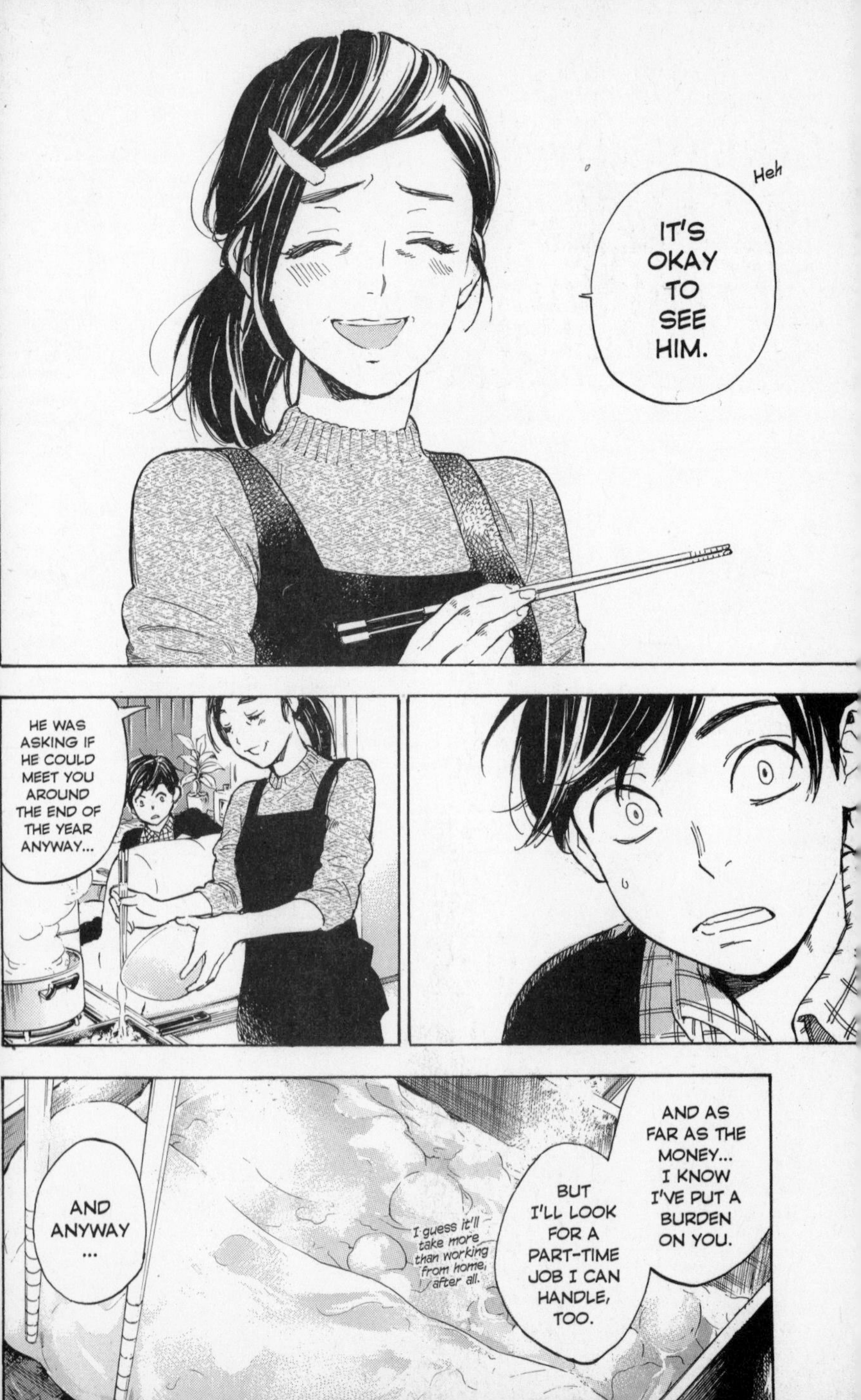
Heh
IT'S OKAY TO SEE HIM.
HE WAS ASKING IF HE COULD MEET YOU AROUND THE END OF THE YEAR ANYWAY...
AND AS FAR AS THE MONEY... I KNOW I'VE PUT A BURDEN ON YOU.
BUT I'LL LOOK FOR A PART-TIME JOB I CAN HANDLE, TOO.
I guess it'll take more than working from home, after all.
AND ANYWAY...

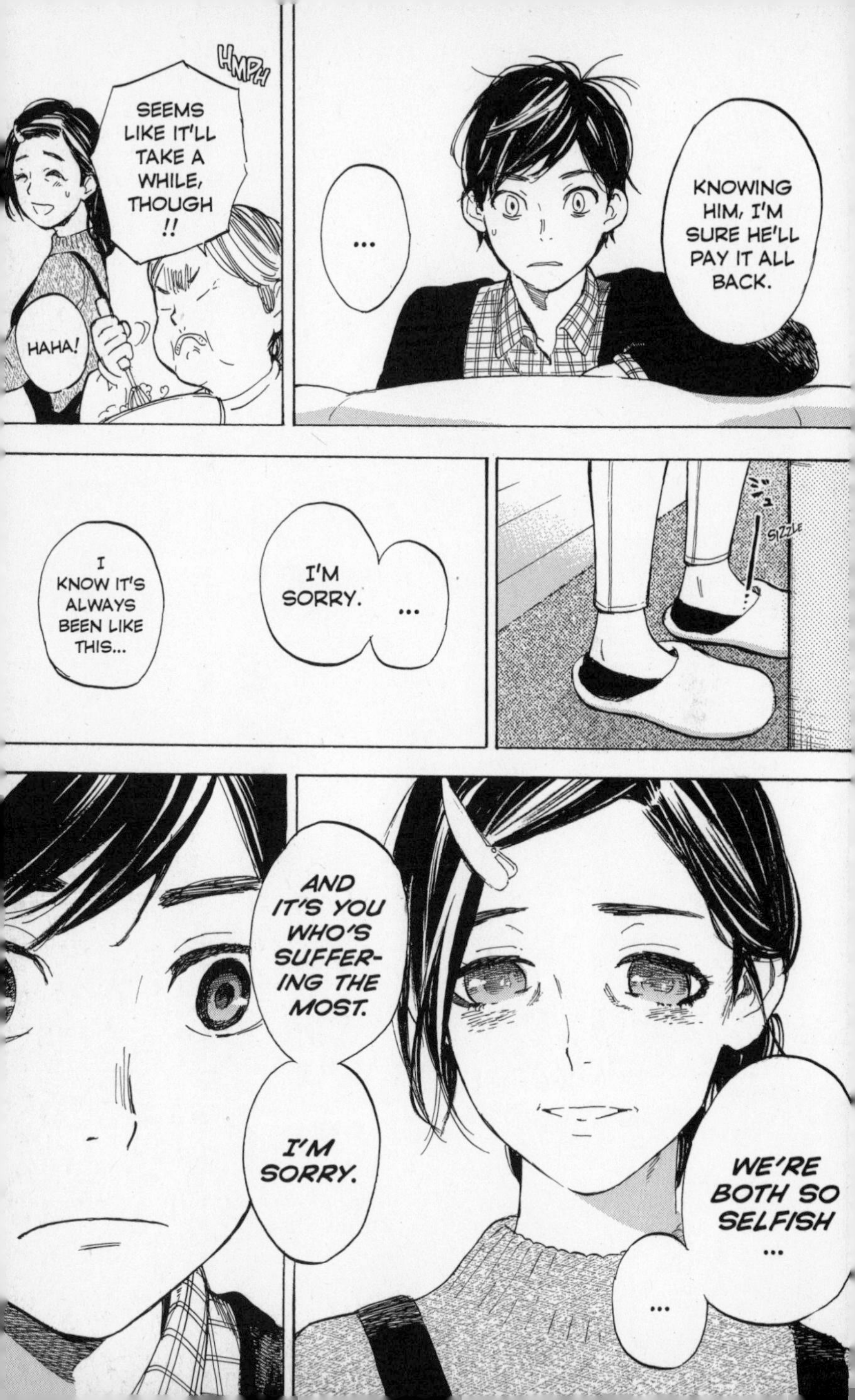
KNOWING HIM, I'M SURE HE'LL PAY IT ALL BACK.
...
HMPH
SEEMS LIKE IT'LL TAKE A WHILE, THOUGH !!
HAHA!
SIZZLE
I'M SORRY.
...
I KNOW IT'S ALWAYS BEEN LIKE THIS...
AND IT'S YOU WHO'S SUFFER-ING THE MOST.
I'M SORRY.
WE'RE BOTH SO SELFISH ...
...

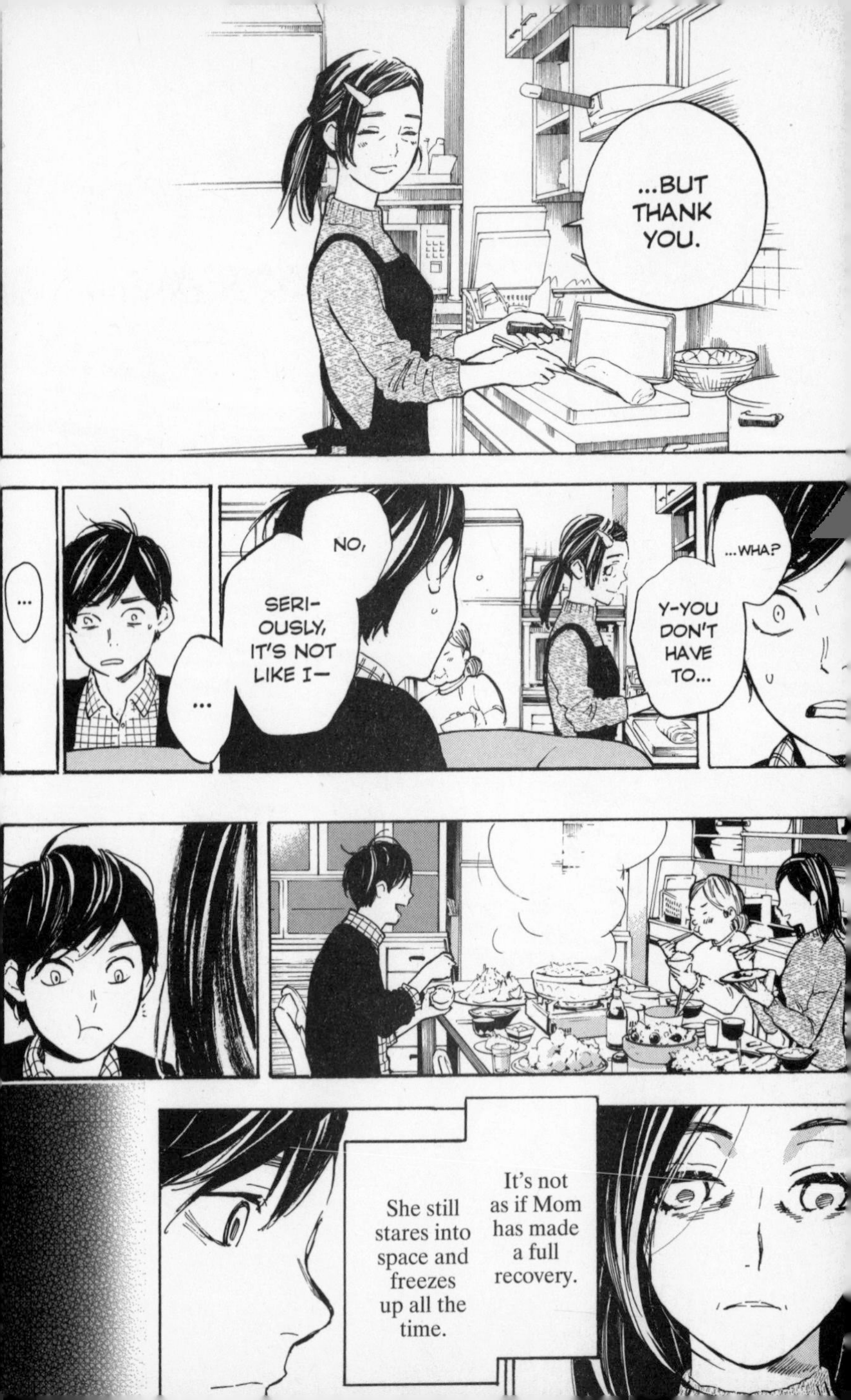
...BUT THANK YOU.
...WHA?
Y-YOU DON'T HAVE TO...
NO,
SERI-OUSLY, IT'S NOT LIKE I—
...
...
It's not as if Mom has made a full recovery.
She still stares into space and freezes up all the time.

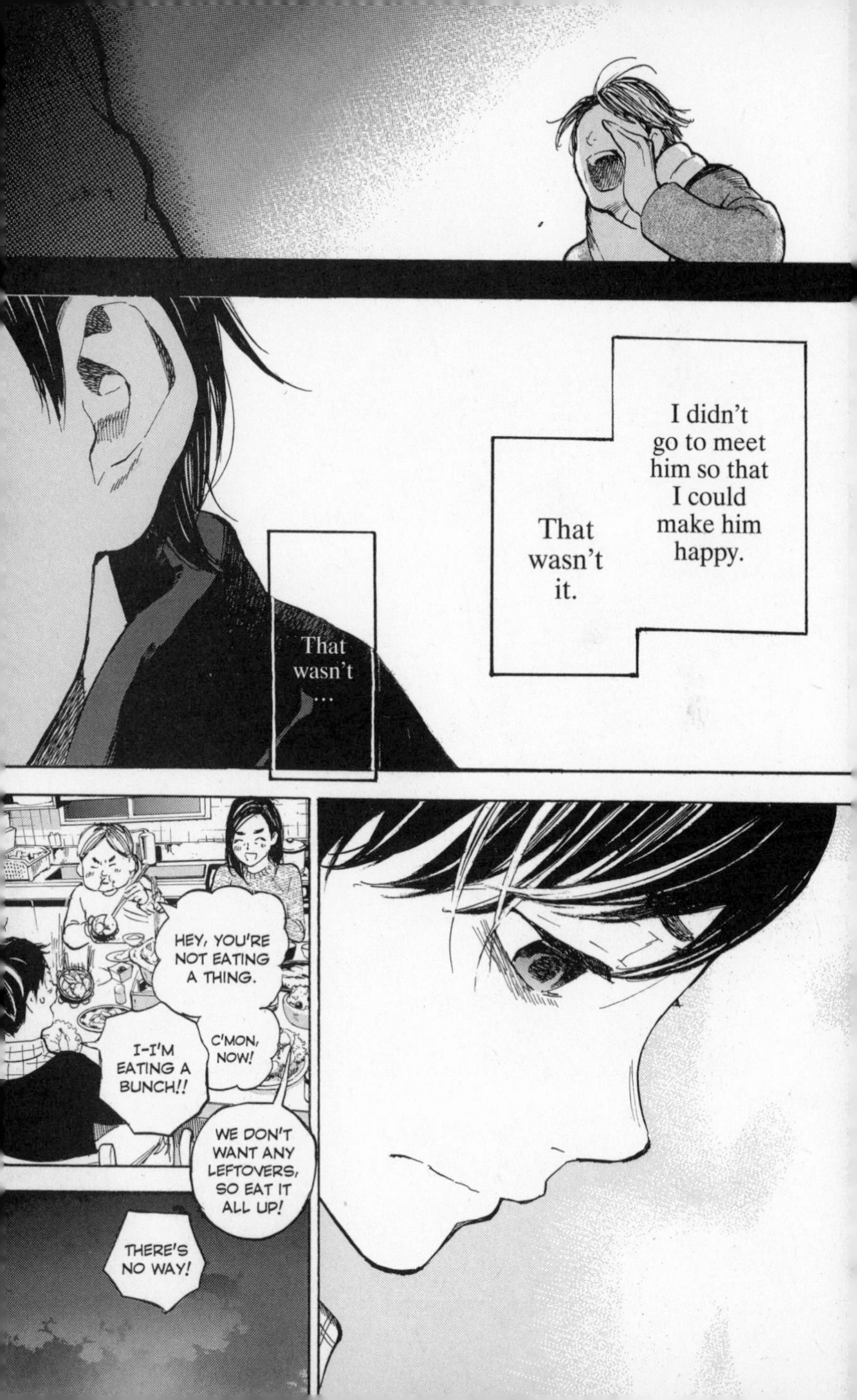
I didn't go to meet him so that I could make him happy.
That wasn't it.
That wasn't …
HEY, YOU'RE NOT EATING A THING.
C'MON, NOW!
I-I'M EATING A BUNCH!!
WE DON'T WANT ANY LEFTOVERS, SO EAT IT ALL UP!
THERE'S NO WAY!

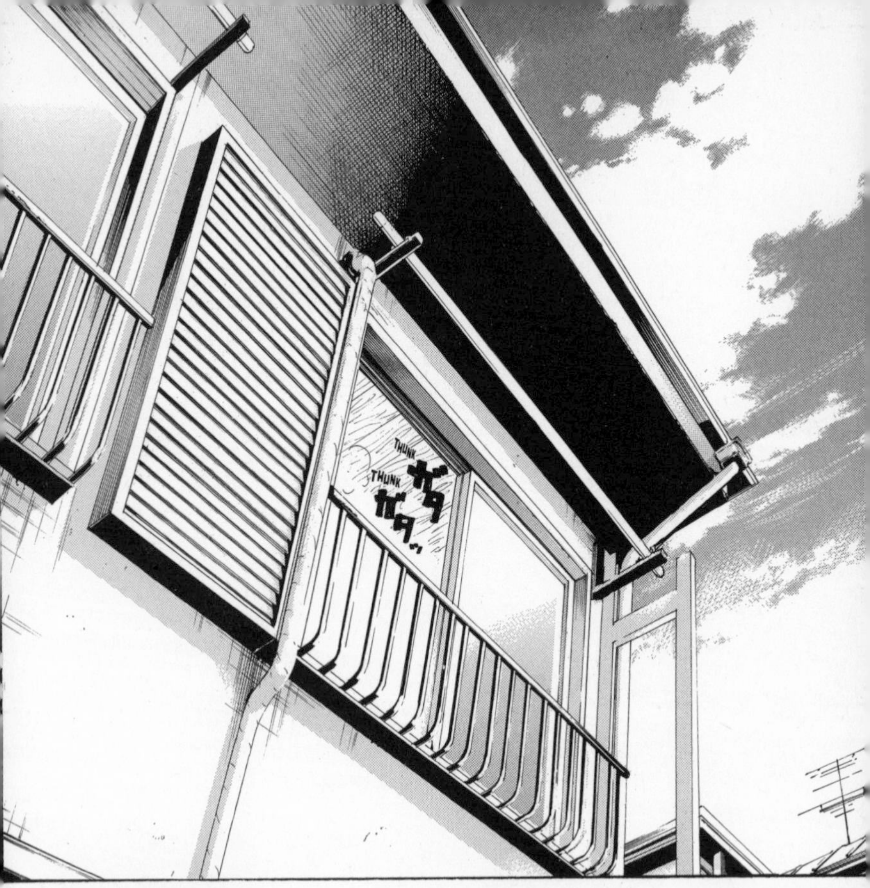
THUNK
ガタ
THUNK
ガタッ

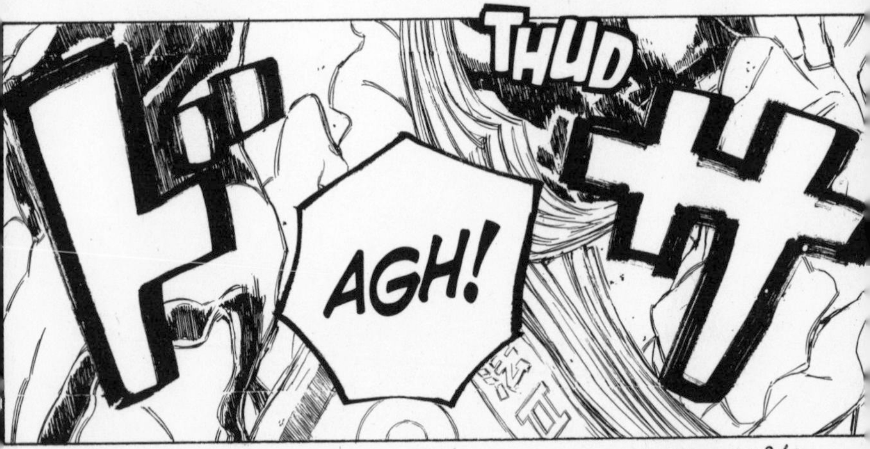
THUD
ドサッ
AGH!

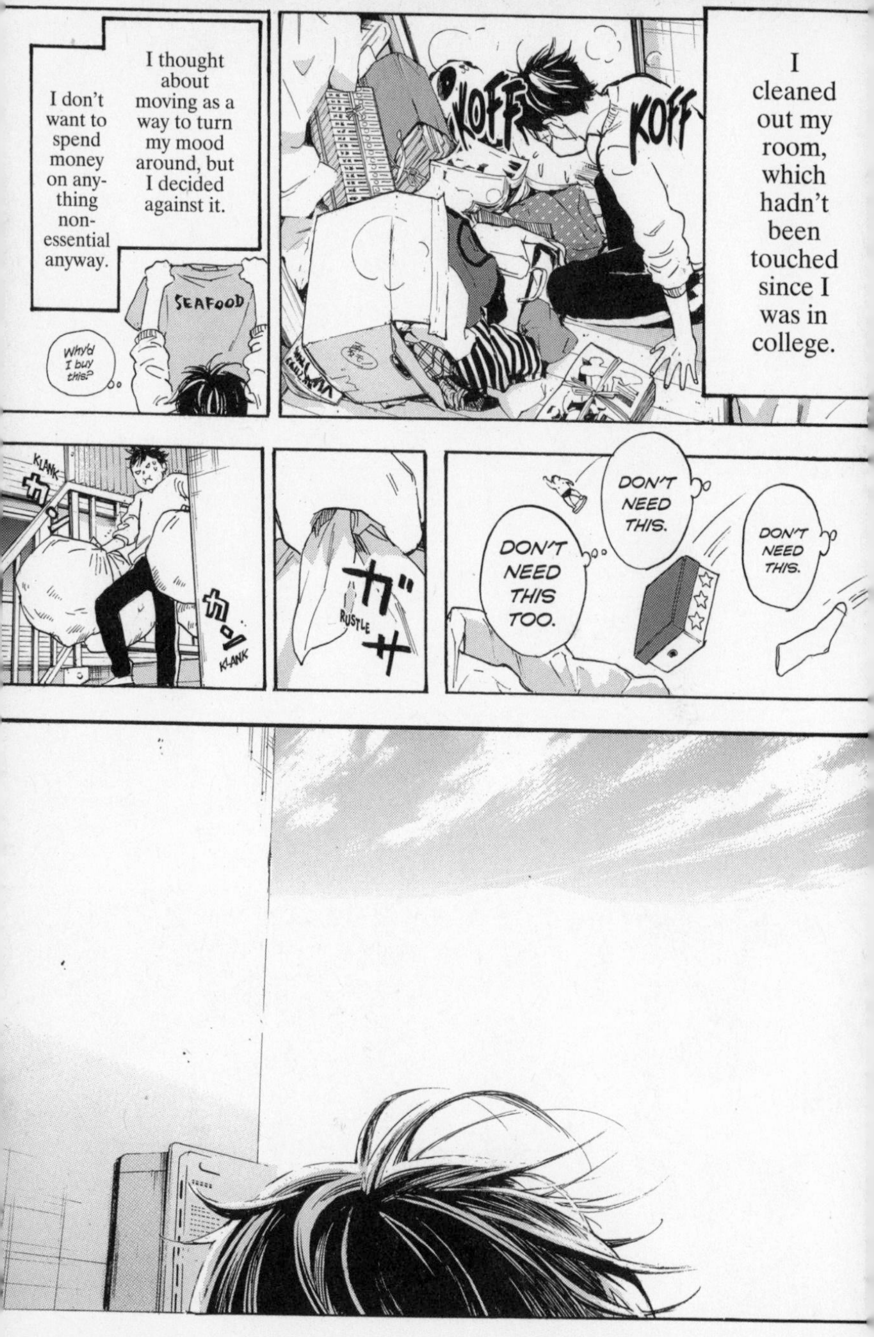
I cleaned out my room, which hadn't been touched since I was in college.
KOFF
KOFF
I thought about moving as a way to turn my mood around, but I decided against it.
I don't want to spend money on anything non-essential anyway.
SEAFOOD
Why'd I buy this?
DON'T NEED THIS.
DON'T NEED THIS.
DON'T NEED THIS TOO.
ガサ
RUSTLE
カン
KLANK
KLANK

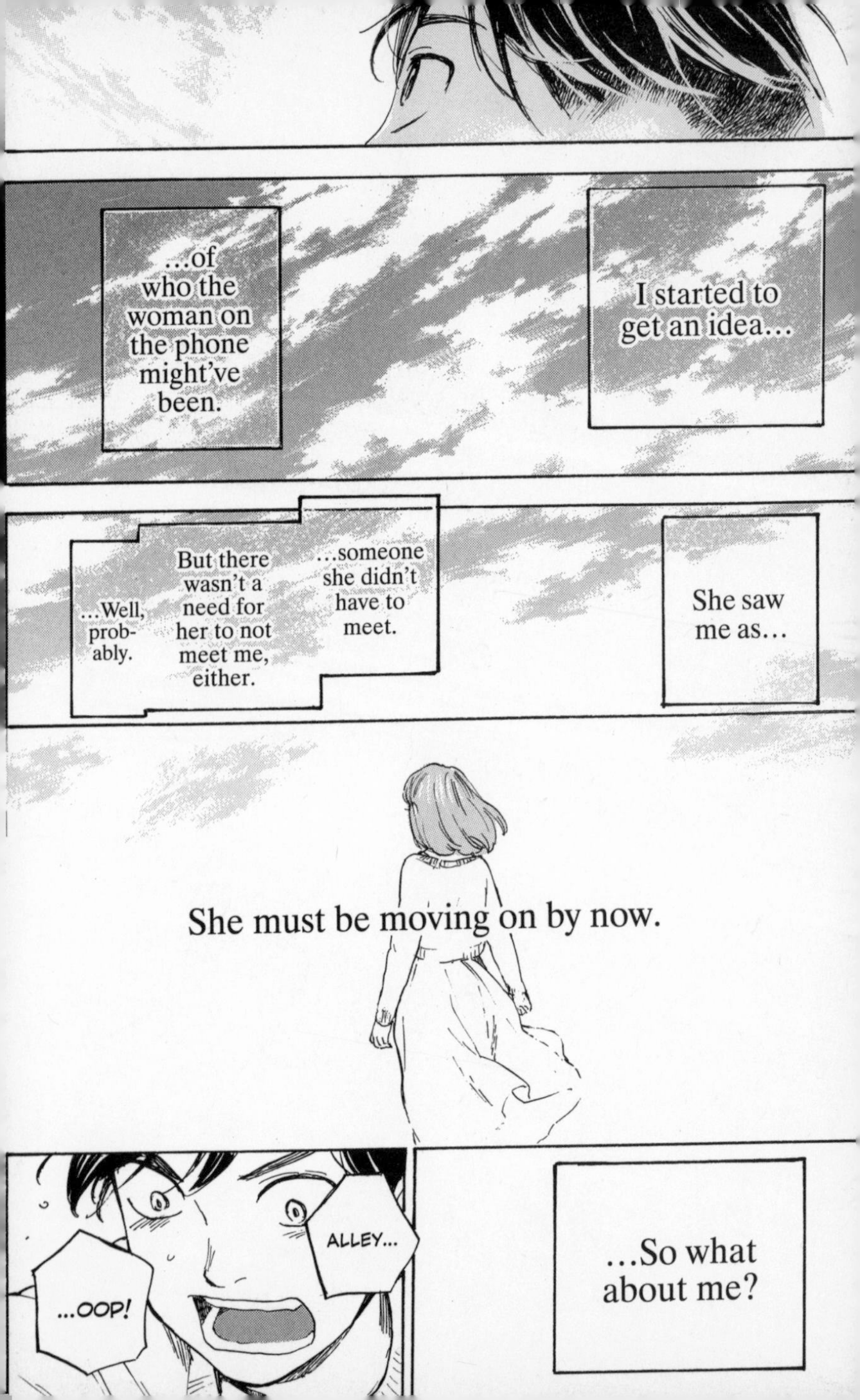
I started to get an idea…
…of who the woman on the phone might've been.
She saw me as…
…someone she didn't have to meet.
But there wasn't a need for her to not meet me, either.
…Well, probably.
She must be moving on by now.
…So what about me?
ALLEY…
…OOP!

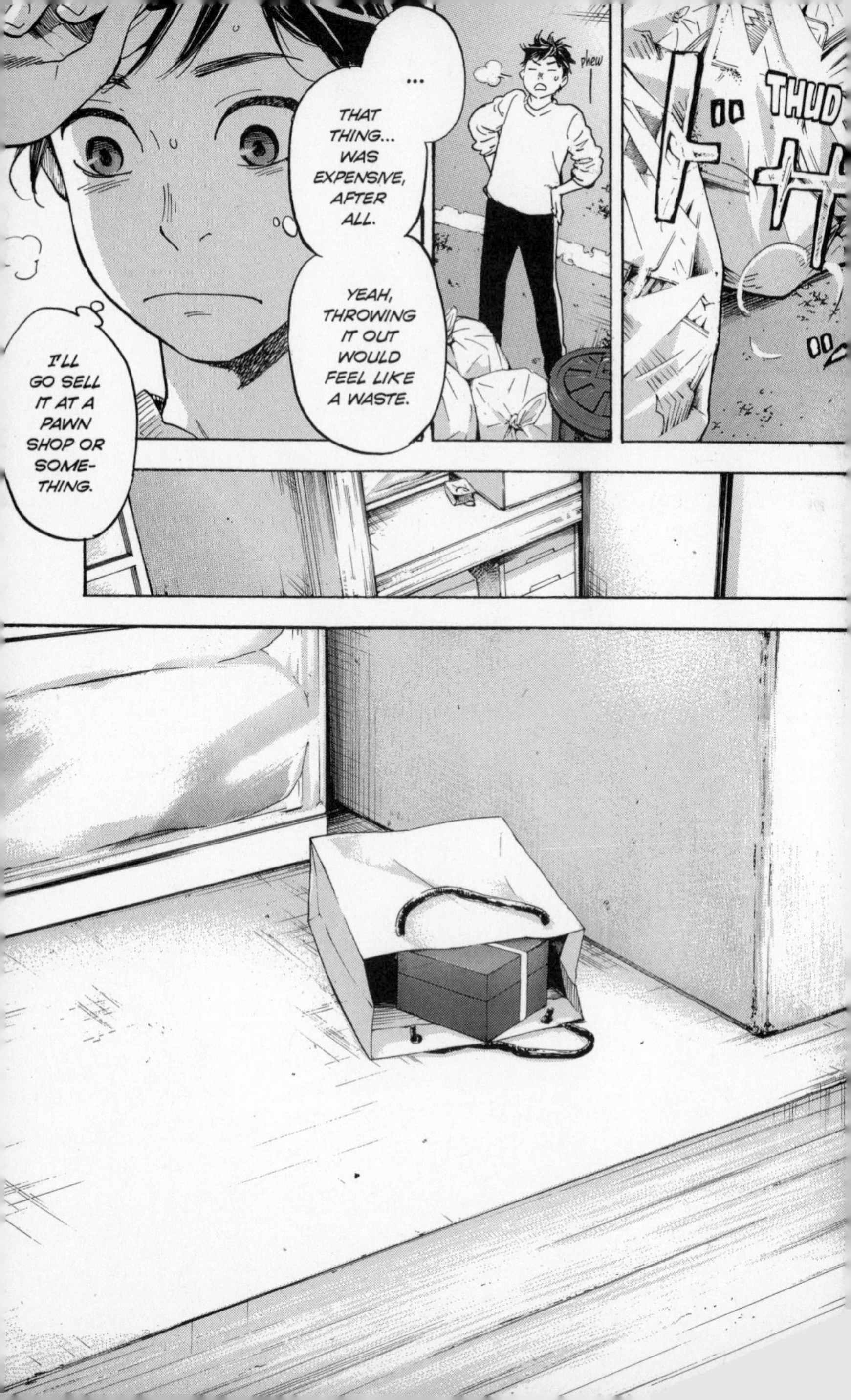
THUD
phew
...
THAT THING... WAS EXPENSIVE, AFTER ALL.
YEAH, THROWING IT OUT WOULD FEEL LIKE A WASTE.
I'LL GO SELL IT AT A PAWN SHOP OR SOME-THING.

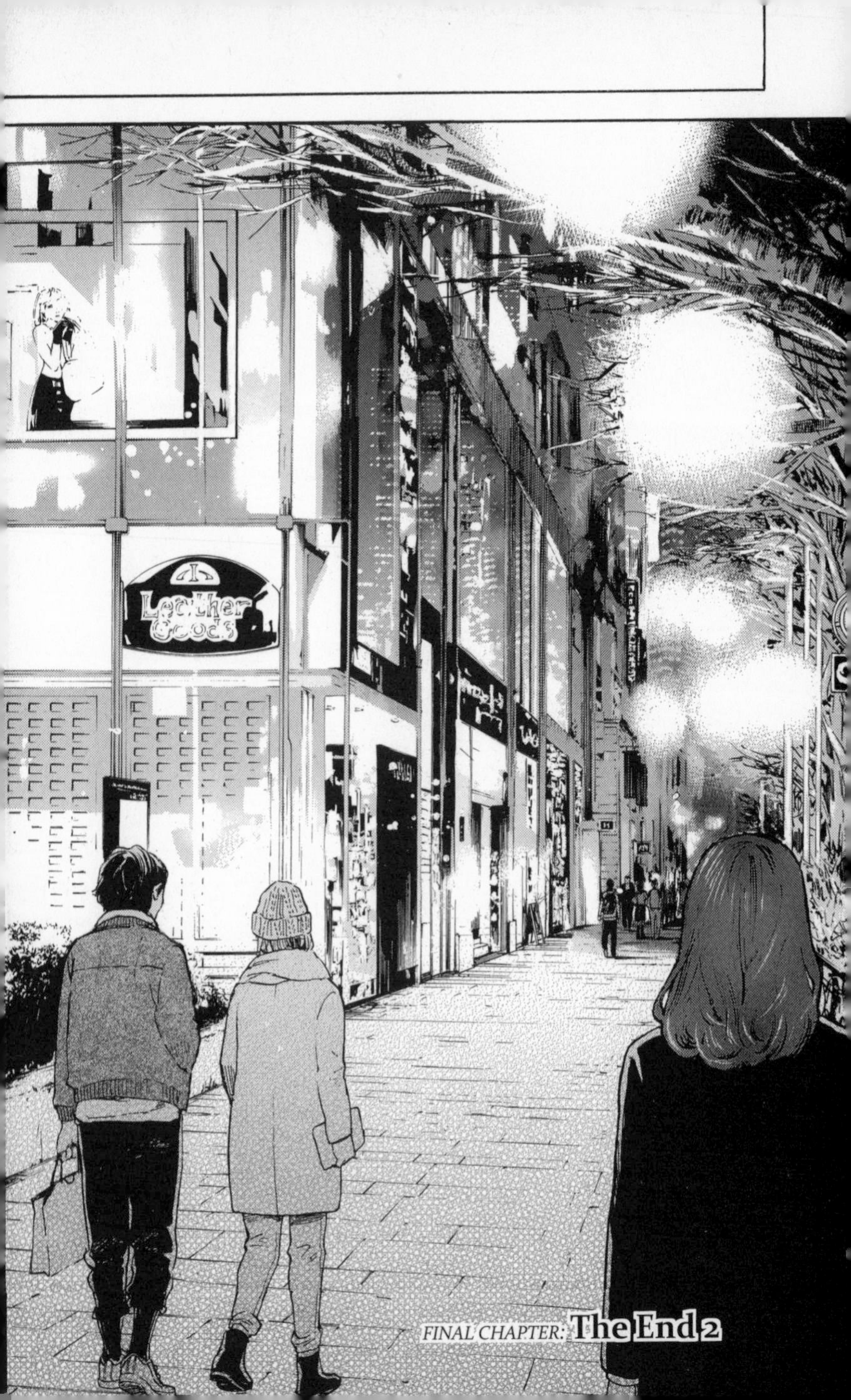
Leather Goods

FINAL CHAPTER: The End 2

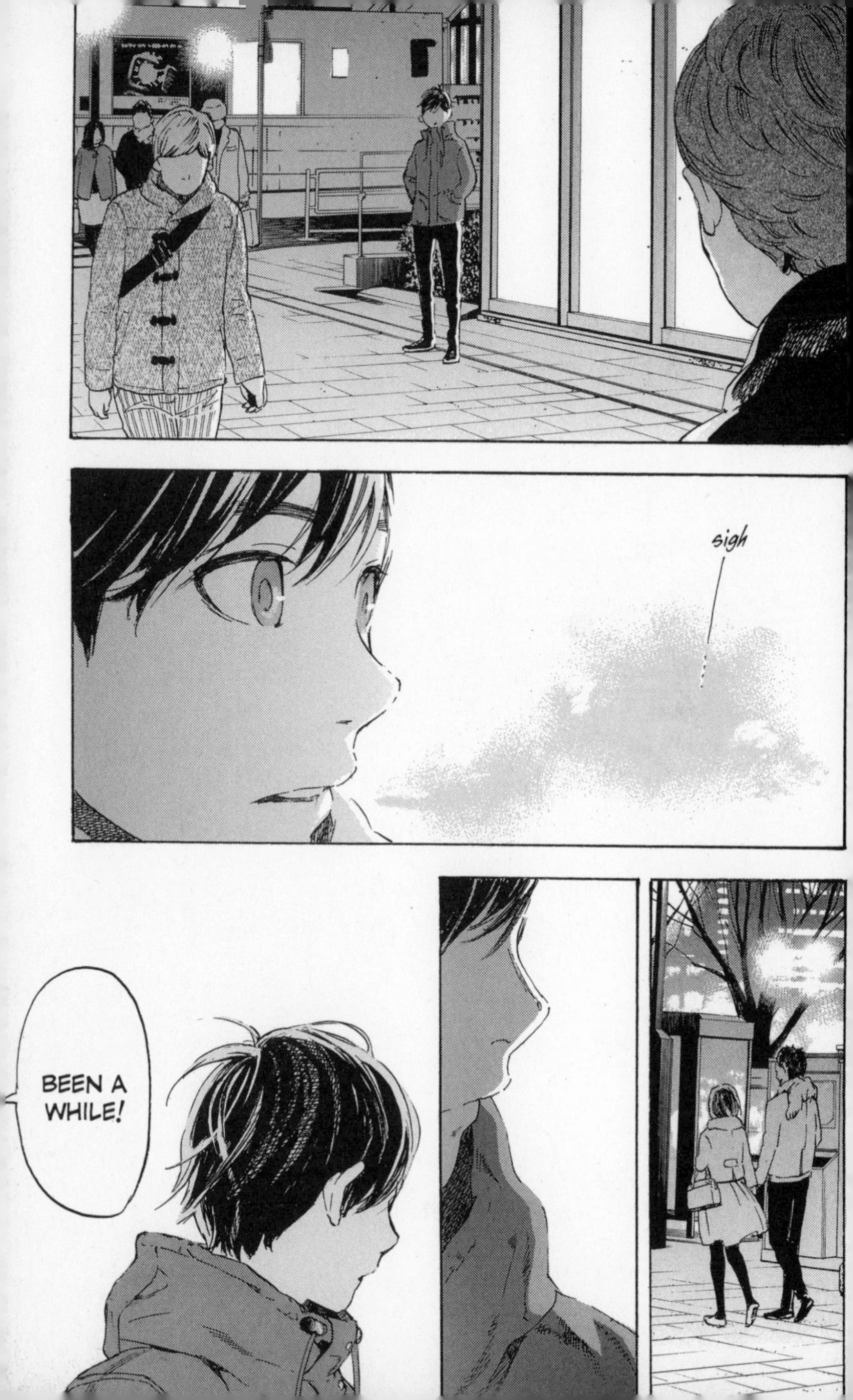
sigh
BEEN A WHILE!

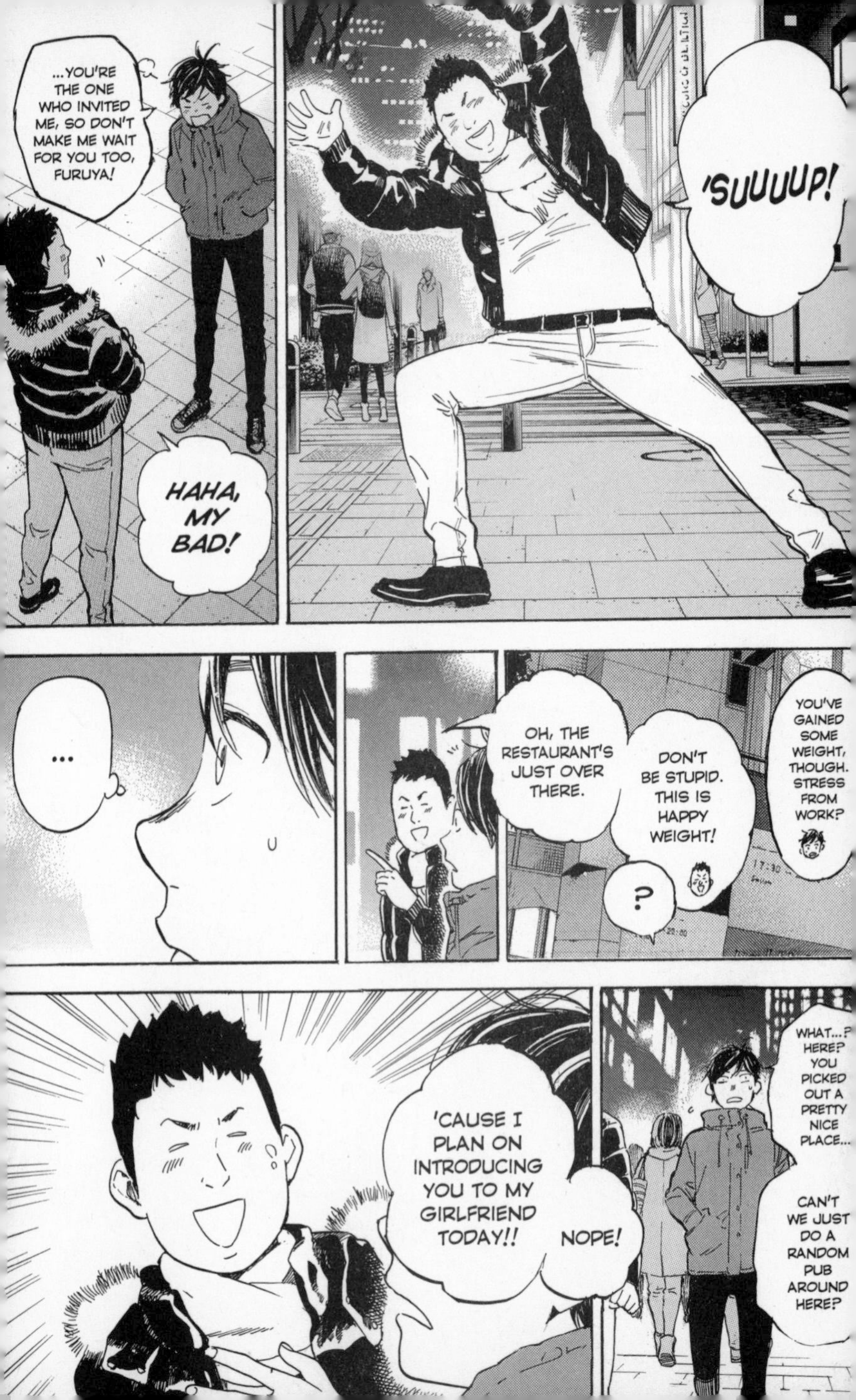
'SUUUUP!
...YOU'RE THE ONE WHO INVITED ME, SO DON'T MAKE ME WAIT FOR YOU TOO, FURUYA!
HAHA, MY BAD!
YOU'VE GAINED SOME WEIGHT, THOUGH. STRESS FROM WORK?
DON'T BE STUPID. THIS IS HAPPY WEIGHT!
?
OH, THE RESTAURANT'S JUST OVER THERE.
...
WHAT...? HERE? YOU PICKED OUT A PRETTY NICE PLACE...
CAN'T WE JUST DO A RANDOM PUB AROUND HERE?
NOPE!
'CAUSE I PLAN ON INTRODUCING YOU TO MY GIRLFRIEND TODAY!!

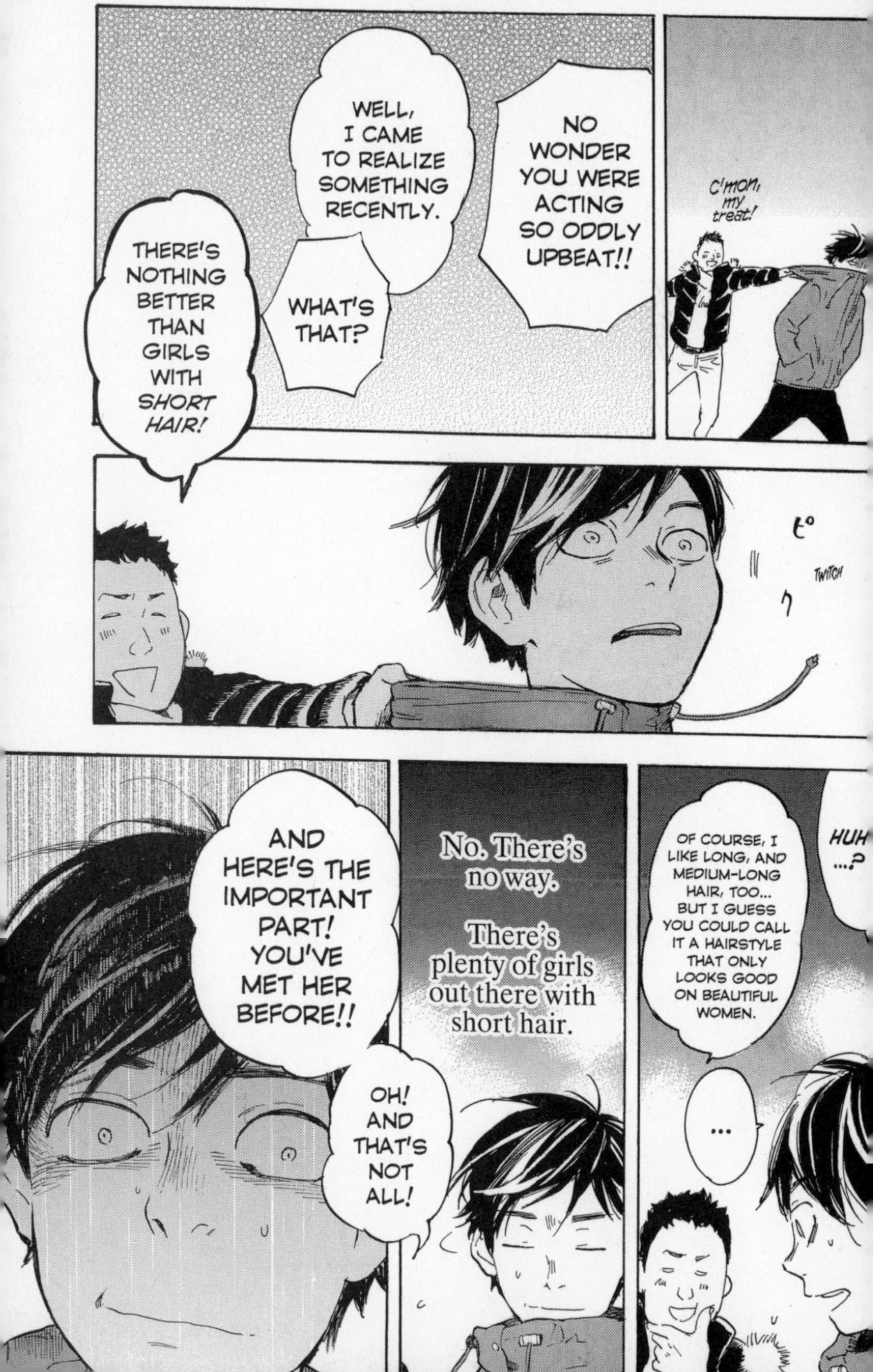
C'mon, my treat!
NO WONDER YOU WERE ACTING SO ODDLY UPBEAT!!
WELL, I CAME TO REALIZE SOMETHING RECENTLY.
WHAT'S THAT?
THERE'S NOTHING BETTER THAN GIRLS WITH *SHORT HAIR!*
TWITCH
HUH ...?
OF COURSE, I LIKE LONG, AND MEDIUM-LONG HAIR, TOO... BUT I GUESS YOU COULD CALL IT A HAIRSTYLE THAT ONLY LOOKS GOOD ON BEAUTIFUL WOMEN.
...
No. There's no way.
There's plenty of girls out there with short hair.
OH! AND THAT'S NOT ALL!
AND HERE'S THE IMPORTANT PART! YOU'VE MET HER BEFORE!!

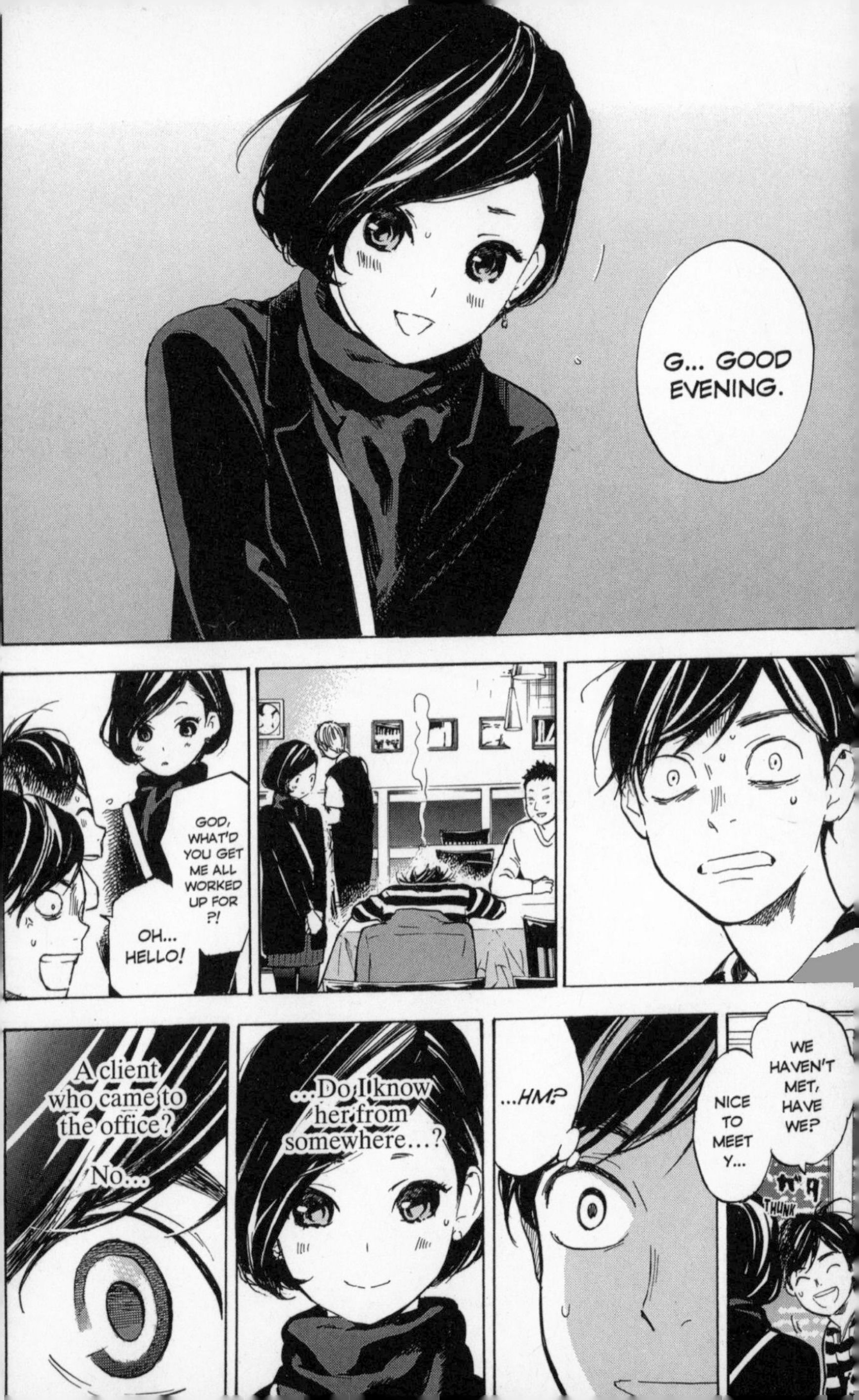
G... GOOD EVENING.
GOD, WHAT'D YOU GET ME ALL WORKED UP FOR ?!
OH... HELLO!
WE HAVEN'T MET, HAVE WE?
NICE TO MEET Y...
ガタ
THUNK
...HM?
...Do I know her from somewhere...?
A client who came to the office?
No...

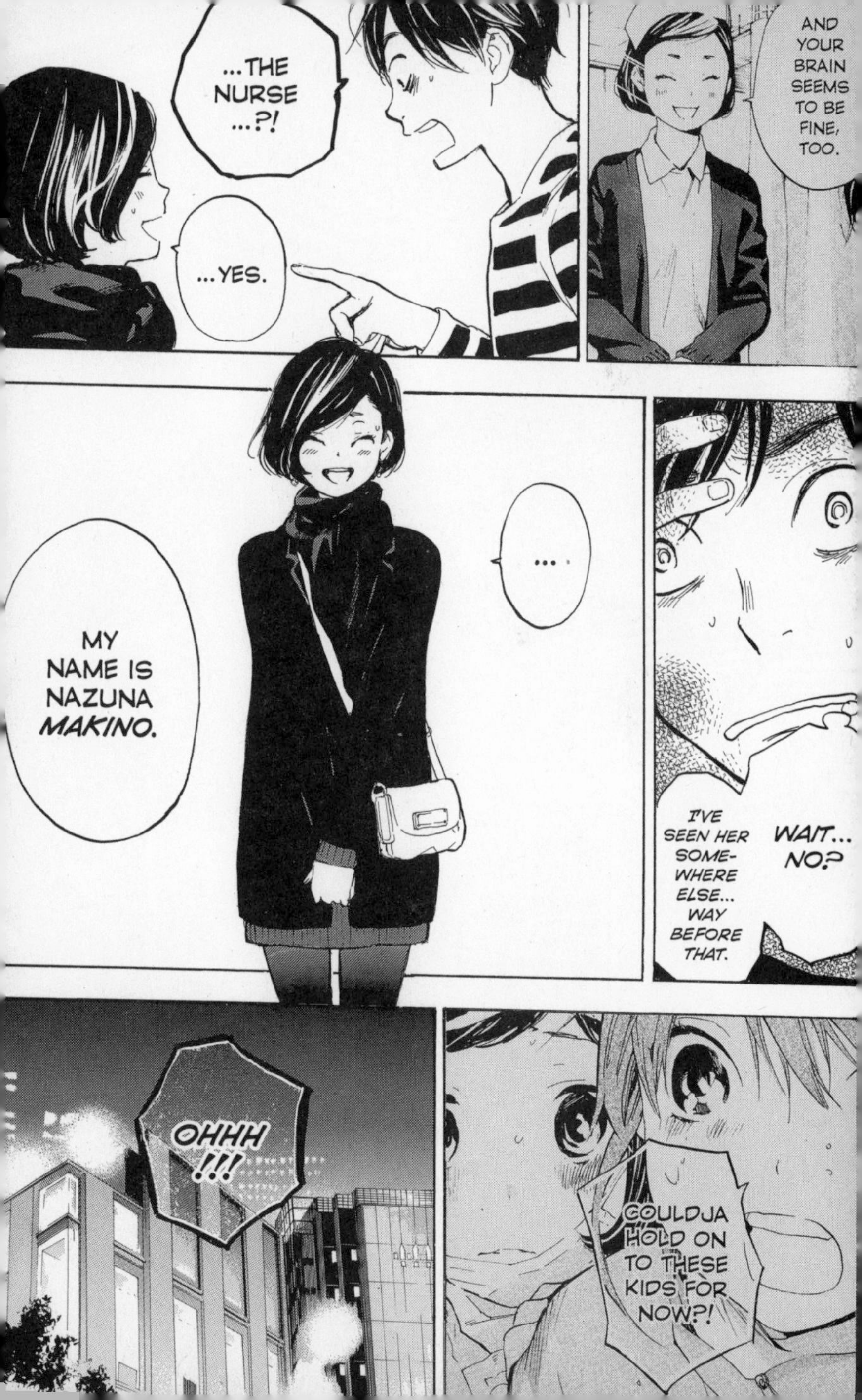
AND YOUR BRAIN SEEMS TO BE FINE, TOO.
...THE NURSE ...?!
...YES.
WAIT... NO?
I'VE SEEN HER SOMEWHERE ELSE... WAY BEFORE THAT.
...
MY NAME IS NAZUNA *MAKINO.*
COULDJA HOLD ON TO THESE KIDS FOR NOW?!
OHHH !!!

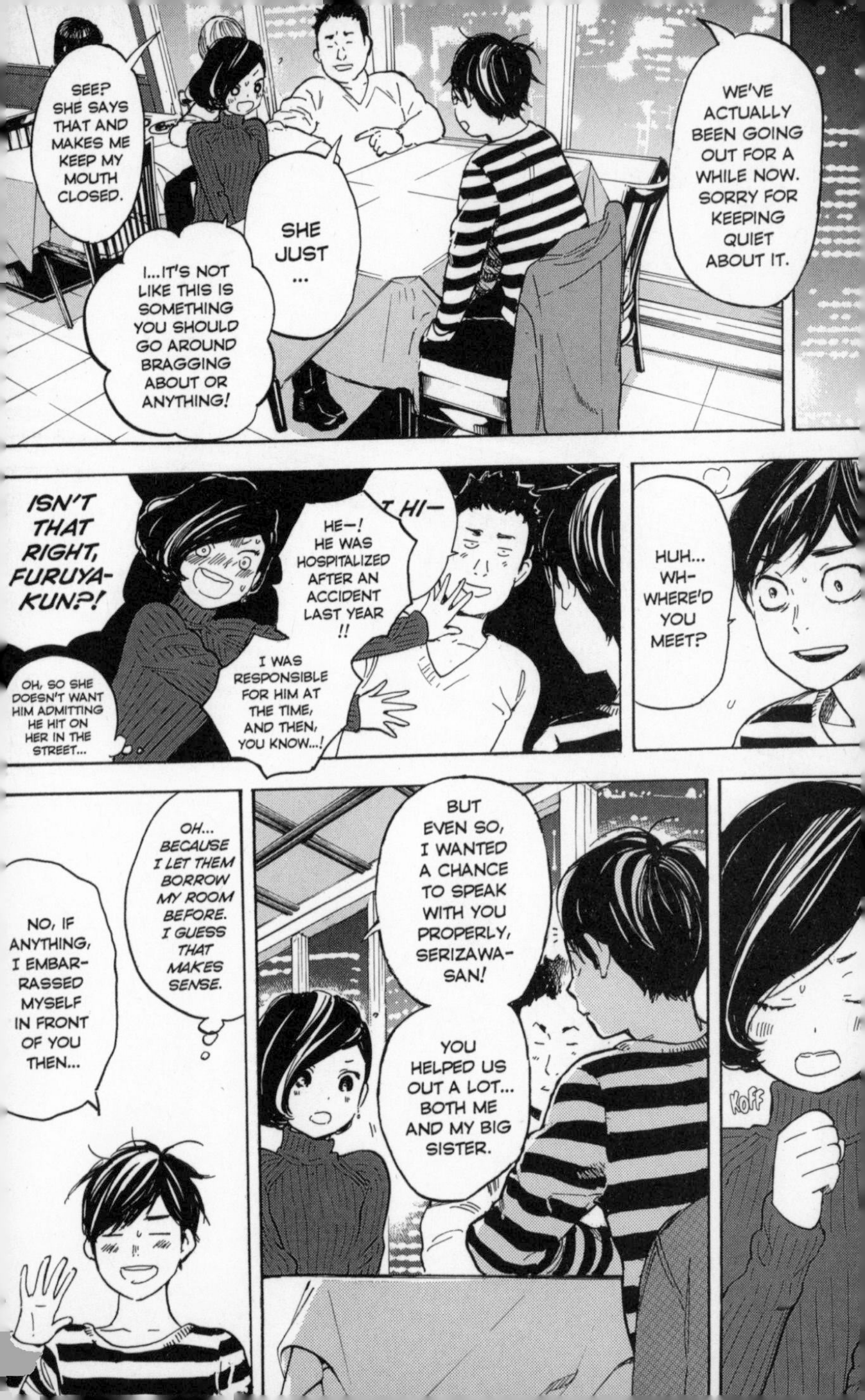
WE'VE ACTUALLY BEEN GOING OUT FOR A WHILE NOW. SORRY FOR KEEPING QUIET ABOUT IT.
SEE? SHE SAYS THAT AND MAKES ME KEEP MY MOUTH CLOSED.
SHE JUST ...
I...IT'S NOT LIKE THIS IS SOMETHING YOU SHOULD GO AROUND BRAGGING ABOUT OR ANYTHING!
HUH... WH- WHERE'D YOU MEET?
T HI—
HE—! HE WAS HOSPITALIZED AFTER AN ACCIDENT LAST YEAR !!
ISN'T THAT RIGHT, FURUYA-KUN?!
I WAS RESPONSIBLE FOR HIM AT THE TIME, AND THEN, YOU KNOW...!
OH, SO SHE DOESN'T WANT HIM ADMITTING HE HIT ON HER IN THE STREET...
KOFF
BUT EVEN SO, I WANTED A CHANCE TO SPEAK WITH YOU PROPERLY, SERIZAWA-SAN!
YOU HELPED US OUT A LOT... BOTH ME AND MY BIG SISTER.
OH... BECAUSE I LET THEM BORROW MY ROOM BEFORE. I GUESS THAT MAKES SENSE.
NO, IF ANYTHING, I EMBARRASSED MYSELF IN FRONT OF YOU THEN...

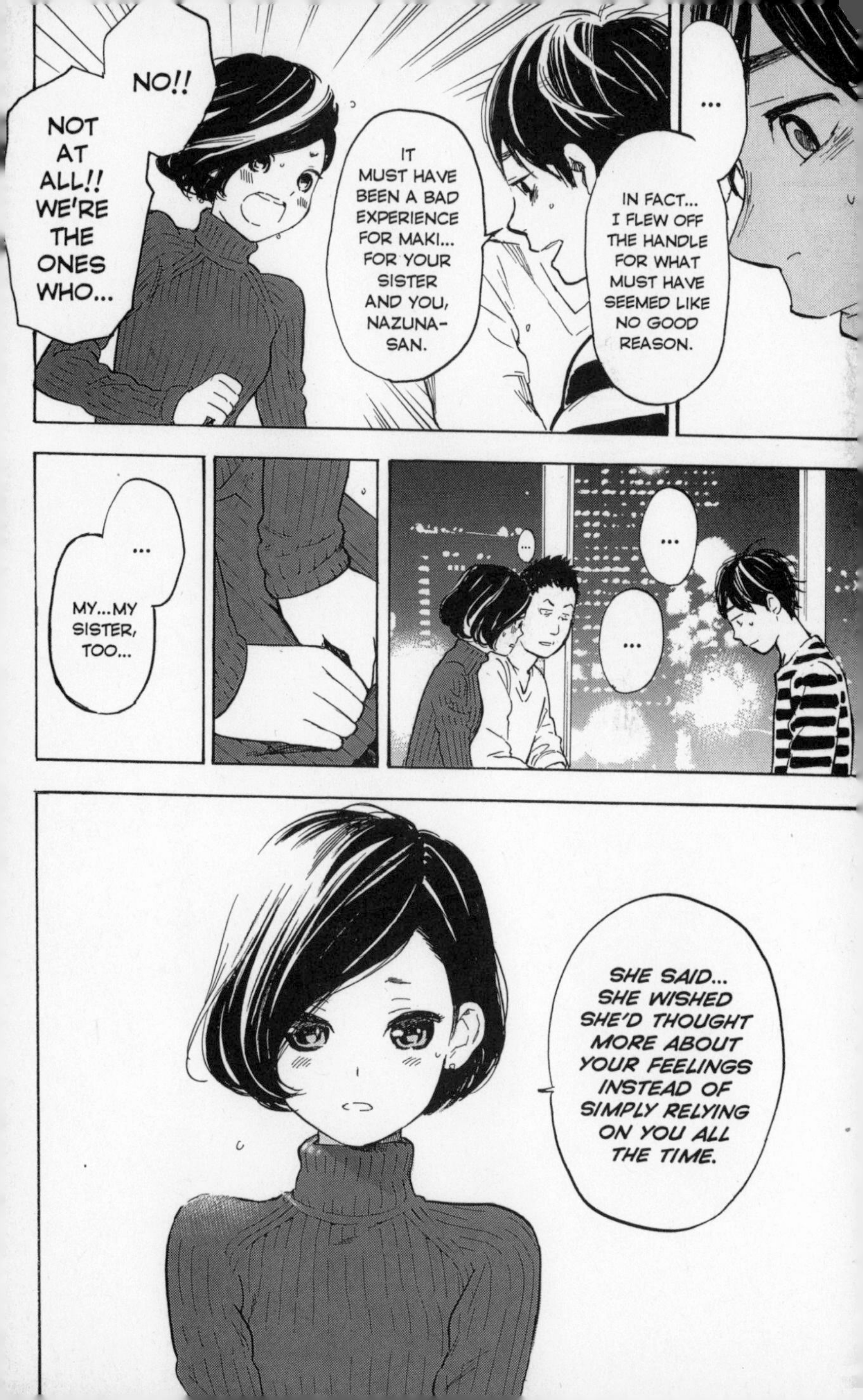
...
IN FACT... I FLEW OFF THE HANDLE FOR WHAT MUST HAVE SEEMED LIKE NO GOOD REASON.
IT MUST HAVE BEEN A BAD EXPERIENCE FOR MAKI... FOR YOUR SISTER AND YOU, NAZUNA-SAN.
NO!!
NOT AT ALL!! WE'RE THE ONES WHO...
...
...
...
...
MY...MY SISTER, TOO...
SHE SAID... SHE WISHED SHE'D THOUGHT MORE ABOUT YOUR FEELINGS INSTEAD OF SIMPLY RELYING ON YOU ALL THE TIME.

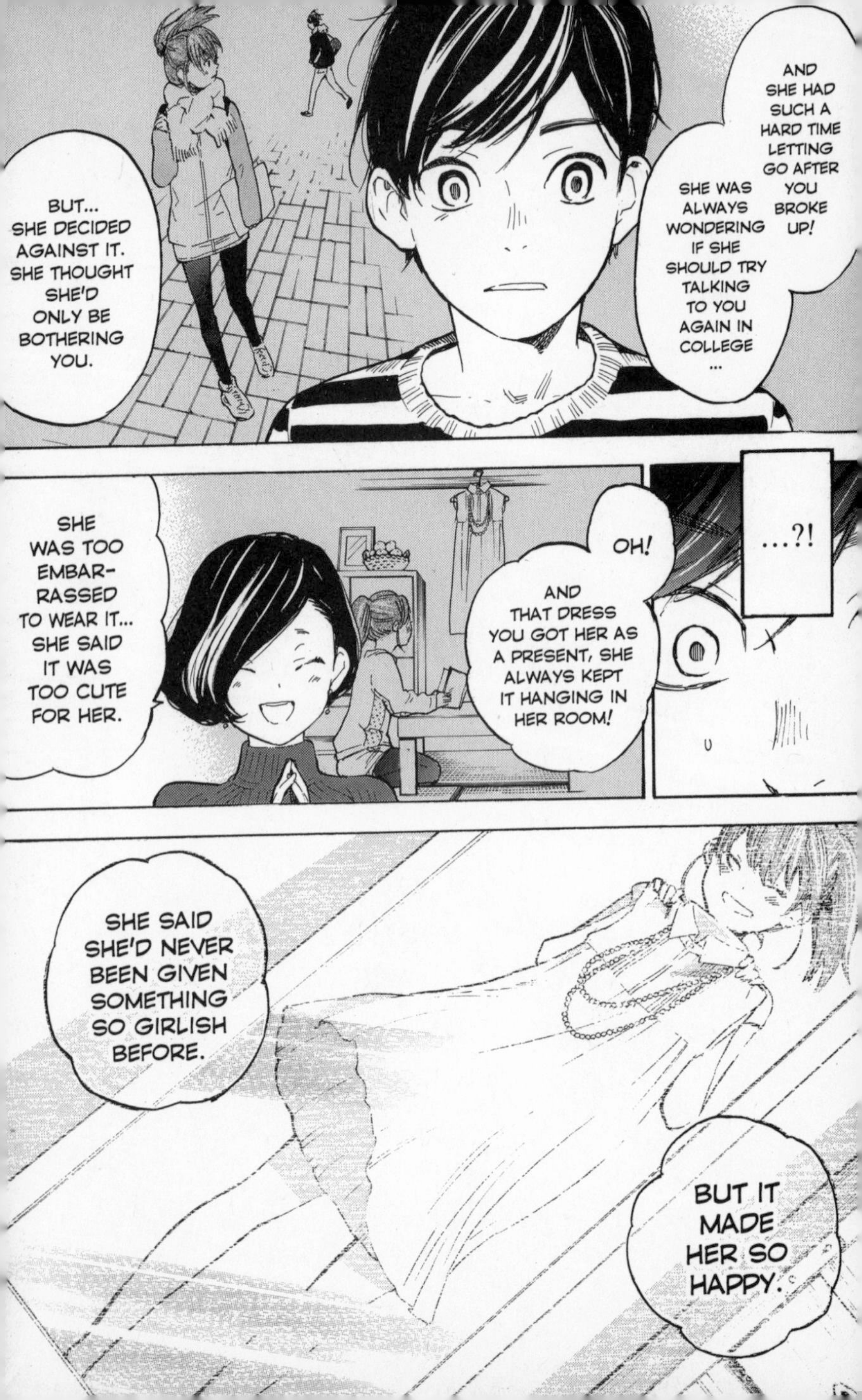

AND SHE HAD SUCH A HARD TIME LETTING GO AFTER YOU BROKE UP!
SHE WAS ALWAYS WONDERING IF SHE SHOULD TRY TALKING TO YOU AGAIN IN COLLEGE ...
BUT... SHE DECIDED AGAINST IT. SHE THOUGHT SHE'D ONLY BE BOTHERING YOU.
...?!
OH!
AND THAT DRESS YOU GOT HER AS A PRESENT, SHE ALWAYS KEPT IT HANGING IN HER ROOM!
SHE WAS TOO EMBAR-RASSED TO WEAR IT... SHE SAID IT WAS TOO CUTE FOR HER.
SHE SAID SHE'D NEVER BEEN GIVEN SOMETHING SO GIRLISH BEFORE.
BUT IT MADE HER SO HAPPY.

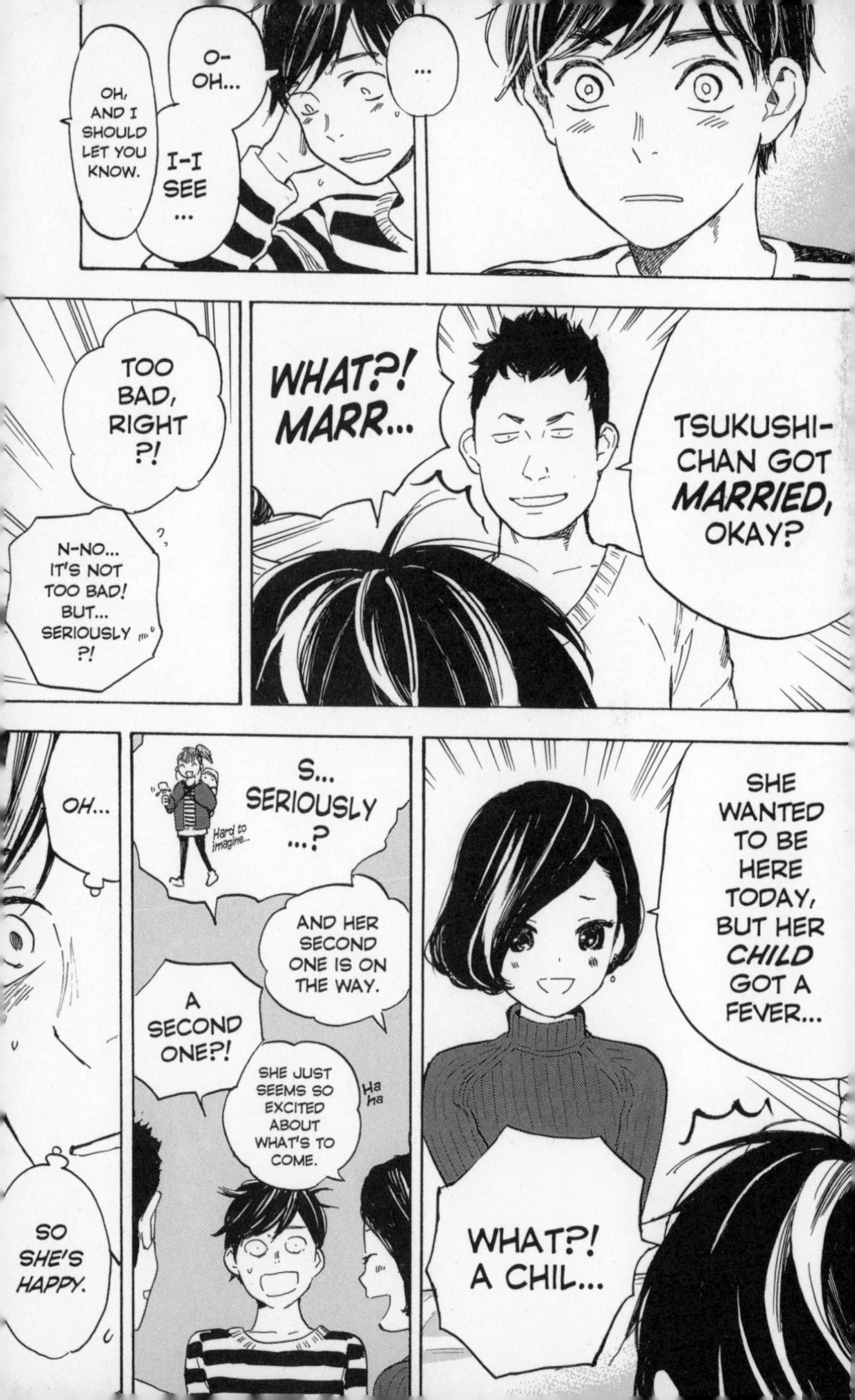
...
O-OH...
I-I SEE...
OH, AND I SHOULD LET YOU KNOW.
TSUKUSHI-CHAN GOT *MARRIED*, OKAY?
WHAT?! MARR...
TOO BAD, RIGHT?!
N-NO... IT'S NOT TOO BAD! BUT... SERIOUSLY?!
SHE WANTED TO BE HERE TODAY, BUT HER *CHILD* GOT A FEVER...
WHAT?! A CHIL...
S... SERIOUSLY...?
Hard to imagine...
AND HER SECOND ONE IS ON THE WAY.
A SECOND ONE?!
SHE JUST SEEMS SO EXCITED ABOUT WHAT'S TO COME.
Ha ha
OH...
SO SHE'S HAPPY.

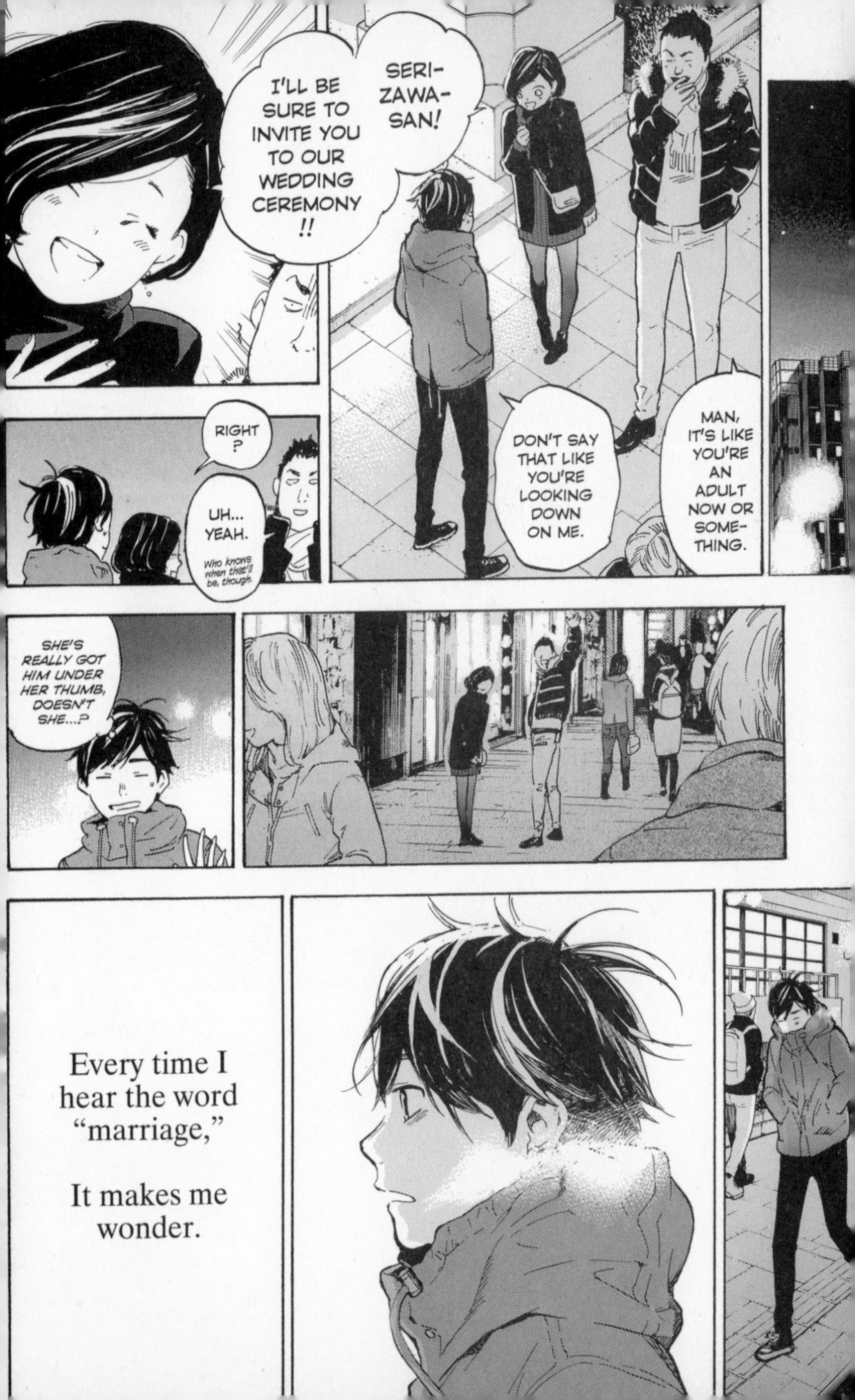
MAN, IT'S LIKE YOU'RE AN ADULT NOW OR SOME-THING.
DON'T SAY THAT LIKE YOU'RE LOOKING DOWN ON ME.
SERI-ZAWA-SAN!
I'LL BE SURE TO INVITE YOU TO OUR WEDDING CEREMONY !!
RIGHT ?
UH... YEAH.
Who knows when that'll be, though.
SHE'S REALLY GOT HIM UNDER HER THUMB, DOESN'T SHE...?
Every time I hear the word "marriage,"
It makes me wonder.

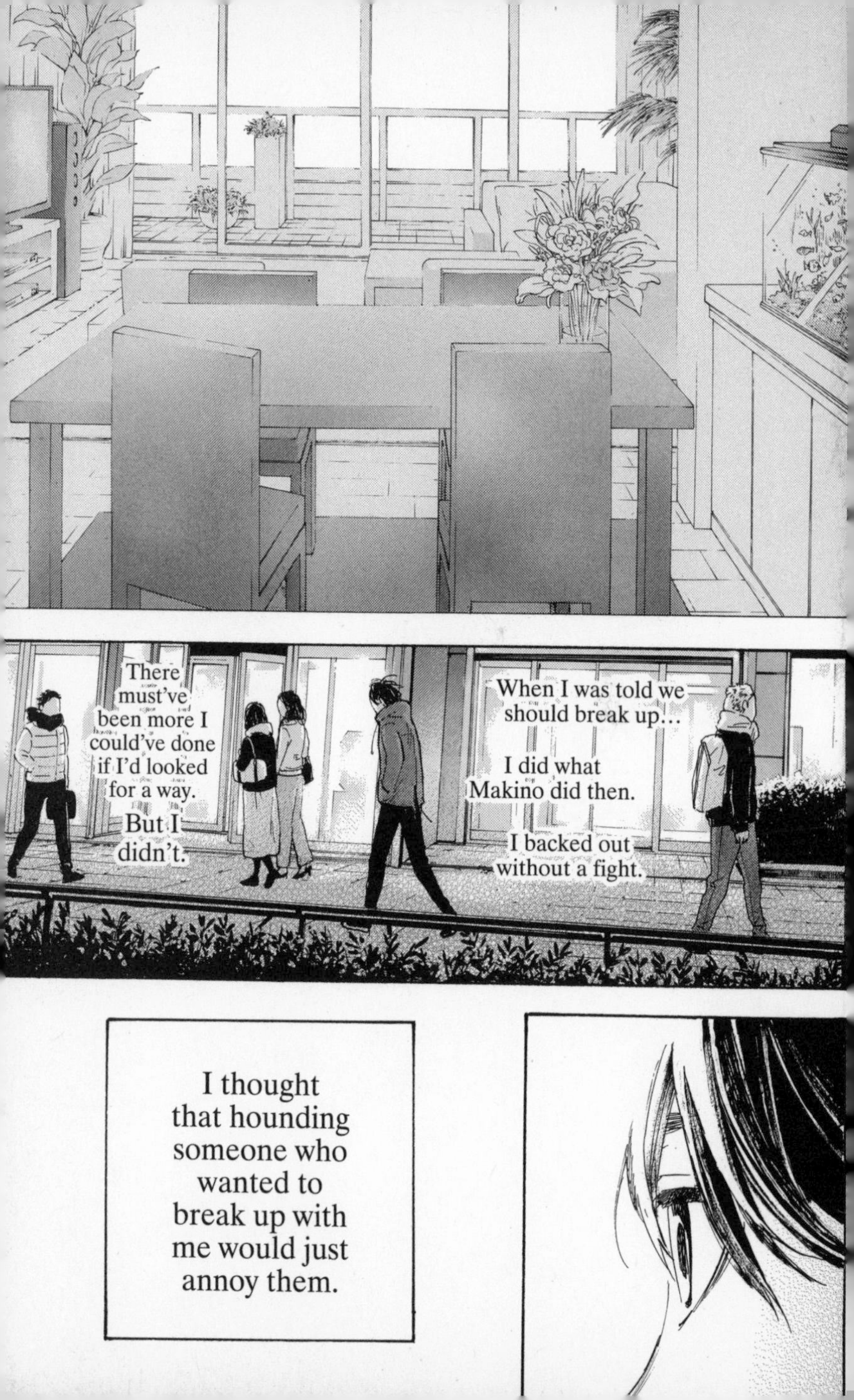
When I was told we should break up…
I did what Makino did then.
I backed out without a fight.
There must've been more I could've done if I'd looked for a way.
But I didn't.
I thought that hounding someone who wanted to break up with me would just annoy them.

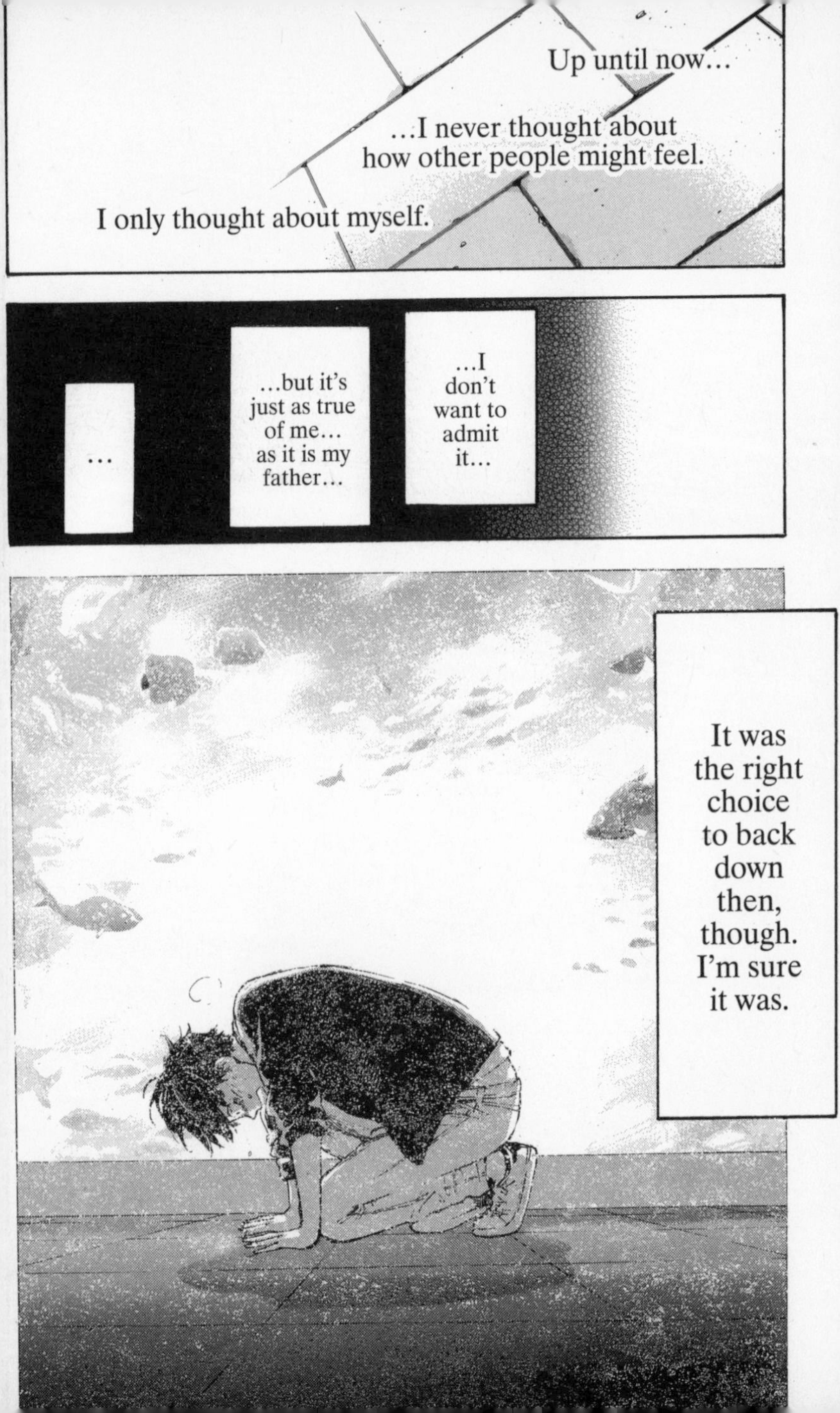
Up until now...
...I never thought about how other people might feel.
I only thought about myself.
...I don't want to admit it...
...but it's just as true of me... as it is my father...
...
It was the right choice to back down then, though. I'm sure it was.

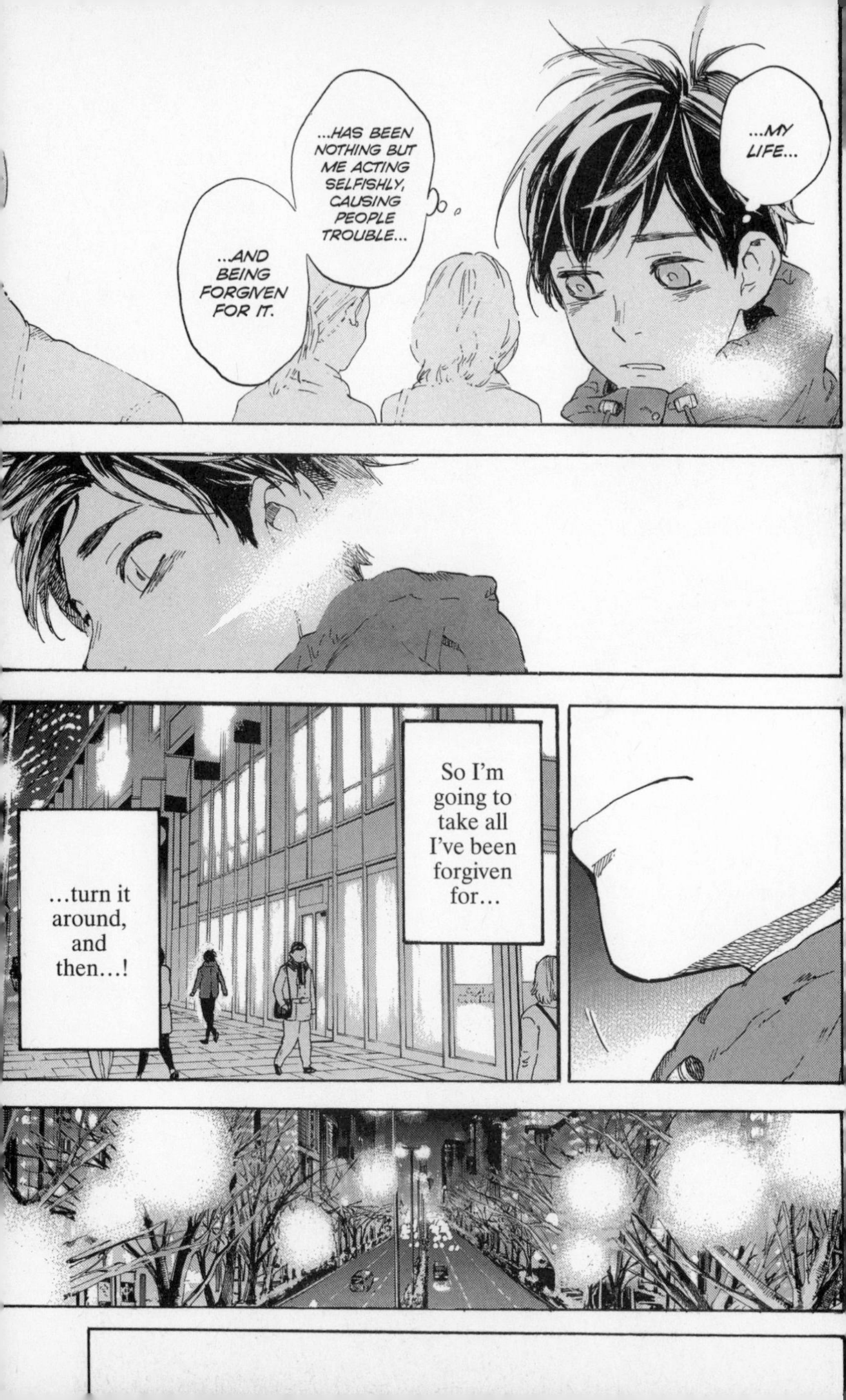
...MY LIFE...
...HAS BEEN NOTHING BUT ME ACTING SELFISHLY, CAUSING PEOPLE TROUBLE...
...AND BEING FORGIVEN FOR IT.
So I'm going to take all I've been forgiven for...
...turn it around, and then...!

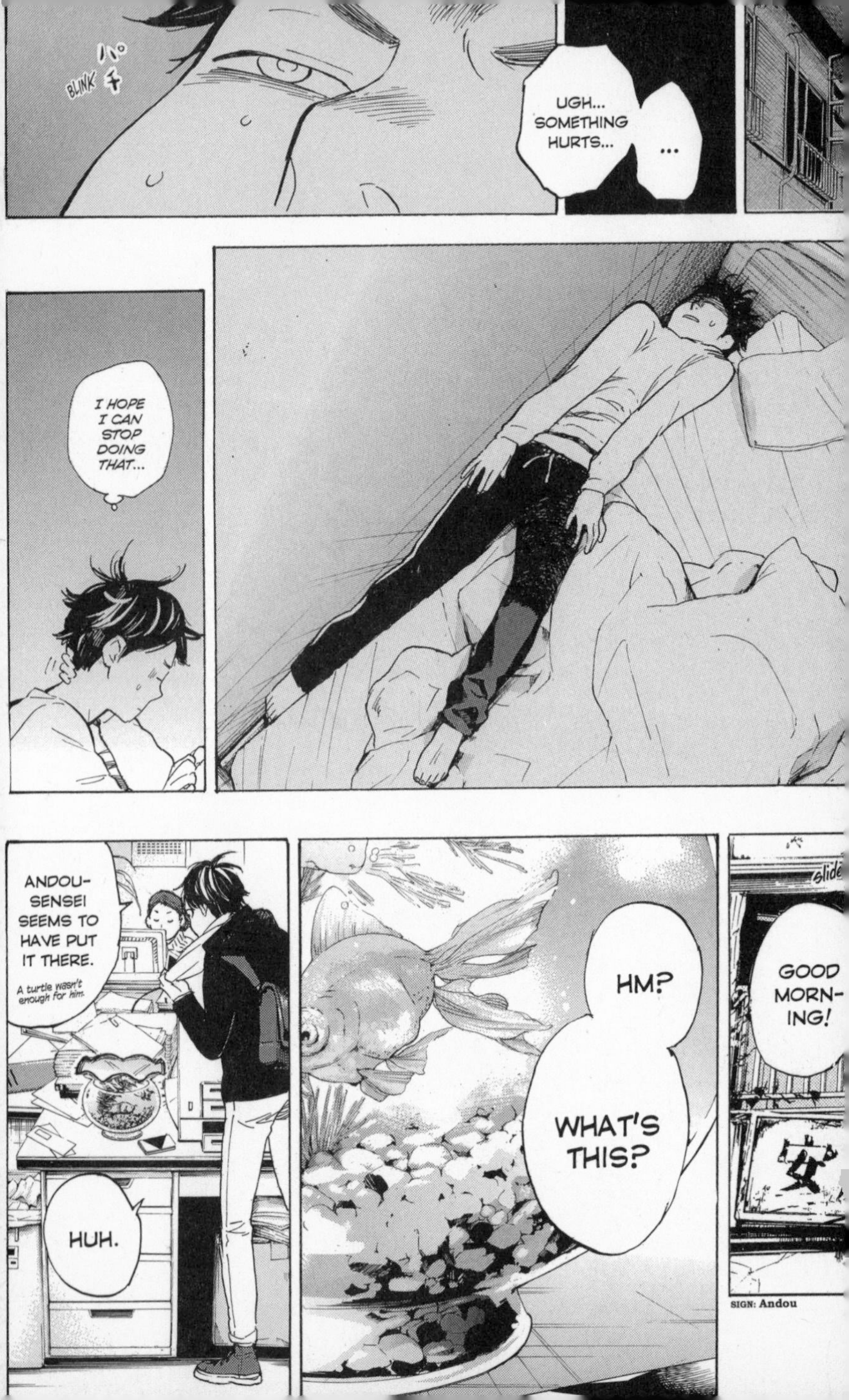
UGH... SOMETHING HURTS...
...
BLINK パチ
I HOPE I CAN STOP DOING THAT...
GOOD MORNING!
HM?
WHAT'S THIS?
ANDOU-SENSEI SEEMS TO HAVE PUT IT THERE.
A turtle wasn't enough for him.
HUH.

SIGN: Andou

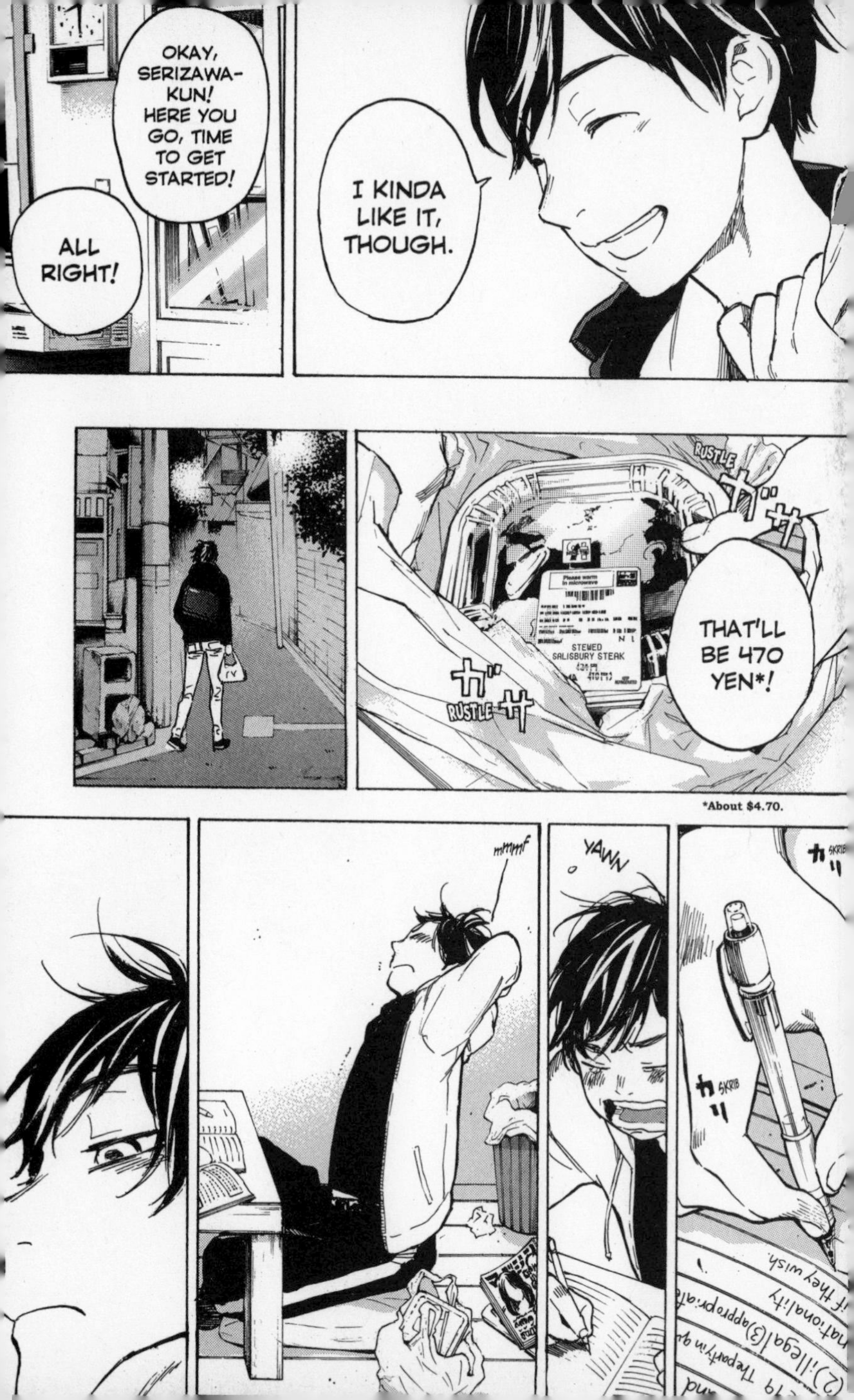
I KINDA LIKE IT, THOUGH.
OKAY, SERIZAWA-KUN! HERE YOU GO, TIME TO GET STARTED!
ALL RIGHT!
RUSTLE
THAT'LL BE 470 YEN*!
Please warm in microwave
STEWED SALISBURY STEAK
RUSTLE
SKRIB
SKRIB
YAWN
mmmf
*About $4.70.

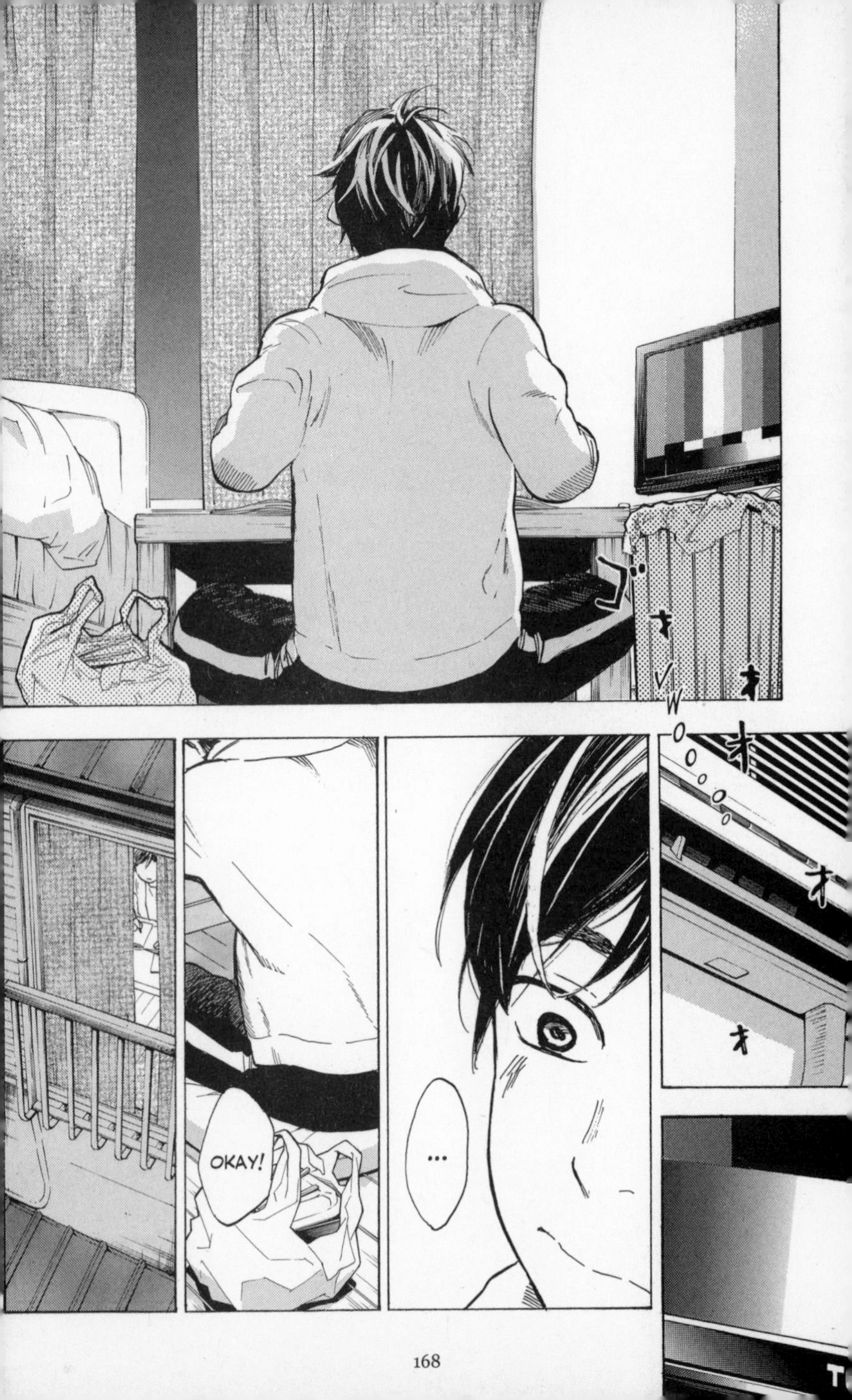
VWOOOOO
...
OKAY!

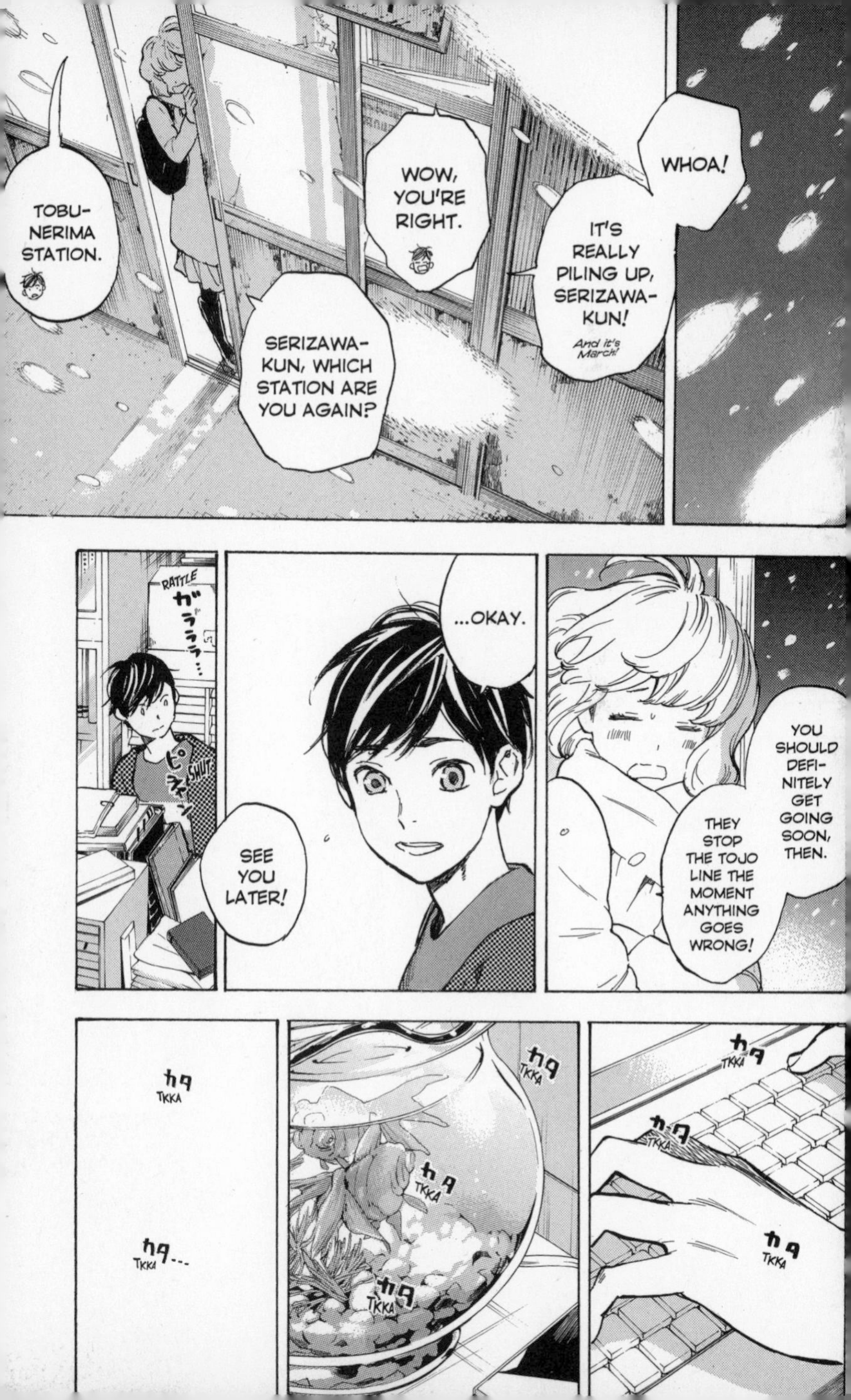
WHOA!
IT'S REALLY PILING UP, SERIZAWA-KUN!
And it's March!
WOW, YOU'RE RIGHT.
SERIZAWA-KUN, WHICH STATION ARE YOU AGAIN?
TOBU-NERIMA STATION.
YOU SHOULD DEFINITELY GET GOING SOON, THEN.
THEY STOP THE TOJO LINE THE MOMENT ANYTHING GOES WRONG!
...OKAY.
SEE YOU LATER!
RATTLE
SHUT
カタ TKKA
カタ TKKA
カタ TKKA
カタ TKKA
カタ TKKA
カタ TKKA
カタ TKKA
カタ TKKA...

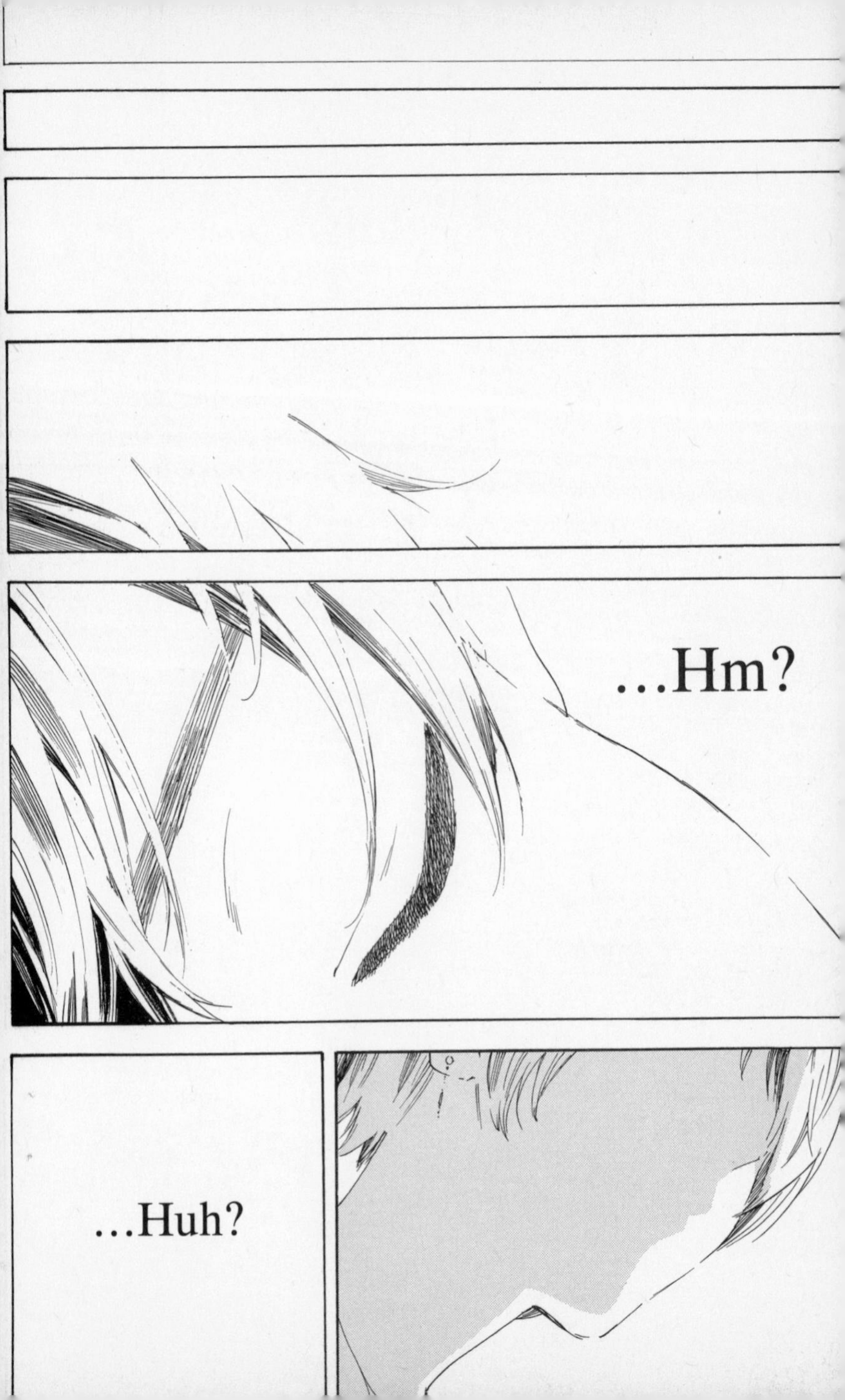
...Hm?
...Huh?

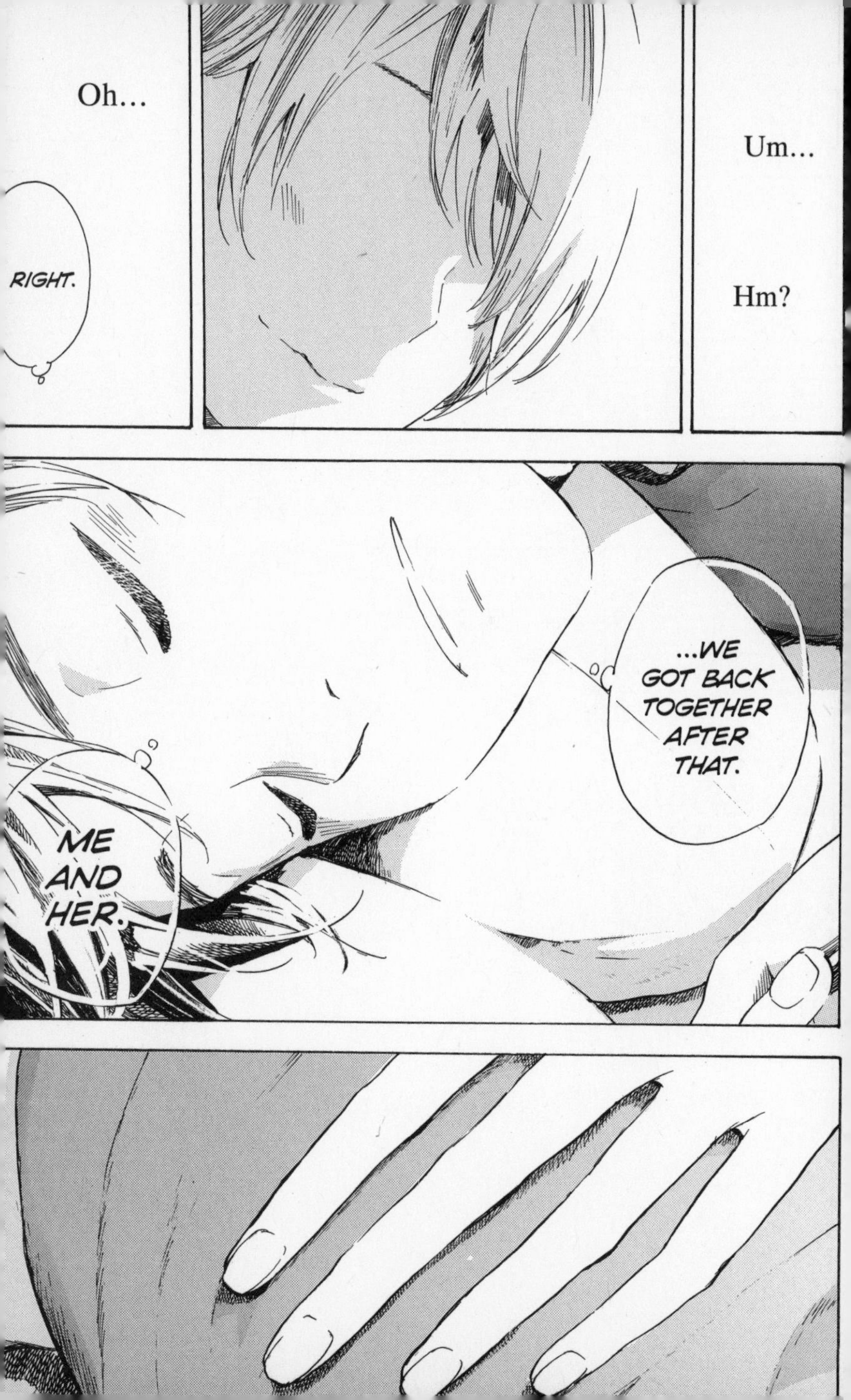
Um…
Hm?
Oh…
RIGHT.
...WE GOT BACK TOGETHER AFTER THAT.
ME AND HER.

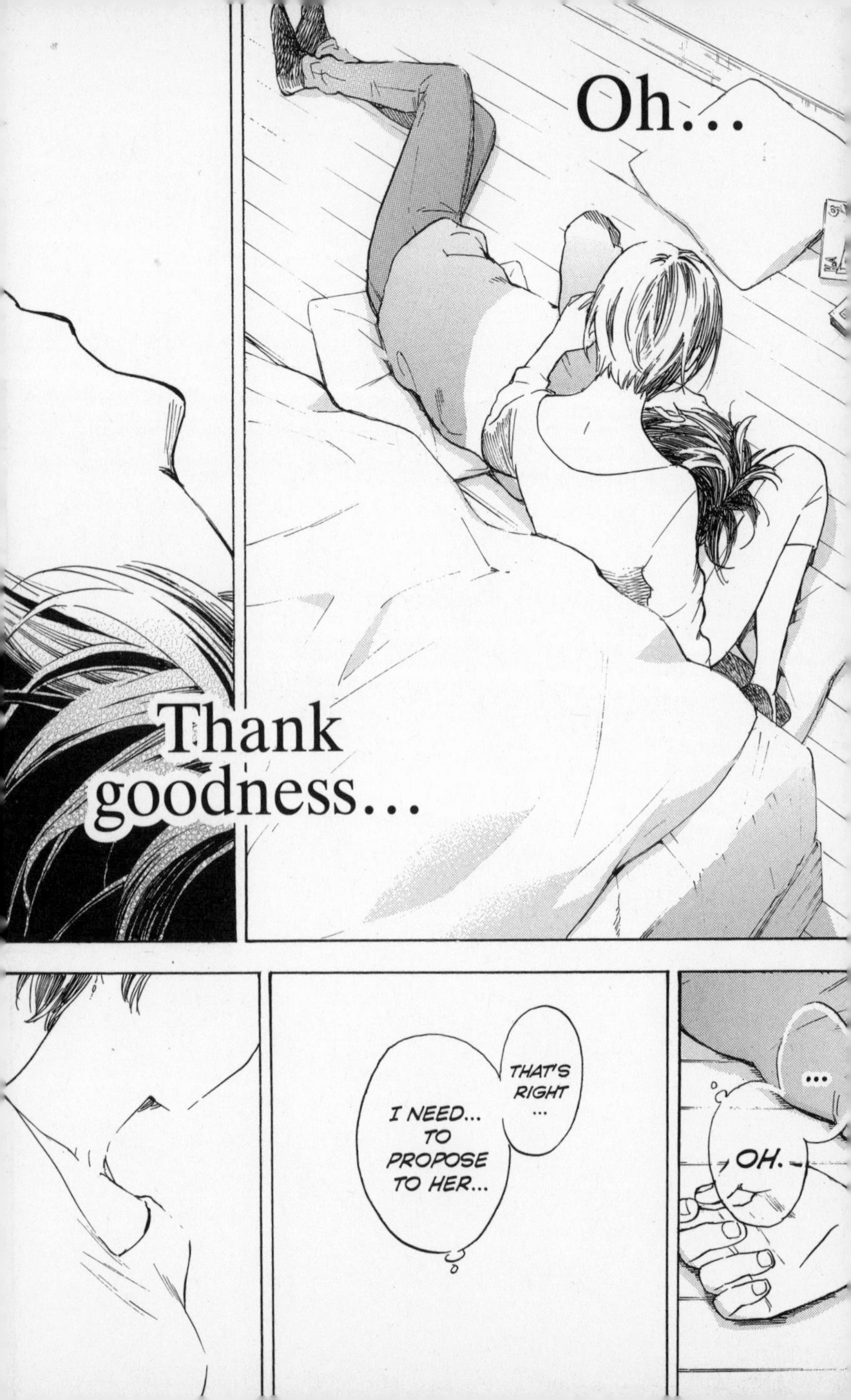
Oh...
Thank goodness...
...
OH.
THAT'S RIGHT ...
I NEED... TO PROPOSE TO HER...

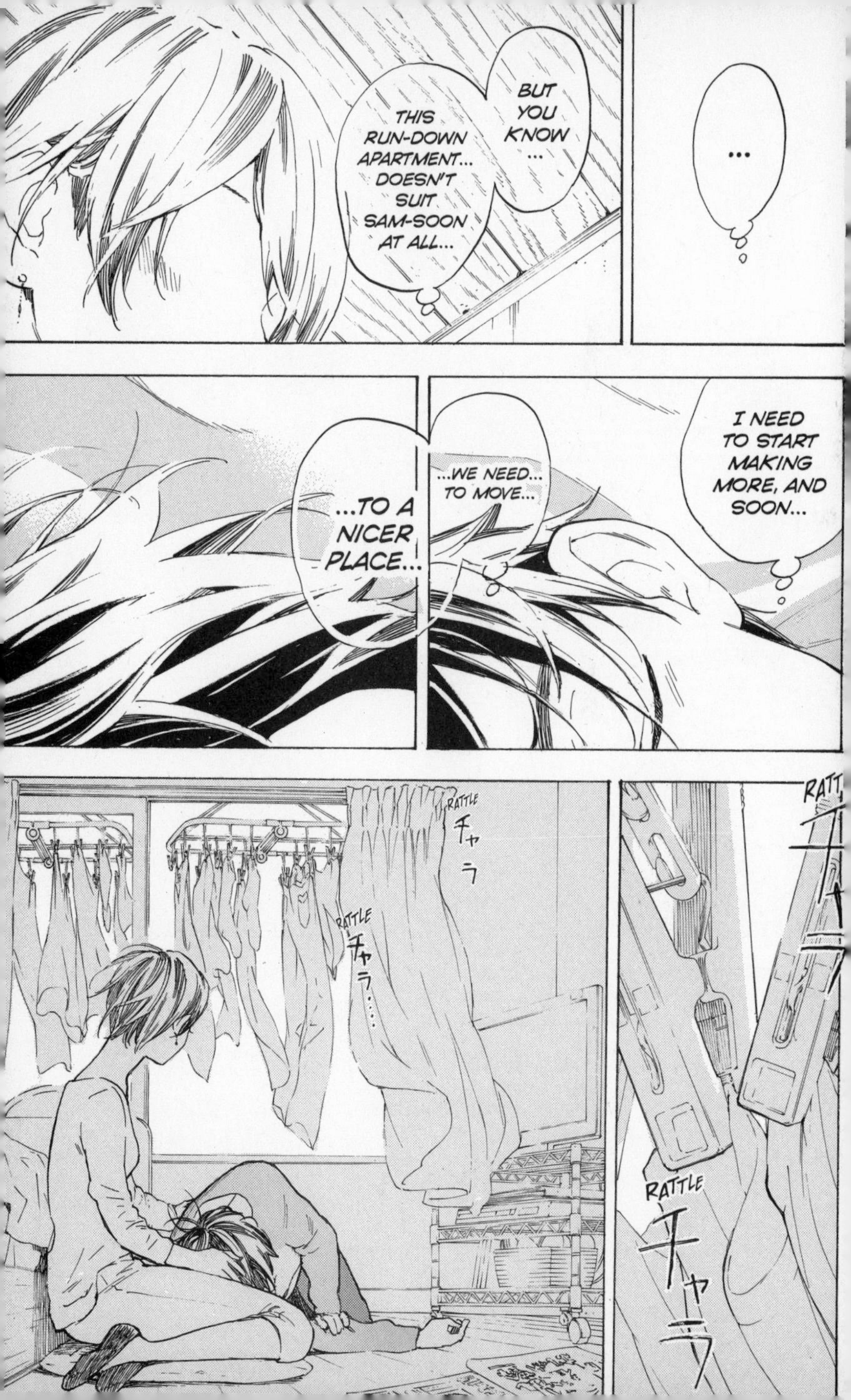
...
BUT YOU KNOW ...
THIS RUN-DOWN APARTMENT... DOESN'T SUIT SAM-SOON AT ALL...
I NEED TO START MAKING MORE, AND SOON...
...WE NEED... TO MOVE...
...TO A NICER PLACE...
RATT
RATTLE
チャラ
RATTLE
チャラ
RATTLE
チャラ....

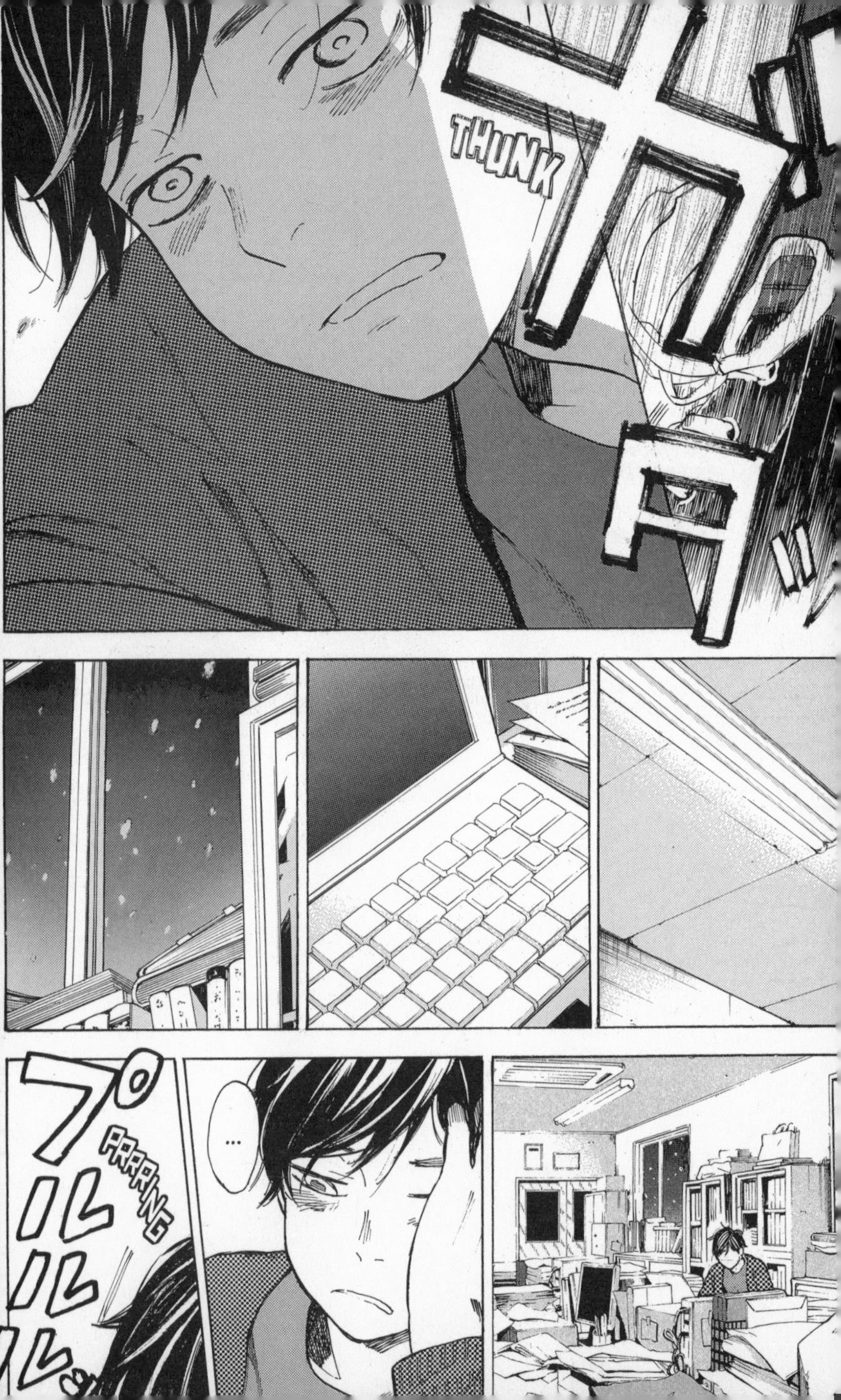
THUNK
...
プルルル
PRRRING

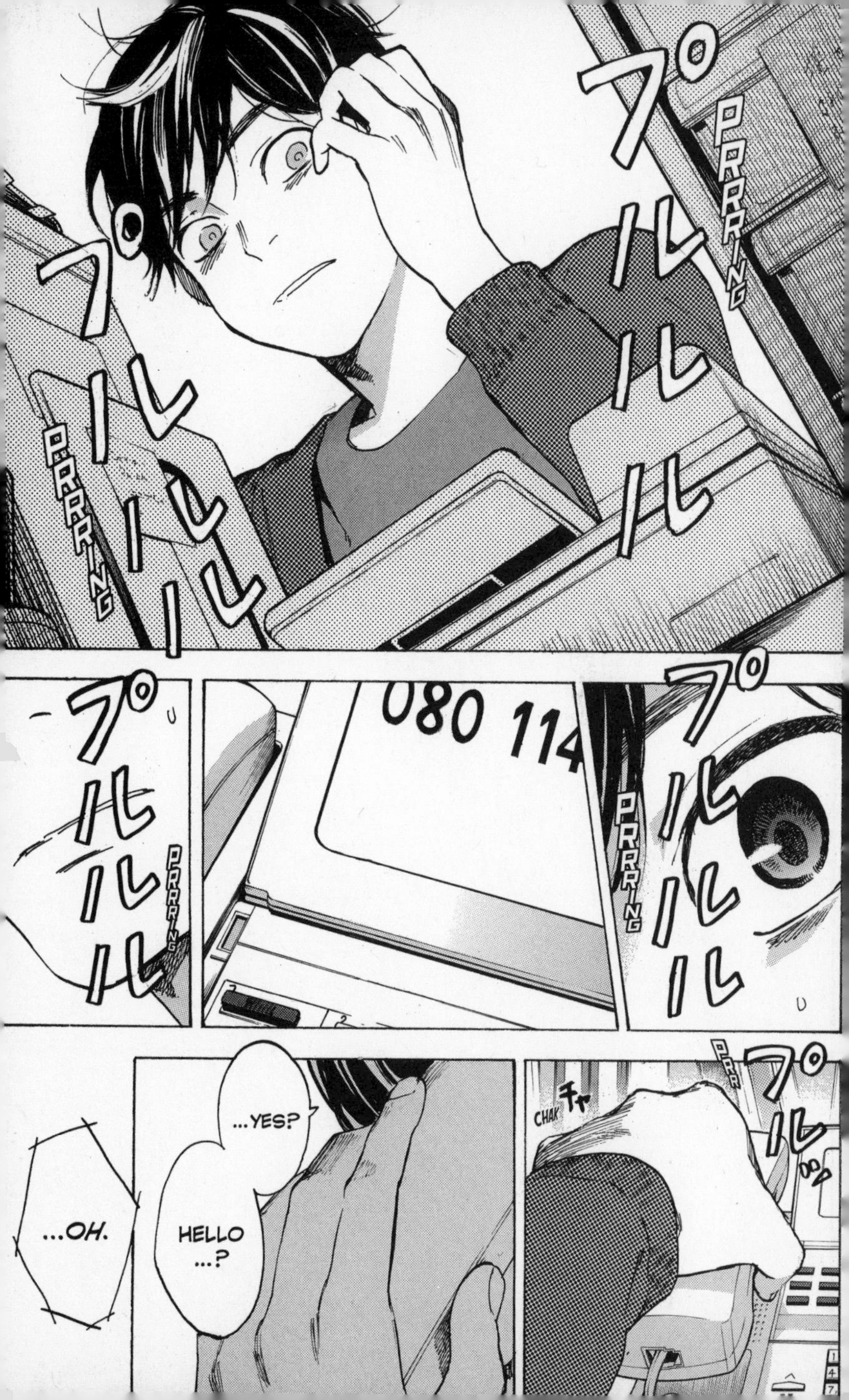
プルルル
PRRRING
プルルルル
PRRRING
プルルル
PRRRING
080 114
プルルル
PRRRING
プル
PRRR
チャ
CHAK
...YES?
HELLO ...?
...OH.

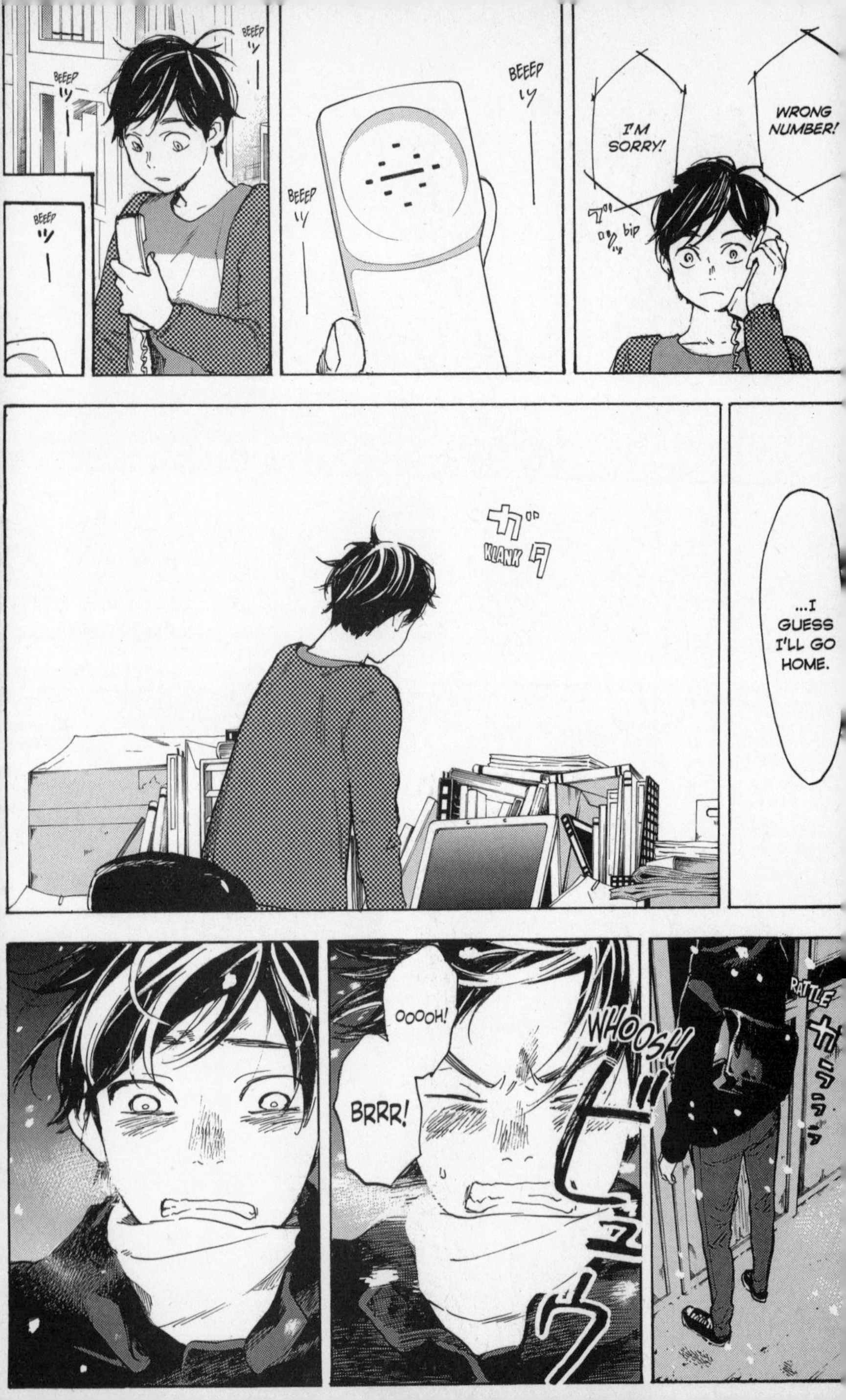
WRONG NUMBER!
I'M SORRY!
bip
BEEEP
ツー
BEEEP
ツー
BEEEP
ツー
BEEEP
ツー
BEEEP
ツー
...I GUESS I'LL GO HOME.
KLANK
ガタ
RATTLE
カラララ
WHOOSH
ビュウ
OOOOH!
BRRR!

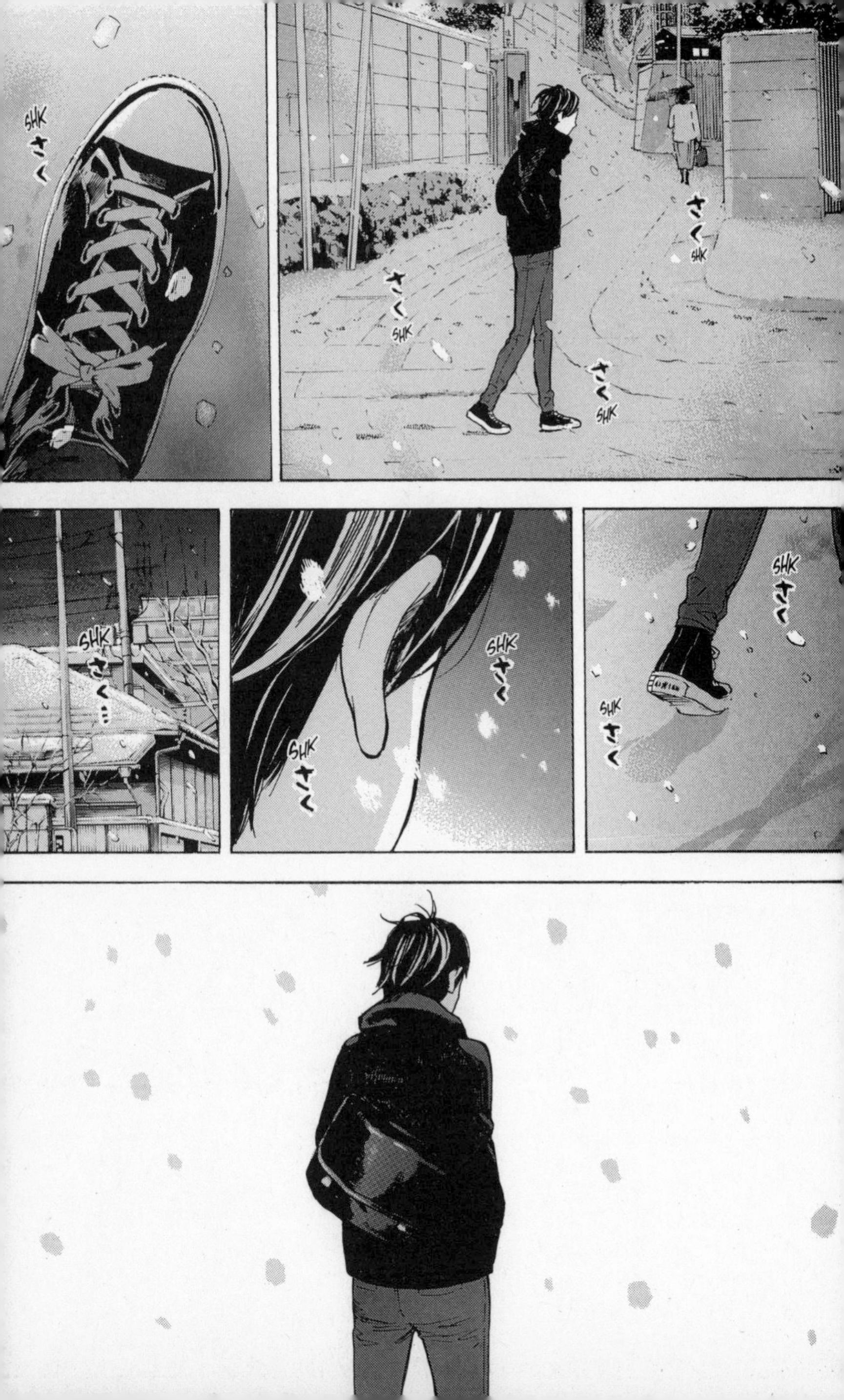
さく SHK
さく SHK
さく SHK
SHK さく
SHK さく
SHK さく
SHK さく
SHK さく
SHK さく…

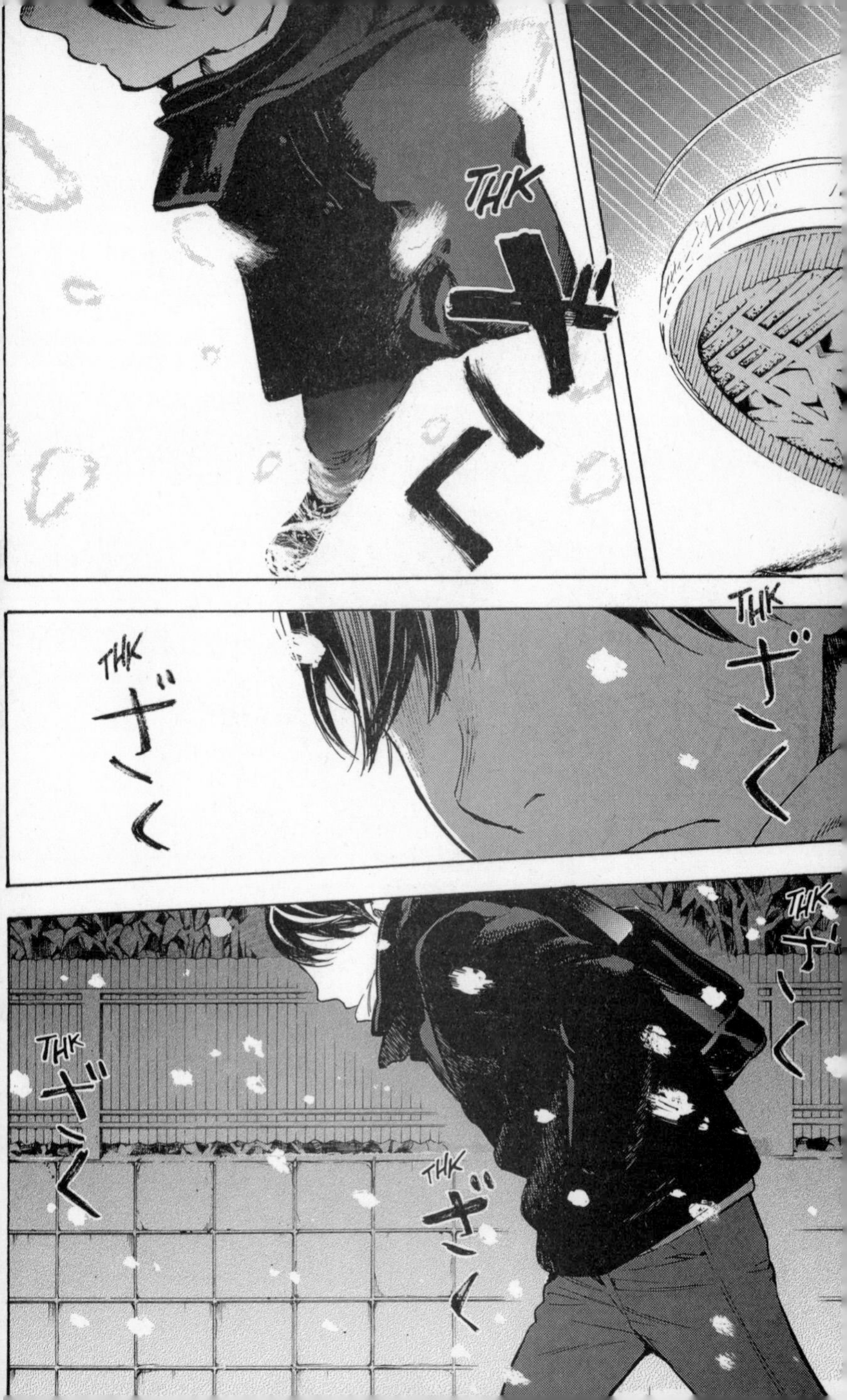
THK
ざく
THK
ざく
THK
ざく
THK
ざく
THK
ざく
THK
ざく

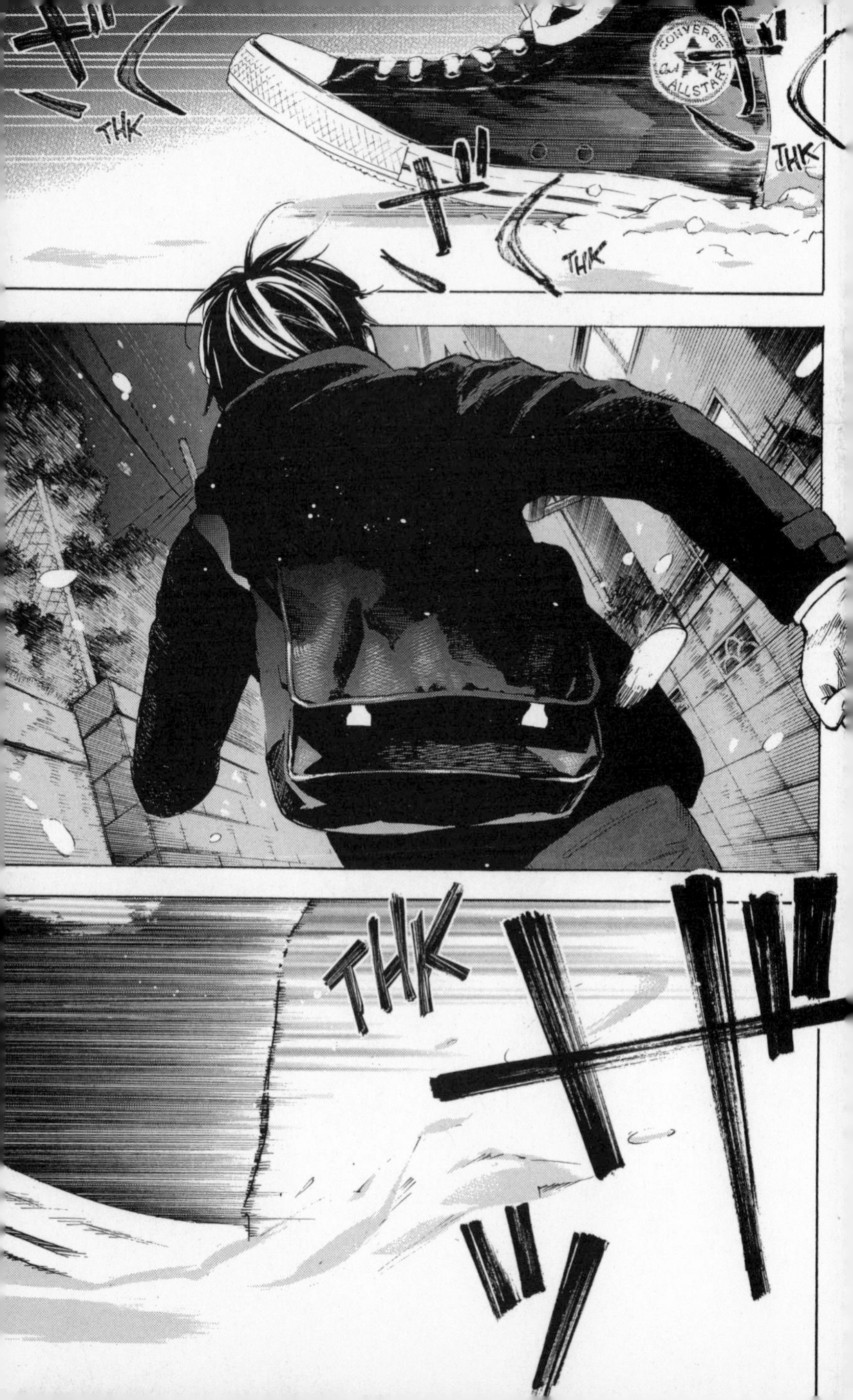
CONVERSE
ALLSTAR
THK
THK
THK
THK

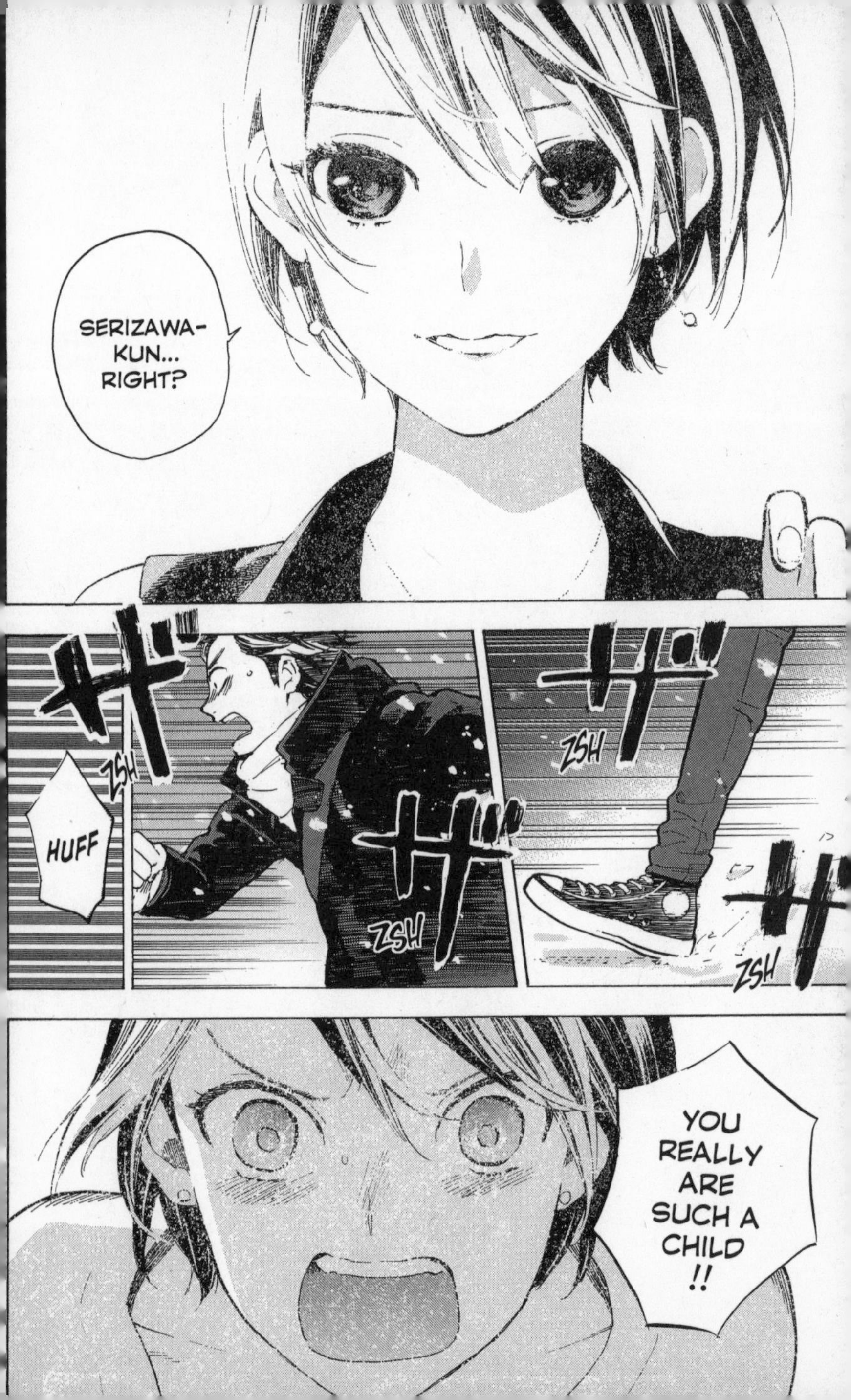
SERIZAWA-KUN... RIGHT?
ZSH
ZSH
ZSH
HUFF
ZSH
YOU REALLY ARE SUCH A CHILD!!

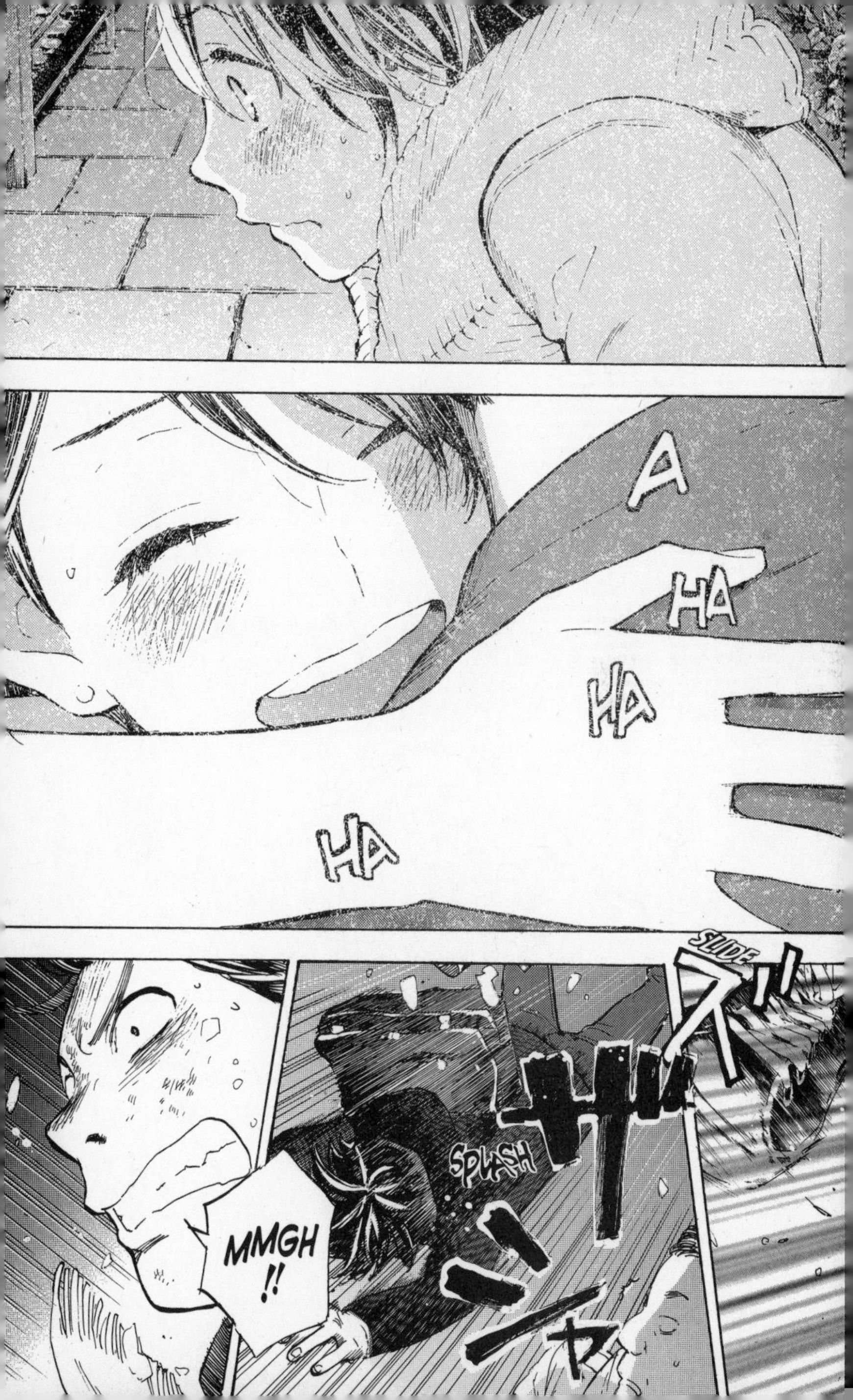
A
HA
HA
HA
SLIDE
SPLASH
MMGH
!!

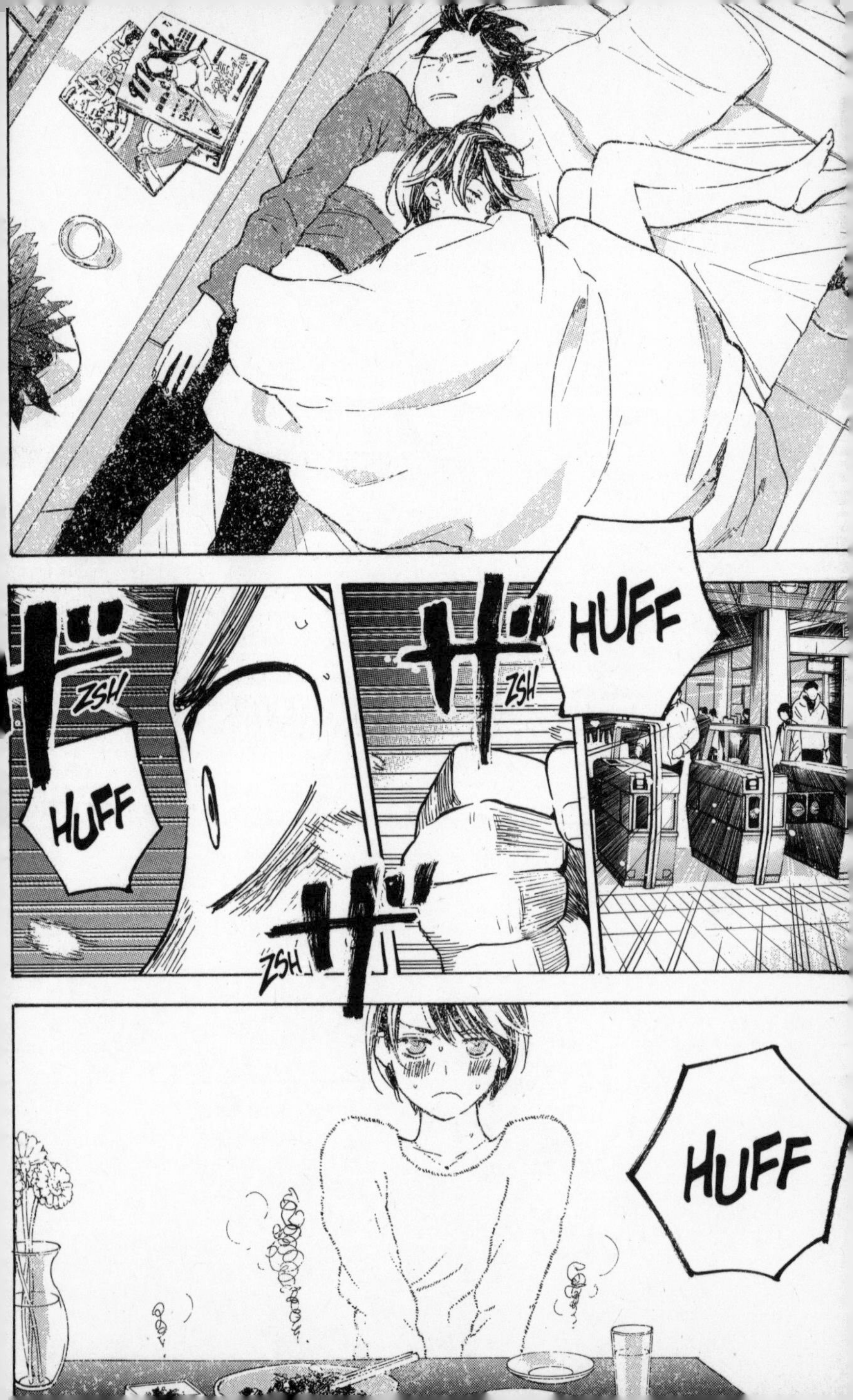
HUFF
ZSH
ZSH
ZSH
HUFF
HUFF

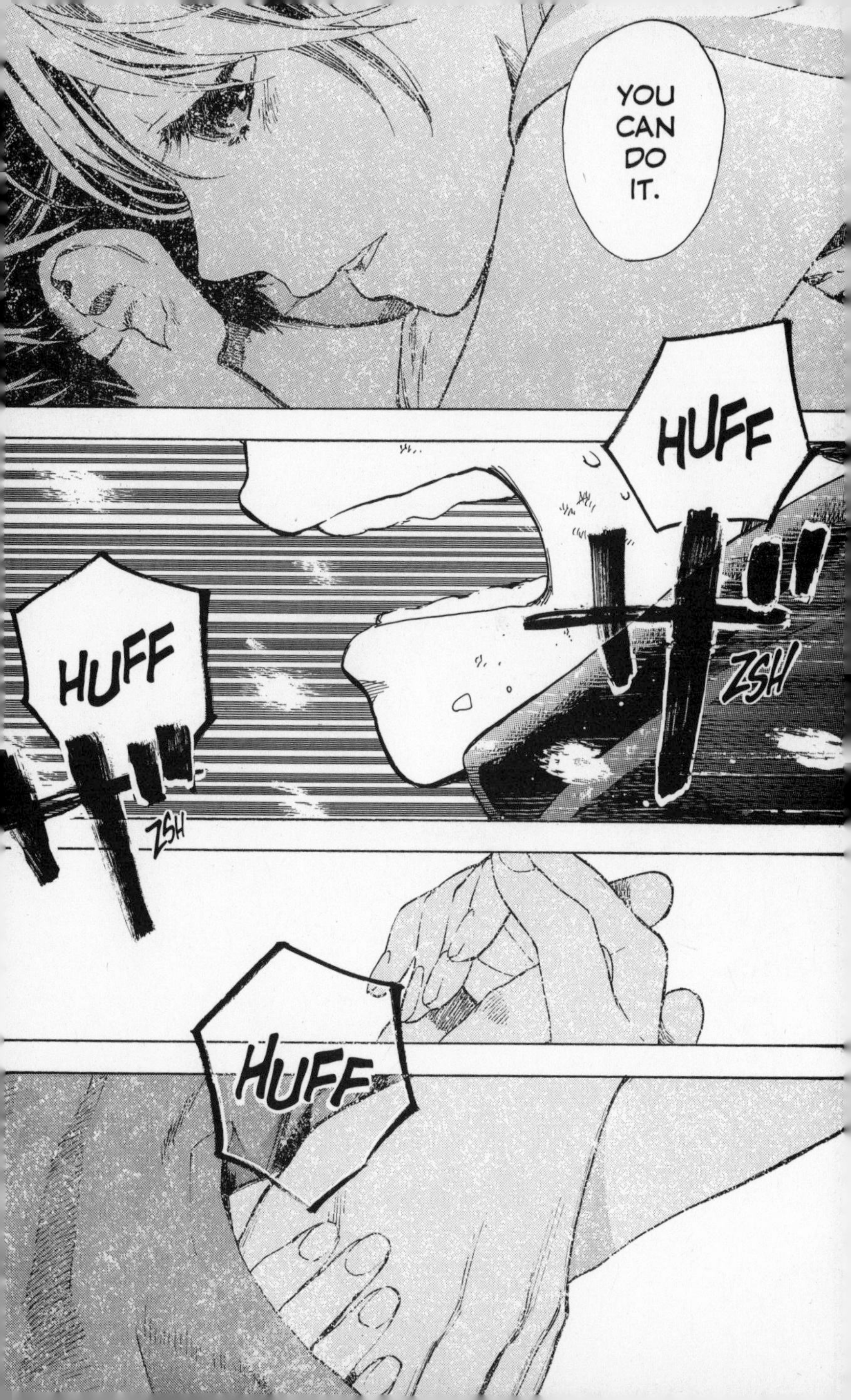
YOU CAN DO IT.
HUFF
ZSH
HUFF
ZSH
HUFF

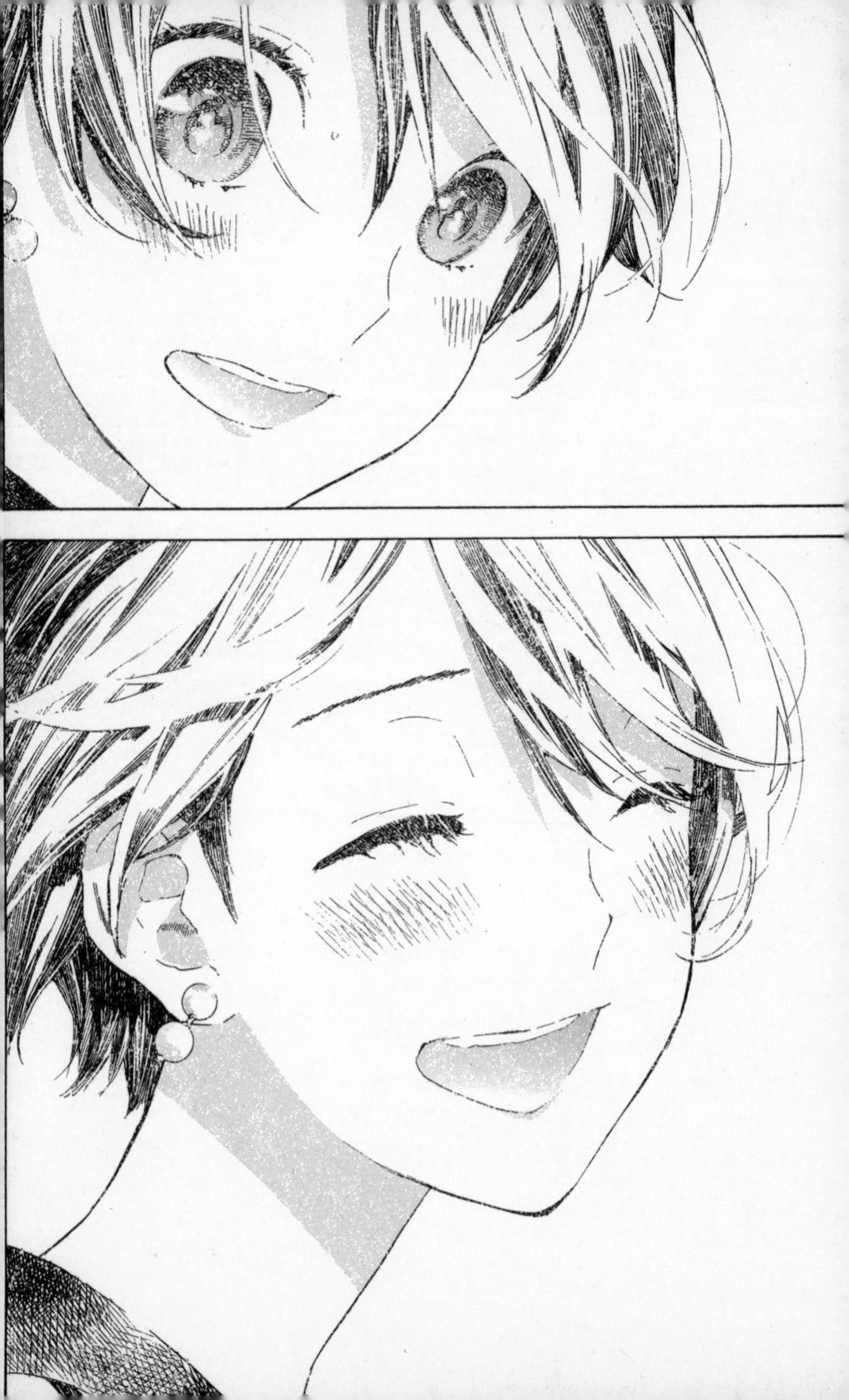

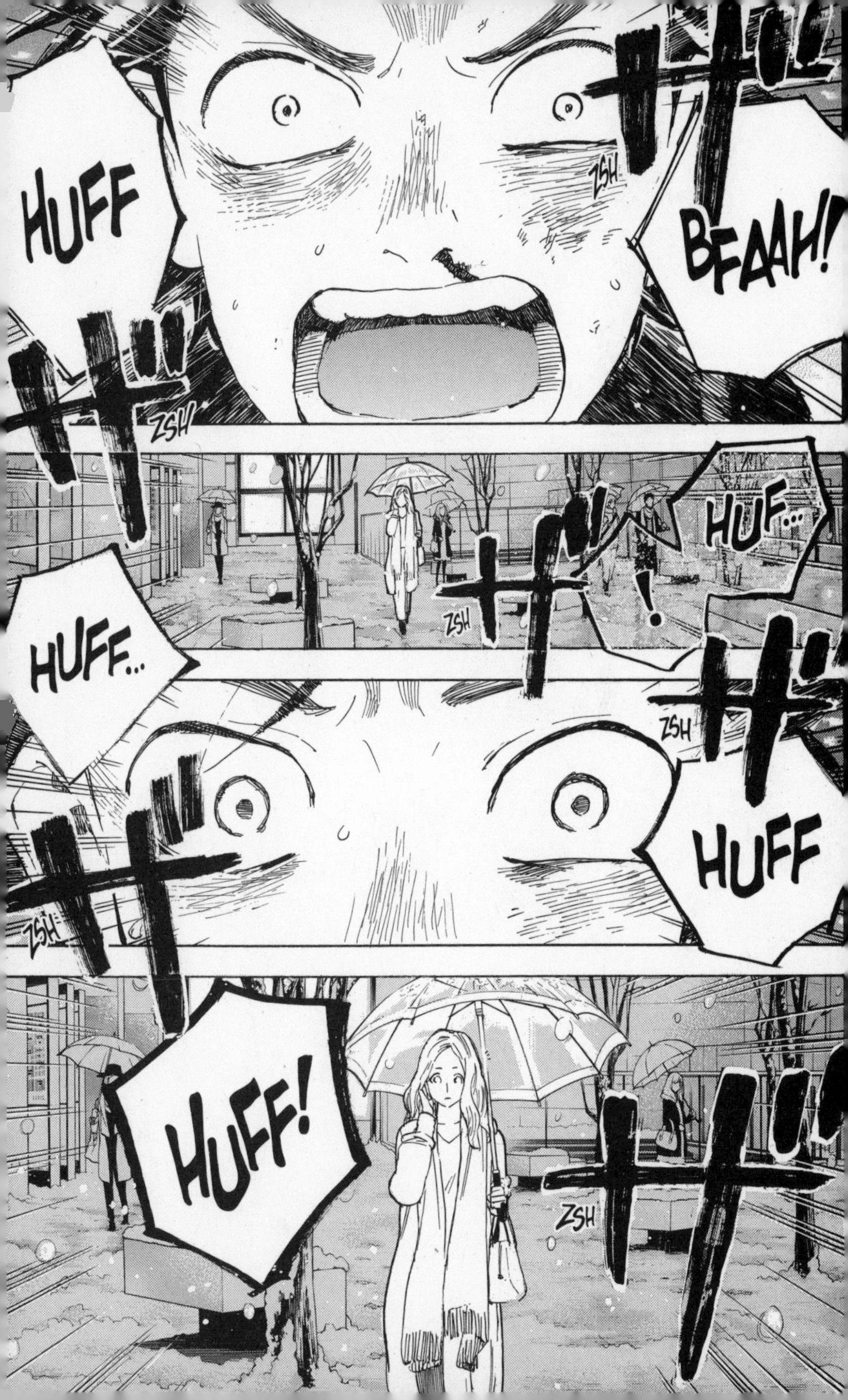
ZSH
BFAAH!
HUFF
ZSH
HUF...
ZSH
HUFF...
ZSH
HUFF
ZSH
ZSH
HUFF!

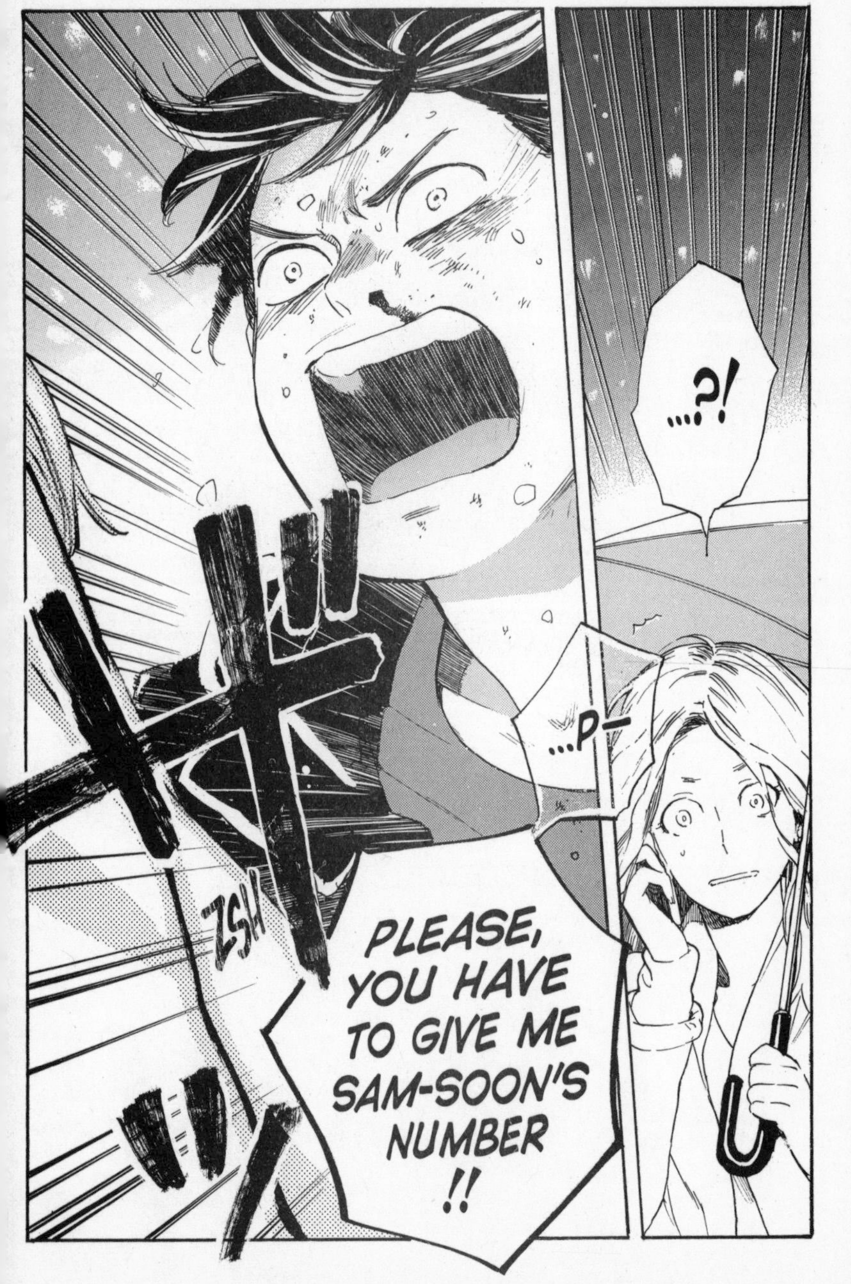
...?!
...P—
PLEASE, YOU HAVE TO GIVE ME SAM-SOON'S NUMBER !!
ZSH

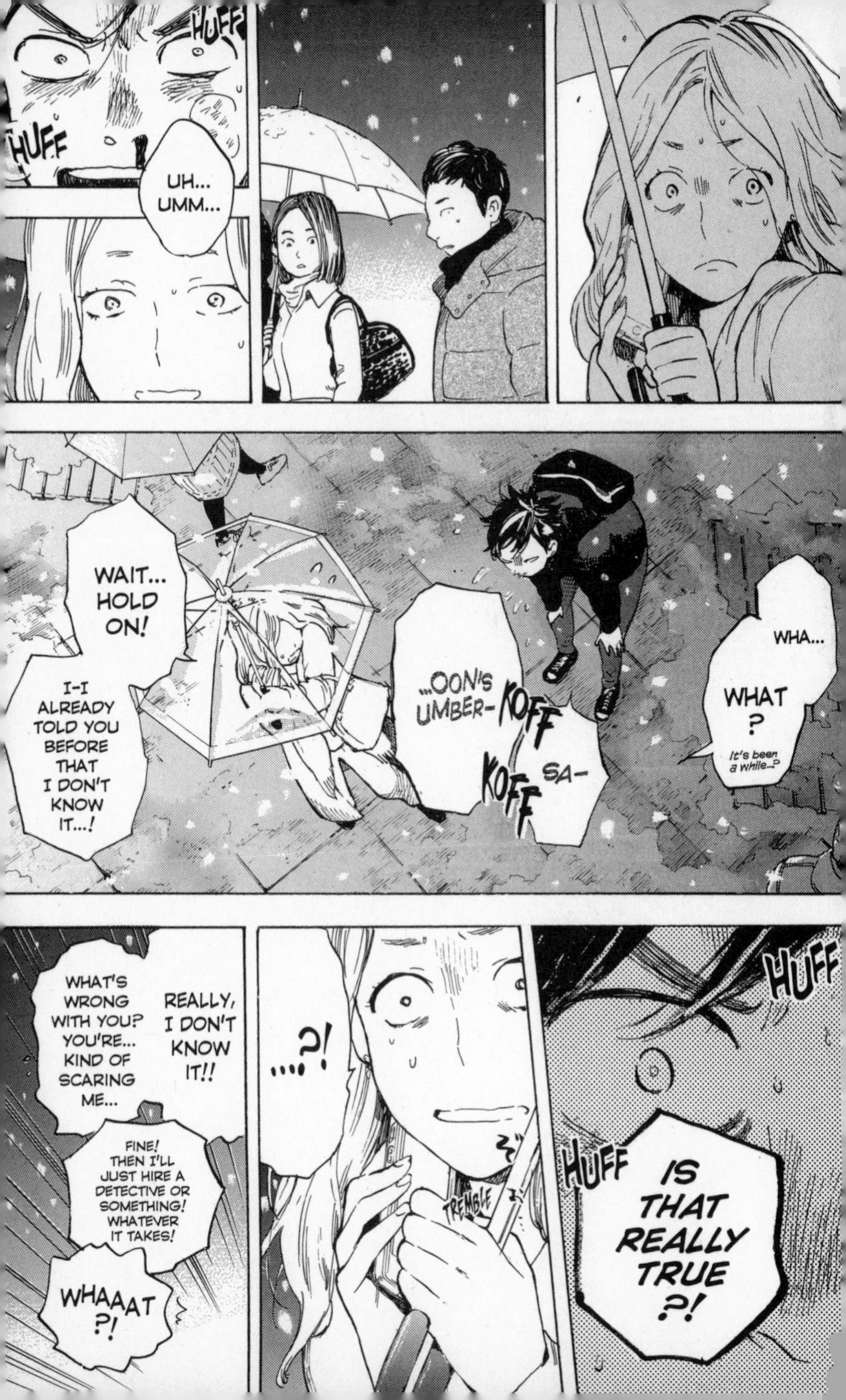
HUFF
HUFF
UH... UMM...
WHA... WHAT?
It's been a while...?
...OON'S UMBER- KOFF KOFF SA-
WAIT... HOLD ON!
I-I ALREADY TOLD YOU BEFORE THAT I DON'T KNOW IT...!
HUFF
HUFF
IS THAT REALLY TRUE?!
...?!
TREMBLE
REALLY, I DON'T KNOW IT!!
WHAT'S WRONG WITH YOU? YOU'RE... KIND OF SCARING ME...
FINE! THEN I'LL JUST HIRE A DETECTIVE OR SOMETHING! WHATEVER IT TAKES!
WHAAAT?!

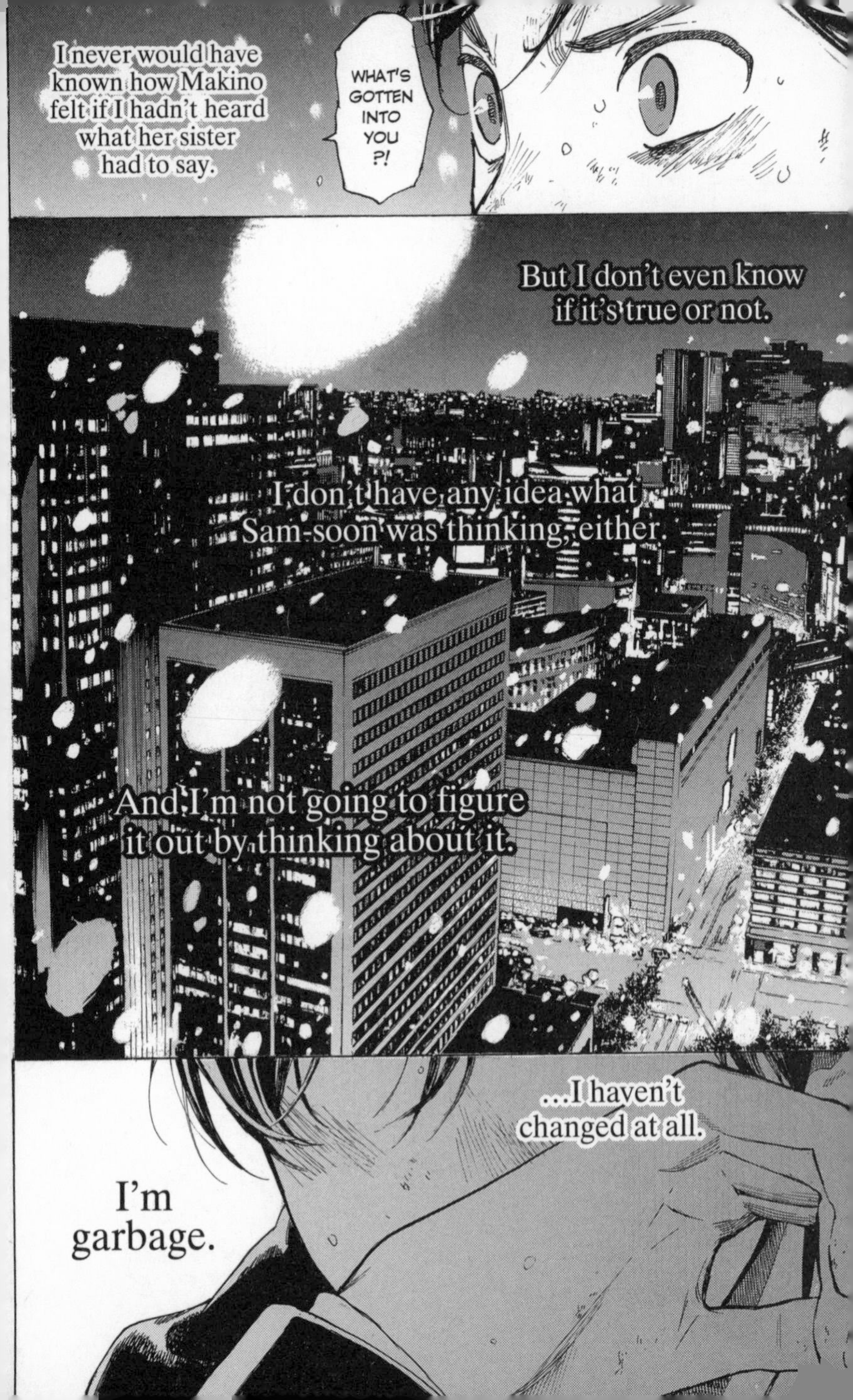
WHAT'S GOTTEN INTO YOU ?!
I never would have known how Makino felt if I hadn't heard what her sister had to say.
But I don't even know if it's true or not.
I don't have any idea what Sam-soon was thinking, either.
And I'm not going to figure it out by thinking about it.
...I haven't changed at all.
I'm garbage.

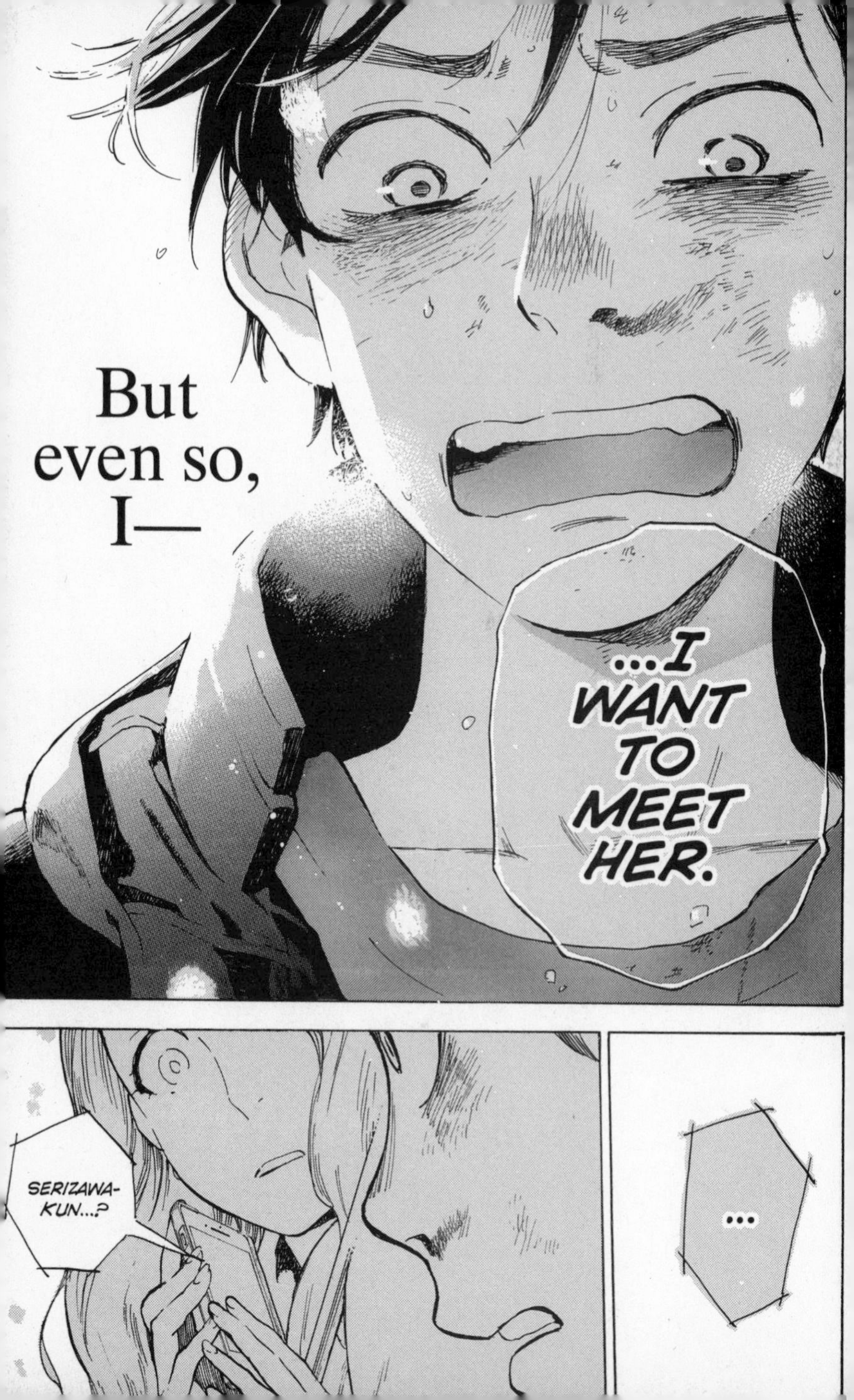
But even so, I—
...I WANT TO MEET HER.
...
SERIZAWA-KUN...?

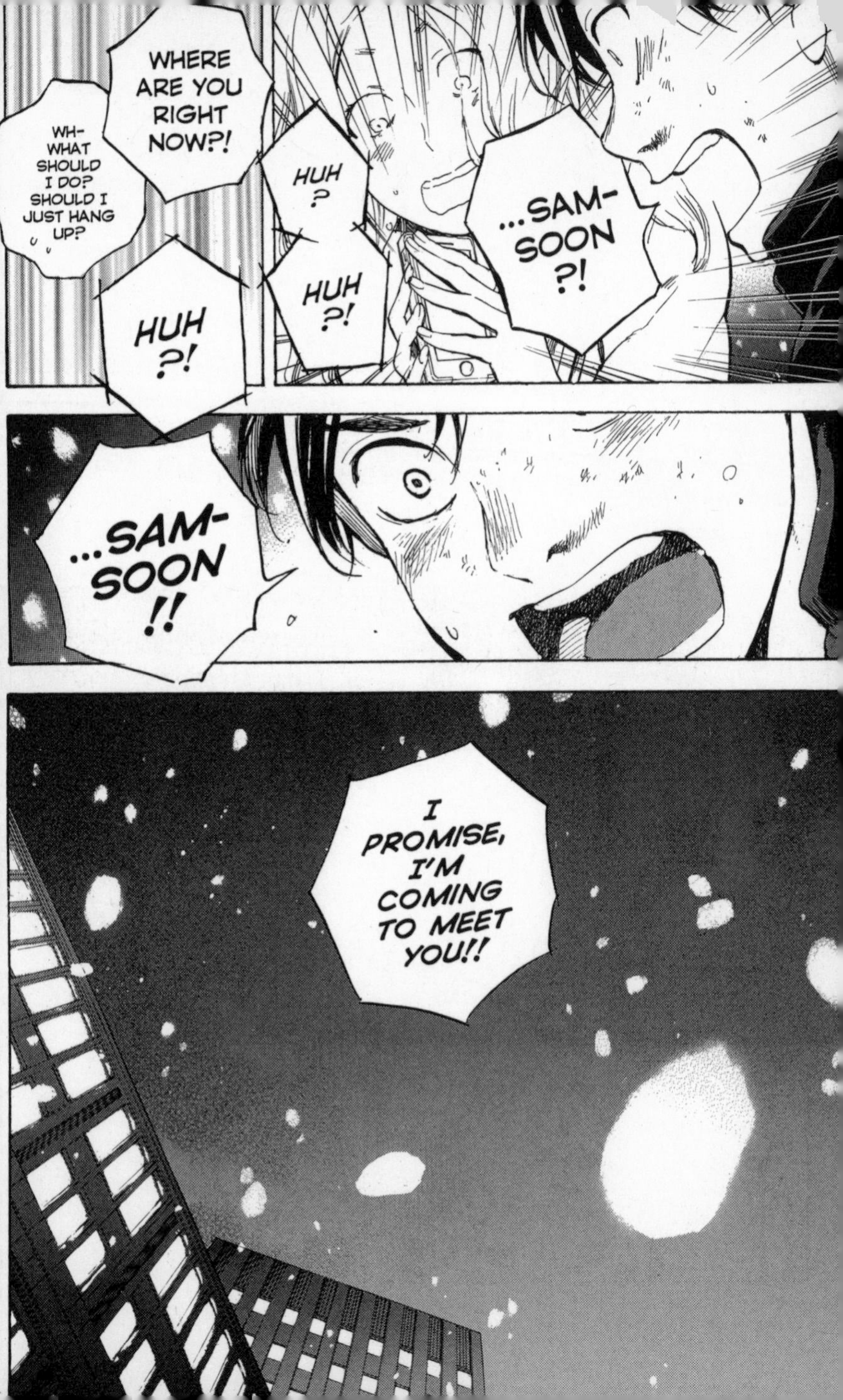
...SAM-SOON?!
HUH?
HUH?!
WHERE ARE YOU RIGHT NOW?!
WH-WHAT SHOULD I DO? SHOULD I JUST HANG UP?
HUH?!
...SAM-SOON!!
I PROMISE, I'M COMING TO MEET YOU!!

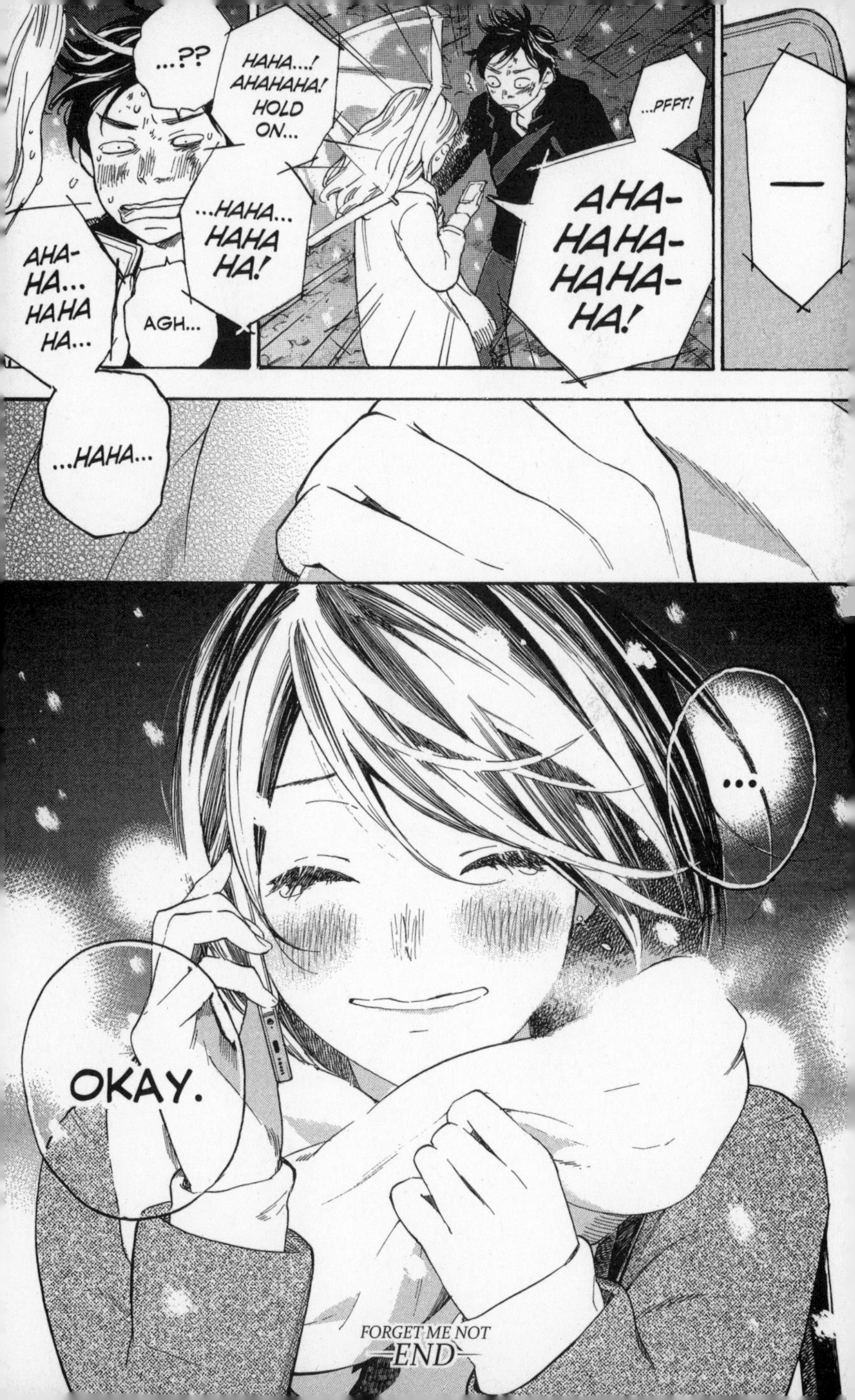
—
...PFFT!
AHA-HAHA-HAHA-HA!
HAHA...! AHAHAHA! HOLD ON...
...HAHA... HAHA HA!
...??
AHA-HA... HAHA HA...
AGH...
...HAHA...
...
OKAY.
FORGET ME NOT
END

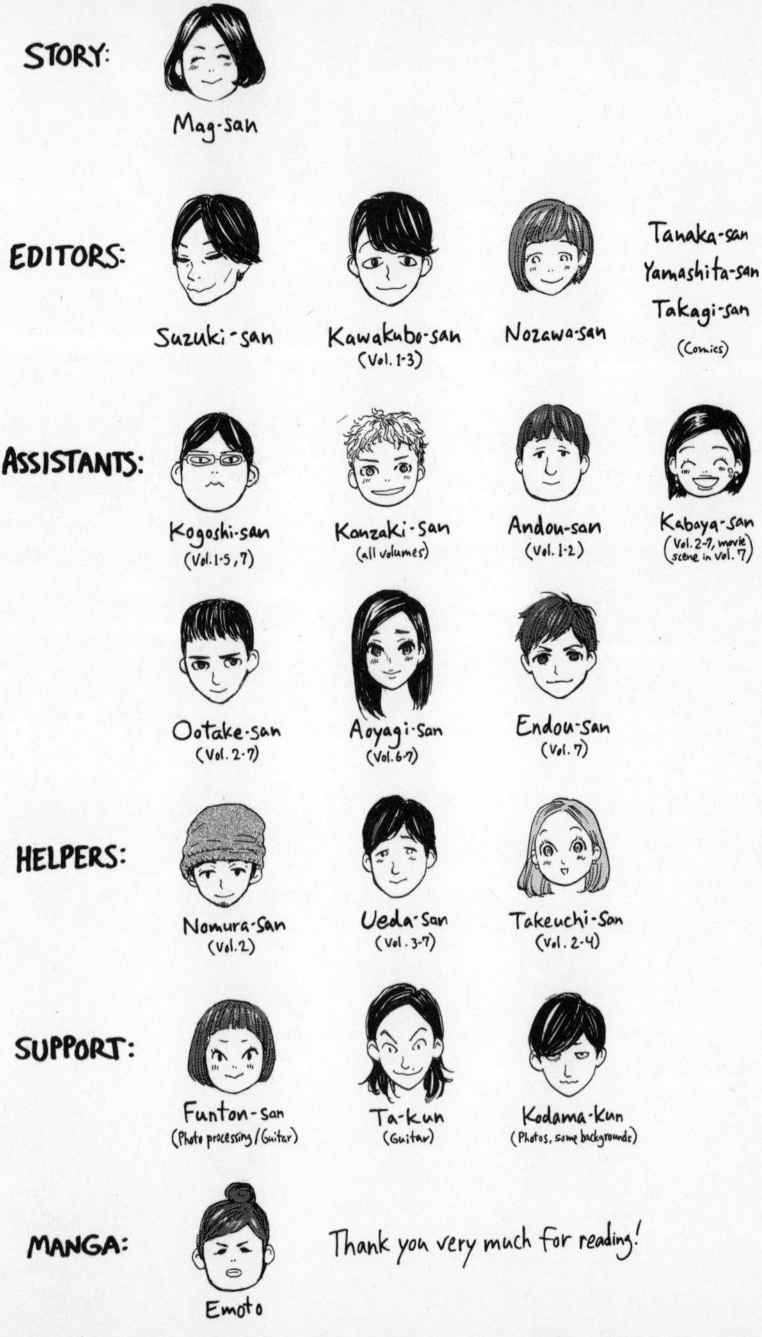
STORY:
Mag-san
EDITORS:
Suzuki-san
Kawakubo-san
(Vol. 1-3)
Nozawa-san
Tanaka-san
Yamashita-san
Takagi-san
(Comics)
ASSISTANTS:
Kogoshi-san
(Vol. 1-5, 7)
Kanzaki-san
(all volumes)
Andou-san
(Vol. 1-2)
Kabaya-san
(Vol. 2-7, movie scene in Vol. 7)
Ootake-san
(Vol. 2-7)
Aoyagi-san
(Vol. 6-7)
Endou-san
(Vol. 7)
HELPERS:
Nomura-san
(Vol. 2)
Ueda-san
(Vol. 3-7)
Takeuchi-san
(Vol. 2-4)
SUPPORT:
Funton-san
(Photo processing / Guitar)
Ta-kun
(Guitar)
Kodama-kun
(Photos, some backgrounds)
MANGA:
Emoto
Thank you very much for reading!

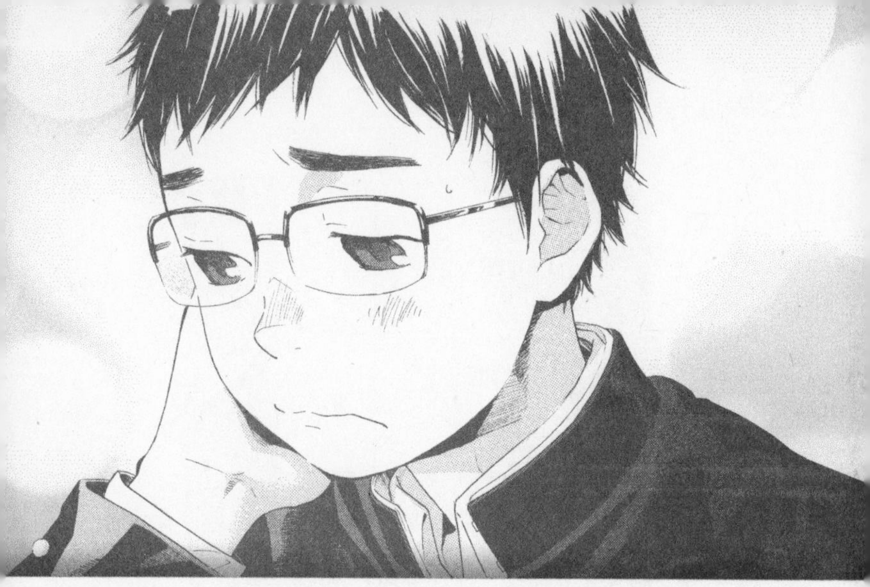

Forget Me Not

TRANSLATION NOTES

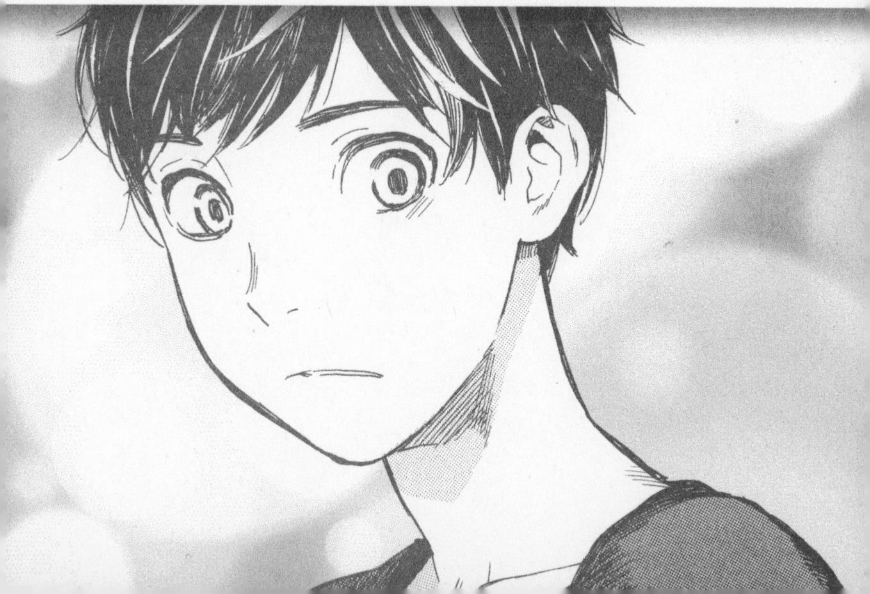

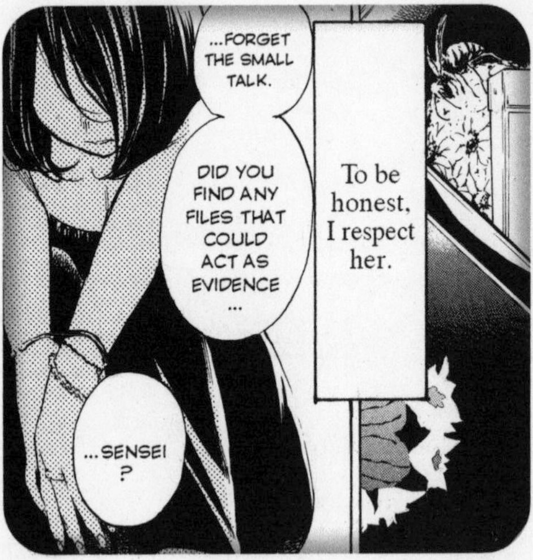
To be honest, I respect her.
...FORGET THE SMALL TALK.
DID YOU FIND ANY FILES THAT COULD ACT AS EVIDENCE ...
...SENSEI ?

SENSEI page 12

The word *sensei* is recognizable as a term used for teachers, but it can also be a form of address for people in certain occupations, such as doctors, artists, and in this case, a lawyer.

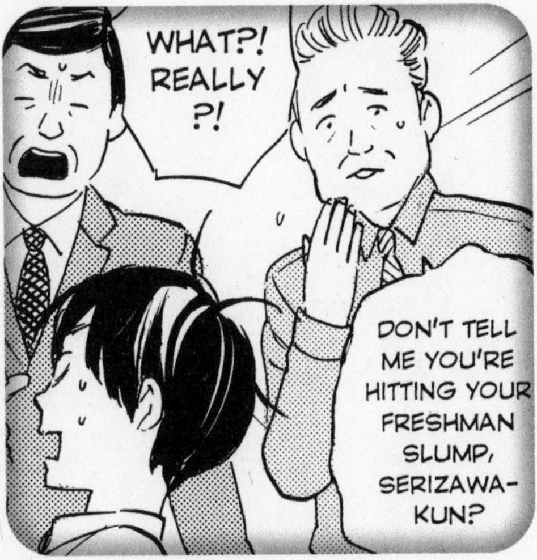
WHAT?! REALLY ?!
DON'T TELL ME YOU'RE HITTING YOUR FRESHMAN SLUMP, SERIZAWA-KUN?

FRESHMAN SLUMP page 21

In Japanese, they're actually talking about *gogatsu-byou,* which literally translates to "May illness." A more fitting translation would be "freshman apathy" or "new-employee blues." This condition occurs when new employees, usually fresh out of college, are overcome with depression due to the difference between their hopes for their new job or life in contrast to the reality or the inability to keep up with things. The "May" part comes from the fact that most companies welcome new employees in April and the subsequent hard-hitting realizations come in May, after the Japanese, week-long holiday called "Golden Week."

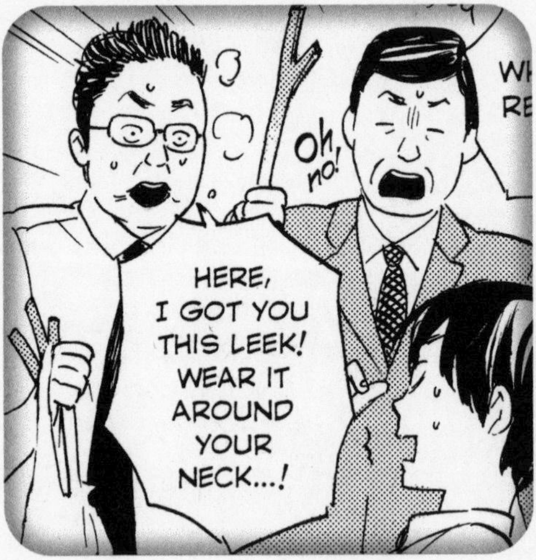
Oh, no!
HERE, I GOT YOU THIS LEEK! WEAR IT AROUND YOUR NECK...!

LEEK AROUND THE NECK page 21

One Japanese folk-remedy for the common cold is to wrap a leek around one's neck. There doesn't seem to be any conclusive evidence that this is true, but the fact that plants in the allium family (onions, garlic, etc.) have antibacterial and anti-inflammatory effects may convince some people that it's a true cure.

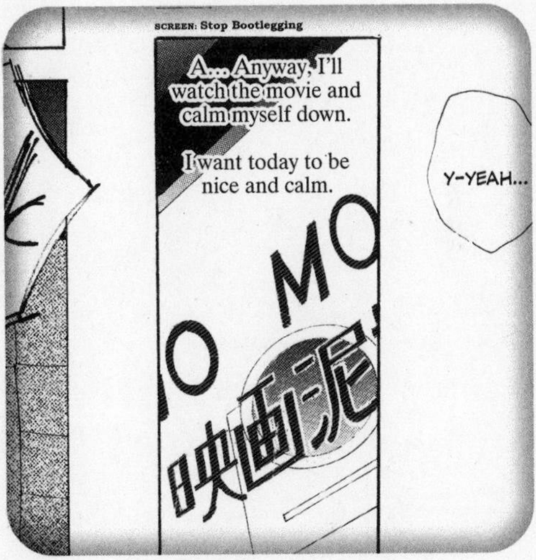
SCREEN: Stop Bootlegging
A... Anyway, I'll watch the movie and calm myself down.
I want today to be nice and calm.
Y-YEAH...
NO MO
映画泥

STOP BOOTLEGGING page 58

This appears to be a frame from an advertisement that is typically shown before movies in Japan. The short video usually features a man in a suit with a video camera for a head who tries to film a movie in the theater but is caught and captured by the police. These advertisements are part of a nationwide campaign to prevent bootlegging in movie theaters and the slogan for the campaign is *NO MORE Eiga Dorobou* (No more film thieves).

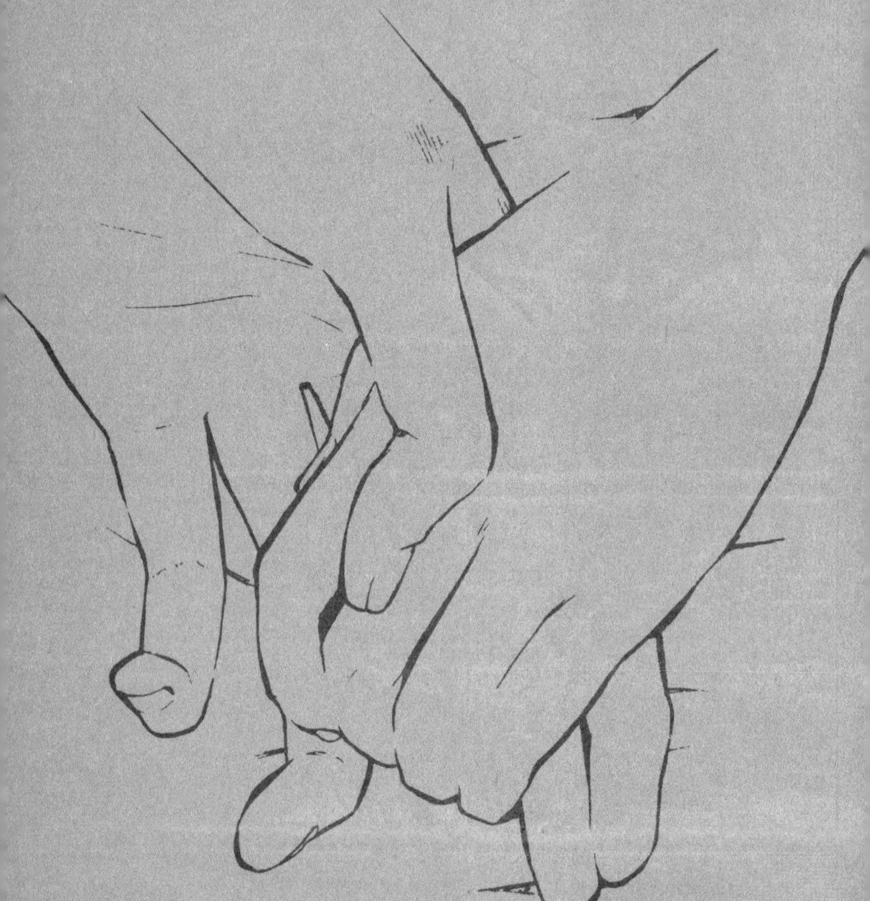

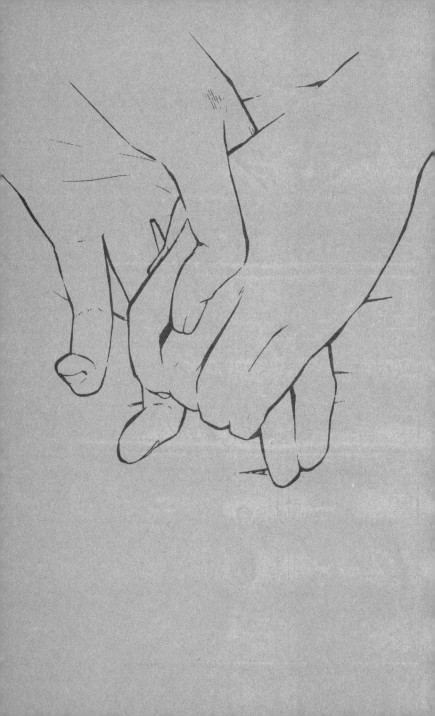

Forget Me Not

BONUS ART GALLERY

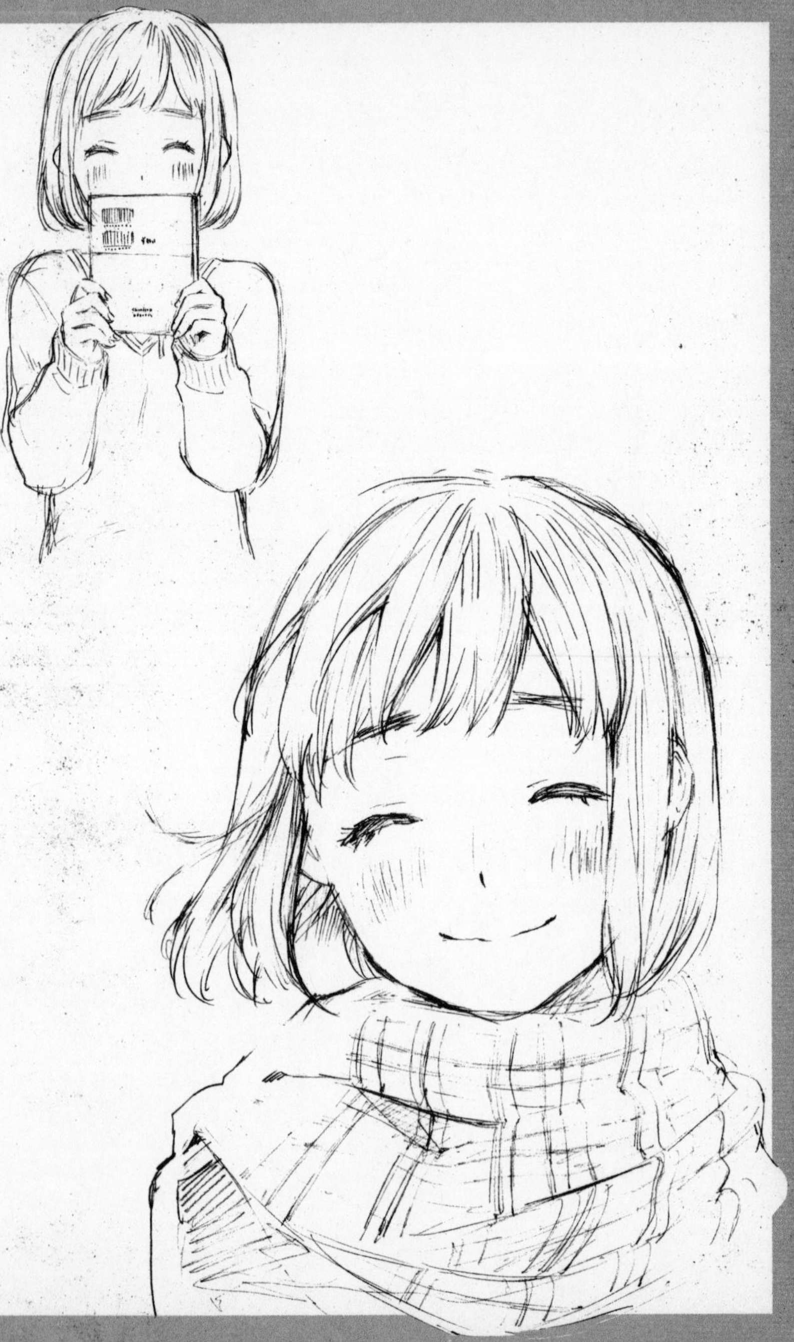

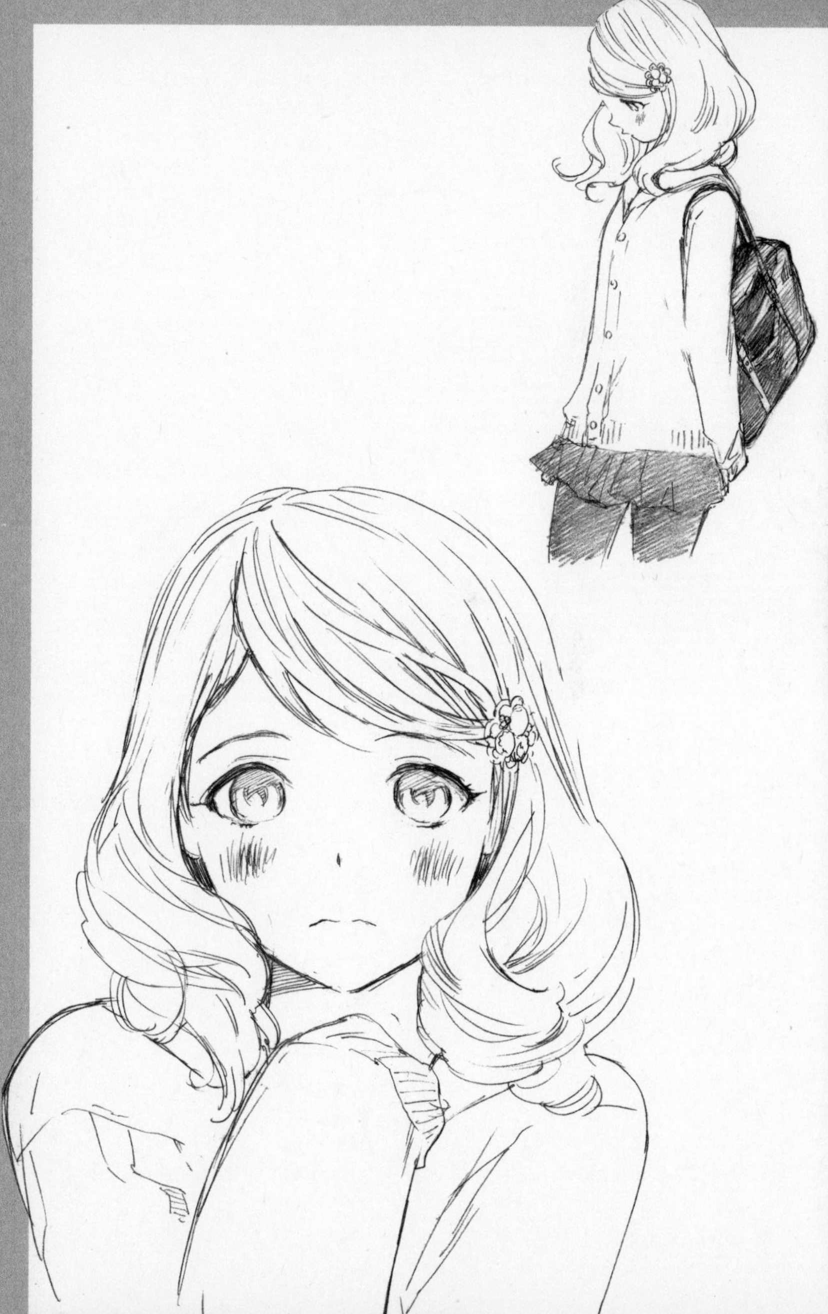

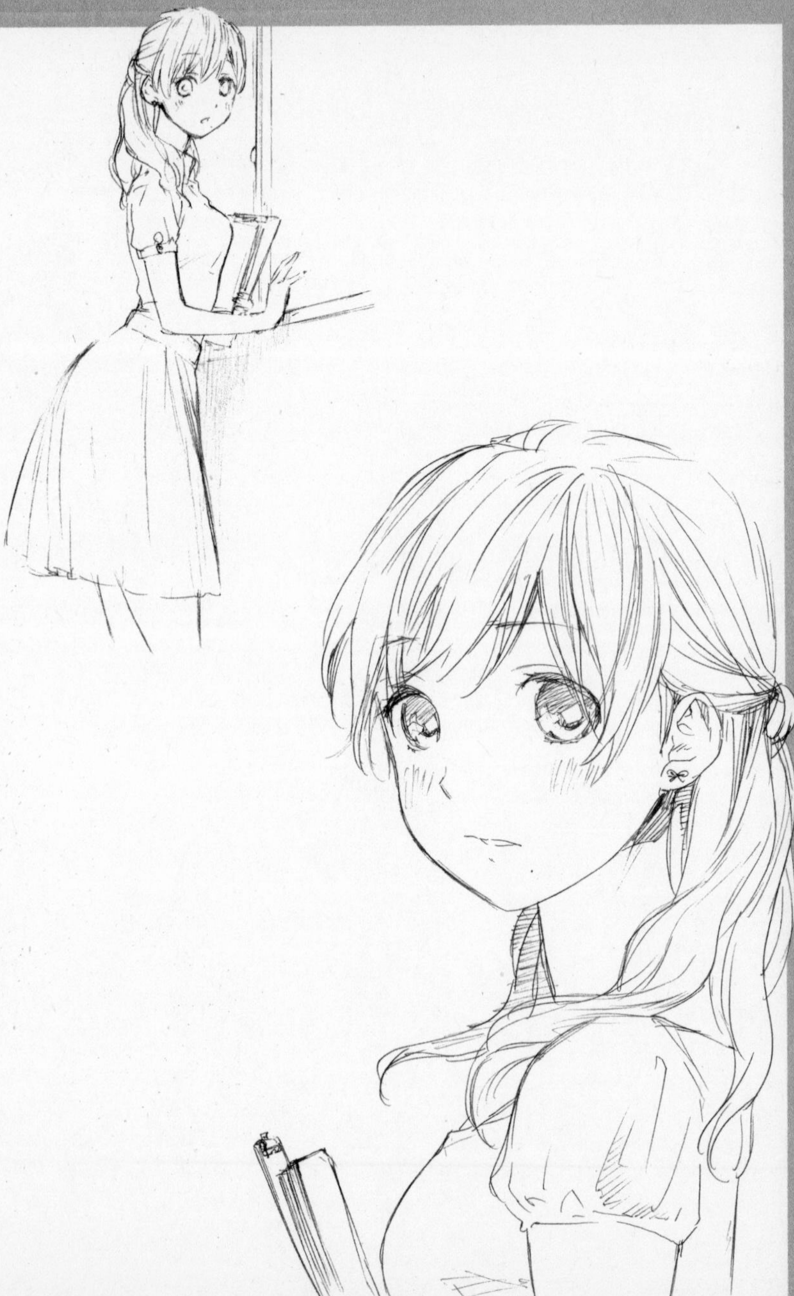

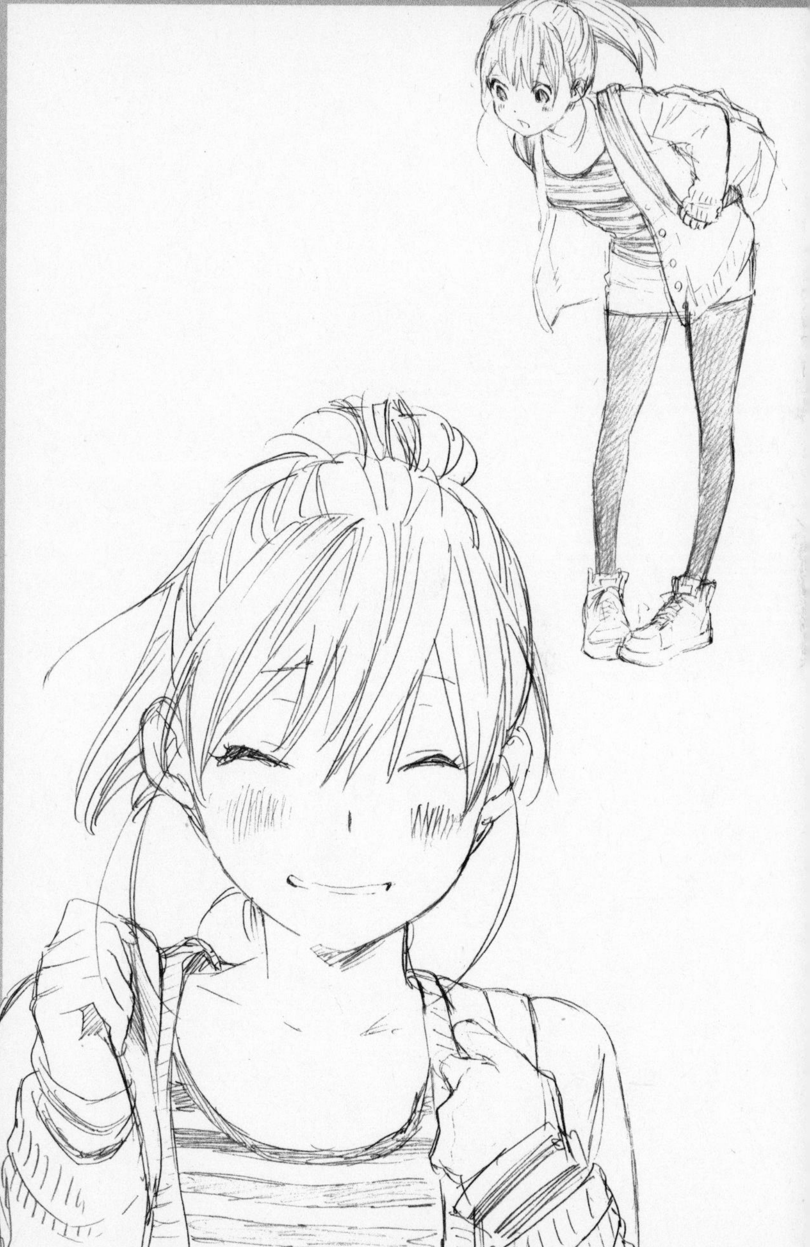

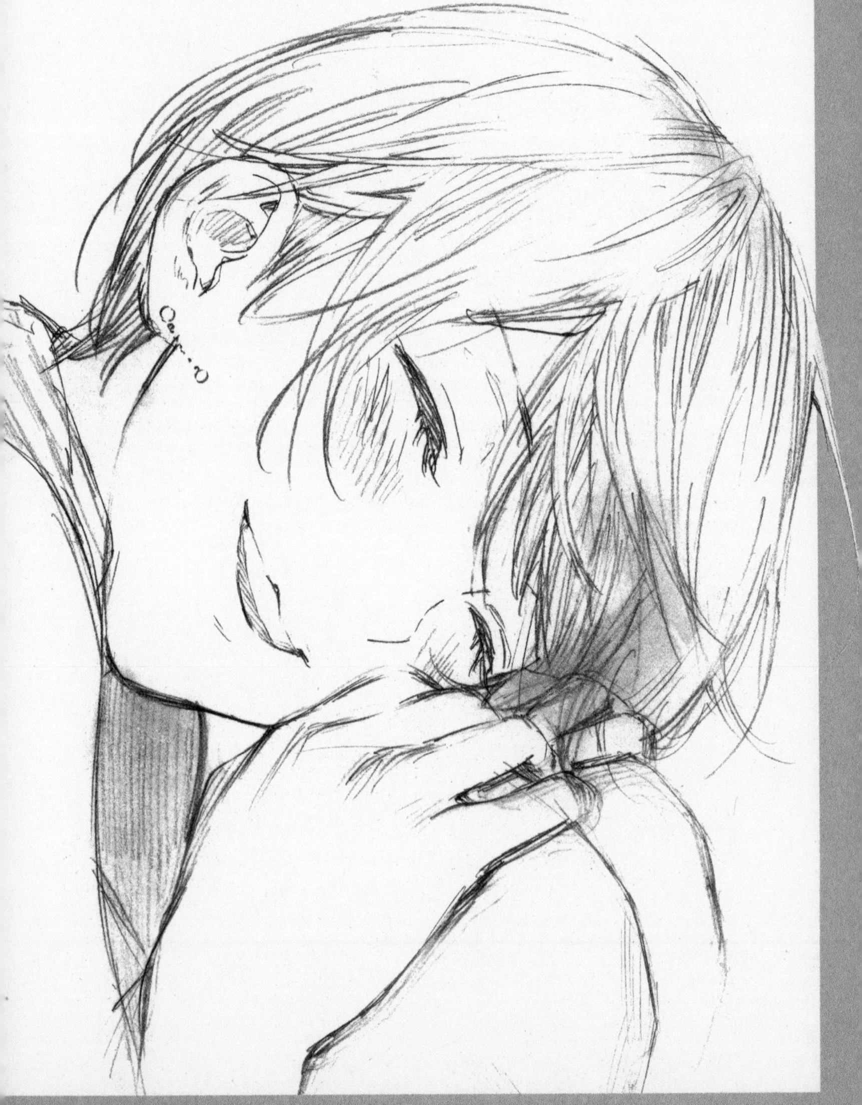

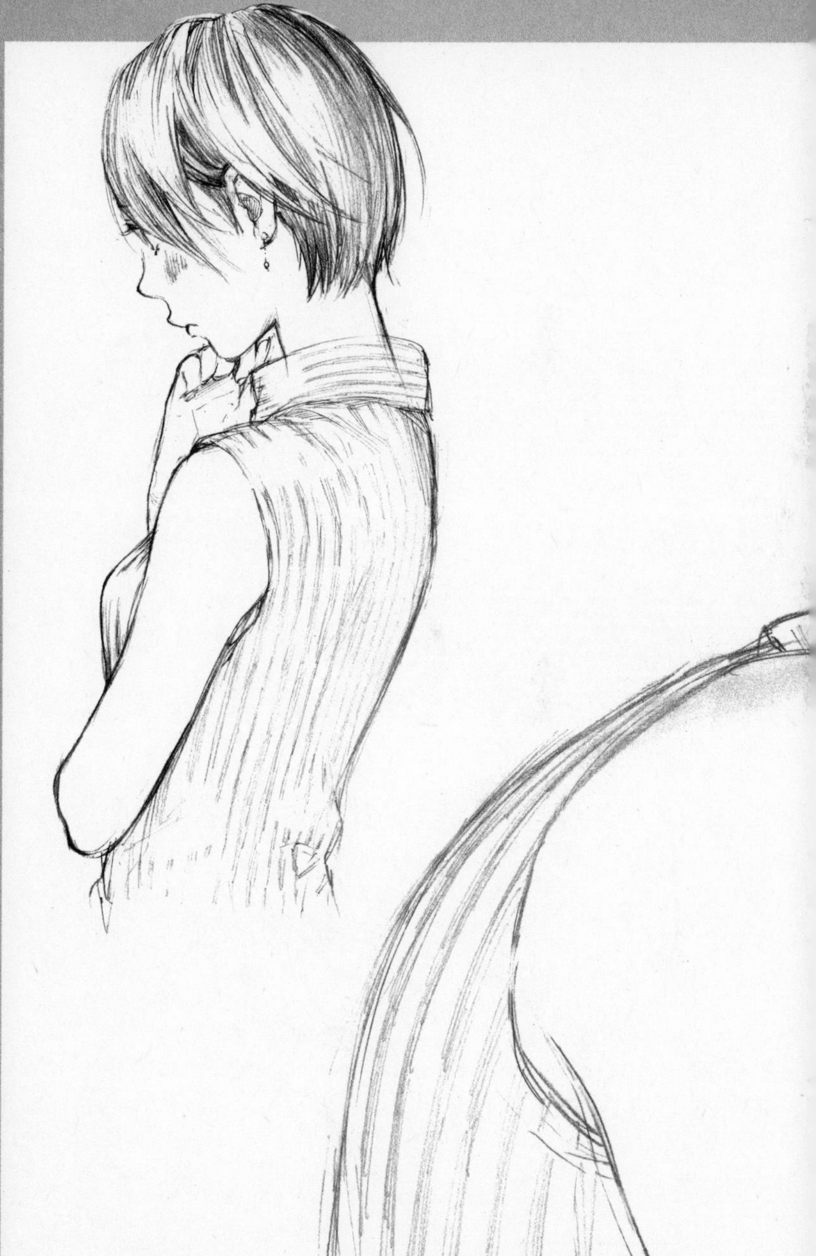

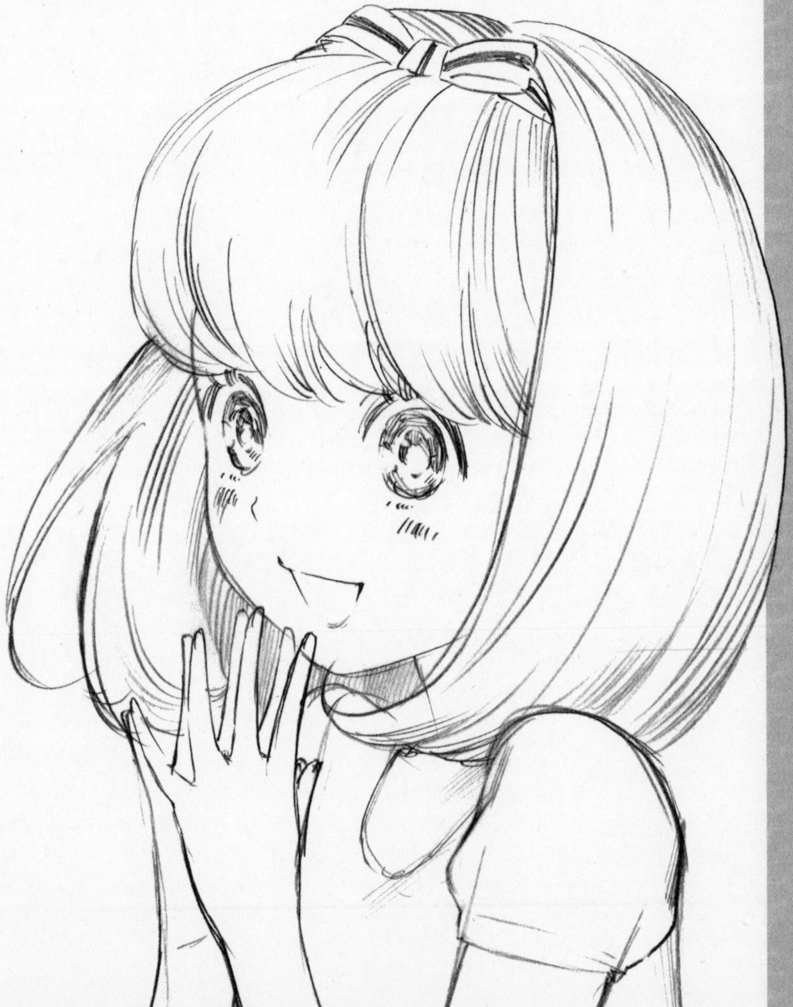

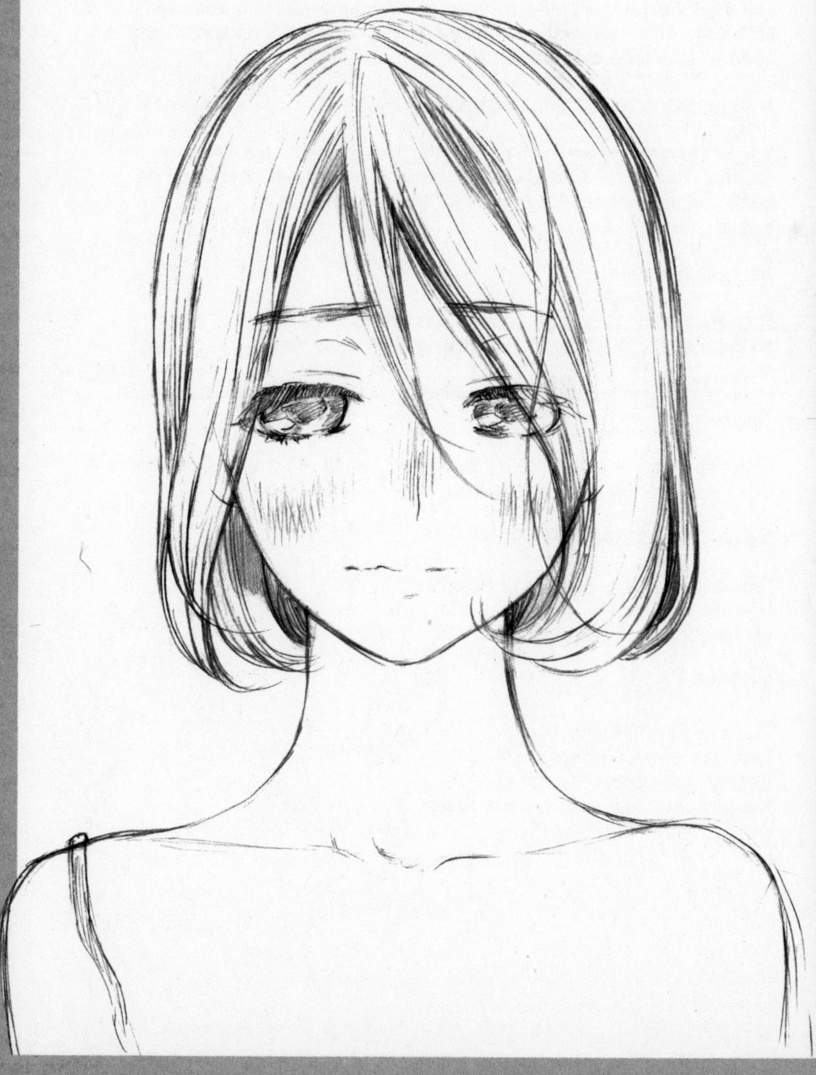

Forget Me Not volume 7 is a work of fiction. Names, characters, places, and incidents are the products of the author's imagination or are used fictitiously. Any resemblance to actual events, locales, or persons, living or dead, is entirely coincidental.

A Kodansha Comics Trade Paperback Original.

Published in the United States by Kodansha Comics,
an imprint of Kodansha USA Publishing, LLC, New York.

Publication rights for this English edition arranged through Kodansha Ltd., Tokyo.

First published in Japan in 2016 by Kodansha Ltd., Tokyo, as *Sore Demo Boku Wa Kimi Ga Suki* volume 7.

ISBN 978-1-63236-339-8

Printed in the United States of America.

www.kodanshacomics.com

9 8 7 6 5 4 3 2 1

Translation: Ko Ransom
Lettering: Evan Hayden
Editing: Ajani Oloye
Kodansha Comics edition cover design: Phil Balsman